Fodor's

SAN DIEGO

WELCOME TO SAN DIEGO

San Diego is a vacationer's paradise, with year-round temperatures in the seventies and near-constant sunshine. One of America's most family-friendly cities, San Diego is home to LEGOLAND, the New Children's Museum, and the famous San Diego Zoo. Sunbathers and surfers are guaranteed to find their perfect beach, and foodies find delights in artisanal breweries, local bistros, and gourmet restaurants. From the Broadway excitement of La Jolla Playhouse to the European feel of Little Italy to the nouveau-chic of the Gaslamp Quarter, San Diego has something for everyone.

TOP REASONS TO GO

★ **Sun and Surf:** Legendary beaches and surfing in La Jolla, Coronado, and Point Loma.

★ **Golf:** A concentration of beautiful courses with sweeping ocean views and light breezes.

★ **Outdoor Sports:** A perfect climate for biking, hiking, sailing—anything—outdoors.

★ **Family Time:** Fun for all ages at LEGOLAND, Balboa Park, the San Diego Zoo, and more.

★ **Great Eats:** Brewpubs, a wide mix of ethnic cuisines, and modern cafes delight diners.

★ **Shopping:** From hip boutiques and fine Mexican crafts to the upscale Fashion Valley Mall.

Fodor's SAN DIEGO

Publisher: Amanda D'Acierno, *Senior Vice President*

Editorial: Arabella Bowen, *Editor in Chief*; Linda Cabasin, *Editorial Director*

Design: Tina Malaney, *Associate Art Director*; Chie Ushio, *Senior Designer*; Ann McBride, *Production Designer*

Photography: Jennifer Arnow, *Senior Photo Editor*; Mary Robnett, *Photo Researcher*

Production: Linda Schmidt, *Managing Editor*; Evangelos Vasilakis, *Associate Managing Editor*; Angela L. McLean, *Senior Production Manager*

Maps: Rebecca Baer, *Senior Map Editor*; David Lindroth and Mark Stroud (Moon Street Cartography), *Cartographers*

Sales: Jacqueline Lebow, *Sales Director*

Marketing & Publicity: Heather Dalton, *Marketing Director*; Katherine Punia, *Publicity Director*

Business & Operations: Susan Livingston, *Vice President, Strategic Business Planning*; Sue Daulton, *Vice President, Operations*

Fodors.com: Megan Bell, *Executive Director, Revenue & Business Development*; Yasmin Marinaro, *Senior Director, Marketing & Partnerships*

Copyright © 2015 by Fodor's Travel, a division of Random House LLC

Writers: Claire Deeks van der Lee, Maren Dougherty, Bobbi Zane, Jeff Terich, Casey Hatfield-Chiotti, Mary Hellman James, Ron James

Editor: Kristan Schiller

Production Editor: Jennifer DePrima

30th Edition

ISBN 978-1-101-87815-6

ISSN 1053–5950

SPECIAL SALES

This book is available at special discounts for bulk purchases for sales promotions or premiums. For more information, e-mail specialmarkets@penguinrandomhouse.com

PRINTED IN THE UNITED STATES OF AMERICA

10 9 8 7 6 5 4 3 2 1

CONTENTS

1 EXPERIENCE SAN DIEGO......9
San Diego Today 10
What's Where 12
San Diego Planner 16
San Diego Top Attractions 18
Top Experiences. 20
Great Itineraries. 22
Like a Local. 25
San Diego with Kids 26
Free (and Almost Free)
in San Diego 27
A Walk Through San Diego's
Past .28
Farmers' Markets 30

2 DOWNTOWN. 31

3 BALBOA PARK AND
SAN DIEGO ZOO 43

4 OLD TOWN AND UPTOWN. . . . 65
Old Town 68
Hillcrest 73
Mission Hills 76
Mission Valley 76
University Heights. 77
North Park 77
South Park 78

5 MISSION BAY AND
THE BEACHES 79
SeaWorld San Diego 82

6 LA JOLLA 89
Northern San Diego: Clairemont and
Kearny Mesa 96

7 POINT LOMA AND
CORONADO 97
Cabrillo National Monument 100
Ocean Beach. 104
Shelter Island 104

Fodor's Features

San Diego Zoo 55

Harbor Island. 104
Coronado 105

8 WHERE TO EAT 107
San Diego Dining Planner. 110
Restaurant Reviews. 111
Best Bets for
San Diego Dining 112

9 WHERE TO STAY 161
Planning. 163
Best Bets for
San Diego Lodging 164
Hotel Reviews 166

10 NIGHTLIFE 179
Planning. 182
Nightlife by Neighborhood 183

11 THE ARTS 199

12 BEACHES 209
San Diego's Best Beaches. 210
La Jolla's Beaches and Beyond. . .212
Beach Planner. 216
Beaches by Neighborhood 218

13 SPORTS AND THE
OUTDOORS. 227

CONTENTS

Surfing San Diego. 228

Sports and the
Outdoors Planner. 230

Participation Sports. 232

Spectator Sports. 253

14 SHOPPING 255

Shopping Planner. 257

Shopping by Neighborhood. 259

15 NORTH COUNTY AND
AROUND. 277

Welcome to
North County. 278

Planner 280

North Coast: Del Mar
to Oceanside. 282

Inland North County and
Temecula 301

The Backcountry and Julian. . . . 314

The Desert 323

TRAVEL SMART SAN DIEGO. . 331

INDEX. 342

ABOUT OUR WRITERS. 352

MAPS

A Walk Through San Diego's Past . .29

Downtown 32

Balboa Park and San Diego Zoo. . .44

Old Town and Uptown 66

Mission Bay, Beaches, and
SeaWorld 80

La Jolla 90

Point Loma and Coronado 98

Dining in San Diego 109

Where to Eat and Stay
in San Diego 151–159

Nightlife in San Diego 181

San Diego Beaches. 215

South Bay to
Coronado Beaches 218

Point Loma to Mission
Bay Beaches. 221

La Jolla Beaches 222

North County Beaches. 224

Shopping in San Diego. 258

Del Mar to Oceanside 283

Inland North County, the
Backcountry, and Desert. 302

San Diego MTS Trolley 330

ABOUT THIS GUIDE

Fodor's Recommendations

Everything in this guide is worth doing—we don't cover what isn't—but exceptional sights, hotels, and restaurants are recognized with additional accolades. Fodor'sChoice★ indicates our top recommendations; and **Best Bets** call attention to notable hotels and restaurants in various categories. Care to nominate a new place? Visit Fodors.com/contact-us.

Trip Costs

We list prices wherever possible to help you budget well. Hotel and restaurant price categories from **$** to **$$$$** are noted alongside each recommendation. For hotels, we include the lowest cost of a standard double room in high season. For restaurants, we cite the average price of a main course at dinner or, if dinner isn't served, at lunch. For attractions, we always list adult admission fees; discounts are usually available for children, students, and senior citizens.

Hotels

Our local writers vet every hotel to recommend the best overnights in each price category, from budget to expensive. Unless otherwise specified, you can expect private bath, phone, and TV in your room. For expanded hotel reviews, facilities, and deals visit Fodors.com.

Top Picks	Hotels & Restaurants
★ Fodor'sChoice	🏨 Hotel
Listings	⤵ Number of rooms
✉ Address	⦿I Meal plans
✉ Branch address	✕ Restaurant
☎ Telephone	⟋ Reservations
🖷 Fax	👔 Dress code
⊕ Website	▭ No credit cards
✎ E-mail	$ Price
🎫 Admission fee	**Other**
⊙ Open/closed times	⇨ See also
Ⓜ Subway	☞ Take note
✛ Directions or Map coordinates	🏌 Golf facilities

Restaurants

Unless we state otherwise, restaurants are open for lunch and dinner daily. We mention dress code only when there's a specific requirement and reservations only when they're essential or not accepted. To make restaurant reservations, visit Fodors.com.

Credit Cards

The hotels and restaurants in this guide typically accept credit cards. If not, we'll say so.

EUGENE FODOR

Hungarian-born Eugene Fodor (1905–91) began his travel career as an interpreter on a French cruise ship. The experience inspired him to write *On the Continent* (1936), the first guidebook to receive annual updates and discuss a country's way of life as well as its sights. Fodor later joined the U.S. Army and worked for the OSS in World War II. After the war, he kept up his intelligence work while expanding his guidebook series. During the Cold War, many guides were written by fellow agents who understood the value of insider information. Today's guides continue Fodor's legacy by providing travelers with timely coverage, insider tips, and cultural context.

EXPERIENCE SAN DIEGO

SAN DIEGO TODAY

Although most visitors know little about San Diego beyond its fun-in-the-sun reputation, locals are talking about much more than the surf forecast and their tan lines. San Diego politics made international headlines when Mayor Bob Filner resigned in 2013 amidst a sexual harassment scandal. Taking it all in stride, the city was quick to move on and, in the words of *Anchorman's* Ron Burgundy, "Stay Classy, San Diego." Beyond the scandal, issues such as public infrastructure, unions, and affordable housing are all topics of heated political debate. After several years of tough economic times, San Diegans have managed to keep the city's forecast sunny. The buzz around San Diego's science and biotech industry continues to grow, and several large companies, including Qualcomm, PETCO, and Bridgepoint Education, continue to call San Diego home base. San Diego has been busy shedding its image as LA's less sophisticated neighbor, and coming into an urban identity of its own. Across the region, residents are embracing new trends in the local art, shopping, dining, and cultural scenes.

Today's San Diego:

is eating well. Once considered somewhat of a culinary wasteland, the San Diego dining scene is enjoying a renaissance. All over town, new and exciting restaurants are popping up, celebrating both the local bounty and the region's diversity. Healthy and fresh California Modern cuisine remains a feature on many menus, while neighboring Baja Mexico has given rise to the new trend of BajaMed, a fusion of Mexican and Mediterranean styles. San Diego's sizable Asian population has introduced everything from dim sum carts to Mongolian hot pot, while local sushi chefs take advantage of San Diego's reputation for some of the finest sea urchin in the world. The locavore trend has become somewhat of an obsession for San Diegans, and many restaurants are happy to highlight how and where they source their ingredients.

is toasting the town. San Diego continues to gain recognition as one of the most exciting beer towns in the nation. Craft brewers creating a buzz include AleSmith, Ballast Point, and Lost Abbey, just to name a few, and Stone Brewing Company (⇨ *Nightlife*), creator of the notorious Arrogant Bastard Ale, has several locations. All

WHAT WE'RE TALKING ABOUT

Construction on Phase 1 of the North Embarcadero Visionary Plan is nearly complete. The project promises to transform the landscape of San Diego's waterfront and better connect the Embarcadero with downtown. Public art installations, green spaces, shade pavilions, and ample room to stroll should help transform the Embarcadero into one of the world's great urban waterfronts.

The buzz surrounding the San Diego winemaking community is growing louder. The recent easing of requirements for boutique wineries gave a major boost to the local winemaking community, including several small wine producers around the town of Ramona in North San Diego country. In addition, wine production facilities known as urban wineries are cropping

this enthusiasm for San Diego's suds has given rise to a beer tourism industry, from bus tours of local brewers to large beer-themed events such as the popular San Diego Beer Week. There's even an app to help you find the perfect pint: inspired by the local brewing scene, a San Diego couple created the TapHunter website and mobile application, which helps beer lovers find what's on tap and where.

is building for the future, and conserving its past. A drive around San Diego reveals a huge range of architecture, from hip to historic to downright hideous. Urban planning from half a century ago, such as the decision to run Interstate 5 right through Little Italy and Downtown, is hard to undo but other efforts to conserve the city's architectural integrity have been more successful. Downtown's Gaslamp Quarter is the most famous conservation area, but the residential neighborhoods of Uptown, Kensington, and South Park delight early-20th-century architecture buffs with streets full of historically designated homes. New projects making waves in San Diego today include the revitalization of the Embarcadero and the recent transformation of the old San

Diego Police Headquarters across from Seaport Village

is getting outside. San Diego's near-perfect climate and gorgeous natural landscape make it hard to find an excuse not to get outside and exercise. In fact, San Diego is home to one of the most active populations in the country. Year-round opportunities to surf, sail, bike, or hike offer something for everyone. On weekends and throughout the summer, beaches and parks teem with locals enjoying the great weather and fresh air. Gas barbecues, bouncy houses, and huge shade tents take the concept of the picnic to a whole new level. So when visitors hailing from harsher climates wonder if San Diegans appreciate how good they have it, the answer is a resounding yes.

up in towns around the county. Until now, San Diego's primary wine region, Temecula, was actually over the border in neighboring Riverside County. Before long, locals and visitors alike may be exploring a San Diego wine country that is actually located in San Diego County itself.

San Diego is gearing up for the Centennial Celebration of Balboa Park in 2015. Planning got off to a rocky start, with the original group in charge of planning stepping down amid claims of mismanaged funds.

A scaled-back set of celebrations began in December 2014 and will continue throughout 2015, with specifics detailed at ⊕ *celebratebalboapark.org*.

WHAT'S WHERE

1 Downtown. Downtown used to be a real downer, a mix of bland office towers and seedy sidewalks after sundown. Preservationists and entrepreneurs saved the day, starting with Horton Plaza, a six-block shopping and dining complex. Now, the streets are lined with nightclubs, boutiques, and restaurants, from the glam Gaslamp Quarter (a former red-light district) to the edgier East Village (where Padres fans get their baseball fix at PETCO Park). Also nearby are Seaport Village, the Embarcadero, and trendy yet authentic Little Italy.

2 Balboa Park. In the center of the city, this 1,200-acre patch of greenery is home to world-class museums and performing arts, stunning Spanish colonial revival architecture, and the famed San Diego Zoo. Paths wind around gardens, fountains, and groves of shady trees. It's a sort of Central Park of the west—a leafy getaway for locals, and a must for tourists. Bankers Hill, just west of the park, is a gentrifying neighborhood with hip dining options.

3 Old Town. Before there was a sprawling city, there was an Old Town, home to the remnants of San Diego's—and California's—first permanent European settlement. The former pueblo is now a pedestrian-friendly state historic park, with original and reconstructed buildings and sites, along with a tourist bazaar of souvenir shops, art galleries, and Mexican eateries with margaritas and mariachi aplenty.

4 Uptown. Uptown is a catchall for a cluster of trendy neighborhoods near downtown and north of Balboa Park. Hillcrest is the heart of the city's gay and lesbian community, while in North Park, a hip and edgy set keeps boutiques, galleries, eateries, and bars hopping. The cool crowd has also converged on University Heights, with its eclectic mix of dining and nightlife. Mission Hills is a lovely historic neighborhood between Old Town and Hillcrest, while Mission Valley, northeast of Uptown, is mostly known for office towers, shopping malls, and Qualcomm Stadium.

5 Mission Bay and the Beaches. Home to SeaWorld, Mission Bay also boasts a 4,600-acre aquatic park perfect for boating, jet skiing, swimming, and fishing, plus activities like biking, basketball, and kite-flying. It's neighbored by bustling Mission Beach and Pacific Beach, where streets are lined with surf shops, ice-cream stands, and beach bars.

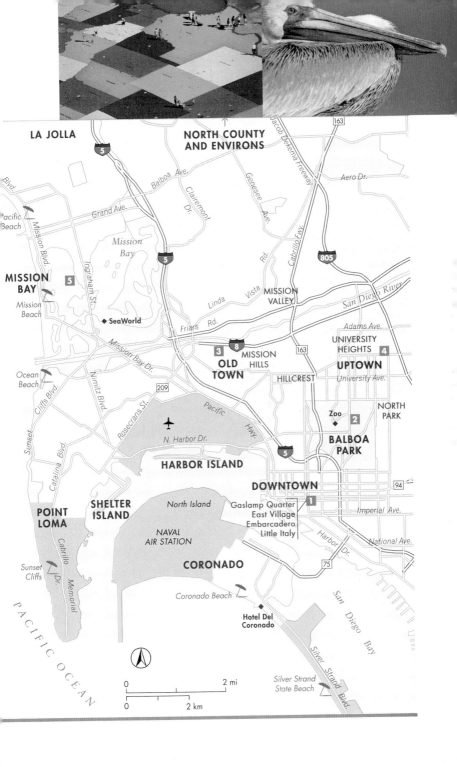

LA JOLLA

NORTH COUNTY
AND ENVIRONS

MISSION
BAY

Mission
Bay

Mission
Beach

◆ SeaWorld

Pacific
Beach

Grand Ave.

Balboa Ave.

Clairemont Dr.

Genesee Ave.

Aero Dr.

Jacob Dekema Freeway

163

805

Linda Vista Rd.

MISSION
VALLEY

San Diego River

Friars Rd.

Mission Bay Dr.

OLD
TOWN

MISSION
HILLS

Adams Ave.

UNIVERSITY
HEIGHTS

UPTOWN
University Ave.

HILLCREST

163

4

Ocean
Beach

Cliffs Blvd.

Sunset

Catalina Blvd.

Nimitz Blvd.

Rosecrans St.

209

Pacific Hwy.

N. Harbor Dr.

HARBOR ISLAND

Zoo ◆

2

NORTH
PARK

BALBOA
PARK

DOWNTOWN

94

POINT
LOMA

SHELTER
ISLAND

North Island

NAVAL
AIR STATION

CORONADO

Gaslamp Quarter
East Village
Embarcadero
Little Italy

1

Imperial Ave.

Harbor Dr.

National Ave.

75

Cabrillo Memorial Dr.

Sunset
Cliffs

Coronado Beach

Hotel Del
Coronado

San Diego Bay

Silver Strand Blvd.

PACIFIC OCEAN

Silver Strand
State Beach

0   2 mi

0   2 km

WHAT'S WHERE

6 La Jolla. This neighborhood lands lavish praise for its picturesque cliffs and beaches, not to mention a bevy of the finest hotels, restaurants, art galleries, and shopping. From Windansea's locals-only surf scene to cocktails at a grand hotel where the Hollywood elite once retreated, there's something for everyone.

7 Point Loma. Curving crescentlike along the bay, Point Loma has main drags cluttered with fast-food joints and budget motels, but farther back, grand old houses give way to ocean views. At the southern tip of the peninsula, the majestic Cabrillo Monument commemorates the landing of explorer Juan Rodríguez Cabrillo at San Diego Bay in 1542; the 360-degree vista sometimes includes glimpses of migrating gray whales. Farther north, make time for tide pools at Ocean Beach's Sunset Cliffs.

8 Harbor and Shelter Islands. Harbor Island is a man-made strip of land in the bay across from the airport, while to the west, Shelter Island is known for its yacht-building and sport-fishing industries. Both have a handful of hotels and restaurants, plus unsurpassed views of the downtown skyline in one direction and Coronado in the other.

9 Coronado. Historic Coronado, an islandlike peninsula across from the San Diego waterfront, came of age as a Victorian resort community. Its seaside centerpiece is the fabled (and gabled) Hotel Del Coronado, a favorite haunt of celebs, A-listers, and—well—ghosts, if you believe local lore. The upscale area, also home to a naval base, offers plenty of shopping, dining, and pleasant stretches of sand. Drive across the bridge or take the ferry to reach it.

10 North County and Environs. Getting outside of San Diego proper is a must for beach towns like Del Mar and family attractions like LEGOLAND and the San Diego Zoo Safari Park. There are a growing number of wineries to visit in Ramona and Temecula, while the Anzo-Borrego Desert offers a variety of exploring opportunities.

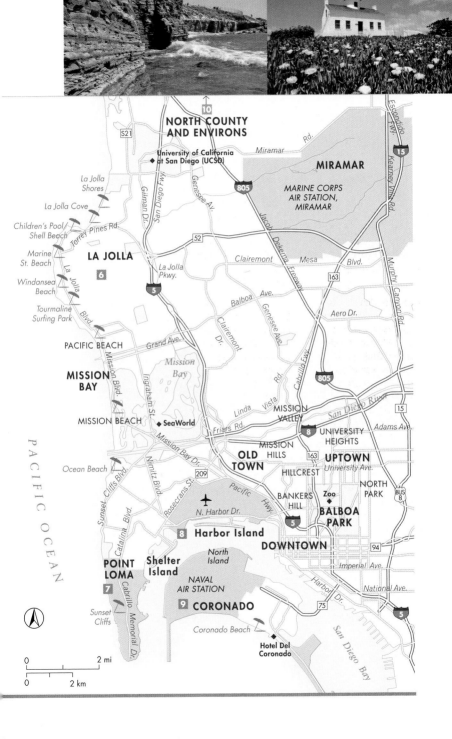

NORTH COUNTY
AND ENVIRONS

University of California
at San Diego (UCSD)

MIRAMAR

MARINE CORPS
AIR STATION,
MIRAMAR

La Jolla
Shores

La Jolla Cove

Children's Pool/
Shell Beach

Marine
St. Beach

LA JOLLA

Miramar Rd.

Escondido Fwy

Clairemont Mesa Blvd.

Torrey Pines Rd.

San Diego Fwy.

Gilman Dr.

Genesee Av.

Jacob Dekema Freeway

Kearney Villa Rd.

Murphy Canyon Rd.

La Jolla
Pkwy.

6

Windansea
Beach

Balboa Ave.

Aero Dr.

Tourmaline
Surfing Park

Clairemont Dr.

Genesee Ave.

Cabrillo Fwy.

PACIFIC BEACH

Grand Ave.

Mission Blvd.

La Jolla Blvd.

MISSION
BAY

Mission
Bay

Ingraham St.

Linda Vista Rd.

MISSION
VALLEY

San Diego River

Adams Ave.

MISSION BEACH

SeaWorld

Mission Bay Dr.

Friars Rd.

MISSION
HILLS

UNIVERSITY
HEIGHTS

OLD
TOWN

UPTOWN

University Ave.

Ocean Beach

Sunset Cliffs Blvd.

Nimitz Blvd.

Rosecrans St.

HILLCREST

NORTH
PARK

PACIFIC OCEAN

Catalina Blvd.

Pacific Hwy.

N. Harbor Dr.

BANKERS
HILL

Zoo

BALBOA
PARK

8 Harbor Island

DOWNTOWN

POINT
LOMA

Shelter
Island

North
Island

NAVAL
AIR STATION

Imperial Ave.

National Ave.

Harbor Dr.

7

Cabrillo Memorial Dr.

9 CORONADO

Sunset
Cliffs

Coronado Beach

Hotel Del
Coronado

San Diego Bay

0   2 mi

0   2 km

SAN DIEGO PLANNER

When to Go

San Diego's weather is so ideal that most locals shrug off the high cost of living and relatively low wages as a "sunshine tax." Along the coast, average temperatures range from the mid-60s to the high 70s, with clear skies and low humidity. Annual rainfall is minimal, less than 10 inches per year.

The peak season for sunseekers is July through October. In July and August, the mercury spikes and everyone spills outside. Beaches are a popular daytime destination, as is Balboa Park, thanks to its shady groves and air-conditioned museums. Summer's nightlife scene thrives with the usual bars and clubs, plus outdoor concerts, theater, and movie screenings. Early fall is a pleasant time to visit, as many tourists have already left town and the temperature is nearly perfect. From mid-December to mid-March, whale-watchers can glimpse migrating gray whales frolicking in the Pacific. In spring and early summer, a marine layer hugs the coastline for much or all of the day (locals call it "June Gloom"), which can be dreary and disappointing for those who were expecting to bask in Southern California sunshine. However, wildflowers also blanket the mountainsides and desert in early spring.

Getting Around

Car Travel: To fully explore sprawling San Diego—especially with kids in tow—consider renting a car. Nearly everything of interest can be found off I–5 or I–163, and the county's freeways are wide and easy to use. Traffic isn't a major issue if you avoid rush hour. Parking in urban areas is typically metered, Monday through Saturday, 8 to 6, unless otherwise marked. You may park for free outside those hours, and on Sunday and holidays. ■TIP→ Yellow commercial loading zones are fair game for parking after 6. During special downtown events, such as Padres games, you'll likely have to settle for one of the many paid parking structures—they cost around $20 close to the action. Parking at beaches is free for the most part, though tough to come by on sunny days unless you stake out a spot early.

Foot Travel: Walking is the way to go once you've reached a destination area. Balboa Park and the zoo are walkers' paradises, and all of downtown is pedestrian friendly.

Pedicab Travel: These pedal-powered chariots are a great way to get around downtown. Just be sure to agree on a price before you start moving, or you could get taken for the wrong kind of ride. Many pedicab drivers offer up their own unique commentary on the sights, though take what they say with a grain of salt—fibbing is par for the course.

Public Transportation: Visit *www.sdcommute.com*, which lists routes and timetables for the Metropolitan Transit System and North County Transit District.

The "Trip Planner" section is a terrific resource.

Local/urban bus fare is $2.25 one-way, but you can pick up an unlimited day pass for $5 (exact change only; pay when you board). A one-way ride on the city's iconic red trolleys is $2.50; get your ticket at any trolley vending machine.

Taxi Travel: Cabs are a fine choice for trips to and from the airport and short jaunts around town. The approximate rates are: $2.80 for the first 1/10 mile, $3 each additional mile, and $24 per hour of waiting time. You can find taxicab stands at the airport, hotels, major attractions, and shopping centers. Downtown, your best bet is to flag one down, New York City–style.

What to Wear

You won't find a more casual big city. Flip-flops are the favored footwear, shorts and beachy skirts comprise the summer uniform, and designer jeans qualify as dressing up. Despite the city's easygoing vibe, San Diegans value labels—just look at Fashion Valley's lineup of high-end outposts like Jimmy Choo and Louis Vuitton. Dining out warrants a little research; some eateries barely toe the "no shirt, no shoes" rule, while others require more elegant attire.

Safety

San Diego has some sketchy areas, although tourists typically encounter few problems. Downtown can get a little rowdy at night, especially toward 2 am, when bars boot drunken patrons out on the sidewalks. The city also has a large homeless population, who often camp out on shadowy side streets not far from East Village. Most are harmless, aside from the occasional panhandling, but it's safest to stick to well-lighted, busy areas. Certain pockets of Balboa Park are frequented by drug dealers and prostitutes after hours; if you're attending a nighttime theater performance or art event, park nearby or use the valet.

Where to WWW

Browse these online options for more about what's on. *www.fodors.com*, check out the forums on our site for answers to your travel questions and tips.
www.sandiego.org for the San Diego visitor bureau.
www.sandiegoreader.com posts tons of event listings, from big concerts to little community to-dos.
www.utsandiego.com is where the scaled-down *San Diego Union-Tribune* posts all its daily newspaper and original online content, including a searchable entertainment section.
www.sdcitybeat.com for the online version of the alternative weekly *San Diego CityBeat,* a guide to the city's edgier side, from regional politics to the hottest local bands.
www.urbanistguide.com is the ultimate how-to for hip urban explorers, including curated calendar picks, Q&As with local scene-makers, and an interactive map feature.

Festivals

Pencil in these festivals when you're in town.

Winter: Drawing 100,000 visitors the first Friday and Saturday of December, **Balboa Park December Nights** offers festive carolers, food, music, and dance. The **San Diego Bay Parade of Lights,** also in December, lights up the harbor with boats decked out for the holidays.

January's **Farmers Insurance Open** is the Holy Grail for golf fans; the celeb-heavy tourney has been held at the scenic Torrey Pines Golf Course for decades. In February, the **Mardi Gras** block party in the Gaslamp Quarter invites revelers to let the good times roll.

Spring: Adams Avenue Unplugged gives music fans a weekend of free acoustic music, while Little Italy's annual **ArtWalk** showcases local art talent on tent-lined streets.

Summer: The **San Diego County Fair,** the Old Globe's **Summer Shakespeare Festival,** the city's huge **LGBT Pride Festival,** racing season at the **Del Mar Fairgrounds,** and outdoor classical concerts at the **Embarcadero** all take place in summer.

Fall: Music fans eagerly wait for the **Adams Avenue Street Fair,** a weekend of concerts and a carnival.

SAN DIEGO
TOP ATTRACTIONS

Balboa Park
(A) Oasis is hardly hyperbole when it comes to describing this 1,200-acre cultural heart of San Diego. Take a peaceful stroll or plan a full day of perusing Balboa Park's many museums, theater spaces, gardens, trails, and playing fields. And don't forget the park's famous San Diego Zoo.

Beaches
(B) San Diego boasts 70 miles of coastline, with beaches for everybody, from pail-and-shovel-toting toddlers to hard-bodied adventurous types—even nudists have their own sheltered spot at Black's Beach. Coronado is a family favorite, twentysomethings soak up some sun at Pacific Beach, and surfers swear by various stretches of shore, including Windansea Beach. Life's a beach, here, literally.

Cabrillo National Monument
(C) On the southern tip of the Point Loma peninsula, this landmark commemorates the 1542 landing of explorer Juan Rodríguez Cabrillo in San Diego Bay. Unparalleled harbor and skyline views, a military history museum, tidal pools, and an old lighthouse are among the offerings. In winter, you may even catch sight of migrating gray whales along the coast.

Carlsbad Flower Fields
(D) Fifty acres of flowers, mostly ranunculus, bloom in Technicolor hues every March on a hillside perched above the Pacific Ocean. Timing is everything, but if you visit in spring, don't miss this showy display of stunning natural beauty.

La Jolla
First things first: It's pronounced La Hoya. Next you need to know that it's one of the prettiest places in California, a wealthy enclave with a small-town feel and world-class scenic coastline. Visit the

Children's Pool, populated by sunbathing seals, or watch locals ride waves at the beach. Then again, you could just shop and nosh the day away.

LEGOLAND California

(E) A whole universe of LEGO fun awaits the pint-size set and their chaperones in Carlsbad, including more than 60 rides and attractions. Especially cool is Miniland USA, scaled-down cities built entirely from LEGO bricks, as well as Dino Island and the Egyptian-theme Dune Raiders, a 30-foot racing slide.

San Diego Zoo

(F) One word: pandas. The San Diego Zoo has several of the roly-poly crowd-pleasers. And yes, they're that cute. But the conservation-minded zoo offers much more, from Polar Bear Plunge, the arctic creature's recently revamped habitat, to oh-so-close encounters of lions, tigers, and bears. Explore the huge, hilly attraction by foot, or take advantage of the guided bus tours, aerial tram, and seated shows. Also a roaring good time: Escondido's Safari Park.

Torrey Pines State Natural Reserve

(G) The nation's rarest pine tree calls this area home, as do the last salt marshes and waterfowl refuges in Southern California. Hikers can wind their way down wind-swept trails that stretch from the high coastal bluffs to sandy Torrey Pines State Beach below. Panoramic views abound.

TOP EXPERIENCES

Did we mention the beach?

If stretching out on the sand with a sun-screen-stained paperback sounds like a snooze, there's always swimming, snorkeling, surfing, diving, and deep-sea fishing. And that's just in the water. On the sand, serve and spike in a friendly beach volleyball pickup or pal around with your pooch at a leash-free dog beach. The truly adventurous should sign up for Over-the-Line, a massive beach softball tourney that takes place every July—the title refers as much to blood alcohol levels as the rules of the game.

Sail away

So you don't own a historic tall ship. Who says you can't experience the thrill of sailing the seas in high style? Several times a year, the **San Diego Maritime Museum** offers public adventure sails aboard the *Star of India,* the *Californian,* and the HMS *Surprise.* And, on very rare occasions, the ships even stage cannon battle reenactments in the San Diego Bay. *Master and Commander* wannabes, consider it your shot at combat glory.

Culture vulture

San Diego's artistic scene gets short shrift compared to the city's outdoorsy offerings, which is a shame. Truly top-notch theater dominates the dance cards of local culturati, like **La Jolla Playhouse,** which routinely hosts Broadway-bound shows before they head east. The **Old Globe**—the oldest professional theater in the state—stages everything from Shakespeare to the avant-garde at its cluster of spaces, including the state-of-the-art Conrad Prebys Theatre Center. Both locations (downtown and La Jolla) of the **Museum of Contemporary Art San Diego** showcase thought-provoking exhibitions, from regionally focused to international retrospectives, while niche galleries throughout the county cater to the visually curious. And no matter what the season, visitors will find something fetching from area performing-arts staples such as the **San Diego Symphony Orchestra, San Diego Opera,** and **San Diego Ballet.**

Bogey bliss

Whether you're timid at the tee or an aspiring golf pro, San Diego's wide-ranging golf options will wow you. Never mind the fact that water restrictions have left some greens a little less, er, green. Golfing in San Diego is an experience par none, no matter what your price range and ability. If you can swing the fees, splurge at Carlsbad's **Park Hyatt Resort Aviara** or at the **Rancho Bernardo Resort & Spa.** La Jolla's **Torrey Pines Golf Course,** home to the 2008 U.S. Open and every Buick Invitational (now the Farmers Insurance Open) since 1968, is one of the finest 18-hole public courses in the country, and a more affordable outing. Just be sure to book tee times well in advance.

Sky high

Sometimes, soaring above the earth is the best way to get a sense of its mind-blowing scale—to wit, the colorful hot-air balloons that dot the horizon at sunrise and sunset. Tiny and toylike from the ground, they offer big bird's-eye views to those who take flight. The annual **Temecula Balloon & Wine festival,** typically in June, is a favorite among fliers. If standing beneath an open flame makes you a basket case, perhaps tandem paragliding will put you in your proper airborne place. At the **Torrey Pines Gliderport,** an instructor handles the hard work. All you have to do is shout in glee as the winged glider climbs and dips above cliff-bordered beaches.

Charge it

When your Visa bill reads like a vacation diary, you know you're a serious shopaholic. Jimmy Choo, Hermès, and Louis Vuitton? That was just an afternoon at **Fashion Valley!** San Diego has options to suit every style of shopper. For unique, edgy scores, scour boutiques in neighborhoods like **Hillcrest, Little Italy,** and **North Park.** Sleek storefronts in **La Jolla** and other well-heeled areas carry all variety of luxury goods, while downtown's **Westfield Horton Plaza** stocks standard mall fare. For souvenirs—seashells and such—try **Seaport Village,** or browse festive Mexican arts and crafts at Old Town's **Fiesta de Reyes.**

Hang loose, dude

Only a grom (a newbie) would say "hang loose," but "dude" is definitely a prominent part of the local surfer's vocabulary (as in, duuuuude). If you have the courage to wriggle into a wetsuit and waddle into knee-deep white water with a big foam board, you might just catch a wave—or at least stand up for a few seconds. Learning to surf is hard work, so your best bet is to take lessons, either private instruction or group-based. Try La Jolla's **Surf Diva Surf School,** geared primarily toward ladies, or Carlsbad's **San Diego Surfing Academy** in North County.

Sample the fish tacos

The humble fish taco is a local foodie favorite. Beer-battered and fried or lightly grilled, topped with salsa or white sauce and cabbage, tacos around town appeal to every palate. Sample the different styles from simple storefront restaurants and mobile taco trucks, and be prepared for a heated discussion. The only thing most San Diegans agree on is that fish tacos taste even better with a cold beer.

Spa-tacular

Money may not buy happiness, but it can definitely purchase a day of pampering at one of San Diego's many upscale spas. There's no limit to the luxuriating, from youth-restoring facials to aromatherapy massages that unkink months' worth of muscle aches. If cost is no concern, book an afternoon at Carlsbad's idyllic **La Costa Resort and Spa,** or at the historic **Hotel Del Coronado,** a beauty-boosting seaside retreat since the Victorian days.

Skip town

San Diego's allure extends well beyond its famous coastline. To the east, visitors will find forested mountains and an otherworldly desert landscape. The tiny town of **Julian,** in the Cuyamaca Mountains, charms with olden-day bed-and-breakfasts and ample slices of apple pie. In winter, weather allowing, visitors can even take horse-drawn sleigh rides. One of San Diego's most underrated natural attractions is the vast **Anza-Borrego Desert State Park,** 600,000 beautiful acres of protected land crisscrossed with hiking trails. Rough it at a campground or hole up at a hotel. Spring, which blankets the valleys with desert wildflowers, is peak season. Just steer clear of summer, when temperatures skyrocket into the 100s.

GREAT ITINERARIES

ONE DAY IN SAN DIEGO

If you've only got 24 hours to spare, start at **Balboa Park,** the cultural heart of San Diego. Stick to El Prado, the main promenade, where you'll pass by peaceful gardens and soaring Spanish colonial revival architecture (Balboa Park's unforgettable look and feel date to the 1914 Panama–California Exposition). Unless you're a serious museum junkie, pick whichever of the park's many offerings most piques your interest—choices range from photography to folk art.

If you're with the family, don't even think of skipping the **San Diego Zoo.** You'll want to spend the better part of your day there, but make an early start of it so you can head for one of San Diego's **beaches** afterward while there's still daylight. Kick back under the late afternoon sun and linger for sunset. Or wander around **Seaport Village** and the **Embarcadero** before grabbing a bite to eat in the **Gaslamp Quarter,** which pulses with nightlife until last call (around 1:40 am).

Alternate plan: Start your day at SeaWorld and wrap it up with an ocean-view dinner in **La Jolla.**

FOUR DAYS IN SAN DIEGO

Day 1

The one-day itinerary *above* also works for the first day of an extended visit. If you're staying in North County, though, you may want to bypass the zoo and head for the **San Diego Safari Park,** a vast preserve with huge open enclosures. Here, you'll see herds of African and Asian animals acting as they would in the wild. It's the closest thing in the States to an exotic safari. Not included in the general admission, but worth the extra cost if it's in the budget, are the park's "special experiences"—guided photo caravans, rolling Segway tours, mule rides, and the Flightline, which sends harnessed guests soaring down a zip-line cable high above earthbound animals.

Another North County option for families with little ones: **LEGOLAND** in Carlsbad. **Note:** The San Diego Zoo, the San Diego Safari Park, and LEGOLAND are all-day, wipe-those-kids-right-out kind of adventures.

Day 2

Your first day was a big one so you might want to ease into your second with a leisurely breakfast—and there are some great places to eat in the city—followed by a 90-minute tour aboard the **SEAL Amphibious Tour,** which departs from Seaport Village daily. The bus-boat hybrid explores picturesque San Diego neighborhoods before rolling right into the water for a cruise around the bay, all with fun-facts narration.

Back on land, you can devote an hour or so to **Seaport Village** itself, a 14-acre waterfront entertainment complex with around 50 shops and more than a dozen restaurants. Meant to look like a harbor in the 19th century, Seaport features 4 miles of cobblestone pathways bordered by lush landscaping and water features.

From there, stroll north to the **Embarcadero,** where you'll marvel at the **Maritime Museum's** historic vessels, including the *Star of India* (the world's oldest active sailing ship), *Berkeley, Californian, Medea,* and *Pilot.*

Explore San Diego's military might at the **USS Midway Museum,** aboard the permanently docked aircraft carrier with more than 60 exhibits and 25 restored aircraft.

Spend the rest of your afternoon and evening in **Coronado,** a quick jaunt by ferry or bridge, or walk a few blocks north to the **Gaslamp Quarter,** where the shopping and dining will keep you busy for hours.

Day 3

Set out early enough, and you might snag a parking spot near **La Jolla Cove,** where you can laugh at the sea lions lounging on the beach like lazy couch potatoes at the **Children's Pool.** Then head up one block to Prospect Street, where you'll find the vaunted **La Valencia** hotel (called the "Pink Lady" for its blush-hue exterior) and dozens of posh boutiques and galleries.

Head east to the **Museum of Contemporary Art San Diego**'s La Jolla location, which impresses as much with its ocean views as it does with its world-class collection of artwork. MCASD's Museum Café is a casual but elegant spot for a light lunch.

If you're with kids, skip the museum and head for **La Jolla Shores,** a good beach for swimming and making sand castles, followed by a visit to the **Birch Aquarium** and a fresh bite to eat at **El Pescador Fish Market** ($\Rightarrow$ *For this and other restaurant reviews, see Where to Eat*), an always-crowded lunchtime favorite.

Once you've refueled, head for **Torrey Pines State Natural Reserve,** where you can be rewarded for hiking down the cliffs to the state beach with breathtaking views in every direction. (If you're with small children, the trek might prove too challenging, but you can still take in the views from the top.)

For dinner, swing north to **Del Mar**—during racing season, the evening scene is happening—or, for families, head down to **Ocean Beach** for a juicy burger at the surf-theme **Hodad's.**

Day 4

Start the day with a morning visit to **Cabrillo National Monument,** a national park with a number of activities. Learn about 16th-century explorer Juan Rodríguez Cabrillo, take a gentle 2-mile hike on the beautiful Bayside Trail, look around the Old Point Loma Lighthouse, and peer at tide pools, which teem with sea life (remember: look but don't touch). ■ TIP→ Find out if low tide is in the morning or afternoon before planning your itinerary.

After Cabrillo, hop in your car and head to **Old Town,** where San Diego's early history comes to carefully reconstructed life. Old Town's Mexican restaurants aren't the city's best, but they're definitely bustling and kid-friendly, and frosty margaritas make an added incentive for grown-ups.

After that, spend a few hours exploring whatever cluster of neighborhoods appeals to you most. If you like casual coastal neighborhoods with a youthful vibe, head to **Pacific, Mission,** or **Ocean Beach,** or venture up to **North County** for an afternoon in **Encinitas,** which epitomizes the old California surf town.

If edgy and artsy are more your thing, check out the hip and ever-changing neighborhoods in **Uptown,** where you'll find super-cool shops, bars, and eateries.

ALTERNATIVES

If you're an adventure junkie, you might want to ignore all of the above suggestions and just skip to the Fodor's Sports and the Outdoors listings. You can easily fill four days or more with every imaginable outdoor activity, from swimming, surfing, and sailing to hiking, golfing,

TIPS

■ Sure, it's fun to dip those toes in the sand and saunter through one of the world's most incredible zoos. But don't overlook San Diego's somewhat underrated performing arts scene. It's extremely easy to add a theater performance or a concert to any of the four days described here. Some of the city's top performance venues are in Balboa Park (Day 1), downtown (Day 2), and La Jolla (Day 3).

■ If you plan to tour more than a couple of museums in Balboa Park, buy the **Balboa Park Explorer Pass**, which gets you into 14 attractions for just $53, or the **Balboa Park Explorer Combo Pass**, which also gets you into the zoo (it costs $89). You can buy these at the **Balboa Park Visitor Center** (☎ 619/239–0512 ⊕ www.balboapark.org).

■ Locals complain about public transportation as often as they complain about the price of fuel, but the **Trolley** and the **Coaster** are a hassle-free way to get to foot-friendly neighborhoods up and down the coast. Public transportation saves you the headache of traffic and parking, and includes free sightseeing along the way. You can head almost anywhere from the historic **Santa Fe Depot** downtown (don't miss the cutting-edge Museum of Contemporary Art next door to the station).

paragliding, and stand-up paddling. San Diego is an athletic enthusiast's heaven—unless you're a skier, that is.

In **winter,** adjust the itineraries to include more indoor activities—the museums are fantastic—as well as a whale-watching boat tour.

In **summer,** check local listings for outdoor concerts, theater, and movie screenings, the perfect way to relax and enjoy a warm evening outdoors.

LIKE A LOCAL

Just because San Diego has tourist attractions at every turn doesn't mean you shouldn't stray from the beaten path and pretend you're a local for a day.

A pared-down pace
Balboa Park is the city's preferred playground. Visitors with detailed agendas (Museums? Check. Zoo? Check.) often miss out on the sweet spots that keep locals coming back time and again. Grab a map from the visitor center and explore the park's nooks and crannies. Or throw down a blanket on the lawn and laugh at the other tourists with their impossibly long to-do lists.

The hoppiest place on Earth
Cold beer seems to suit San Diego's chill personality, which may be why their craft-brewing scene has been lauded as one of the most cutting-edge in the world. You could easily spend an entire day visiting breweries, from the tiny **Alpine Beer Company**—to Escondido's venerable **Stone Brewing**, which started off as a pet project and now ships nationwide. If a full-fledged beer tour is out of the question, try a bold double IPA—a San Diego specialty—at **O'Brien's**, a Kearny Mesa pub that's low on personality but high on hops, or head to **30th Street** in North Park, which is lined with so many brewpubs that it's been nicknamed the "Belgian Corridor" by in-the-know imbibers.

Fill your heart with art
MCASD Downtown's **Thursday Night Thing**—aka TNT—is a boisterous quarterly museum party that puts to rest all notions of an artless art scene.

Sunrise, sunset
The beaches can't be beat, but battling the crazy summer crowds for a spot on the sand is far from relaxing. Take a brisk stroll just after dawn, and savor the views without distraction. Or, find a secluded spot on the cliffs for a sunset happy hour. Booze is banned at beaches, but a little creativity will have you toasting in no time (hint: wash and save a couple of paper coffee cups).

Break for breakfast
Even fitness freaks—and San Diegans are among the country's fittest—will agree that a slow-paced morning meal is a lovely start to the weekend, which explains the long lines at any place worth the wait.

The **Mission** has locations in Mission Beach (✉ 3795 Mission Blvd. ☎ 858/488–9060), North Park (✉ 2801 University Ave. ☎ 619/220–8992), and the East Village (✉ 1250 J St. ☎ 619/232–7662). The café food is simple and hearty, ranging from traditional fare (eggs, pancakes) to the Latino-inspired (the Papas Locas or "crazy potatoes" will burn a hole in your tongue).

Hash House A Go Go (✉ 3628 5th Ave., Hillcrest ☎ 619/298–4646) specializes in Southern-accented favorites, in large portions. There are a variety of the namesake hashes and eggs Benedict, as well as fluffy pancakes and French toast. Weekends mean long lines, so try to visit during the week.

Kono's Surf Club Café (✉ 704 Garnet Ave. ☎ 858/483–1669) in Pacific Beach lures locals with an outdoor patio and ocean views, but the last thing you'll want to do after eating one of Kono's massive breakfast burritos is slip into a bikini. There's a reason for the expression "burrito belly"—but it's a small price to pay for brazenly overindulgent pleasure.

SAN DIEGO WITH KIDS

Beach fun

A pail and shovel can keep kids entertained for hours at the beach—**Coronado Beach** is especially family-friendly. Be liberal with the sunscreen, even if it's cloudy.

If you're visiting in summer, check out the **Imperial Beach Sun and Sea Festival's** sand castle competition, which usually takes place in late July or early August. There is even a kids' competition.

Drop off the tweens and teens for a morning **surf lesson** and enjoy some guilt-free grown-up time. Or rent bikes for a casual family ride along the **Mission Bay boardwalk**. If that's not enough of an adventure, take your daring offspring on the **Giant Dipper**, an old wooden roller coaster at Mission Bay's **Belmont Park**, also home to a huge arcade.

Top attractions

LEGOLAND California is a full day of thrills for kids 12 and under, while the **San Diego Zoo** and **San Diego Safari Park** satisfy all age groups and every kind of kid, from the curious (plenty of educational angles) to the boisterous (room to run around and lots of animals to imitate). They even have family sleepover nights in summer.

Winter sightings

If you're visiting in winter, try a **whale-watching** tour. Even if you don't see any migrating gray whales, the boat ride is fun. La Jolla's **Birch Aquarium** has enough glowing and tentacled creatures to send imaginations plummeting leagues under the sea.

Museums geared to kids

An afternoon at the museum might elicit yawns until they spy all the neat stuff. Balboa Park's **San Diego Air and Space Museum** celebrates aviation and flight history with exhibitions that include actual planes, while **Reuben H. Fleet Science Center** inspires budding scientists with interactive exhibits and its IMAX dome theater. The **San Diego Model Railroad Museum** features miles and miles of model trains and track, including an incredibly detailed reproduction of the Tehachapi railroad circa 1952.

Downtown's **New Children's Museum** appeals to all age groups; too-cool teens can even retreat to the edgy Teen Studio. With installations geared just for them and dry and wet art-making areas (less mess for you), kids can channel all that excess vacation energy into something productive. While they color and craft, you can admire the museum's ultracontemporary, sustainable architecture.

Take me out to the ball game

Baseball buffs will have a blast at **PETCO Park**, where the San Diego Padres play all spring and summer. PETCO's Park at the Park, a grassy elevated area outside the stadium, offers stellar center-field views—plus all the action on a big-screen—with a sandy play space if your kids get bored after a few innings.

Treating your tots

Pacific Beach's yummy **The Baked Bear** (*4516 Mission Blvd.* ⊕ *www.thebakedbear.com*) offers customized ice cream sandwiches that are sure to please. Also delish is Hillcrest's **Babycakes** (✉ *3766 5th Ave.* ⊕ *www.babycakessandiego.com*), a stylish spot nestled in an 1889 Craftsman near Balboa Park. Bonus: Babycakes serves beer and wine for weary moms and dads. If toys trump sweet treats, check out the classics at **Geppetto's** (⊕ *www.geppettostoys.com*), a family-run business with eight locations throughout San Diego, including Old Town, La Jolla, and the Fashion Valley Mall.

FREE (AND ALMOST FREE) IN SAN DIEGO

San Diego may levy an unofficial "sunshine tax," but it makes up for it with plenty of free stuff. Aside from the beaches, backcountry trails, and verdant city parks—all as free as the steadfast sun and endless blue skies—a little careful planning can land you cost-free (or very cheap) fun for the whole family.

Free in Balboa Park

Balboa Park hosts its one-hour **Twilight in the Park** concert series from June to August, Tuesday through Thursday at 6:15 pm. Sit under the stars and take in everything from Dixieland Jazz to Latin salsa. Also at the park, check out the **Spreckels International Organ Festival** concerts Monday at 7:30 pm, from June to August, as well as 2 pm Sunday matinee concerts throughout the year. Balboa Park's **Film in the Garden,** an outdoor movie screening, runs throughout summer. The **Timken Museum of Art** in Balboa Park is free but a donation is suggested.

Free concerts

The Del Mar Fairgrounds' summertime **4 O'Clock Fridays** series features big-name local and national bands; it's technically free, though you still have to pay a few bucks for racetrack admission.

Also worth catching: Carlsbad's **TGIF Jazz in the Parks,** Friday at 6 pm; **Coronado Summer Concerts-in-the-Park,** Sunday at 6 pm, May through September; **La Jolla Concerts by the Sea,** Sunday at 2 pm, July and August; the **Del Mar Twilight Concert Series,** Tuesday at 7 pm, June through September; and Encinitas' **Sunday Summer Concerts by the Sea,** 3 pm, July and August.

The annual **Adams Avenue Unplugged** festival in spring and **Adams Avenue Street Festival** in September both hit pay dirt: blues, folk, country, jazz, indie, world, and more—all for free.

Free (or inexpensive) tastings

Beer aficionados can take a $3, 45-minute tour of the 55,000-square-foot **Stone Brewing Company**—groups fill up fast, maybe because of the free tastings at the end. At **Alpine Beer Company**, it's not free, but it's cheap: up to four tasters are just $1.50 each. Wine lovers might pack a lunch and head for **Orfila Vineyards & Winery,** where picnic tables dot the pastoral landscape—the wine's not free, but the views are. Or spend an entire afternoon in **Temecula Wine Country.** Tastings typically aren't free, but you can find twofer coupons and other discounts at ⊕ *www.temeculawines.org.*

October freebies

October is Kids Free Month at the **San Diego Zoo** and the **San Diego Safari Park;** all children under 11 get in free.

Free museums

Both locations of **MCASD** are always free for patrons under 25, and for everyone else the third Thursday of the month from 5 to 7 pm.

In February, you can pick up a free **Museum Month Pass** at Macy's that offers half-off admission to 40 museums for the entire month.

Many of San Diego's museums offer a once-a-month free Tuesday, on a rotating schedule (see ⊕ *www.balboapark.org* for the schedule) to San Diego city and county residents and active military, and their families; special exhibitions often require separate admission.

Discounts and deals

Try **Just My Ticket** (⊕ *www.justmyticket. com*) for deals on last-minute theater, concert, and sporting event tickets, as well as restaurant coupons.

A WALK THROUGH SAN DIEGO'S PAST

Downtown San Diego is a living tribute to history and revitalization. The Gaslamp Quarter followed up its boomtown years—the late 1800s, when Wyatt Earp ran gambling halls and sailors frequented brothels lining 4th and 5th avenues—with a long stint of seediness, emerging only recently as a glamorous place to live and play. Little Italy, once a bustling fishing village, got a fresh start when the city took its cause to heart.

Where It All Started

Begin at the corner of 4th and Island. This is the location of the 150-year-old **William Heath Davis House**, a saltbox structure shipped around Cape Horn and assembled in the Gaslamp Quarter. Among its famous former residents: Alonzo Horton, the city's founder. Take a tour, keeping a lookout for the house's current resident: a lady ghost.

From there walk a block east to 5th Avenue and head north. Along the way, you'll see some of the 16½-block historic district's best-known Victorian-era commercial beauties, including the Italianate **Marston Building** (at F Street), the **Keating Building**, the **Spencer-Ogden Building**, and the **Old City Hall**. Architecture buffs should pick up a copy of *San Diego's Gaslamp Quarter*, a self-guided tour published by the Historical Society.

At E Street, head back over to 4th Avenue and you'll behold the **Balboa Theatre**, a striking Spanish Renaissance–style building that was constructed in 1923 and restored in 2007. Right next to it is **Westfield Horton Plaza** mall, which opened its doors in 1985. This multilevel mall played a huge role in downtown's revitalization, as entrepreneurs and preservationists realized the value of the Gaslamp Quarter. Pop across Broadway to check out the stately **U.S. Grant Hotel,** built in 1910 by the son of President Ulysses S. Grant.

Art Stop

Follow Broadway west to Kettner Boulevard, where the **Museum of Contemporary Art San Diego (MCASD)** makes a bold statement with its steel-and-glass lines. It's definitely worth a wander, as is MCASD's newest addition across the street, situated in the renovated baggage depot of the 1915 **Santa Fe Depot** (the station itself is also a stunner).

From Fishermen to Fashionistas

From there, head north on Kettner to A Street, make a quick right, and then take a left on India Street. This is the heart of **Little Italy**, which at the turn of the 20th century was a bustling Italian fishing village. The area fell into disarray in the early 1970s due to a decline in the tuna industry and the construction of I–5, which destroyed 35% of the area. In 1996, a group of forward-thinking architects—commissioned by the city—developed new residential, retail, and public areas that coexist beautifully with the neighborhood's historic charms. Now, it's a vibrant urban center with hip eateries, bars, and shops. There are remnants of retro Little Italy, from authentic cafés (check out **Pappalecco,** a popular gelateria) to boccie ball matches played by old-timers at **Amici Park.**

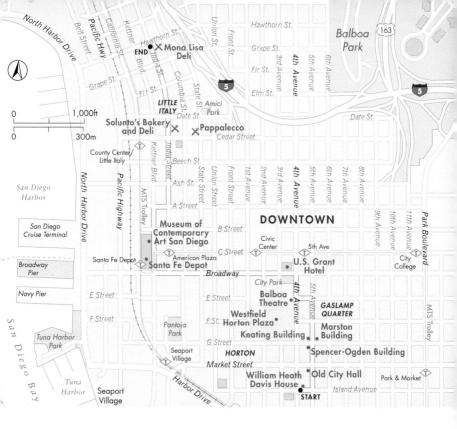

Highlights:	The restored gas lamps that give the Gaslamp its name; the juxtaposition of old and new architecture; Little Italy's sidewalk cafés.
Where to Start:	At the corner of 4th and Island avenues, at the William Heath Davis House. It's a short walk from most downtown hotels. If you drive, park in a paid lot or at nearby Horton Plaza, which offers three free hours with validation (get your ticket stamped at one of the validation machines).
Length:	About 3 miles and three to four hours round-trip with stops. Take the Orange Line trolley from Santa Fe Depot back if you're tired.
Where to Stop:	From Little Italy follow the same path back or head down Laurel Street to Harbor Drive and wander along the waterfront until you hit Broadway.
Best Time to Go:	Morning or early afternoon.
Worst Time to Go:	In the evening, when it's just too crowded.
Where to Refuel:	If your stomach is growling, Little Italy is waiting for you like an Italian mamma: mangia, mangia! Try Solunto's Bakery and Deli (⊠ 1643 India St.) or Mona Lisa (⊠ 2061 India St.).

FARMERS' MARKETS

Take advantage of San Diego's year-round gorgeous weather and visit a farmers' market or flea market during your stay. You'll have a chance to mingle with locals and pick up some bargains on things that are hard to find downtown or at the mall. Enjoy the festive atmosphere with live entertainment as you browse the tempting selection of fresh produce, gourmet foods, arts and crafts, fresh flowers, and more. *Below are a few of our favorite markets.* You can find more on ⊕ *www. sdfarmbureau.org.*

■TIP→ Before you head out, be sure you wear comfortable shoes and bring a tote bag to carry your purchases. Arrive early for the best selection, and assume that you'll have to pay with cash rather than plastic. A little haggling is expected, but be sure to do it politely, and with a smile.

Cedros Avenue Farmers' Market. Located at the south end of the Cedros Design District, this upscale market offers organic veggies and herbs, local fruit, healthy juices, California wines, smoked salmon, to-die-for chocolates, freshly baked bread, and, for your canine pals, all-natural dog treats. If you arrive hungry, the food court opens an hour early. ⊠ *444 S. Cedros Ave., at the corner of S. Cedros Ave. and Rosa St., Solana Beach* ⊕ *www.solana beachfarmersmarket.com* ☉ *Sun. 1–5.*

Coronado Farmers' Market. This small market, in the parking lot of Il Fornaio restaurant, boasts a scenic bayside setting and more than a dozen vendors selling a variety of fresh produce and exotic flowers from local farms. ⊠ *Ferry Landing, First and B Sts., Coronado* ⊕ *www. sdfarmbureau.org* ☉ *Tues. 2:30–6.*

Hillcrest Farmer's Market. At one of the city's best farmer's markets there's farm-fresh produce, of course, but also handmade clothing and jewelry, and other handicrafts. Come browse and plan to stay for lunch: there are all sorts of vendors selling top-notch food, from fresh crêpes to tamales and just about everything in between. ⊠ *3960 Normal St., at Lincoln Ave., Hillcrest* ⊕ *www.hillcrestfarmersmarket.com* ☉ *Sun. 9–2.*

La Jolla Open Aire Market. With a county-fair atmosphere and proceeds benefiting local children, this large market features not only fresh produce and flowers, but also paintings from local artists, handmade clothing and jewelry, and a tempting food court serving everything from crêpes and tacos to gyros and roasted corn on the cob. ⊠ *La Jolla Elementary School playground, at corner of Girard St. and Genter St., 7335 Girard St., La Jolla* ⊕ *www.lajollamarket.com* ☉ *Sun. 9–1.*

Little Italy Mercato. This festive market is one of the largest and liveliest in San Diego. Enjoy a panino or Italian pastry as you stroll the aisles, shopping for handcrafted gifts, cheese, nuts, Mexican candy, and olive oil. ⊠ *Date St. (between India and Columbia Sts.), Little Italy* ⊕ *www. littleitalymercato.com* ☉ *Sat. 8–2.*

Ocean Beach Farmers' Market. Voted "Best Farmers Market in California" by *Sunset* magazine, this bustling midweek event features live music, fresh produce, samples from local restaurants, crafts, and more. Other popular offerings are the handmade apparel and accessories, holistic products, and the bouncy house for kids. ⊠ *Newport Ave. between Cable and Bacon Sts., 4900 Newport Ave., Ocean Beach* ⊕ *https://oceanbeachsandiego.com/ attractions/annual-events/farmers-market-wednesdays* ☉ *Wed., Apr.–early Dec., Jan.–early Mar.*

2

DOWNTOWN

East Village, Embarcadero, Gaslamp
Quarter, and Little Italy

GETTING ORIENTED

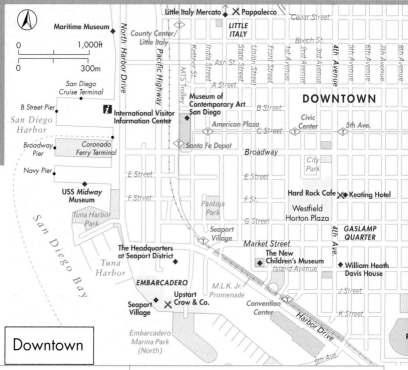

Little Italy Mercato ✕ Pappalecco · Cedar Street

Maritime Museum

County Center/
Little Italy

LITTLE
ITALY

Beech St.

0 ——— 1,000ft
0 ——— 300m

North Harbor Drive · Pacific Highway · MTS Trolley · Kettner St. · India Street · Ash St. · State Street · Union Street · Front Street · 1st Avenue · 2nd Avenue · 3rd Avenue · 4th Avenue · 5th Avenue · 6th Avenue · 7th Avenue · 8th Avenue

San Diego
Cruise Terminal

A Street

Museum of
Contemporary Art
San Diego

DOWNTOWN

B Street Pier

International Visitor
Information Center

B Street

San Diego
Harbor

American Plaza
C Street

Civic
Center

5th Ave.

Broadway
Pier

Coronado
Ferry Terminal

Santa Fe Depot

Broadway

City
Park

Navy Pier

E Street

E Street

USS Midway
Museum

F Street

F St.

Hard Rock Cafe ✕◆ Keating Hotel

Tuna Harbor
Park

Pantoja
Park

G Street

Westfield
Horton Plaza

San Diego Bay

Seaport
Village

Market Street

GASLAMP
QUARTER

Tuna
Harbor

The Headquarters
at Seaport District

The New
Children's Museum
Island Avenue

4th Ave.

◆ William Heath
Davis House

EMBARCADERO

M.L.K. Jr.
Promenade

J Street

Upstart
✕ Crow & Co.

Convention
Center

K Street

Seaport ◆
Village

Harbor Drive

Embarcadero
Marina Park
(North)

5th Ave.

Downtown

GETTING HERE	TOP REASONS TO GO
It's an easy drive into downtown, especially from the nearby airport. There are reasonably priced parking lots (about $10 per day) along Harbor Drive, Pacific Highway, and lower Broadway and Market Street. Most restaurants offer valet parking at night, but beware of fees of $15 and up. If you tire of exploring downtown on foot, hop aboard a pedicab, the San Diego Trolley, or a GoCar (three-wheel cars equipped with a GPS-guided audio tour).	**Waterfront delights:** Stroll along the Embarcadero, explore Seaport Village, or enjoy a harbor cruise. **Contemporary art for all ages:** From the stunning galleries of the Museum of Contemporary Art to the clever incorporation of art and play at the New Children's Museum, downtown is the place for art. **Maritime history:** Climb aboard and explore a wide array of vessels from sailing ships to submarines. **Delicious dining:** The hip and high-style restaurants of Little Italy, the Gaslamp Quarter and the East Village make downtown San Diego a diner's delight. **Happening Gaslamp:** It's hard to believe this hip neighborhood filled with street art, galleries, restaurants, and buzzing nightlife was once slated for the wrecking ball.

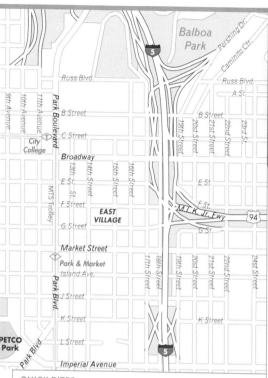

PLANNING YOUR TIME

Most downtown attractions are open daily, but the Museum of Contemporary Art is closed Wednesday and the New Children's Museum is closed on Tuesday during the school year. For guided tours of the Gaslamp Quarter Historic District, visit on Saturday. A boat trip on the harbor, or at least a hop over to Coronado on the ferry, is a must at any time of year. From December through March, when gray whales migrate between the Pacific Northwest and southern Baja, consider booking a whale-watching excursion from the Broadway Pier.

QUICK BITES

Pappalecco. Kids and adults alike will swoon over the addictive gelato at Pappalecco, while those seeking something savory can choose from a selection of panini and other snacks. ⊠ *1602 State St., Little Italy* ☎ *619/238–4590* ⊕ *www.pappalecco.com.*

Upstart Crow & Co. This combination bookstore and coffeehouse serves good cappuccino and espresso with pastries and cakes. ⊠ *835 W. Harbor Dr., #C, Seaport Village, Central Plaza, Embarcadero* ☎ *619/232–4855* ⊕ *www. upstartcrowtrading.com.*

You can get everything from cinnamon rolls to sushi at the food court on **Westfield Horton Plaza's top level.**

VISITOR INFORMATION

International Visitor Information Center. This office is a great resource for information and discounts on hotels, restaurants, and local attractions. As part of the Embarcadero redevelopment, this office will soon relocate to its new and stylish home farther south on North Harbor Drive. ⊠ *1140 N. Harbor Dr., Embarcadero* ☎ *619/236–1212* ⊕ *www.sandiego.org* ☼ *June–Sept., daily 9–5; Oct.–May, daily 9–4.*

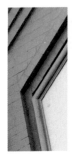

Sightseeing
★★★★★
Nightlife
★★★★★
Dining
★★★★★
Lodging
★★★★☆
Shopping
★★★★☆

Nearly written off in the 1970s, today downtown San Diego is a testament to conservation and urban renewal. Once derelict Victorian storefronts now house the hottest restaurants, and the *Star of India*, the world's oldest active sailing ship, almost lost to scrap, floats regally along the Embarcadero. Like many modern U.S. cities, downtown San Diego's story is as much about its rebirth as its history. Although many consider downtown to be the 16½-block Gaslamp Quarter, it's actually comprised of eight neighborhoods, including East Village, Little Italy, and Embarcadero.

GASLAMP QUARTER

Updated by
Claire Deeks
van der Lee

Considered the liveliest of the downtown neighborhoods, the Gaslamp Quarter's 4th and 5th avenues are peppered with trendy nightclubs, swanky lounge bars, chic restaurants, and boisterous sports pubs. The Gaslamp has the largest collection of commercial Victorian-style buildings in the country. Despite this, when the move for downtown redevelopment gained momentum in the 1970s, there was talk of bulldozing them and starting from scratch. In response, concerned history buffs, developers, architects, and artists formed the Gaslamp Quarter Council to clean up and preserve the quarter.

The majority of the quarter's landmark buildings are on 4th and 5th avenues, between Island Avenue and Broadway. If you don't have much time, stroll down 5th Avenue, where highlights include **Louis Bank of Commerce** (No. 835), **Old City Hall** (No. 664), **Nesmith-Greeley** (No. 825), and **Yuma** (No. 631) buildings. The Romanesque Revival **Keating Hotel** at 432 F Street was designed by the same firm that created the famous Hotel Del Coronado, the Victorian grande dame that presides over Coronado's beach. At the corner of 4th Avenue and F Street, peer into the **Hard Rock Cafe,** which occupies a restored turn-of-the-20th-century tavern with a 12-foot mahogany bar and a spectacular stained-glass domed ceiling.

The section of G Street between 6th and 9th avenues has become a haven for galleries; stop in one of them to pick up a map of the downtown arts district. The **Urban Art Trail** has added pizzazz to drab city thoroughfares by transforming such things as trash cans and traffic controller boxes into works of

WORD OF MOUTH

"Did you visit Seaport Village? It can be so beautiful on a sunny day. There are tons of casual restaurants to restaurants that overlook the bay. There are also tons of great attractions like the USS *Midway* (which you can tour) and the *Star of India*." —kenem

art. The Gaslamp is a lively place—during baseball season, the streets flood with Padres fans, and festivals, such as Mardi Gras in February, ShamROCK on St. Patrick's Day, and Monster Bash in October, keep the party atmosphere going throughout the year.

TOP ATTRACTIONS

Westfield Horton Plaza. This downtown shopping, dining, and entertainment mecca fronts Broadway and G Street from 1st to 4th avenues and covers more than six city blocks. Designed by Jon Jerde and completed in 1985, Westfield Horton Plaza is a collage of colorful tile work, banners waving in the air, and modern sculptures. The complex rises in uneven, staggered levels to five floors; great views of downtown from the harbor to Balboa Park and beyond can be had here.

Macy's and Nordstrom department stores anchor the plaza that also houses clothing, sporting-goods, jewelry, and gift shops. Other attractions include a movie complex, restaurants, and the respected San Diego Repertory Theatre below ground level. In 2008 the **Balboa Theater**, contiguous with the shopping center, reopened its doors after a $26.5-million renovation. The historic 1920s theater seats 1,400 and offers live arts and cultural performances throughout the week.

The mall has a multilevel parking garage; even so, lines to find a space can be long. ■TIP➡ Entering the parking structure on G Street rather than 4th Avenue generally means less traffic and more parking space. Parking validation is complimentary whether you spend a bundle or just window-shop. Validation machines throughout the center allow for three hours' free parking; after that it's $8 per hour (or $2 per 15-minute increment). If you use this notoriously confusing fruit-and-vegetable–themed garage, be sure to remember at which produce level you've left your car. If you're staying downtown, the Old Town Trolley Tour will drop you directly in front of Westfield Horton Plaza. ✉ *324 Horton Plaza, Gaslamp Quarter* ☎ *619/239–8180* ⊕ *www.westfield. com/hortonplaza* ☉ *Weekdays 10–9, Sat. 10–8, Sun. 11–6.*

WORTH NOTING

Gaslamp Museum at the William Heath Davis House. The oldest wooden house in San Diego is the site of the Gaslamp Quarter Historical Foundation, the district's curator. Before developer Alonzo Horton came to town, Davis, a prominent San Franciscan, had made an unsuccessful attempt to develop the waterfront area. In 1850 he had this prefab saltbox-style house, built in Maine, shipped around Cape Horn and assembled in San Diego (it originally stood at State and Market streets). Ninety-minute walking tours of the historic district leave from the house on Saturday at 11 am and cost $15. If you can't time your visit with the tour, a self-guided tour map is available for $2. ✉ *410 Island Ave., at 4th Ave., Gaslamp Quarter* ☎ *619/233–4692* ⊕ *www.gaslampquarter. org* ✉ *$5* ⊙ *Tues.–Sat. 10–5, Sun. noon–4.*

EMBARCADERO

The **Embarcadero** cuts a scenic swath along the harborfront and connects today's downtown San Diego to its maritime routes. The bustle of Embarcadero comes less these days from the activities of fishing folk than from the throngs of tourists, but this waterfront walkway, stretching from the Convention Center to the Maritime Museum, remains the nautical soul of the city. There are several seafood restaurants here, as well as sea vessels of every variety—cruise ships, ferries, tour boats, and Navy destroyers.

On the north end of the Embarcadero at Ash Street you'll find the **Maritime Museum.** South of it, the **B Street Pier** is used by ships from major cruise lines while tickets for harbor tours and whale-watching

> ### GONE TO THE DOGS
>
> In 2007 two life-size dog statues took center stage in San Diego's downtown park next to the William Heath Davis House on the corner of 4th and Island avenues. Dedicated to San Diego's official town dog, "Bum," the bronze statue shares a prominent place alongside "Greyfriars Bobby," the official dog of Edinburgh, Scotland. When the citizens of Edinburgh discovered that, like them, San Diego had an official town dog, they presented a Greyfriars Bobby replica. In 2008, a replica of Bum was installed in Edinburgh, symbolizing the friendship between the sister cities.

trips are sold at the foot of **Broadway Pier.** The terminal for the Coronado Ferry lies in between. Docked at the **Navy Pier** is the decommissioned **USS** *Midway.* At the foot of G Street, **Tuna Harbor** was once the hub of one of San Diego's earliest and most successful industries, commercial tuna fishing. The pleasant Tuna Harbor Park offers a great view of boating on the bay and across to any aircraft carriers docked at the North Island naval base. A few blocks south, **Embarcadero Marina Park North** is an 8-acre extension into the harbor from the center of **Seaport Village.** It's usually full of kite fliers, in-line skaters, and picnickers. Seasonal celebrations, including San Diego's Parade of Lights, the Port of San Diego Big Balloon Parade and the Big Bay July 4 Celebration, are held here and at the similar **Embarcadero Marina Park South.** The **San Diego Convention Center,** on Harbor Drive between 1st and 6th avenues, is a waterfront landmark designed by Canadian architect Arthur Erickson. The backdrop of blue sky and sea complements the building's nautical lines. The center often holds trade shows that are open to the public, and tours of the building are available.

A huge revitalization project is underway along the northern Embarcadero. The overhaul will create a wide esplanade with gardens, shaded pavilions, and public art installations along the water as well as a new information center building. In mid-2014, San Diego unveiled the new Waterfront Park located adjacent to the County Administration Building. This 12-acre expanse includes a large green space, sprawling children's play area and a spectacular interactive fountain that's perfect for cooling off on hot sunny days.

TOP ATTRACTIONS

FAMILY **Maritime Museum.**
Fodor'sChoice ⇨ *See the highlighted listing in this*
★ *chapter.*

Fodor'sChoice **Museum of Contemporary Art San**
★ **Diego (MCASD).** At the Downtown branch of the city's contemporary art museum (the original is in La Jolla), explore the works of international and regional artists in a modern, urban space. The Jacobs Building—formerly the baggage building at the historic Santa Fe Depot—features large gallery spaces, high ceilings, and natural lighting, giving artists the flexibility to create large-scale installations. MCASD's collection includes many Pop Art, minimalist, and conceptual works from the 1950s to the present. The museum showcases both established and emerging artists in temporary exhibitions, and has permanent, site-specific commissions by Jenny Holzer and Richard Serra. ■TIP→ Admission, good for seven days, includes the Downtown and La Jolla locations. ⊠ *1100 and 1001 Kettner Blvd., Downtown* ☎ *858/454–3541* ⊕ *www.mcasd.org* ⌂ *$10; free 3rd Thurs. of the month 5–7* ⊙ *Thurs.–Tues., 11–5; 3rd Thurs. until 7* ⊙ *Closed Wed.*

FAMILY **The New Children's Museum (NCM).** The NCM blends contemporary
Fodor'sChoice art with unstructured play to create an environment that appeals to
★ children as well as adults. The 50,000-square-foot structure was constructed from recycled building materials, operates on solar energy, and is convection-cooled by an elevator shaft. It also features a nutritious and eco-conscious café. Interactive exhibits include designated areas for toddlers and teens, as well as plenty of activities for the entire family. Several art workshops are offered each day, as well as hands-on studios where visitors are encouraged to create their own art. The studio projects change frequently and the entire museum changes exhibits every 18 to 24 months, so there is always something new to explore. The adjoining 1-acre park and playground is across from the convention center

TROLLEY DANCES

Every city has street performers, but during the fall in San Diego, the commuter experience comes alive with dance performances at select trolley stops. A partnership between the Jean Isaacs Dance Theater and the city's Metropolitan Transit System, Trolley Dances combines human movement with the ever-changing scenery of the city as a backdrop. At six different stops, dancers give site-specific performances inspired by their environments, from historic Barrio Logan to the newly opened downtown library. Get on the trolley for a tour ($35) to all of the sites to see each performance. Learn more at ⊕ *www.sandiegodancetheater.org/trolleydances2013.html.*

MARITIME MUSEUM

✉ *1492 N. Harbor Dr., Embarcadero* ☎ *619/234–9153*
⊕ *www.sdmaritime.org* ✉ *$16 includes entry to all ships except Californian, $5 more for Pilot Boat Bay Cruise* ☉ *Daily 9–8.*

TIPS

■ Weekend sails (and Friday in summer) on the Californian, typically from noon to 4, cost $60 for adults; buy tickets online or at the museum on the day of sail. Arrive at least an hour early on sunny days for a spot onboard.

■ Cruise San Diego Bay for only $5 plus museum admission on the 1914 Pilot boat. The 45-minute narrated tours are offered at several times.

■ Partnering with the museum, the renowned yacht America also offers sails on the bay, and whale-watching excursions in winter. Times and prices vary.

■ Parties of eight or more should call ahead for special group admission and a guided two-hour tour. Exploring the submarines requires climbing through several midsize hatches; wear flat shoes and pants.

■ Keep an eye out for the workshop onboard the Berkley where volunteers build extraordinary model ships.

From sailing ships to submarines, the Maritime Museum is a must for anyone with an interest in nautical history. This collection of restored and replica ships affords a fascinating glimpse of San Diego during its heyday as a commercial seaport.

Highlights

The jewel of the collection, the *Star of India*, is often considered a symbol of the city. An iron windjammer built in 1863, the *Star of India* made 21 trips around the world in the late 1800s, when it traveled the East Indian trade route, shuttled immigrants from England to New Zealand, and served the Alaskan salmon trade. Saved from the scrap yard and painstakingly restored, the *Star of India* is the oldest active iron sailing ship in the world.

The popular HMS *Surprise*, purchased in 2004, is a replica of an 18th-century British Royal Navy frigate and was used in the Academy Award–winning *Master and Commander: The Far Side of the World.*

The museum's headquarters are on the *Berkeley*, an 1898 steam-driven ferryboat, which served the Southern Pacific Railroad in San Francisco until 1958. Its ornate detailing carefully restored, the main deck serves as a floating museum, with permanent exhibits on West Coast maritime history and complementary rotating exhibits.

Two submarines are featured at the museum: a *Soviet B-39 "Foxtrot"* class submarine and the USS *Dolphin* research submarine. Take a peek at the harbor from a periscope, get up close with the engine control room, and wonder at the tight living quarters onboard.

trolley stop. ✉ *200 W. Island Ave., Embarcadero* ☎ *619/233–8792* ⊕ *www.thinkplaycreate.org* 🎟 *$10; 2nd Sun. each month free 10–4* ⏱ *During school year: Mon. and Wed.–Sat. 10–4, Sun. noon–4; closed Tues.; summer hours: Mon.–Sat. 10-4, Sun. noon–4.*

FAMILY **Seaport Village.** You'll find some of the best views of the harbor at Seaport Village, three bustling shopping plazas designed to reflect the New England clapboard and Spanish Mission architectural styles of early California. On a prime stretch of waterfront the dining, shopping, and entertainment complex connects the harbor with hotel towers and the convention center. Specialty shops offer everything from a kite store and swing emporium to a shop devoted to hot sauces. You can dine at snack bars and restaurants, many with harbor views.

Live music can be heard daily from noon to 4 at the main food court. Additional free concerts take place every Sunday from 1 to 4 at the East Plaza Gazebo. If you happen to visit San Diego in late November or early December, you might be lucky enough to catch Surfing Santa's Arrival and even have your picture taken with Santa on his wave. In late March or early April, the Seaport Buskers Fest presents an array of costumed street performers. The **Seaport Village Carousel** (rides $3) has 54 animals, hand-carved and hand-painted by Charles Looff in 1895.

Across the street, the newly opened **Headquarters at Seaport District** converted the historic police headquarters into several trendsetting shops and restaurants, including the local Urban Beach House for surfer-chic apparel, alongside outposts of Mario Batali's Pizzeria Mozza and LA celeb boutique Kitson.

Seaport Village's shops are open daily 10 to 9 in winter and 10 to 10 in summer; a few eateries open early for breakfast. The Headquarters' shops are open Monday to Saturday from 10 to 9, and 10 to 8 on Sunday; restaurants may have extended hours. ✉ *849 W. Harbor Dr., Downtown* ☎ *619/235–4014 office and events hotline* ⊕ *www.seaportvillage.com.*

Fodor'sChoice **USS Midway Museum.** After 47 years of worldwide service, the retired ★ USS *Midway* began a new tour of duty on the south side of the Navy pier in 2004. Launched in 1945, the 1,001-foot-long ship was the largest in the world for the first 10 years of its existence. The most visible landmark on the north Embarcadero, it now serves as a floating interactive museum—an appropriate addition to the town that is home to one-third of the Pacific fleet and the birthplace of naval aviation. A free audio tour guides you through the massive ship while offering insight from former sailors. As you clamber through passageways and up and down ladder wells, you'll get a feel for how the *Midway*'s 4,500 crew members lived and worked on this "city at sea."

Though the entire tour is impressive, you'll really be wowed when you step out onto the 4-acre flight deck—not only the best place to get an idea of the ship's scale, but also one of the most interesting vantage points for bay and city skyline views. An F-14 Tomcat jet fighter is just one of many vintage aircraft on display. Free guided tours of the bridge and primary flight control, known as "the Island," depart every 10 minutes from the flight deck. Many of the docents stationed

Docked off the Navy pier, the USS *Midway* aircraft carrier was once home to 4,500 crew members.

throughout the ship served in the Navy, some even on the *Midway*, and they are eager to answer questions or share stories. The museum also offers multiple flight simulators for an additional fee, climb-aboard cockpits, and interactive exhibits focusing on naval aviation. There is a gift shop and a café with pleasant outdoor seating. This is a wildly popular stop, with most visits lasting several hours. ⚠ Despite efforts to provide accessibility throughout the ship, some areas can only be reached via fairly steep steps; a video tour of these areas is available on the hangar deck. ✉ *910 N. Harbor Dr., Embarcadero* ☎ *619/544–9600* ⊕ *www.midway.org* 🎫 *$20* 🕐 *Daily 10–5; opens at 9:30 in July and August; last admission 4 pm.*

EAST VILLAGE

The most ambitious of the downtown projects is **East Village**, not far from the Gaslamp Quarter, and encompassing 130 blocks between the railroad tracks up to J Street, and from 6th Avenue east to around 10th Street. Sparking the rebirth of this former warehouse district was the 2004 construction of the San Diego Padres' baseball stadium, **PETCO Park.** As the city's largest downtown neighborhood, East Village is continually broadening its boundaries with its urban design of redbrick cafés, spacious galleries, rooftop bars, sleek hotels, and warehouse restaurants.

Chicano Park and Barrio Logan. San Diego's Mexican-American community is centered in Barrio Logan, under the San Diego–Coronado Bay Bridge on the downtown side. Chicano Park, spread along National Avenue from Dewey to Crosby streets, is the barrio's recreational hub. It's worth taking a short detour to see the huge murals of Mexican history painted on the bridge supports at National Avenue and Dewey Street; they're among the best examples of folk art in the city. Art enthusiasts will also enjoy the burgeoning gallery scene in the Barrio Logan neighborhood, rapidly becoming a hub for artists in San Diego. ⚠ With its somewhat isolated location under a bridge, visitors should exercise caution visiting the Chicano Park murals after dark. ✉ *National Ave. at S. Evans St., Barrio Logan.*

WESTERN METAL SUPPLY

Initially scheduled for demolition to make room for PETCO Park, the historic Western Metal Supply Co. was instead incorporated into the ballpark and supports the left-field foul pole. Great care was taken to retain the historic nature of the building's exterior despite extensive interior renovations. Built in 1909, the four-story structure originally manufactured wagon wheels and war supplies, and today holds the Padres' Team Store, the Padres' Hall of Fame Bar and Grill, and rooftop seating.

WORTH NOTING

FAMILY **PETCO Park.** Opened in 2004, PETCO Park is a state-of-the-art major league ballpark and home to the San Diego Padres. Built at a cost of $450 million, the stadium features a 30- x 53-foot LED video board and more than 1,000 televisions, and is strategically designed to give fans a view of San Diego Bay, the skyline, and Balboa Park. Reflecting San Diego's beauty, the stadium is clad in sandstone from India to evoke the area's cliffs and beaches; the 42,000 seats are dark blue, reminiscent of the ocean, and the exposed steel is painted white to reflect the sails of harbor boats on the bay. The family-friendly lawnlike berm, "Park at the Park," is a popular and affordable place for fans to view the game. Behind-the-scenes guided tours of PETCO, including the press box and the dugout, are offered throughout the year. ✉ *100 Park Blvd., East Village* ☎ *619/795–5011 Tour hotline* ⊕ *sandiego.padres.mlb.com* 💲 *$12 tour* ☉ *Tours offered 7 days a wk; times vary seasonally, call ahead.*

LITTLE ITALY

Unlike many tourist-driven communities, the charming neighborhood of **Little Italy** is authentic to its roots, from the Italian-speaking residents to the imported delicacies. The main thoroughfare, India Street, is filled with lively cafés, gelato shops, bakeries, and restaurants. Art lovers can browse gallery showrooms, while shoppers adore the Fir Street cottages. Home to many in San Diego's design community, Little Italy exudes a sense of urban cool. The neighborhood bustles each Saturday during the wildly popular Mercato farmers' market, and at special events throughout the year such as Artwalk in spring and FESTA! each fall. Yet

Home of the San Diego Padres, PETCO Park offers behind-the-scenes tours.

the neighborhood is also marked by old-country charms: church bells ring on the half-hour, and Italians gather daily to play bocce in Amici Park. After an afternoon of gelati and espresso, you may just forget that you're in Southern California.

WORTH NOTING

FAMILY **Firehouse Museum.** Firefighting artifacts of all sorts fill this converted fire station, which at one time also served as the repair shop for all of San Diego's firefighting equipment. Three large rooms contain everything from 19th-century horse- and hand-drawn fire engines to 20th-century motorized trucks, the latest dating from 1943. ✉ *1572 Columbia St., Little Italy* ☎ *619/232–3473* ⊕ *www.sandiegofirehousemuseum.com* 🎟 *$3* ⊙ *Thurs. and Fri. 10–2, weekends 10–4.*

BALBOA PARK
AND SAN
DIEGO ZOO

GETTING ORIENTED

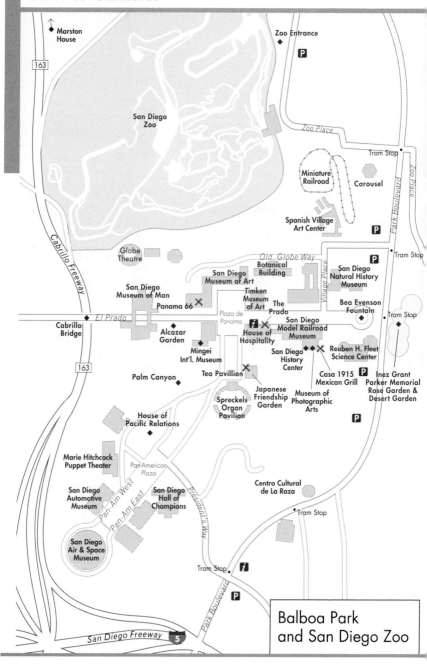

Marston House

163

Zoo Entrance

San Diego Zoo

Zoo Place

Tram Stop

Miniature Railroad

Carousel

Spanish Village Art Center

Cabrillo Freeway

Globe Theatre

Old Globe Way

Botanical Building

San Diego Museum of Art

Village Place

San Diego Natural History Museum

Tram Stop

San Diego Museum of Man

Timken Museum of Art

Panama 66

The Prado

Bea Evenson Fountain

Plaza de Panama

El Prado

San Diego Model Railroad Museum

Tram Stop

Cabrillo Bridge

Alcazar Garden

House of Hospitality

163

Mingei Int'l. Museum

San Diego History Center

Reuben H. Fleet Science Center

Palm Canyon

Tea Pavillion

Casa 1915 Mexican Grill

Inez Grant Parker Memorial Rose Garden & Desert Garden

Spreckels Organ Pavilion

Japanese Friendship Garden

Museum of Photographic Arts

House of Pacific Relations

Marie Hitchcock Puppet Theater

Pan-American Plaza

San Diego Automotive Museum

Pan-Am West

Pan-Am East

San Diego Hall of Champions

President's Way

Centro Cultural de La Raza

Tram Stop

San Diego Air & Space Museum

Tram Stop

Park Boulevard

San Diego Freeway   5

Balboa Park and San Diego Zoo

TOP REASONS TO GO

San Diego Zoo: San Diego's best-loved attraction, the world-renowned zoo, is set amidst spectacular scenery in the heart of Balboa Park.

Museums galore: Automobiles and spacecraft, international folk art and baroque masters, dinosaur fossils and mummified humans—there is something for everyone at Balboa Park's many museums.

The great outdoors: Escape down a hiking trail, try your hand at a new sport, or just soak in the sunshine from your own stretch of grass. You may even forget you are in the middle of the city.

Gorgeous gardens: From the lush tropical feel of the Botanical Building to the refined design of the Rose Garden, Balboa Park's intricate gardens and landscaping are sure to delight.

Free cultural events: The park is full of freebies, from weekly concerts at the organ pavilion to annual events like Earth Day and December Nights.

QUICK BITES

Quick snacking opportunities abound throughout the park, from cafés tucked in among the museums and grounds, to hot dog, tamale, or ice-cream carts along the walkways and plazas. Good bets include the sushi, noodles, and, of course, tea at the **Tea Pavilion** outside the Japanese Friendship Garden, or customized burritos, bowls or salads at the **Casa 1915 Mexican Grill,** inside the Casa de Balboa.

The Prado. Enjoy inventive cuisine in a gracious setting inside the House of Hospitality. An extensive lunch and dinner menu is offered in the dining room; casual bites are served in the bar. ✉ *1549 El Prado, Balboa Park* ☎ *619/557–9441* ✕ *No dinner Mon.*

GETTING HERE

Located just north of downtown, Balboa Park is easily reached from both Interstate 5 and Highway 163. The most spectacular approach is from 6th Avenue over the Cabrillo Bridge. There are also several entrances off Park Boulevard.

Balboa Park is served by public buses, particularly the No. 3, 7, and 120 lines. Taxis can often be found inside the park near the visitor center and lined up outside the zoo.

Although Balboa Park is massive, many of its star attractions are located quite close to each other. That said, exploring the park can lead to a lot of walking, particularly if you throw in a trip to the zoo or take on one of the many hiking trails. The park's free tram service stops at several spots around the park, and can give tired feet a welcome rest at the end of a long day.

VISITOR INFORMATION

House of Hospitality. The visitor center located here is an excellent resource for planning your visit to the park. Check the website before you go or spend a few minutes at the center when you arrive. There's usually a special event happening on the weekend, from festivals to fun runs. ✉ *1549 El Prado, Balboa Park* ☎ *619/239–0512* ⊕ *www.balboapark.org* ✕ *Daily 9:30–4:30 (until 5 pm from July 4th—Labor Day).*

3

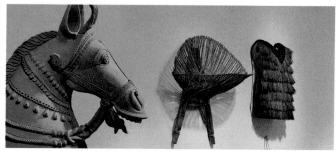

Sightseeing
★★★★★

Nightlife
★☆☆☆☆

Dining
★★★☆☆

Lodging
☆☆☆☆☆

Shopping
★★★☆☆

Overlooking downtown and the Pacific Ocean, 1,200-acre Balboa Park is the cultural heart of San Diego. Ranked as one of the world's best parks by the Project for Public Spaces, it's also where you can find most of the city's museums, art galleries, the Tony Award–winning Old Globe Theatre, and the world-famous San Diego Zoo. Often referred to as the "Smithsonian of the West" for its concentration of museums, Balboa Park is also a series of botanical gardens, performance spaces, and outdoor playrooms endeared in the hearts of residents and visitors alike.

Updated by
Claire Deeks
van der Lee

Thanks to the "Mother of Balboa Park," Kate Sessions, who suggested hiring a landscape architect in 1889, wild and cultivated gardens are an integral part of the park, featuring 350 species of trees. What Balboa Park would have looked like had she left it alone can be seen at Florida Canyon (between the main park and Morley Field, along Park Boulevard)—an arid landscape of sagebrush, cactus, and a few small trees.

In addition, the captivating architecture of Balboa's buildings, fountains, and courtyards gives the park an enchanted feel. Historic buildings dating from San Diego's 1915 Panama–California International Exposition are strung along the park's main east–west thoroughfare, El Prado, which leads from 6th Avenue eastward over the Cabrillo Bridge (formerly the Laurel Street Bridge), the park's official gateway. If you're a cinema fan, many of the buildings may be familiar—Orson Welles used exteriors of several Balboa Park buildings to represent the Xanadu estate of Charles Foster Kane in his 1941 classic, *Citizen Kane*. Prominent among them was the California Building, whose 200-foot tower, housing a 100-carillon bell that tolls the hour, is El Prado's tallest structure. Missing from the black-and-white film, however, was the magnificent blue of its tiled dome shining in the sun.

The parkland across the Cabrillo Bridge, at the west end of El Prado, is set aside for picnics and athletics. Rollerbladers zip along Balboa Drive, which leads to the highest spot in the park, Marston Point, overlooking downtown. At the green beside the bridge, ladies and gents in all-white outfits meet on summer afternoons for lawn-bowling tournaments.

East of Plaza de Panama, El Prado becomes a pedestrian mall and ends at a footbridge that crosses over Park Boulevard, the park's main north–south thoroughfare, to the perfectly tended Rose Garden, which has more than 2,000 rosebushes. In the adjacent Desert Garden, trails wind around cacti and succulents from around the world. Palm Canyon, north of the Spreckels Organ Pavilion, has more than 50 varieties of palms along a shady bridge. Pepper Grove, along Park Boulevard south of the museums, has lots of picnic tables as well as play equipment.

BALBOA PARK PLANNER

BEST TIMES TO VISIT
San Diego's ideal climate and sophisticated horticultural planning make visiting Balboa Park a year-round delight. However, summer brings longer opening hours, additional concerts at the Spreckels Organ Pavilion, and the beloved Shakespeare Festival at the Old Globe's outdoor stage.

OPEN HOURS
Most of the park's museums and attractions are open from 10 or 11 am until 4 or 5 pm, with the zoo opening earlier. Some offer extended hours during the summer. Many of the park's museums are closed on Monday. Balboa Park is beautiful by night, with the buildings along El Prado gorgeously illuminated. The Prado restaurant and the Old Globe Theatre keep this portion of the park from feeling deserted after dark.

PLANNING YOUR TIME
It's impossible to cover all Balboa Park's museums and attractions in one day, so choose your focus before you head out. If you plan on visiting the San Diego Zoo, expect to spend at least half the day there, leaving no more than a couple of hours to explore Balboa's other attractions afterward. ⇨ *See the highlighted listing for more information about the San Diego Zoo.* Otherwise, check out these itineraries.

Two Hours: To help maximize your time, rent one of the audio headsets that guide you on a 60-minute tour of the park's history, architecture, and horticulture. Pick a garden of interest to explore or drop down into Palm Canyon. Spend the remainder of your time relaxing in front of the Botanical Building or around the Bea Evenson Fountain.

Half Day: Spend a little more time at the sights above, then select a museum to explore. Alternatively, catch a puppet show at the Marie Hitchcock Theater. Afterward, you might have time for a quick ride on the carousel or a browse around the studios of the Spanish Village Art Center. Cap things off with lunch at the café in the Sculpture Garden.

Full Day: Consider purchasing a one-day discount pass from the visitor center if you want to tackle several museums. Depending on when you visit, enjoy a free concert at the Spreckels Organ Pavilion, a cultural dance at the House of Pacific Relations International Cottages, or join a guided walking tour. Active types can hit one of the more intensive hiking trails, while others can rest their feet at an IMAX or 3-D movie in the Fleet Center or Natural History Museum, respectively. In the evening, dine at the beautiful Prado restaurant or catch a show at the Old Globe Theatre.

WHAT'S FREE WHEN

Many freebies can be found in Balboa Park, both on a weekly basis and at special times of the year. Free **Ranger Tours** depart from the visitor center Tuesday and Sunday at 11 am providing an overview of the history, architecture, and horticulture of the park. On Saturday at 10 am, volunteers offer a rotating selection of thematic **Offshoot Tours,** also free of charge and departing from the visitor center. If you prefer to explore on your own, head to the visitor center to pick up a free garden tour map.

The free concerts at the **Spreckels Organ Pavilion** take place Sunday afternoons at 2 pm year-round and on Monday evenings in summer. Also at the Speckels Organ Pavilion, the **Twilight in the Park Summer Concert Series** offers various performances Tuesday, Wednesday, and Thursday from 6:15 to 7:15.

The **Timken Museum of Art** is always free (a donation is suggested), as is admission to the **House of Pacific Relations International Cottages,** although the latter are only open on Sunday. You can explore the studios at the **Spanish Village Art Center** at no charge, although you just might be tempted to purchase a unique souvenir.

A fantastic deal for residents of San Diego County and active-duty military and their families is **Free Tuesdays in the Park,** a rotating schedule of free admission to most of Balboa Park's museums.

The **San Diego Zoo** is free for kids under 12 the whole month of October.

The **December Nights** festival on the first Friday and Saturday of that month includes free admission (and later hours) to most of the Balboa Park museums. The outdoor events during the festival make it something not to miss.

DISCOUNT: EXPLORER PASS

The visitor center offers a selection of Balboa Park Explorer passes that are worth considering if you plan on visiting several museums. The Passport ($53 adult, $29 children ages 3–12) offers one-time admission to 14 museums and attractions over the course of seven days. If you are also planning on visiting the zoo, the Zoo/Passport Combo might be a good choice ($89 adult/$52 child). A single-day pass includes entry to your choice of 5 out of the 14 options ($43 adult, $25 child).

TIPS

■ Hop aboard the free trams that run every 10 to 20 minutes, 9 am to 6 pm daily, with extended summer hours.

■ Wear comfortable shoes—you'll end up walking more than you might expect. Bring a sweater or light jacket for the evening drop in temperature.

■ Don't be afraid to wander off the main drag. Discovering a hidden space of your own is one of the highlights of a trip to Balboa.

■ Balboa Park is a good bet for the odd rainy day—the museums are nice and dry, and many of the park's buildings are connected by covered walkways.

■ Make reservations for the Prado restaurant; it's popular with both visitors and locals alike.

■ If you aren't receiving a discount at one of the museums where San Diego residents get in for free on Tuesday, consider avoiding them on Tuesday, as they can become overcrowded.

■ Don't overlook the 6th Avenue side of the park, between the Marston House and the Cabrillo Bridge. There are several pathways and open fields that make for a quiet escape.

PARKING

Parking within Balboa Park, including at the zoo, is free. From the Cabrillo Bridge, the first parking area you come to is off El Prado to the right. Don't despair if there are no spaces here; you'll see more lots as you continue along toward Pan American Plaza. Alternatively, you can park at Inspiration Point on the east side of the park, off Presidents Way. Free trams run from Inspiration Point to the visitor center and museums. Valet parking is available outside the House of Hospitality on weekends and on weekday evenings, except Monday.

EXPLORING BALBOA PARK

BALBOA PARK WALK

Although Balboa Park as a whole is huge, many of its top attractions are located within reasonable walking distance. A straight shot across the **Cabrillo Bridge**, through the **Plaza de Panama**, and on to the **Bea Evenson Fountain** will take you past several of the park's architectural gems, including the **House of Hospitality.** Many of the park's museums are housed in the buildings lining the way. This route also encompasses the **Alcazar Garden** and **Botanical Building.** From the fountain, a quick jaunt across the pedestrian footbridge leads you into the **Desert Garden** and the **Inez Grant Parker Memorial Rose Garden.** Back at the fountain, your walking tour can continue by heading north toward the **San Diego Zoo.** This will take you past the **Spanish Village Art Center, Carousel,** and **Miniature Railroad.** Alternatively, double back to the Plaza de Panama and head south toward the **Spreckels Organ Pavilion.** Continuing on from here, a loop will take you past **Palm Canyon,** the **International Cottages,** the **Marie Hitchcock Puppet Theater,** several more museums, and the **Japanese Friendship Garden.**

While the aforementioned routes provide a broad overview, there are several walking opportunities for those seeking more focused explorations of the park. Those wishing to experience the numerous gardens in depth will appreciate the excellent "Gardens of Balboa Park Self-Guided Walk," available free of charge at the visitor center. History and architecture buffs might consider buying a self-guided walking tour pamphlet from the visitor center, or taking the briefer audio tour. Opportunities for hiking abound, from a brief journey through **Palm Canyon** to more strenuous hikes through **Florida Canyon** or on the **Old Bridle Trail**. Stop in the visitor center for maps and guidance before setting out.

TOP ATTRACTIONS

Alcazar Garden. You may feel like royalty here as you rest on the benches by the exquisitely tiled fountains—the garden's highlight—and it's no wonder: the garden's landscaping was inspired by the gardens surrounding the Alcazar Castle in Seville, Spain. The garden is open year-round, allowing for a seasonally shifting color palette. The flower beds, for example, are ever-changing horticultural exhibits featuring more than 7,000 annuals for a nearly perpetual bloom. ⊠ *1439 El Prado, Balboa Park* ⊕ *www.balboapark.org.*

Bea Evenson Fountain. A favorite of barefoot children, this fountain shoots cool jets of water upwards of 50 feet. Built in 1972 between the Fleet Center and Natural History Museum, the fountain offers plenty of room to sit and watch the crowds go by. ⊠ *East end of El Prado, Balboa Park* ⊕ *www.balboapark.org.*

Fodor's Choice
★
Botanical Building. The graceful redwood-lath structure, built for the 1915 Panama–California International Exposition, now houses more than 2,000 types of tropical and subtropical plants plus changing seasonal flower displays. Ceiling-high tree ferns shade fragile orchids and feathery bamboo. There are benches beside miniature waterfalls for resting in the shade. The rectangular pond outside, filled with lotuses and water lilies that bloom in spring and fall, is popular with photographers. ⊠ *1549 El Prado, Balboa Park* ☎ *619/239–0512* ⊕ *www. balboapark.org* ⌨ *Free* ☾ *Fri.–Wed. 10–4* ☾ *Closed Thurs.*

Cabrillo Bridge. The official gateway into Balboa Park soars 120 feet above a canyon floor. Pedestrian-friendly, the 1,500-foot bridge provides inspiring views of the California Tower and El Prado beyond. ■ TIP→ This is a great spot for a photo-capturing a classic image of the park. ⊠ *On El Prado, at 6th Ave. park entrance, Balboa Park* ⊕ *www. balboapark.org.*

FAMILY
Fodor's Choice
★
Carousel. Suspended an arm's length away on this antique merry-go-round is the brass ring that could earn you an extra free ride (it's one of the few carousels in the world that continues this bonus tradition). Hand-carved in 1910, the carousel features colorful murals, big-band music, and bobbing animals including zebras, giraffes, and dragons; real horsehair was used for the tails. ⊠ *1889 Zoo Pl., behind zoo parking lot, Balboa Park* ☎ *619/239–0512* ⊕ *www.balboapark.org* ⌨ *$2.50* ☾ *Mid-June–Labor Day, 11–5:30 daily; Labor Day–Mid-June, 11–5:30 Sat.–Sun. and school holidays.*

The lily pond outside the Botanical Building is a beautiful spot to take a break.

Fodor's Choice

★ **Inez Grant Parker Memorial Rose Garden and Desert Garden.** These neighboring gardens sit just across the Park Boulevard pedestrian bridge and offer gorgeous views over Florida Canyon. The formal rose garden contains 2,500 roses representing nearly 200 varieties; peak bloom is usually in April and May. The adjacent Desert Garden provides a striking contrast, with 2.5 acres of succulents and desert plants seeming to blend into the landscape of the canyon below. ⊠ *2525 Park Blvd., Balboa Park* ⊕ *www.balboapark.org.*

Japanese Friendship Garden. A koi pond with a cascading waterfall, a tea pavilion, and a large activity center are highlights of the park's authentic Japanese garden, designed to inspire contemplation and evoke tranquillity. You can wander the various peaceful paths and meditate in the traditional stone and Zen garden. The development of an additional 9 acres is well underway, with several acres already open and the rest scheduled for completion in 2015. The expanded garden features a cherry tree grove and, when complete, a traditional teahouse, which will be the crown jewel of this serene escape. ⊠ *2215 Pan American Rd., Balboa Park*

CLOSE UP

Balboa's Best Bets

With so much on offer, Balboa Park truly has something for everyone. Here are some best bets based on area of interest.

ARCHITECTURE BUFFS
Bea Evenson Fountain

Cabrillo Bridge

House of Hospitality

ARTS AFICIONADOS
Museum of Photographic Arts

San Diego Museum of Art

Spanish Village Art Center

Spreckels Organ Pavilion

Timken Museum of Art

CULTURAL EXPLORERS
House of Pacific Relations

Mingei International Museum

HISTORY JUNKIES
San Diego Museum of Man

San Diego History Center

KIDS OF ALL AGES
Carousel

Marie Hitchcock Puppet Theater

Miniature Railroad

San Diego Model Railroad Museum

San Diego Zoo

NATURE LOVERS
Alcazar Garden

Botanical Building

Inez Grant Parker Memorial Rose Garden

Japanese Friendship Garden

Palm Canyon

SCIENCE AND TECHNOLOGY GEEKS
Reuben H. Fleet Science Center

San Diego Air & Space Museum

San Diego Automotive Museum

☎ 619/232–2721 ⊕ www.niwa.org ☞ $6 ⊙ 10–4:30, last admission at 3:30.

Mingei International Museum. The name "Mingei" comes from the Japanese words *min,* meaning "all people," and *gei,* meaning "art." Thus the museum's name describes what's found under its roof: "art of all people." The Mingei's colorful exhibits of folk art feature toys, pottery, textiles, costumes, jewelry, and curios from around the globe. Traveling and permanent exhibits in the museum include everything from a history of surfboard design and craft to the latest in Japanese ceramics. The gift shop carries items related to major exhibitions as well as artwork from cultures worldwide, such as Zulu baskets, Turkish ceramics, and Mexican objects. ⊠ *House of Charm, 1439 El Prado, Balboa Park* ☎ 619/239–0003 ⊕ www.mingei.org ☞ $8 ⊙ Tues.–Sun. 10–5.

Palm Canyon. Enjoy an instant escape from the buildings and concrete of urban life in this Balboa Park oasis. Lush and tropical, with hundreds of palm trees, the 2-acre canyon has a shaded path perfect for those who love walking through nature. ⊠ *South of House of Charm, 1549 El Prado, Balboa Park.*

FAMILY **Reuben H. Fleet Science Center.** Interactive exhibits here are artfully educational and for all ages: older kids can get hands-on with inventive projects in the Tinkering Studio, while the five-and-under set can be easily entertained with interactive play stations like the Ball Wall and Fire Truck in the center's Kid City. The IMAX Dome Theater, which screens exhilarating nature and sci-

> **HISTORY REVEALED**
>
> While demurely posing as a butterfly garden today, the Zoro Garden has a racy history—tucked between the Casa de Balboa and the Fleet Center, this area showcased a nudist colony during the 1935–36 Exposition.

ence films, was the world's first, as was the Fleet's "NanoSeam" (seamless) dome ceiling that doubles as a planetarium. ⊠ *1875 El Prado, Balboa Park* 🕾 *619/238–1233* ⊕ *www.rhfleet.org* ✉ *Gallery exhibits $13; gallery exhibits and 1 IMAX film $17, or 2 IMAX films $24* ⊗ *Daily 10–5.*

FAMILY **San Diego Air & Space Museum.** By day, the streamlined edifice looks like
Fodor's Choice any other structure in the park; at night, outlined in blue neon, the
★ round building appears—appropriately enough—to be a landed UFO. In all, there are more than 60 full-size aircraft on the floor and hanging from the rafters. In addition to exhibits from the dawn of flight to the jet age, the museum displays a growing number of space-age exhibits, including the actual *Apollo 9* command module. To test your own skills, you can ride in a two-seat Max Flight simulator or try out the F-35 interactive simulator. Movies in the 3D/4D theater are included with admission. ⊠ *2001 Pan American Pl., Balboa Park* 🕾 *619/234–8291* ⊕ *www.sandiegoairandspace.org* ✉ *Museum $18 (more for special exhibitions), Flight Simulators $5–$8 extra, restoration tour $7 extra and subject to availability* ⊗ *Daily 10–5, last admission 4:30.*

Fodor's Choice **San Diego Museum of Art.** Known primarily for its Spanish baroque and
★ Renaissance paintings, including works by El Greco, Goya, Rubens, and van Ruisdael, San Diego's most comprehensive art museum also has strong holdings of South Asian art, Indian miniatures, and contemporary California paintings. The museum's exhibits tend to have broad appeal, and if traveling shows from other cities come to town, you can expect to see them here. Free docent tours are offered throughout the day. An outdoor Sculpture Court and Garden exhibits both traditional and modern pieces. ⊠ *1450 El Prado, Balboa Park* 🕾 *619/232–7931* ⊕ *www.sdmart.org* ✉ *$12* ⊗ *Mon., Tues., and Thurs.–Sat. 10–5, Sun. noon–5*

FAMILY **San Diego Museum of Man.** If the facade of this building—the landmark California Building—looks familiar, it's because filmmaker Orson Welles used it and its dramatic tower as the principal features of the Xanadu estate in his 1941 classic, *Citizen Kane.* Inside, exhibits at this highly respected anthropological museum focus on Southwestern, Mexican, and South American cultures. Carved monuments from the Mayan city of Quirigua in Guatemala, cast from the originals in 1914, are particularly impressive. ⊠ *California Bldg., 1350 El Prado, Balboa Park* 🕾 *619/239–2001* ⊕ *www.museumofman.org* ✉ *$12.50* ⊗ *Daily 10–5; until 7:30 Thurs.–Sat. Memorial Day–Labor Day.*

Continued on page 62

Polar bear, San Diego Zoo

LIONS AND TIGERS AND PANDAS:
The World-Famous San Diego Zoo

From cuddly pandas and diving polar bears to 6-ton elephants and swinging great apes, San Diego's most famous attraction has it all. Nearly 4,000 animals representing 800 species roam the 100-acre zoo in expertly crafted habitats that replicate the animals' natural environments. While the pandas get top billing, there are plenty of other cool creatures to see here, from teeny-tiny mantella frogs to two-story-tall giraffes. But it's not all just fun and games. Known for its exemplary conservation programs, the zoo educates visitors on how to go green and explains its efforts to protect endangered species.

SAN DIEGO ZOO TOP ATTRACTIONS

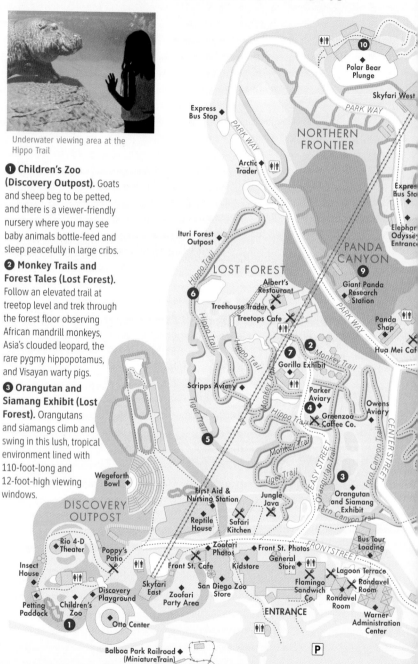

Underwater viewing area at the Hippo Trail

❶ **Children's Zoo (Discovery Outpost).** Goats and sheep beg to be petted, and there is a viewer-friendly nursery where you may see baby animals bottle-feed and sleep peacefully in large cribs.

❷ **Monkey Trails and Forest Tales (Lost Forest).** Follow an elevated trail at treetop level and trek through the forest floor observing African mandrill monkeys, Asia's clouded leopard, the rare pygmy hippopotamus, and Visayan warty pigs.

❸ **Orangutan and Siamang Exhibit (Lost Forest).** Orangutans and siamangs climb and swing in this lush, tropical environment lined with 110-foot-long and 12-foot-high viewing windows.

4 **Scripps, Parker, and Owens Aviaries (Lost Forest).** Wandering paths climb through the enclosed aviaries where brightly colored tropical birds swoop between branches inches from your face.

5 **Tiger Trail (Lost Forest).** The mist-shrouded trails of this simulated rainforest wind down a canyon. Tigers, Malayan tapirs, and Argus pheasants wander among the exotic trees and plants.

6 **Hippo Trail (Lost Forest).** Glimpse huge but surprisingly graceful hippos frolicking in the water through an underwater viewing window and buffalo cavorting with monkeys on dry land.

7 **Gorilla Exhibit (Lost Forest).** The gorillas live in one of the zoo's bioclimatic zone exhibits modeled on their native habitat with waterfalls, climbing areas, and an open meadow. The sounds of the tropical rain forest emerge from a 144-speaker sound system that plays CDs recorded in Africa.

8 **Sun Bear Forest (Asian Passage).** Playful beasts claw apart the trees and shrubs that serve as a natural playground for climbing, jumping, and general merrymaking.

9 **Giant Panda Research Station (Panda Canyon).** An elevated pathway provides visitors with great access

Lories at Owen's Aviary

to the zoo's most famous residents in their side-by-side viewing areas. The adjacent discovery center features lots of information about these endangered animals and the zoo's efforts to protect them.

10 **Polar Bear Plunge (Northern Frontier).** Watch polar bears take a chilly dive from the underwater viewing room. There are also Siberian reindeer, white foxes, and other Arctic creatures here. Kids can learn about the Arctic and climate change through interactive exhibits.

11 **Elephant Odyssey.** Get a glimpse of the animals that roamed Southern California 12,000 years ago and meet their living counterparts. The 7.5-acre, multispecies habitat features elephants, California condors, jaguars, and more.

12 **Koala Exhibit (Outback).** The San Diego Zoo houses the largest number of koalas outside Australia. Walk through the exhibit for photo ops of these marsupials from Down-Under curled up on their perches or dining on eucalyptus branches.

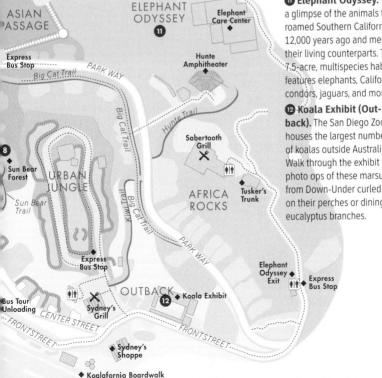

ASIAN PASSAGE

Express Bus Stop

Big Cat Trail

8
Sun Bear Forest

Sun Bear Trail

URBAN JUNGLE

PARK WAY

Big Cat Trail

Big Cat Trail

ELEPHANT ODYSSEY
11

Elephant Care Center

Hunte Amphitheater

Hunte Trail

Sabertooth Grill

AFRICA ROCKS

Tusker's Trunk

Express Bus Stop

Bus Tour Unloading

CENTER STREET

Sydney's Grill

OUTBACK

Koala Exhibit

12

Elephant Odyssey Exit

Express Bus Stop

FRONT STREET

FRONT STREET

PARK WAY

Sydney's Shoppe

Koalafornia Boardwalk

MUST-SEE ANIMALS

❶ GORILLA

This troop of primates engages visitors with their human-like expressions and behavior. The youngsters are sure to delight, especially when hitching a ride on mom's back. Up-close encounters might involve the gorillas using the glass partition as a backrest while peeling cabbage. By dusk the gorillas head inside to their sleeping quarters, so don't save this for your last stop.

❷ ELEPHANT

Asian and African elephants coexist at the San Diego Zoo. The larger African elephant is distinguished by its big flapping ears—shaped like the continent of Africa—which it uses to keep cool. An elephant's trunk has over 40,000 muscles in it—that's more than humans have in their whole body.

❸ GIANT PANDA

The San Diego Zoo is well-known for its giant panda research and conservation efforts, and has had five successful panda births. You'll likely see parents Bai Yun ("White Cloud") and Gao-Gao ("Big-Big") with their youngest baby Xiao Liwu ("little gift").

❹ KOALA

While this collection of critters is one of the cutest in the zoo, don't expect a lot of activity from the koala habitat. These guys spend most of their day curled up asleep in the branches of the eucalyptus tree—they can sleep up to 20 hours a day. Although eucalyptus leaves are poisonous to most animals, bacteria in koalas' stomachs allow them to break down the toxins.

❺ POLAR BEAR

The trio of polar bears is one of the San Diego Zoo's star attractions, and their brand-new exhibit gets you up close and personal. Visitors sometimes worry about polar bears living in the warm San Diego climate, but there is no cause for concern. The San Diego-based bears eat a lean diet, thus reducing their layer of blubber and helping them keep cool.

DID YOU KNOW?

Bamboo is the panda's dietary staple—they can consume 84 pounds of it a day—and the zoo grows 69 species of bamboo to ensure they have plenty of variety.

PLANNING YOUR DAY AT THE ZOO

Left: Main entrance of the San Diego Zoo. Right: Sunbear

PLANNING YOUR TIME

Plan to devote at least a half-day to exploring the zoo, but with so much to see it is easy to stay a full day or more.

If you're on a tight schedule, opt for the guided **35 minute bus tour** that lets you zip through three-quarters of the exhibits. However, lines to board the busses can be long, and you won't get as close to the animals.

Another option is to take the **Skyfari Aerial Tram** to the far end of the park, choose a route, and meander back to the entrance. The Skyfari trip gives a good overview of the zoo's layout and a spectacular view.

The **Elephant Odyssey,** while accessible from two sides of the park, is best entered from just below the Polar Rim. The extremely popular **Panda exhibit** can develop long lines, so get there early.

The zoo offers several entertaining **live shows** daily. Check the website or the back of the map handed out at the zoo entrance for the day's offerings and showtimes.

BEFORE YOU GO

■ To avoid ticket lines, purchase and print tickets online using the zoo's Web site.

■ To avoid excessive backtracking or a potential meltdown, plan your route along the zoo map before setting out. Try not to get too frustrated if you lose your way, as there are exciting exhibits around every turn and many paths intersect at several points.

■ The zoo offers a variety of program extras, including behind-the-scenes tours, backstage pass animal encounters, and sleepover events. Call in advance for pricing and reservations.

AT THE ZOO

■ Don't forget to explore at least some of the exhibits on foot—a favorite is the lush Tiger Trail.

■ If you visit on the weekend, find out when the Giraffe Experience is taking place. You can purchase leaf–eater biscuits to hand feed the giraffes!

■ Splurge a little at the gift shop: your purchases help support zoo programs.

■ The zoo rents strollers, wheelchairs, and lockers; it also has a first-aid office, a lost and found, and an ATM.

Fern Canyon, San Diego Zoo

GETTING HERE AND AROUND
The zoo is easy to get to, whether by bus or car.

Bus Travel: Take Bus No. 7 and exit at Park Boulevard and Zoo Place.

Car Travel: From Downtown, take Route 163 north through Balboa Park. Exit at Zoo/Museums (Richmond Street) and follow signs.

Several options help you get around the massive park: express buses loop through the zoo and the Skyfari Aerial Tram will take you from one end to the other. The zoo's topography is fairly hilly, but moving sidewalks lead up the slopes between some exhibits.

QUICK BITES
There is a wide variety of food available for purchase at the zoo from food carts to ethnic restaurants such as the Pan-Asian **Hua Mei Cafe.**

One of the best restaurants is **Albert's** ($), near the Gorilla exhibit, which features grilled fish, homemade pizza, and fresh pasta along with a full bar.

SERVICE INFORMATION

✉ 2920 Zoo Dr., Balboa Park

☎ 619/234-3153; 888/697-2632 Giant panda hotline

🌐 www.sandiegozoo.org

Gorilla

SAN DIEGO ZOO SAFARI PARK

About 45 minutes north of the zoo in Escondido, the 1,800-acre San Diego Zoo Safari Park is an extensive wildlife sanctuary where animals roam free—and guests can get close in escorted caravans and on backcountry trails. This park and the zoo operate under the auspices of the San Diego Zoo's nonprofit organization; joint tickets are available. ⇨ *See Chapter 15: North County and Environs for more information.*

Stairs lead down to the lush Palm Canyon, which has more than 58 species of palms.

FAMILY **San Diego Natural History Museum.** There are 7.5 million fossils, dinosaur models, and even live reptiles and other specimens under this roof. Favorite exhibits include the Foucault Pendulum, suspended on a 43-foot cable and designed to demonstrate the Earth's rotation, and *Ocean Oasis,* the world's first large-format film about Baja California and the Sea of Cortés. Included in admission are 3-D films shown at the museum's giant-screen theater. ✉ *1788 El Prado, Balboa Park* ☎ *619/232–3821* ⊕ *www.sdnhm.org* ✉ *$17; extra for special exhibits* ☉ *Daily 10–5.*

⟳ **San Diego Zoo.**
Fodor's Choice ⇨ *See the highlighted listing in this chapter.*
★
Fodor's Choice **Spanish Village Art Center.** More than 200 local artists, including glass-
★ blowers, enamel workers, woodcarvers, sculptors, painters, jewelers, and photographers work and give demonstrations of their craft on a rotating basis in these red tile–roof studio-galleries that were set up for the 1935–36 exposition in the style of an old Spanish village. The center is a great source for memorable gifts. ✉ *1770 Village Pl., Balboa Park* ☎ *619/233–9050* ⊕ *www.spanishvillageart.com* ✉ *Free* ☉ *Daily 11–4.*

Fodor's Choice **Spreckels Organ Pavilion.** The 2,400-bench-seat pavilion, dedicated in
★ 1915 by sugar magnates John D. and Adolph B. Spreckels, holds the 4,518-pipe Spreckels Organ, the largest outdoor pipe organ in the world. You can hear this impressive instrument at one of the year-round, free, 2 pm Sunday concerts, regularly performed by civic organist Carol Williams and guest artists—a highlight of a visit to Balboa Park. On Monday evenings from late June to mid-August, internationally renowned organists play evening concerts. At Christmastime the

park's Christmas tree and life-size Nativity display turn the pavilion into a seasonal wonderland. ✉ *2211 Pan American Rd., Balboa Park* ☎ *619/702–8138* ⊕ *spreckelsorgan.org.*

WORTH NOTING

House of Pacific Relations. This is not really a house but a cluster of red tile–roof stucco cottages representing some 30 foreign countries. The word "pacific" refers to the goal of maintaining peace. The cottages, decorated with crafts and pictures, are open Sunday afternoons, when you can chat with transplanted natives and try out different ethnic foods. From the first Sunday in March through the last Sunday in October, folk-song and dance performances are presented on the outdoor stage around 2 pm. Across the road from the cottages is the Spanish colonial–style **United Nations Building.** Inside, the United Nations Association's International Gift Shop, open daily, has reasonably priced crafts, cards, and books. ✉ *2191 Pan American Pl., Balboa Park* ☎ *619/234–0739* ⊕ *www.sdhpr.org* ✎ *Free, donations accepted* ☉ *Sun. noon–4.*

FAMILY **Marie Hitchcock Puppet Theater.** Performances incorporate marionettes, hand puppets, rod puppets, shadow puppets, and ventriloquism, while the stories range from traditional fairy tales to folk legends and contemporary puppet plays. Kids stare wide-eyed at the short, energy-filled productions. ✉ *2130 Pan American Pl., Balboa Park* ☎ *619/544–9203* ⊕ *www.balboaparkpuppets.com* ✎ *$5* ☉ *Wed.–Sun., one or more shows each morning and afternoon.*

Marston House Museum & Gardens. George W. Marston (1850–1946), a San Diego pioneer and philanthropist who financed the architectural landscaping of Balboa Park—among his myriad other San Diego civic projects—lived in this 16-room home at the northwest edge of the park. Designed in 1905 by San Diego architects Irving Gill and William Hebbard, it's a classic example of the American Arts and Crafts style, which emphasizes simplicity and functionality of form. On the 5-acre grounds is a lovely English Romantic garden, as interpreted in California. The house may only be visited by guided tour. ✉ *3525 7th Ave., Balboa Park* ☎ *619/298–3142* ⊕ *www.marstonhouse.org* ✎ *$10* ☉ *Thurs.– Mon. 10–4:30 in summer, Fri.–Mon. 10–3:30 in winter, guided tours every half-hour. Call for info about weekend specialty tours of gardens, historic 7th Ave. and the Bankers Hill neighborhood.*

FAMILY **Miniature Railroad.** Adjacent to the zoo parking lot and across from the carousel, a pint-size 48-passenger train runs a ½-mile loop through four tree-filled acres of the park. The engine of this rare 1948 model train is one of only 50 left in the world. ✉ *2885 Zoo Pl., Balboa Park* ☎ *619/239–0512* ✎ *$3* ☉ *June–Aug., daily 11–6:30; Sept.–May, Sat.– Sun. and school holidays 11–4:30.*

Museum of Photographic Arts. World-renowned photographers such as Ansel Adams, Imogen Cunningham, Henri Cartier-Bresson, and Edward Weston are represented in this museum's permanent collection, which includes everything from 19th-century daguerreotypes to contemporary photojournalism prints. ✉ *Casa de Balboa, 1649 El Prado,*

Balboa Park ☎ *619/238–7559* ⊕ *www.mopa.org* ✎ *$8* ⊙ *Tues.–Sun. 10–5; Memorial Day–Labor Day, open until 9 Thurs.*

San Diego Automotive Museum. Even if you don't know a choke from a chassis, you're bound to admire the sleek designs of the autos in this impressive museum. On display are gems from the museum's core collection of vintage motorcycles and cars—ranging from a Porsche, a Ferrari, and a Glitz & Gam to a 1981 silver DeLorean (remember the time machine in *Back to the Future?*)—as well as a series of international rotating exhibits. ⊠ *2080 Pan American Plaza, Balboa Park* ☎ *619/231–2886* ⊕ *www.sdautomuseum.org* ✎ *$8.50* ⊙ *Daily 10–5; last admission 4:30.*

San Diego History Center. The San Diego Historical Society maintains its research library in the basement of the Casa de Balboa and organizes shows on the first floor. Permanent and rotating exhibits, which are often more lively than you might expect, survey local urban history after 1850, when California entered the Union. A 100-seat theater hosts public lectures, workshops, and educational programs, and a gift shop carries books on local history. ⊠ *Casa de Balboa, 1649 El Prado, Balboa Park* ☎ *619/232–6203* ⊕ *www.sandiegohistory.org* ✎ *$8* ⊙ *Tues.–Sun. 10–5 (last admission 4:30), open daily in summer.*

FAMILY **San Diego Model Railroad Museum.** When the exhibits at this 27,000-square-foot museum are in operation, you can hear the sounds of chugging engines, screeching brakes, and shrill whistles. Local model railroad clubs built and maintain the four main displays, which represent California railroads in miniature, with the track laid on scale models of San Diego County terrain. A Toy Train Gallery contains an interactive Lionel exhibit. ⊠ *Casa de Balboa, 1649 El Prado, Balboa Park* ☎ *619/696–0199* ⊕ *www.sdmrm.org* ✎ *$8* ⊙ *Tues.–Fri. 11–4, Sat.–Sun. 11–5.*

Timken Museum of Art. Though somewhat out of place architecturally, this small and modern structure, made of travertine imported from Italy, is a jewelbox. The museum houses works by major European and American artists as well as a superb collection of Russian icons. ⊠ *1500 El Prado, Balboa Park* ☎ *619/239–5548* ⊕ *www.timkenmuseum.org* ✎ *$10 suggested donation; audio tours $5* ⊙ *Tues.–Sat. 10–4:30, Sun. noon–4:30.*

OLD TOWN
AND UPTOWN

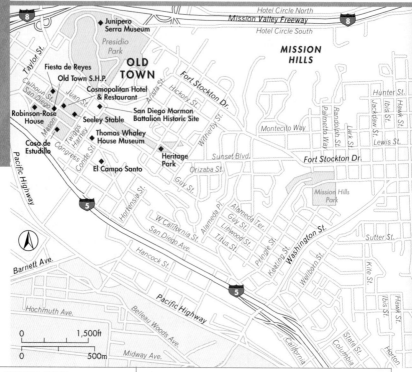

GETTING HERE

Old Town and Uptown are north-west and north of Balboa Park, respectively. Access to Old Town is easy thanks to the nearby Old Town Transit Center. Ten bus lines stop here, as do the San Diego Trolley and the Coaster commuter rail line. Two large parking lots linked to the Old Town Historic Park by an underground pedestrian walkway ease some of the parking congestion.

Uptown is best explored by car, although several bus routes do serve the area. Both metered street parking and pay-and-display lots are available.

TOP REASONS TO GO

Step back in time: Experience the early days of San Diego, from its beginnings as a remote military outpost and mission to the development of the first town plaza.

Architectural delights: Take an architectural journey through San Diego's history. Discover the pueblo- and clapboard-style structures of Old Town and the ornate Victorian gems in Heritage Park. Then head up the hill to view wonderfully preserved early-20th-century homes in Uptown.

Scare yourself silly: A nighttime visit to the Thomas Whaley House Museum, "the most haunted house in America," is sure to give you goose bumps.

Tortillas and margaritas: Enjoy the convivial atmosphere at one of the many Mexican eateries in Old Town.

Live like a local: Explore the vibrant shopping, dining, and nightlife of Uptown's unique neighborhoods.

MISSION BASILICA SAN DIEGO DE ALCALÁ TO ↑

Bachman Pl.

UNIVERSITY HEIGHTS

163

Dickinson St.

TO NORTH PARK →

3rd Ave.

Bachman Pl.

Arbor Dr.

Montecito Way

Hayes Ave.

Lincoln Ave.

Lewis St.

Albatross St.

HILLCREST

6th Ave.

Washington Street

Cleveland Ave.

W University Ave.

Bread & Cie Cafe ✕

5th Ave.
6th Ave.
7th Ave.
8th Ave.

University Ave.

Dove St.

Front St.

1st Ave.

3rd Ave.

Pennsylvania Ave.

4th Ave.

Robinson Ave.

163

Cypress Ave.

UPTOWN

Goldfinch St.

Reynard Way

Brant St.

Brookes Ave.

Walnut Ave.

Dove St.

Upas St.

Old Town and Uptown

Thorn St.

Spruce St.

QUICK BITES

Bread and Cie Café. Its delicious loaves are distributed around San Diego, but visitors to Hillcrest can go to the source at Bread and Cie Café. Pastries, soups, salads, sandwiches, and plenty of bread are served in a bustling atmosphere. Enjoy a heavenly cappuccino alfresco, or sit inside to watch the commotion from the open kitchen. ⌧ *350 University Ave., Hillcrest* ☎ *619/683-9322* ⊕ *www.breadandcie.com.*

Fiesta de Reyes Snacks. If traveling back in time has left you tired and hungry, Old Town's Fiesta de Reyes has several options for a quick recharge. To the right when you enter from the plaza, La Panadería serves a variety of sweet and savory empanadas as well as homemade *churros* (strips of fried dough) and hot chocolate. Viva el Café, toward the rear of the courtyard, features decadent desserts and specialty coffee drinks. If you are visiting between Friday and Sunday, look for the simple booth marked Street Tacos for a quick meal on the go. ⌧ *4016 Wallace St., Old Town* ☎ *619/297-3100* ⊕ *www.fiestadereyes.com.*

PLANNING YOUR TIME

It takes about two hours to walk through Old Town. Try to time your visit to coincide with the free daily tours given by costumed park staff. They depart at 11 and 2 from the Robinson-Rose House Visitor Center and take about one hour. If you go to Presidio Park, definitely consider driving up the steep hill from Old Town.

The highlight of an Uptown tour is exploring the heart of Hillcrest, located at the intersection of University and 5th avenues. Plan to drive or catch a bus between neighborhoods, then explore on foot.

FESTIVALS

The Uptown neighborhoods host a variety of events throughout the year, such as free summer concerts at Trolley Barn Park. Hillcrest hosts the annual LGBT Pride event every July. In late summer, Cityfest rocks the neighborhood with live music, food stalls, and beer gardens. Old Town celebrates Cinco de Mayo and the Old Town Art Festival held in early fall.

Sightseeing
★★★★☆

Nightlife
★★★★☆

Dining
★★★★★

Lodging
★★☆☆☆

Shopping
★★★★☆

San Diego's Spanish and Mexican roots are most evident in Old Town and the surrounding hillside of Presidio Park. Visitors can experience settlement life in San Diego from Spanish and Mexican rule to the early days of U.S. statehood. Nearby Uptown is composed of several smaller neighborhoods near downtown and around Balboa Park: the vibrant neighborhoods of Hillcrest, Mission Hills, University Heights, North Park and South Park showcase their unique blend of historical charm and modern urban community.

OLD TOWN

Updated by
Claire Deeks
van der Lee

As the first European settlement in Southern California, **Old Town** began to develop in the 1820s. However, its true beginnings took place on a nearby hillside in 1769 with the establishment of a Spanish military outpost and the first of California's missions, San Diego de Alcalá. In 1774 the hilltop was declared a presidio reál, a fortress built by the Spanish empire, and the mission was relocated along the San Diego River. Over time, settlers moved down from the presidio to establish Old Town. A central plaza was laid out, surrounded by adobe and, later, wooden structures. San Diego became an incorporated U.S. city in 1850, with Old Town as its center. In the 1860s, however, the advent of Alonzo Horton's New Town to the southeast caused Old Town to wither. Efforts to preserve the area began early in the 20th century, and Old Town became a state historic park in 1968.

Today Old Town is a lively celebration of history and culture. The **Old Town San Diego State Historic Park** re-creates life during the early settlement, while San Diego Avenue buzzes with art galleries, gift shops, festive restaurants, and open-air stands selling inexpensive Mexican handicrafts.

Old Town celebrates Mexican culture with live music and entertainment at the Cinco de Mayo festival.

TOP ATTRACTIONS

FAMILY
Fodor's Choice
★

Fiesta de Reyes. North of San Diego's Old Town Plaza lies the area's unofficial center, built to represent a colonial Mexican plaza. The collection of more than a dozen shops and restaurants around a central courtyard in blossom with magenta bougainvillea, scarlet hibiscus, and other flowers in season reflects what early California might have looked like from 1821 to 1872. Shops are even stocked with items reminiscent of that era. Mariachi bands and folklorico dance groups frequently perform on the plaza stage—check the website for times and upcoming special events. ■TIP→ Casa de Reyes is a great stop for a margarita and some chips and guacamole. ⊠ 4016 Wallace St., Old Town ☎ 619/297–3100 ⊕ www.fiestadereyes.com ☯ Shops 10–9 daily.

Heritage Park. A number of San Diego's important Victorian buildings are the focus of this 7.8-acre park on the Juan Street hill near Harney Street. Among the buildings is Southern California's first synagogue, a one-room Classical Revival structure built in 1889 for Congregation Beth Israel. The most interesting of the park's six former residences might be the Sherman-Gilbert House, which has a widow's walk and intricate carving on its decorative trim. It was built for real estate dealer John Sherman in 1887 at the then-exorbitant cost of $20,000—indicating just how profitable the booming housing market could be. All the houses, some of which may seem surprisingly colorful, accurately represent the bright tones of the era. The synagogue and the Senlis Cottage are open to visitors daily from 9 to 5; the latter contains a small exhibit with information on the history and original locations of the houses. The McConaughy House hosts the Coral Tree Tea House and

Old Town Gift Emporium, offering traditional tea service Thursday through Sunday from 11 to 5. Save Our Heritage Organization moved the buildings to this park from their original locations and also restored them. ✉ *2454 Heritage Park Row, Old Town* ☎ *858/565–3600* ⊕ *www.sdparks.org.*

FAMILY

Fodor's Choice ★

Old Town San Diego State Historic Park. The six square blocks on the site of San Diego's original pueblo are the heart of Old Town. Most of the 20 historic buildings preserved or re-created by the park cluster around **Old Town Plaza,** bounded by Wallace Street on the west, Calhoun Street on the north, Mason Street on the east, and San Diego Avenue on the south. The plaza is a pleasant place to rest, plan your tour of the park, and watch passers-by. San Diego Avenue is closed to vehicle traffic here.

Some of Old Town's buildings were destroyed in a fire in 1872, but after the site became a state historic park in 1968, reconstruction and restoration of the remaining structures began. Five of the original adobes are still intact. The tour pamphlet available at Robinson-Rose House gives details about all the historic houses on the plaza and in its vicinity; *a few of the more interesting ones are noted below.* Several reconstructed buildings serve as restaurants or as shops purveying wares reminiscent of those that might have been available in the original Old Town.

Racine & Laramie, a painstakingly reproduced version of San Diego's first cigar store in 1868, is especially interesting. Free tours depart daily from the Robinson-Rose House at 11 and 2. ■ TIP→ The covered wagon located near the intersection of Mason and Calhoun streets provides a great photo opp. 2737 San Diego Ave.

Casa de Estudillo. San Diego's first county assessor, Jose Antonio Estudillo, built this home in 1827 in collaboration with his father, the commander of the San Diego Presidio, José Maria Estudillo. The largest and most elaborate of the original adobe homes, it was occupied by members of the Estudillo family until 1887. It was purchased and restored in 1910 by sugar magnate and developer John D. Spreckels, who advertised it in bold lettering on the side as "Ramona's Marriage Place." Spreckels's claim that the small chapel in the house was the site of the wedding in Helen Hunt Jackson's popular novel *Ramona* had no basis; that didn't stop people from coming to see it, however. 4001 Mason St.

Cosmopolitan Hotel and Restaurant. A Peruvian, Juan Bandini, built a hacienda on this site in 1829, and the house served as Old Town's social center during Mexican rule. Albert Seeley, a stagecoach entrepreneur, purchased the home in 1869, built a second story, and turned it into the Cosmopolitan Hotel, a way station for travelers on the daylong trip south from Los Angeles. It later served as a cannery before being revived (a few times over the years) as a hotel and restaurant. 2660 Calhoun St.

Robinson-Rose House. Facing Old Town Plaza, this was the original commercial center of Old San Diego, housing railroad offices, law offices, and the city's first newspaper press. Built in 1853 but in ruins at the end of the 19th century, it has been reconstructed and now serves as the park's visitor center. Inside are a model of Old Town as it looked in 1872, as well as various historic exhibits. Apparently ghosts came with the rebuild, as the house is now considered haunted. Just behind the Robinson-Rose House is a replica of the Victorian-era Silvas-McCoy house, originally built in 1869. 4002 Wallace St.

Seeley Stable. Next door to the Cosmopolitan Hotel, the stable became San Diego's stagecoach stop in 1867 and was the transportation hub of Old Town until 1887, when trains became the favored mode of travel. The stable houses horse-drawn vehicles, some so elaborate that you can see where the term "carriage trade" came from. Also inside are Western memorabilia, including an exhibit on the California *vaquero*, the original American cowboy, and a collection of Native American artifacts. 2630 Calhoun St.

Also worth exploring: The San Diego Union Museum, Mason Street School, Wells Fargo History Museum, First San Diego Courthouse, Casa de Machado y Silvas Commercial Restaurant Museum, and the Casa de Machado y Stewart. Ask at the visitor center for locations. ✉ *Visitor Center (Robinson-Rose House), 4002 Wallace St., Old Town* ☎ *619/220–5422* ⊕ *www.parks.ca.gov* 🖙 *Free* ☉ *Oct.–Apr., Mon.–Thurs. 10–4, Fri.–Sun. 10–5; May–Sept., daily 10–5; hrs may vary at individual sites.*

Presidio Park. The hillsides of the 50-acre green space overlooking Old Town from the north end of Taylor Street are popular with picnickers, and many couples have taken their wedding vows on the park's long stretches of lawn, some of the greenest in San Diego. The park offers a great ocean view from the top, and more than 2 miles of hiking trails below. It's a nice walk from Old Town to the summit if you're in good shape and wearing the right shoes—it should take about half an hour. You can also drive to the top of the park via Presidio Drive, off Taylor Street.

If you walk, look in at the **Presidio Hills Golf Course** on Mason Street. It has an unusual clubhouse that incorporates the ruins of Casa de Carrillo, the town's oldest adobe, constructed in 1820. At the end of Mason Street, veer left on Jackson Street to reach the **presidio ruins,** where adobe walls and a bastion have been built above the foundations

AMERICA'S MOST HAUNTED

Built on a former gallows site in 1856, the Whaley House is one of 30 houses designated by the Department of Commerce to be haunted. Legend has it that the house is inhabited by seven spirits, making it the "most haunted house in America." Listen for the sound of heavy footsteps, said to belong to the ghost of Yankee Jim Robinson, a convict hanged on the site in 1852. Less ominous are sightings of the Whaley family's fox terrier scampering about the house.

4

of the original fortress and chapel. Also on-site is the 28-foot-high **Serra Cross,** built in 1913 out of brick tiles found in the ruins. Continue up the hill to find the **Junípero Serra Musuem,** built at the site of the original Mission San Diego de Alcalá and often mistaken for the Mission. Then take Presidio Drive southeast to reach the site of **Fort Stockton,** built to protect Old Town and abandoned by the United States in 1848. Plaques and statues also commemorate the Mormon Battalion, which enlisted here to fight in the battle against Mexico. ⊠ *Taylor and Jackson Sts., Old Town* ⊕ *www.sdparks.org.*

Thomas Whaley House Museum. A New York entrepreneur, Thomas Whaley came to California during the gold rush. He wanted to provide his East Coast wife with all the comforts of home, so in 1857 he had Southern California's first two-story brick structure built, making it the oldest double-story brick building on the West Coast. The house, which served as the county courthouse and government seat during the 1870s, stands in strong contrast to the Spanish-style adobe residences that surround the nearby historic plaza and marks an early stage of San Diego's "Americanization." A garden out back includes many varieties of prehybrid roses from before 1867. The place is perhaps most famed, however, for the ghosts that are said to inhabit it. You can tour on your own during the day, but must visit by guided tour starting at 5 pm. The evening tours are geared toward the supernatural aspects of the house. They are offered every half hour, with the last tour departing at 9:30 pm, and last about 45 minutes. ⊠ *2476 San Diego Ave., Old Town* ☎ *619/297–7511* ⊕ *www.whaleyhouse.org* ☞ *$6 before 5 pm, $10 after 5* ☉ *Sept.–May, Sun.–Tues. 10–5, Thurs.–Sat. 10–9:30; June–Aug., daily 10–9:30.*

WORTH NOTING

El Campo Santo cemetery. Now a peaceful stop for visitors to Old Town, the old adobe-wall cemetery established in 1849 was, until 1880, the burial place for many members of Old Town's founding families—as well as for some gamblers and bandits who passed through town. Antonio Garra, a chief who led an uprising of the San Luis Rey Indians, was executed at El Campo Santo in front of the open grave he had been forced to dig for himself. Most of the markers give only approximations of where the people named on them are buried; some of the early settlers laid to rest at El Campo Santo actually reside under San Diego Avenue. ⊠ *North side of San Diego Ave. S, between Arista and Ampudia Sts., Old Town.*

Junípero Serra Museum. In 1929, department store magnate and philanthropist George Marston established Presidio Park and this Spanish Mission–style museum on the hill where San Diego's original Spanish presidio (fortress) and California's first mission were perched. The museum and park commemorate the history of the site from the time it was occupied by the Kumeyaay Indians through its Spanish, Mexican, and American periods. Artifacts include Kumeyaay baskets, Spanish riding gear, and an 18th-century cannon once used to protect Fort Guijarros down the hill in Old Town. The education room has hands-on stations where kids can grind acorns in metates (stones used for grinding grain) and dig for buried artifacts with archaeology tools. Ascend the tower to compare the view you'd have gotten before 1929 with the one you have today. The museum, now operated by the San Diego History Center, is at the north end of Presidio Park, near Taylor Street. ✉ *2727 Presidio Dr., Old Town* ☎ *619/297–3258, 619/232–6203* ⊕ *www. sandiegohistory.org* ✆ *$6* ☉ *Sept.–Mar., weekends 10–4; Mar.–May, weekends 10–5; June–Aug., Fri.–Sun. 10–5; museum closes frequently for special events so call ahead.*

San Diego Mormon Battalion Historic Site. Operated by the Church of Jesus Christ of Latter-day Saints, this engaging museum tells the story of the formation of the Mormon Battalion and the unit's journey to San Diego. During the Mexican-American war, the battalion of nearly 500 men left Council Bluffs, Iowa, in July 1846 for a grueling six-month, roughly 2,000-mile infantry march, accompanied by approximately 80 women and children. Once the group arrived in San Diego, its members helped develop Old Town. The museum features impressive set designs and multimedia exhibits, including talking picture frames. Guides in period costumes lead visitors through a series of rooms representing stages of the journey. At the end of the tour, visitors can learn more about members of the Battalion in the Research Room, or pan for gold out back. ✉ *2510 Juan St., Old Town* ☎ *619/298–3317* ⊕ *www.oldtownsandiegoguide.com/historic_sites/mormonbattalion. html* ✆ *Free* ☉ *Daily 9–9.*

HILLCREST

The large retro Hillcrest sign over the intersection of University and 5th avenues makes an excellent landmark at the epicenter of this vibrant section of Uptown. Strolling along University Avenue between 4th and 6th avenues and from Washington Street to Robinson Avenue will reveal a mixture of retail shops and restaurants. National chains such as American Apparel and Pinkberry coexist with local boutiques, bookstores, bars, and coffee shops. A few blocks east, another interesting stretch of stores and restaurants runs along University Avenue to Normal Street. Long established as the center of San Diego's gay community, the neighborhood bustles both day and night with a mixed crowd of shoppers, diners, and partygoers. If you are visiting Hillcrest on Sunday between 9 and 2, be sure to explore the Hillcrest Farmers Market.

FAMILY **Hillcrest Farmers Market.** One of San Diego's best farmers' markets, this weekly bazaar offers everything from vegan fruit pies and strawberry lemonade to homemade hummus and Turkish kabobs. A wide assortment of fresh produce and flowers are delivered straight from San Diego's farms. Several vendors dish up food to enjoy on the spot, making this an excellent choice for a quick lunch. Since parking can be tight, the market offers free trolley service from the heart of Hillcrest on 5th Avenue, as well as parking in a lot at Washington Street and Campus Avenue. ✉ *3960 Normal St., at Lincoln Ave., Hillcrest* ☎ *619/299–3330* ⊕ *www.hillcrestfarmersmarket.com* ☉ *Sun. 9–2.*

Spruce Street Bridge. This wobbly but scenic bridge is considered one of San Diego's best-kept secrets. Constructed in 1912 by Edwin Capps,

California's Padre President

San Diego, the first European settlement in Southern California, was founded by Father Junípero Serra in July 1769. A member of the Franciscan order, Father Serra was part of a larger expedition chartered by King Charles III of Spain to travel north from Baja California and occupy the territory known as Alta California.

When they arrived in San Diego, the Spaniards found about 20,000 Kumeyaay Indians living in a hundred or so villages. The missionaries attempted to convert them to Christianity, and taught them agricultural and other skills so they could work what would become the missions' vast holdings.

Mission San Diego de Alcalá, established on a hillside above what is now Mission Valley, was the first of the 21 missions that the Franciscans built along the coast of California. After establishing the mission and presidio in San Diego, Serra and Portola moved on, founding the Mission San Carlos Borromeo and presidio at Monterey.

Father Serra, the padre president of California, established nine missions. Besides those at San Diego and Monterey, there were: San Antonio de Padua, 1771; San Gabriel, 1771; San Luis Obispo, 1772; Dolores, 1776; San Juan Capistrano, 1776; Santa Clara, 1777; and San Buenaventura, 1782. He personally oversaw the planning, construction, and staffing of each of these, and conferred the sacraments. His work took him from Carmel to locations up and down the length of California. It's estimated that during this period he walked more than 24,000 miles in visiting missions.

The missions comprised millions of acres and were in fact small self-sufficient cities, with the church as the centerpiece. In addition to converting the Indians to Christianity and teaching them European ways, the padres managed farming, education, and industries such as candle making and tanning. San Diego is the southernmost mission, while the mission at Sonoma, San Francisco Solano, the last to be founded, in 1823, is the northernmost; each was established a day's walk—about 30 miles—from the previous one and was linked to El Camino Highway. The missions were the earliest form of lodging in the Golden State, known far and wide for their hospitality. You can trace the steps of Father Serra along El Camino Real by driving U.S. 101, the historic route that traverses coastal California.

Father Serra spent barely a year in San Diego before embarking on his journey to establish missions across California, but his presence left a lasting imprint. You can see some of the history at the Junípero Serra Museum and at Mission San Diego Alcalá.

—Bobbi Zane

this 375-foot suspension bridge across Kate Sessions Canyon (commonly referred to as Arroyo Canyon) originally served as a passageway between isolated neighborhoods and trolley lines. It's a somewhat hair-raising stroll over the treetops below. ⊠ *Spruce St. and 1st Ave., Hillcrest.*

MISSION HILLS

The route from Old Town to Hillcrest passes through the historic neighborhood of **Mission Hills** with its delightful examples of early-20th-century architecture. From the top of Presidio Park, take Presidio Drive into the heart of this residential area. A left on Arista Street and a right on Fort Stockton Drive takes you past wonderfully

preserved Spanish Revival, Craftsman, and Prairie-style homes, to name a few. Many local residents fine-tune their green thumbs at the **Mission Hills Nursery** (✉ *1525 Ft. Stockton Dr.*), founded in 1910 by Kate Sessions, the "Mother of Balboa Park." Continuing on Fort Stockton Drive, a right on Goldfinch Street leads you to several popular eateries along the neighborhood's burgeoning restaurant row. From there, a left on University Avenue will take you into the Hillcrest section of Uptown. For more information on this historic San Diego neighborhood, contact the Mission Hills Heritage Organization (⊕ *www. missionhillsheritage.org*).

MISSION VALLEY

Although Mission Valley's charms may not be immediately apparent, it offers many conveniences to visitors and residents alike. One of the area's main attractions is the Fashion Valley mall, with its mix of high-end and mid-range retail stores and dining options, and movie theater. Mission Valley is also home to the San Diego Chargers stadium, and traffic is congested on game days and on most days during rush hour. Just beyond the stadium, the Mission Basilica San Diego de Alcalá provides a tranquil refuge from the surrounding suburban sprawl.

Fodor's Choice ★ **Mission Basilica San Diego de Alcalá.** It's hard to imagine how remote California's earliest mission must have once been; these days, however, it's accessible by major freeways (I–15 and I–8) and via the San Diego Trolley. The first of a chain of 21 missions stretching northward along the coast, Mission San Diego de Alcalá was established by Father Junípero Serra on Presidio Hill in 1769 and moved to this location in 1774. In 1775, it proved vulnerable to enemy attack, and Padre Luis Jayme, a young friar from Spain, was clubbed to death by the Kumeyaay Indians he had been trying to convert. He was the first of more than a dozen Christians martyred in California. The present church, reconstructed in 1931 following the outline of the 1813 church, is the fifth built on the site. It measures 150 feet long but only 35 feet wide because, without easy means of joining beams, the mission buildings were only as wide as the trees that served as their ceiling supports were tall. Father Jayme is buried in the sanctuary; a small museum named for him documents mission history and exhibits tools and artifacts from the early days; there is also a gift shop. From

Gay-friendly Hillcrest is one of the hippest neighborhoods in San Diego.

the peaceful, palm-bedecked gardens out back you can gaze at the 46-foot-high *campanario* (bell tower), the mission's most distinctive feature, with five bells. Mass is celebrated on the weekends. ⊠ *10818 San Diego Mission Rd., Mission Valley* ✢ *From I–8 east, exit and turn left on Mission Gorge Rd., then left on Twain Rd.; mission is on right* ☎ *619/281–8449* ⊕ *www.missionsandiego.com* ✉ *$5, $3–$5 audio tours* ☉ *Daily 9–4:30; check website for mass times.*

UNIVERSITY HEIGHTS

Tucked between Hillcrest and North Park, this small but charming neighborhood is centered on Park Boulevard. The tree-lined street is home to several notable bars and restaurants, as well as the acclaimed LGBT Diversionary Theatre. Kids love the playgrounds at Trolley Barn Park, just around the corner on Adams Avenue. The park is also home to free family concerts in the summer.

NORTH PARK

Named for its location north of Balboa Park, this evolving neighborhood is home to an exciting array of restaurants, bars, and shops. High-end condominiums and local merchants are often cleverly disguised behind historic signage from barbershops, bowling alleys, and theater marquees. The stretch of Ray Street near University Avenue is home to several small galleries, as well as the Ray at Night art walk, held the second Saturday of each month. Just around the corner on University

Avenue lies the stunning 1920s-era North Park Theatre. With a steady stream of new openings in the neighborhood, North Park is one of San Diego's top dining and nightlife destinations.

SOUTH PARK

The South Park neighborhood is actually on the east side of Balboa Park, but it's south of North Park, hence the name. The tree-lined neighborhood is largely residential but its collection of interesting galleries, boutiques (⇨ *Specialty Stores in Shopping*), and restaurants make for a nice stroll.

MISSION BAY AND THE BEACHES

GETTING ORIENTED

Mission Bay, Beaches, and SeaWorld

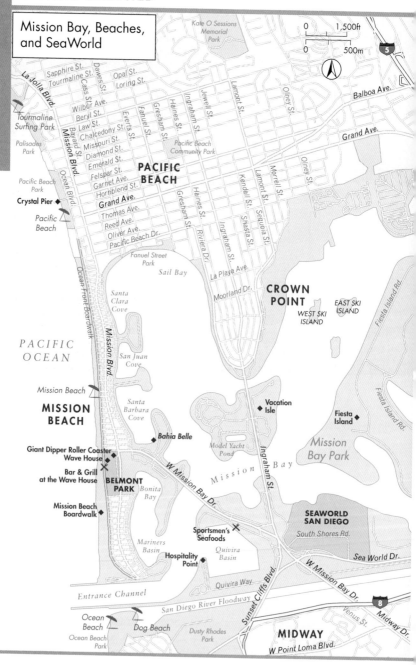

Kate O Sessions Memorial Park

0   1,500ft
0   500m

La Jolla Blvd.

Sapphire St.
Tourmaline St.
Dawes St.
Opal St.
Loring St.
Cass St.

Wilbur Ave.
Beryl St.
Law St.
Chalcedony St.
Missouri St.
Diamond St.
Emerald St.
Felspar St.
Garnet Ave.
Hornblend St.

Bayard St.
Everts St.
Fanuel St.
Gresham St.
Haines St.
Ingraham St.
Jewell St.
Lamont St.
Olney St.

Balboa Ave.

Grand Ave.

PACIFIC BEACH

Pacific Beach Community Park

Mission Blvd.

Ocean Blvd.

Kendall St.
Shasta St.
Morrell St.
Lamont St.
Olney St.
Sequoia St.

Tourmaline Surfing Park

Palisades Park

Pacific Beach Park

Crystal Pier ◆

Pacific Beach △

Grand Ave.
Thomas Ave.
Reed Ave.
Oliver Ave.
Pacific Beach Dr.

Gresham St.
Haines St.
Ingraham St.
Riviera Dr.

Fanuel Street Park

Sail Bay

La Playa Ave.

Moorland Dr.

CROWN POINT

WEST SKI ISLAND

EAST SKI ISLAND

Fiesta Island Rd.

Santa Clara Cove

PACIFIC OCEAN

Ocean Front Boardwalk

Mission Blvd.

San Juan Cove

Mission Beach ⚓

MISSION BEACH

Santa Barbara Cove

Vacation ◆ Isle

Fiesta ◆ Island

Mission Bay Park

Fiesta Island Rd.

◆ Bahia Belle

Model Yacht Pond

Mission Bay

Ingraham St.

Giant Dipper Roller Coaster ◆
Wave House ◆✕

Bar & Grill at the Wave House ✕

BELMONT PARK

Bonita Bay

W. Mission Bay Dr.

Mission Beach Boardwalk ◆

Mariners Basin

Sportsmen's ✕ Seafoods

Quivira Basin

Hospitality ◆ Point

SEAWORLD SAN DIEGO

South Shores Rd.

Sea World Dr.

W. Mission Bay Dr.

Quivira Way

Entrance Channel

San Diego River Floodway

Sunset Cliffs Blvd.

8

Venus St.

Midway Dr.

Ocean Beach ⚓

Dog Beach

Ocean Beach Park

Dusty Rhodes Park

MIDWAY

W. Point Loma Blvd.

5

TOP REASONS TO GO

Sun and sand: With sand stretching as far as the eye can see, Mission and Pacific beaches represent the classic Southern California beach experience.

Bustling boardwalk: College kids partying at the bars, families grilling in front of their vacation homes, and kids playing in the sand—take in the scene with a stroll along the Mission Beach boardwalk.

Bayside delights: A quiet respite from the nearby beaches, Mission Bay is ringed with peaceful pathways, playgrounds, and parks.

Get out on the water: Catch a wave, paddle a kayak, or rev a Jet Ski at this irresistible water-sports playground.

QUICK BITES

The Bar and Grill at the WaveHouse. This spot is a great place to grab a drink or meal while taking in the view of surfers on the nearby wave machine. ⊠ *Mission Beach Boardwalk at Belmont Park, Mission Bay* ☎ *858/228–9304* ⊕ *www.wavehousesandiego.com.*

Sportsmen's Sea Foods. This waterside eatery serves good fish-and-chips, seafood salads, and sandwiches to eat on the inelegant but scenic patio—by the marina, where sportfishing boats depart daily—or to take out to your chosen picnic spot. ⊠ *1617 Quivira Rd., Mission Bay* ☎ *619/224–3551* ⊕ *www. sportsmensseafood.com.*

There is no shortage of dining options inside **SeaWorld**, from burgers at **Café 64**, to Italian fare at **Mama Stella's Pizza Kitchen**, BBQ at the **Calypso Bay Smokehouse**, or baked goods at **Seaside Coffee and Bakery.**

GETTING HERE

SeaWorld, Mission Bay, and Mission and Pacific beaches are all served by public bus routes 8 and 9. Many local hotels offer shuttle service to and from SeaWorld. There is a free parking lot at Belmont Park, although it can quickly fill during busy times.

PLANNING YOUR TIME

You may not find a visit to SeaWorld fulfilling unless you spend at least half a day; a full day is recommended.

Belmont Park is open daily, but not all its rides are open year-round.

The Mission Beach Boardwalk and the miles of trails around Mission Bay are great for a leisurely bike ride. On foggy days, particularly in late spring or early summer, the beaches can be overcast in the morning with the fog burning off as the day wears on.

5

SEAWORLD SAN DIEGO

SeaWorld is one of the world's largest marine-life amusement parks, and is a popular family destination.

(above) Acrobatic dolphins perform at SeaWorld's Blue Horizons. (lower right) Shamu steals the show at One Ocean. (upper right) You can purchase food to feed the flamingos at Flamingo Cove.

The highlights are the large-arena entertainments. **Blue Horizons** has dolphins, pilot whales, tropical birds, and aerialists together in a spectacular performance.

Most of the exhibits are walk-through marine environments such as **Shark Encounter,** where you come face-to-face with several species of sharks while passing through a 57-foot clear acrylic tube. **Wild Arctic** starts out with a simulated helicopter ride to the North Pole and features beluga whales, walruses, and polar bears.

The park also wows with its adventure rides like **Journey to Atlantis,** with a heart-stopping 60-foot plunge, and **Shipwreck Rapids,** where you careen down a river in an inner tube encountering waterfalls. SeaWorld's newest ride, **Manta,** is a thrilling coaster.

DISCOUNTS AND DEALS

The San Diego Zoo 3-for-1 Pass ($149 for adults, $119 for children ages 3 to 9) offers seven consecutive days of unlimited admission to SeaWorld, the San Diego Zoo, and the San Diego Safari Park. Look for SeaWorld specials at Mission Bay area hotels; some offer admission deals or free shuttle service to and from the park. Be sure to ask when you book.

SEAWORLD IN A DAY

The highlights of any visit to SeaWorld are the shows, so review the current performance schedule (available online or when you arrive at the park) and plan accordingly. Shows are fairly short—about 20 minutes—so you can see several.

SeaWorld is busiest in the middle of the day, so tackle the adventure rides either at the beginning or end of your visit. Coaster lovers will want to carve out time for the popular new **Manta** ride. Unless it's very hot, consider braving the soakers—**Journey to Atlantis, Shipwreck Rapids,** and sitting in the arenas' **Splash Zones**—in close succession, and then changing into dry clothes.

For an interactive experience, focus on the feeding stations and touch pools. The four large touch pools at SeaWorld's newest exhibit, **Explorer's Reef,** greet visitors as they enter the park. More than 4,000 cleaner fish are on hand to give your fingers a friendly little nibble. If you feel emboldened, you can touch rays, horseshoe crabs, and even bamboo sharks. The friendly bottlenose dolphins at **Dolphin Point** just might let you pet them while the hands-on **California Tide Pool** features San Diego's indigenous marine life. At the **Bat Ray Feeding** pool, the friendly rays pop up to the surface for snacks and a gentle pat on the head, while hungry sea lions await you at **Pacific Point.**

The standouts among the walk-through marine exhibits are the **Penguin** and **Shark Encounters, Turtle Reef,** and **Wild Arctic.** Those with tots 42 inches and under should head to the **Sesame Street Bay of Play.**

Note: Theme parks like SeaWorld have been criticized by animal welfare groups. They argue that the conditions and treatment of marine life kept in captivity are harmful for the animals, and that human interaction further exacerbates this. A bill in California's state legislature in 2014 proposed a ban on killer whale shows; it was sent back for further study.

TIPS

■ Pack a change of clothes for after the soaker rides and shows; you can rent lockers to stow belongings. And bring sunscreen and hats.

■ If you get your hand stamped when exiting the park, you can return later that same day.

■ Arrive at shows at least 30 minutes early to get front-row seats, and be prepared to get wet.

■ Steer kids to the **Under the Sun** gift shop, near the Calypso Smoke House, where all items are $10 or less.

■ Eating options include casual spots like the Seaside Coffee and Bakery and Café 64.

SERVICE INFORMATION

✉ *500 SeaWorld Dr., near west end of I–8, Mission Bay* ☎ *800/257–4268* ⊕ *www.seaworld.com* 🎟 *$84 adults, $78 kids; parking $15 cars daily 10–dusk; extended hrs in summer.*

5

Sightseeing
★★★★☆
Nightlife
★★★☆☆
Dining
★★☆☆☆
Lodging
★★★☆☆
Shopping
★☆☆☆☆

Mission Bay and the surrounding beaches are the aquatic playground of San Diego. The choice of activities available is astonishing, and the perfect weather makes you want to get out there and play. If you're craving downtime after all the activity, there are plenty of peaceful spots to relax and simply soak up the sunshine.

MISSION BAY

Mission Bay welcomes visitors with its protected waters and countless opportunities for fun. The 4,600-acre **Mission Bay Park** is the place for water sports like sailing, stand-up paddleboarding, and water-skiing. With 19 miles of beaches and grassy areas, it's also a great place for a picnic. And if you have kids, don't miss **SeaWorld,** one of San Diego's most popular attractions.

TOP ATTRACTIONS

Bahia Belle. At the dock of the Bahia Resort Hotel, on the eastern shores of West Mission Bay Drive, you can board this restored stern-wheeler for a sunset cruise of the bay and a party that continues until the wee hours. There's always music, mostly jazz, rock, and blues, on board, and on Friday and Saturday nights the music is live. You can imbibe at the *Belle*'s full bar, but many revelers like to disembark at the Bahia's sister hotel, the Catamaran Resort, and have a few rounds before reboarding; the boat cruises between the two hotels, which co-own it, stopping to pick up passengers every half hour. Most cruises get a mixed crowd of families, couples, and singles, but cruises after 9:30 pm are adults-only. ⊠ *998 W. Mission Bay Dr., Mission Bay* ☎ *858/539–7779* ⊕ *www. sternwheelers.com/cruise.html* 🖃 *$10 for unlimited cruising; cruisers must be 21-plus after 9:30 pm; free for guests of Bahia and Catamaran hotels* ⊙ *June, Wed.–Sun. 6:30 pm–12:30 am; July–Labor Day, daily*

CLOSE UP

Planning a Day at the Beaches and Bay

A day spent at Mission Bay or the surrounding beaches can be as active or leisurely as you like.

If you want to play in the water, the bay is a great place to kayak, sail, or try some stand-up paddleboarding. If you're into surfing, be sure to check out the waves at **Crystal Pier** in Pacific Beach. A different kind of surfing experience is available at the **WaveHouse** at **Belmont Park,** where the Flow Rider lets you catch a continuous wave.

If you want to keep active on land, the Bayside Walk and Bike Path is a great place to jog or ride along the bay. Beach Cruiser bike rentals are widely available. For a more leisurely stroll and some people-watching, head to the **Mission Beach Boardwalk.** At the south end of Mission Beach try your hand at some typically Californian beach volleyball.

If you'd rather take it easy, just find a spot to lay out your towel anywhere along Mission or Pacific beach and soak up the sun. If you tire of the sand, enjoy a picnic at **Hospitality Point** or enjoy the view from one of the restaurants at Paradise Point Resort and Spa. As the day winds down, the happy-hour crowd is just heating up along Garnet Avenue in Pacific Beach. Alternatively, head to the Bahia Resort Hotel, where you can catch the *Bahia Belle* for a cruise around the bay.

If you are traveling with kids, a day at **SeaWorld** should be high on your list. There is plenty of family fun beyond SeaWorld, too. The protected beaches of the bay are popular spots for youngsters. The well-paved, peaceful Bayside Walk and Bike Path winds past picnic tables, grassy areas, and playgrounds, making it an ideal family spot. For a more lively contrast, cross the street to reach the Mission Beach Boardwalk, a classic boardwalk popular with young, hip surfers. At the south end lies **Belmont Park,** which includes an amusement park, the **WaveHouse,** and the **Giant Dipper** wooden roller coaster.

6:30 pm–12:30 am; Sept., Nov., and Jan. during even-numbered years, and Feb.–May, Fri. and Sat. 6:30 pm–12:30 am. Departures every hr on the ½ hr ☉ Closed Dec. Closed Jan. in odd-numbered years.

Fodor's Choice ★   **Mission Bay Park.** San Diego's monument to sports and fitness, this 4,600-acre aquatic park has 27 miles of shoreline including 19 miles of sandy beaches. Playgrounds and picnic areas abound on the beaches and low, grassy hills. On weekday evenings, joggers, bikers, and skaters take over. In the daytime, swimmers, water-skiers, windsurfers, anglers, and boaters—some in single-person kayaks, others in crowded powerboats—vie for space in the water. ✉ *2688 E. Mission Bay Dr., off I-5 at Exit 22 East Mission Bay Drive, Mission Bay* ☎ *858/581–7602 Park Ranger's Office* ⊕ *www.sandiego.gov/park-and-recreation* ✇ *Free.*

FAMILY   **SeaWorld San Diego.** *See highlighted listing, this chapter.*

Vacation Isle. Ingraham Street bisects this island, providing two distinct experiences for visitors. The west side is taken up by the Paradise Point Resort & Spa, but you don't have to be a guest to enjoy the hotel's lushly landscaped grounds and bay-front restaurants. Boaters and jet-skiers congregate near the launch at **Ski Beach** on the east side of the island, where there's a parking lot as well as picnic areas and restrooms. Ski Beach is the site of the annual Bayfair (formerly called the Thunderboat Regatta), held in September. At the model yacht pond on the south side of the island, children and young-at-heart adults take part year-round in motorized miniature boat races. ⊠ *Mission Bay.*

WORTH NOTING

Fiesta Island. The most undeveloped area of Mission Bay Park, this is popular with bird-watchers (there's a large protected nesting site for the California tern at the northern tip of the island) as well as with dog owners, because it's the only place in the park where pets can run free. At Christmas the island provides an excellent vantage point for viewing the bay's Parade of Lights. In July the annual Over-the-Line Tournament, a competition involving a unique local version of softball, attracts thousands of players and oglers. ⊠ *Access from East Mission Bay Dr., Mission Bay.*

Hospitality Point. This pretty, secluded spot, with a view of sailboats and yachts entering the open sea, is a good place to enjoy a picnic lunch. At the entrance to Hospitality Point, the City of San Diego Mission Bay Park and Recreation Department office supplies area maps and other recreational information. ⊠ *2500 Quivira Ct., Mission Bay.*

MISSION BEACH

Heading west on Mission Bay Drive to the ocean, the Giant Dipper roller coaster rises into view, welcoming visitors to the **Belmont Park** amusement park and to **Mission Beach.** Mission Boulevard runs north along a two-block-wide strip embraced by the Pacific Ocean on the west and the bay on the east. Mission Beach is a famous and lively fun zone for families and young people both; if it isn't party time at the moment, it will be five minutes from now. The pathways in this area are lined with vacation homes, many for rent by the week or month. Those fortunate enough to live here year-round have the bay as their front yard, with wide sandy beaches, volleyball courts, and—less of an advantage—an endless stream of sightseers on the sidewalk.

TOP ATTRACTIONS

FAMILY

Fodor's Choice

★

Belmont Park. The once-abandoned amusement park between the bay and Mission Beach Boardwalk is now a shopping, dining, and recreation complex. Twinkling lights outline the **Giant Dipper,** an antique wooden roller coaster on which screaming thrill-seekers ride more than 2,600 feet of track and 13 hills (riders must be at least 4 feet tall). Created in 1925 and listed on the National Register of Historic Places, this is one of the few old-time roller coasters left in the United States. The **Plunge,** an indoor swimming pool was the largest—60 feet by 125 feet—saltwater pool in the world at the time it opened, in 1935; it's had freshwater since 1951. Johnny Weissmuller and Esther Williams are among the stars who were captured on celluloid swimming here.

DID YOU KNOW?

San Diego has 70 miles of coastline perfect for the time-honored tradition of building sandcastles. All you need is a pail, a shovel, and a little imagination.

Other Belmont Park attractions include miniature golf, a video arcade, bumper cars, a tilt-a-whirl, and an antique carousel. The rock wall challenges both junior climbers and their elders. Belmont Park also has the most consistent wave in the county at the **Wave House,** where the FlowRider provides surfers and bodyboarders a near-perfect simulated wave on which to practice their skills. ⊠ *3146 Mission Blvd., Mission Bay* ☎ *858/488–1549 for rides* ⊕ *www.belmontpark.com* ⊲ *Unlimited ride day package $29 for 48" and taller, $18 for under 48"; individual ride tickets also available* ⊙ *Park opens at 11 daily, ride operation varies seasonally.*

> ### MISSION BAY WARNING
>
> Swimmers at Mission Bay should note signs warning about water pollution; on occasions when heavy rains or other events cause pollution, swimming is strongly discouraged.

Fodor's Choice
★
Mission Beach Boardwalk. The cement pathway lining the sand from the southern end of Mission Beach north to Pacific Beach is always bustling with activity. Cyclists ping the bells on their beach cruisers to pass walkers out for a stroll alongside the oceanfront homes. Vacationers kick back on their patios, while friends play volleyball in the sand. The activity picks up alongside Belmont Park and the WaveHouse, where people stop to check out the action on the FlowRider wave. ⊠ *Alongside the sand from Mission Beach Park to Pacific Beach, Mission Beach.*

PACIFIC BEACH

North of Mission Beach is the college-packed party town of **Pacific Beach,** or "PB" as locals call it. The laid-back vibe of this surfer's mecca draws in free-spirited locals who roam the streets on skateboards and beach cruisers, in the local uniform of board shorts, bikinis, and baseball caps. Lining the main strip of Grand and Garnet avenues are tattoo parlors, smoke shops, vintage stores, and coffeehouses. The energy level peaks during happy hour, when PB's cluster of nightclubs, bars, and 150 restaurants open their doors to those ready to party.

TOP ATTRACTION

Crystal Pier. Stretching out into the ocean from the end of Garnet Avenue, Crystal Pier is Pacific Beach's landmark. A stroll to the end of the pier will likely reveal fishermen hoping for a good catch. Surfers make catches of their own in the waves below. ⊠ *At the end of Garnet Ave., Pacific Beach.*

LA JOLLA

with Northern San Diego:
Clairemont and Kearny Mesa

GETTING ORIENTED

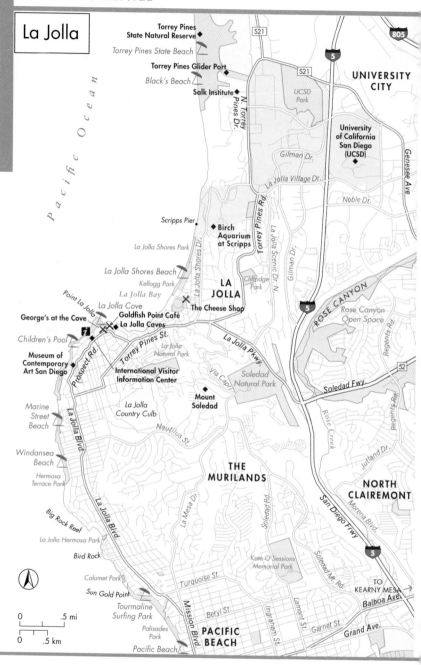

La Jolla

Pacific Ocean

Torrey Pines State Natural Reserve ◆
Torrey Pines State Beach

Torrey Pines Glider Port ◆

Black's Beach

Salk Institute ◆

N. Torrey Pines Dr.

S21

805

5

UNIVERSITY CITY

UCSD Park

University of California San Diego (UCSD)

Gilman Dr.

La Jolla Village Dr.

Noble Dr.

Genesee Ave.

Scripps Pier ◆

◆ Birch Aquarium at Scripps

La Jolla Shores Park

Torrey Pines Rd.

La Jolla Scenic Dr. N.

Gilman Dr.

La Jolla Shores Beach

Kellogg Park

La Jolla Bay

La Jolla Shores Dr.

LA JOLLA

Cliffridge Park

Point La Jolla

La Jolla Cove

×

The Cheese Shop

George's at the Cove

Goldfish Point Café
La Jolla Caves

Children's Pool

Museum of Contemporary Art San Diego

Prospect Rd.

Torrey Pines St.

La Jolla Natural Park

International Visitor Information Center

Via Capri

ROSE CANYON

Rose Canyon Open Space

Regents Rd.

5

La Jolla Pkwy.

52

Soledad Natural Park

Soledad Fwy.

Regents Rd.

◆ Mount Soledad

Marine Street Beach

La Jolla Blvd.

La Jolla Country Culb

Nautilus St.

THE MURILANDS

Rose Creek

Windansea Beach

Hermosa Terrace Park

La Mesa Dr.

Soledad Rd.

San Diego Hwy.

NORTH CLAIREMONT

Morena Blvd.

Jutland Dr.

Big Rock Reef

La Jolla Hermosa Park

La Jolla Blvd.

Bird Rock

Kate O Sessions Memorial Park

Soledad Mt. Rd.

5

Lamont St.

Calumet Park

Sun Gold Point

Turquoise St.

TO KEARNY MESA

Balboa Ave.

Tourmaline Surfing Park

Mission Blvd.

Beryl St.

Ingraham St.

Garnet St.

Grand Ave.

Palisades Park

PACIFIC BEACH

Pacific Beach

0   .5 mi
0   .5 km

TOP REASONS TO GO

Promenade above the cove: The winding pathways above La Jolla Cove offer stunning views of the surf and sea lions below.

Shop 'til you drop: La Jolla's chic boutiques and galleries are San Diego's answer to Rodeo Drive. You may even spot a celebrity as you browse on Prospect Street and Girard Avenue.

Aquatic adventures: Hop in a kayak or strap on scuba gear to explore La Jolla's marine preserve.

Luxe living: Experience the good life at top-notch spas and restaurants. Or just gawk at multimillion-dollar mansions and their denizens running errands in Ferraris.

Torrey Pines State Beach and Reserve: Play the links, hike the trails, relax on the beach, or hang glide off the cliffs.

QUICK BITES

The Cheese Shop. Excellent sandwiches for a quick lunch or picnic on the beach. ⊠ *2165 Avenida de la Playa, La Jolla* ☎ *858/459–3921* ⊕ *www.cheeseshoplajolla.com.*

George's at the Cove. This restaurant complex is one of the best spots in La Jolla for sunset views of La Jolla Cove. The main restaurant, **George's California Modern,** is an upscale affair while the top-level **Ocean Terrace** is a great place for a casual meal. ⊠ *1250 Prospect St., La Jolla* ☎ *858/454–4244* ⊕ *www.georgesatthecove.com.*

Goldfish Point Café. If you are looking for a casual breakfast or lunch overlooking La Jolla Cove, the Goldfish Point Café hits the spot without breaking the bank. ⊠ *1255 Coast Blvd., La Jolla* ☎ *858/459–7407* ⊕ *www.goldfishpointcafe.com.*

GETTING HERE

If you enjoy meandering, the best way to approach La Jolla from the south is to drive on Mission Boulevard through Mission and Pacific beaches, past the in-line skaters, cyclists, and sunbathers. Congestion eases as the street becomes La Jolla Boulevard. Road signs along La Jolla Boulevard and Camino de la Costa direct drivers and cyclists past homes designed by architects such as Irving Gill. As you approach the village, La Jolla Boulevard turns into Prospect Street.

PLANNING YOUR TIME

La Jolla's highlights can be seen in a few hours with a visit to La Jolla Village and the cove followed by a scenic drive along the coast and up through Torrey Pines.

The village and La Jolla Cove are easily explored on foot, but it's a steep walk between the two. Parking can be tough so don't hold out for a better spot. Greater La Jolla is best explored by car or bus route 30.

VISITOR INFORMATION

International Visitor Information Center. The La Jolla branch of the International Visitor Information Center is a great resource. ⊠ *1162 Prospect St., La Jolla* ☎ *858/454–5718* ⊕ *www.lajollabythesea.com* ⊗ *Hrs vary by season, generally 11–4 in winter, 10–5 in summer.*

6

Sightseeing
★★★★☆

Nightlife
★★☆☆☆

Dining
★★★★☆

Lodging
★★★☆☆

Shopping
★★★★☆

La Jollans have long considered their village to be the Monte Carlo of California, and with good cause. Its coastline curves into natural coves backed by verdant hillsides covered with homes worth millions. La Jolla is both a natural and cultural treasure trove. The upscale shops, galleries, and restaurants of La Jolla Village satisfy the glitterati, while secluded trails, scenic overlooks, and abundant marine life provide balance and refuge.

LA JOLLA

Updated by
Claire Deeks
van der Lee

Although **La Jolla** is a neighborhood of the city of San Diego, it has its own postal zone and a coveted sense of class; the ultrarich from around the globe own second homes here and old-money residents maintain friendships with the visiting film stars and royalty who frequent the area's exclusive luxury hotels and private clubs. Development has radically altered the once serene character of the village, but it has gained a cosmopolitan air that makes it a popular vacation resort.

Native Americans called the site "Woholle," or "hole in the mountains," referring to the grottoes that dot the shoreline. The Spaniards changed the name to La Jolla (same pronunciation as La Hoya), "the jewel," which led to the nickname Jewel City.

East of La Jolla, the inland neighborhoods of Clairemont and Kearny Mesa are the center of San Diego's Asian population and offer some interesting specialty restaurants and shops.

TOP ATTRACTIONS

FAMILY **Birch Aquarium at Scripps.** Affiliated with the world-renowned Scripps Institution of Oceanography, this excellent aquarium sits at the end of a signposted drive leading off North Torrey Pines Road and has sweeping views of the La Jolla coast below. More than 60 tanks are filled with colorful saltwater fish, and a 70,000-gallon tank simulates a La Jolla kelp forest. There's a special exhibit on sea horses and a gallery based on the institution's ocean research. ⊠ *2300 Expedition Way, La Jolla* 🕾 *858/534–3474* ⊕ *www. aquarium.ucsd.edu* 🖃 *$17* ⊙ *Daily 9–5; last entry at 4:30.*

FAMILY **La Jolla Caves.** It's a walk of 145 sometimes slippery steps down a tunnel to Sunny Jim, the largest of the caves in La Jolla Cove and the only one reachable by land. This is a one-of-a-kind local attraction; the man-made tunnel took two years to dig, beginning in 1902. Later, a shop was built at its entrance. Today the Sunny Jim Cave Store is still the entrance to the cave. ⊠ *1325 Coast Blvd. S, La Jolla* 🕾 *858/459–0746* ⊕ *www.cavestore.com* 🖃 *$5* ⊙ *Daily 10–5.*

Fodor's Choice ★ **Museum of Contemporary Art San Diego (MCASD).**
⇨ *See the highlighted listing in this chapter.*

Fodor's Choice ★ **Torrey Pines State Natural Reserve.** *Pinus torreyana*, the rarest native pine tree in the United States, enjoys a 1,700-acre sanctuary at the northern edge of La Jolla. About 6,000 of these unusual trees, some as tall as 60 feet, grow on the cliffs here. The park is one of only two places in the world (the other is Santa Rosa Island) where the Torrey pine grows naturally. The reserve has hiking trails leading to the cliffs, 300 feet above the ocean; trail maps are available at the park station. Wildflowers grow profusely in spring, and the ocean panoramas are spectacular. Not permitted: picnicking, smoking, leaving the trails, dogs, alcohol, or collecting plant specimens.

You can unwrap your sandwiches, however, at Torrey Pines State Beach, just below the reserve. When the tide is out, it's possible to walk south all the way past the lifeguard towers to Black's Beach over rocky promontories (avoid the bluffs, however; they're unstable). **Los Peñasquitos Lagoon** at the north end of the reserve is one of the many natural estuaries that flow inland between Del Mar and Oceanside. It's a good place to watch shorebirds. Volunteers lead guided nature walks at 10 and 2 most weekends. ⊠ *N. Torrey Pines Rd. exit off I–5 onto Carmel Valley Rd. going west, then turn left (south) on Coast Hwy. 101, 12600 N. Torrey Pines Rd., La Jolla* 🕾 *858/755–2063* ⊕ *www.torreypine.org* 🖃 *Parking $12–$15* ⊙ *Daily 8–dusk; visitor center has shorter hrs.*

University of California at San Diego. The campus of one of the country's most prestigious research universities spreads over 1,200 acres of coastal canyons and eucalyptus groves, where students and faculty jog, cycle, and rollerblade to class. If you're interested in contemporary art, check out the **Stuart Collection of Sculpture**—18 site-specific works by artists such as Nam June Paik, William Wegman, Niki de St. Phalle, Jenny Holzer, and others arrayed around the campus. UCSD's **Price Center** has a two-level bookstore—the largest in San Diego—and a good coffeehouse, Perks. Look for the postmodern **Geisel Library**, named for longtime La Jolla residents Theodor "Dr. Seuss" Geisel and his wife, Audrey. Bring quarters for the parking meters, or cash for the parking structures, because free parking is only available on weekends. ⊠ *Exit*

6

MUSEUM OF CONTEMPORARY ART SAN DIEGO

✉ *700 Prospect St., La Jolla*
☎ *858/454–3541* ⊕ *www.
mcasd.org* ✉ *$10, good for
1 visit here and at MCASD
downtown within 7 days;
free 3rd Thurs. of month
5–7* ⊗ *Thurs.–Tues. 11–5;
3rd Thurs. of month 11–7*
⊗ *Closed Wed.*

TIPS

■ Be sure to also check out MCASD's downtown branch; admission is good for seven days and valid at both locations.

■ Get in free the third Thursday of every month from 5 to 7. Informative and insightful exhibit tours are offered free of charge weekends at 2 (downtown on Saturday, and in La Jolla on Sunday), and on the third Thursday of the month at 5:30.

■ Head to the museum's X Store for unique cards and gifts.

■ The pleasant courtyard at the museum café is a great spot to relax and recharge.

Driving along Coast Boulevard, it is hard to miss the mass of watercraft jutting out from the rear of the Museum of Contemporary Art San Diego (MCASD) La Jolla location. *Pleasure Point* by Nancy Rubins is just one example of the mingling of art and locale at this spectacular oceanfront setting.

Highlights

The oldest section of La Jolla's branch of San Diego's contemporary art museum was originally a residence, designed by Irving Gill for philanthropist Ellen Browning Scripps in 1916. In the mid-1990s the compound was updated and expanded by architect Robert Venturi, who respected Gill's original structure and clean Mission-style lines while adding distinctive touches. The result is a striking contemporary building that looks as though it's always been here.

The light-filled Axline Court serves as the museum's entrance and does triple duty as reception area, exhibition hall, and forum for special events. Inside, the museum's artwork gets major competition from the setting: you can look out from the top of a grand stairway onto a landscaped garden that contains permanent and temporary sculpture exhibits as well as rare 100-year-old California plant specimens and, beyond that, to the Pacific Ocean.

California artists figure prominently in the museum's permanent collection of post-1950s art, but the museum also includes works by Andy Warhol, Robert Rauschenberg, Frank Stella, Joseph Cornell, and Jenny Holzer, to name a few. Important pieces by artists from San Diego and Tijuana were acquired in the 1990s. The museum also gets major visiting shows.

6

I–5 onto La Jolla Village Dr. going west; take Gilman Dr. off-ramp to right and continue on to information kiosk at campus entrance on Gilman Dr., La Jolla ☎ *858/534–4414 campus tour information* ⊕ *www. ucsd.edu* ☉ *90-min campus tours Sun. at 2 from South Gilman Information Pavilion; reserve before 4 pm Thurs.*

WORTH NOTING

Mount Soledad. La Jolla's highest spot can be reached by taking Nautilus Street to La Jolla Scenic Drive South, and then turning left. Proceed a few blocks to the park, where parking is plentiful and the views are astounding, unless the day is hazy. ⊠ *6905 La Jolla Scenic Dr. S, La Jolla.*

Salk Institute. The world-famous biological-research facility founded by polio vaccine developer Jonas Salk sits on 27 clifftop acres. The twin structures that modernist architect Louis I. Kahn designed in the 1960s in consultation with Dr. Salk used poured concrete to clever effect. The laboratory–office complex faces the Pacific Ocean, an orientation accentuated by a foot-wide "Stream of Life" that flows through the center of a travertine marble courtyard between the buildings. Architecture buffs will enjoy a tour of the property; register online. ⊠ *10010 N. Torrey Pines Rd., La Jolla* ☎ *858/453–4100* ⊕ *www.salk.edu* ✉ *Free; $15 requested donation for tours* ☉ *Grounds open weekdays 8:30–5; architectural tours weekdays at 11:45 (reservations required, see website for details).*

NORTHERN SAN DIEGO: CLAIREMONT AND KEARNY MESA

Located inland from La Jolla and north of Mission Valley, the neighborhoods of Clairemont and Kearny Mesa often fly under the radar of most visitors to San Diego. The shopping centers and restaurants of this area serve as a hub for San Diego's sizeable and diverse Asian population. Though these neighborhoods aren't traditional tourist destinations, those who do venture here will be rewarded as they dine at a myriad of authentic Asian restaurants, relax over a reflexology foot massage, or peruse the aisles of specialty grocery stores.

CLAIREMONT

Centered on Tecolote Canyon, this suburban neighborhood occupies a series of mesas, many with views of Mission Bay. Heading inland, Balboa Avenue serves as the area's commercial hub.

KEARNY MESA

Farther inland, Kearny Mesa is less residential than neighboring Clairemont. The bustling shopping centers lining Convoy Street are home to many popular Asian restaurants and supermarkets.

7

POINT LOMA AND CORONADO

with Harbor and Shelter Islands, and Ocean Beach

GETTING ORIENTED

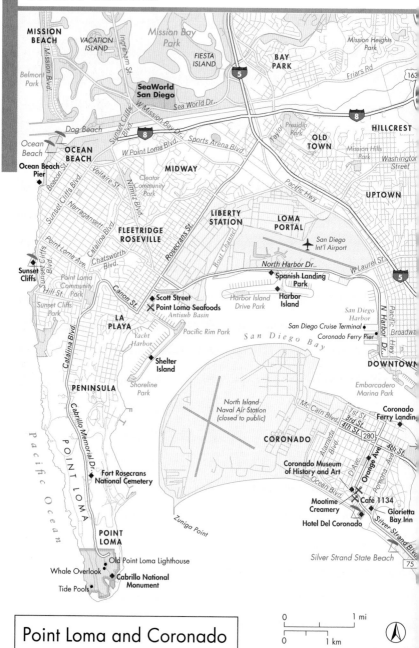

MISSION BEACH

VACATION ISLAND

Mission Bay Park

FIESTA ISLAND

BAY PARK

Mission Heights Park

Ingraham St.

Friars Rd

163

Belmont Park

Mission Blvd.

SeaWorld San Diego

5

Sea World Dr.

W Mission Bay Dr.

Sunset Cliffs Blvd.

Dog Beach

8

Sports Arena Blvd.

Taylor St.

Presidio Park

OLD TOWN

HILLCREST

Ocean Beach

OCEAN BEACH

W Point Loma Blvd.

Mission Hills Park

Washington Street

Ocean Beach Pier

Voltaire St.

MIDWAY

Cleator Community Park

Pacific Hwy

UPTOWN

Beacon St.

Nimitz Blvd.

Narragansett

LIBERTY STATION

LOMA PORTAL

San Diego Int'l Airport

W Laurel St.

Sunset Cliffs Blvd.

Catalina Blvd.

FLEETRIDGE ROSEVILLE

Rosecrans St.

Boat Channel

North Harbor Dr.

5

Point Loma Ave.

Chatsworth Blvd.

Sunset Cliffs

Sunset Cliffs Blvd.

Point Loma Community Park

Canon St.

Spanish Landing Park

Harbor Island

N. Harbor Dr.

Broadway

Sunset Cliffs Park

Hill St.

LA PLAYA

Scott Street

Point Loma Seafoods

Antisub Basin

Harbor Island Drive Park

San Diego Cruise Terminal

San Diego Harbor

Pacific Hwy

Catalina Blvd.

Yacht Harbor

Pacific Rim Park

San Diego Bay

Coronado Ferry Pier

DOWNTOWN

Shelter Island

PENINSULA

Shoreline Park

Embarcadero Marina Park

Cabrillo Memorial Dr.

North Island Naval Air Station (closed to public)

McCain Blvd.

1st St.

3rd St.

Coronado Ferry Landing

P O I N T   L O M A

CORONADO

4th St.

280

Alameda Blvd.

Orange Ave.

Pacific Ocean

Fort Rosecrans National Cemetery

Coronado Museum of History and Art

D Ave.

Ocean Blvd.

4th St.

Pomona Ave.

Zuniga Point

Mootime Creamery

Café 1134

Glorietta Bay Inn

Silver Strand Blvd.

Hotel Del Coronado

POINT LOMA

Old Point Loma Lighthouse

Silver Strand State Beach

75

Whale Overlook

Cabrillo National Monument

Tide Pools

0   1 mi

0   1 km

Point Loma and Coronado

TOP REASONS TO GO

Point Loma's panoramic views: Take in the view from the mountains to the ocean at Cabrillo National Monument. Come evening, watch the sun go down at Sunset Cliffs.

The Hotel Del: As the grande dame of San Diego, the historic Hotel Del Coronado charms guests and visitors alike with her graceful architecture and oceanfront setting.

Boating paradise: San Diego's picturesque marinas are filled with sportfishing charters and ultraluxury yachts.

Sandy beaches: The long stretches of sand on Coronado are family-friendly, while Fido will love swimming at Ocean Beach's Dog Beach.

Military might: From the endless rows of white headstones at Fort Rosecrans National Cemetery to the roar of fighter jets over North Island Naval Air Station, San Diego's strong military ties are palpable.

QUICK BITES

Cafe 1134. You can get a curried tuna sandwich to accompany your espresso at this mini-bistro. ⊠ *1134 Orange Ave., Coronado* ☎ *619/437–1134* ⊕ *www.cafe1134.net.*

Mootime Creamery. Check out the rich ice cream, frozen yogurt, and sorbet made daily here, or dessert nachos made from waffle-cone chips. Just look for the sidewalk statue of Elvis. ⊠ *1025 Orange Ave., Coronado* ☎ *619/435–2422* ⊕ *www.nadolife.com/mootime.*

Point Loma Seafoods. The freshest fish along Point Loma's shores comes from this shop behind the Vagabond Inn. There's also a take-out counter selling prepared foods. ⊠ *2805 Emerson St., Point Loma* ☎ *619/223–1109* ⊕ *www. pointlomaseafoods.com.*

GETTING HERE

Bus 84 serves Cabrillo National Monument on Point Loma, although a transfer is required from Bus 28, near Shelter Island. For Harbor Island, the hearty can walk from the Embarcadero or catch a bus to the airport and walk from there.

Coronado is accessible via the arching blue 2.2-mile-long San Diego–Coronado Bay Bridge, which offers breathtaking views of the harbor and downtown. Alternatively, pedestrians and bikes can reach Coronado via the popular ferry service. Bus 904 meets the ferry and travels as far as Silver Strand State Beach. Bus 901 runs daily between the Gaslamp Quarter and Coronado.

PLANNING YOUR TIME

If you're interested in seeing the tide pools at Cabrillo National Monument, call ahead or check the weather page of the *Union-Tribune* to find out when low tide will occur. Scott Street, with its Point Loma Seafoods, is a good place to find yourself at lunchtime, and Sunset Cliffs Park is where you want to be at sunset.

A leisurely stroll through Coronado takes at least an hour, more if you stop to shop or walk along the family-friendly beaches. Whenever you come, if you're not staying overnight, remember to get back to the dock in time to catch the final ferry out at 9:30 (10:30 on weekends).

7

CABRILLO NATIONAL MONUMENT

Cabrillo National Monument marks the site of the first European visit to San Diego, made by 16th-century explorer Juan Rodríguez Cabrillo. Cabrillo landed at this spot, which he called San Miguel, on September 15, 1542. Today the 160-acre preserve with its rugged cliffs and shores and outstanding overlooks is one of the most frequently visited of all the national monuments.

(above) Point Loma from the water, as Cabrillo would have seen it in 1542. (lower right) Old Point Loma Lighthouse stood watch for 36 years. (upper right) Cabrillo's statue adorns the visitor center.

Catching sight of a whale from the cliffs of Cabrillo National Monument can be a highlight of a wintertime visit to San Diego. More accessible sea creatures can be seen in the tide pools at the foot of the monument's western cliffs.

On land, trails lead down the hillside through sagebrush and cactus. Overlook points offer spectacular views from the desert mountains to downtown and beyond. The informative visitor center and the lighthouse give a historical perspective to this once-remote promontory.

SERVICE INFORMATION

The visitor center, located next to the statue of Cabrillo, presents films and lectures about Cabrillo's voyage, the sea-level tide pools, and migrating gray whales.

✉ *1800 Cabrillo Memorial Dr., Point Loma* ☎ *619/557–5450* ⊕ *www. nps.gov/cabr* ✉ *$5 per car, $3 per person entering on foot or by bicycle, admission good for 7 days* ☉ *Park daily 9–5.*

A HALF DAY AT CABRILLO NATIONAL MONUMENT

A **statue of Cabrillo** overlooks downtown from a windy promontory, where people gather to admire the stunning panorama over the bay, from the snowcapped San Bernardino Mountains, 130 miles north, to the hills surrounding Tijuana to the south. The stone figure standing on the bluff looks rugged and dashing, but he is a creation of an artist's imagination—no portraits of Cabrillo are known to exist.

The moderately steep **Bayside Trail,** 2½ miles round-trip, winds through coastal sage scrub, curving under the cliff-top lookouts and taking you ever closer to the bay-front scenery. You cannot reach the beach from this trail and must stick to the path to protect the cliffs from erosion and yourself from thorny plants and snakes—including rattlers. You'll see prickly pear cactus and yucca, fragrant sage, and maybe a lizard, rabbit, or hummingbird. The climb back is long but gradual, leading up to the old lighthouse.

Old Point Loma Lighthouse's oil lamp was first lighted in 1855 and was visible from the sea for 25 miles. Unfortunately, it was too high above the cliffs to guide navigators trapped in Southern California's thick offshore fog. In 1891 a new lighthouse was built 400 feet below. The restored old light-house is open to visitors. An exhibit in the Assistant Keepers Quarters next door tells the story of the Old Lighthouse, the daily lives of the keepers, how lighthouses work, and the role they played in the development of early maritime commerce along the West Coast. On the edge of the hill near the old lighthouse sits a refurbished radio room containing displays of U.S. harbor defenses at Point Loma used during World War II.

■TIP➜ Restrooms and water fountains are plentiful, but, except for vending machines at the visitor center, there's no food. Exploring the grounds consumes time and calories; pack a picnic and rest on a bench overlooking the sailboats.

WHALE-WATCHING

The western and southern cliffs of Cabrillo National Monument are prime whale-watching territory. A sheltered **viewing station** has wayside exhibits describing the great gray whales' yearly migration from Baja California to the Bering and Chukchi seas near Alaska. High-powered telescopes help you focus on the whales' water-spouts. Whales are visible on clear days from late December through early March, with the highest concentration in January and February. Note that when the whales return north in spring, they are too far out in the ocean to be seen from the monument.

TIDE POOLS

When the tide is low you can walk on the rocks around saltwater pools filled with starfish, crabs, anemones, octopuses, and hundreds of other sea creatures and plants. Tide pooling is best when the tide is at its lowest, so call ahead or check tide charts online before your visit. Exercise caution on the slippery rocks.

7

Sightseeing
★★★☆☆
Nightlife
★☆☆☆☆
Dining
★★★☆☆
Lodging
★★★★☆
Shopping
★★★☆☆

Although Coronado is actually an isthmus, easily reached from the mainland if you head north from Imperial Beach, it has always seemed like an island and is often referred to as such. To the west, Point Loma protects the San Diego Bay from the Pacific's tides and waves. Both Coronado and Point Loma have stately homes, sandy beaches, private marinas, and prominent military installations. Nestled between the two, Harbor and Shelter islands owe their existence to dredging in the bay.

POINT LOMA

Updated by
Claire Deeks
van der Lee

The hilly peninsula of **Point Loma** curves west and south into the Pacific and provides protection for San Diego Bay. Its high elevations and sandy cliffs provide incredible views, and make Point Loma a visible local landmark. Its maritime roots are evident, from its longtime ties to the U.S. Navy to its bustling sport fishing and sailing marinas. The funky community of **Ocean Beach** coexists alongside the stately homes of **Sunset Cliffs** and the honored graves at **Fort Rosecrans National Cemetery.**

TOP ATTRACTIONS

FAMILY   **Cabrillo National Monument.**

Fodor's Choice   ⇨ *See the highlighted listing in this chapter.*
★

Fort Rosecrans National Cemetery. In 1934, 8 of the 1,000 acres set aside for a military reserve in 1852 were designated as a burial site. More than 100,000 people are now interred here; it's impressive to see the rows upon rows of white headstones that overlook both sides of Point Loma just north of the Cabrillo National Monument. Some of those laid to rest at this place were killed in battles that predate California's statehood; the graves of the 17 soldiers and one civilian who died in the 1874 Battle of San Pasqual between troops from Mexico and the United States are marked by a large bronze plaque. Perhaps the most

Point Loma to Harbor Island Driving Tour

Take Catalina Boulevard all the way south to the tip of Point Loma to reach **Cabrillo National Monument.** North of the monument, as you head back into the neighborhoods of Point Loma, you'll see the white headstones of **Fort Rosecrans National Cemetery.** Continue north on Catalina Boulevard to Hill Street and turn left to reach the dramatic **Sunset Cliffs,** at the western side of Point Loma near Ocean Beach. Park to tour the dramatic cliff tops and the boiling seas below, but be cautious because the cliffs can be unstable. Signs generally warn you where not to go. Head north on Sunset Cliffs Boulevard until you reach Newport Avenue, where you will make a left to enter the heart of **Ocean Beach.** If you have your dog with you, head north to **Ocean Beach's Dog Beach** or check out surfers from the **Ocean Beach Pier** off Niagara Avenue. Just before the pier, turn left onto Newport Avenue, OB's main drag.

Return to Sunset Cliffs Boulevard and backtrack south to take a left on Point Loma Avenue. Turn left at Canon Street, which leads toward the peninsula's eastern (bay) side. Almost at the shore you'll see **Scott Street,** Point Loma's main commercial drag. Scott Street is bisected by Shelter Island Drive, which leads to **Shelter Island.** For another example of what can be done with tons of material dredged from a bay, go back up Shelter Island Drive, turn right on Rosecrans Street, another right on North Harbor Drive, and a final right onto **Harbor Island.**

7

impressive structure in the cemetery is the 75-foot granite obelisk called the Bennington Monument, which commemorates the 66 crew members who died in a boiler explosion and fire onboard the USS *Bennington* in 1905. The cemetery, visited by many veterans, is still used for burials. ⊠ *Cabrillo Memorial Dr., Point Loma* ☎ *619/553–2084* ⊗ *Mon.–Fri. 8–4:30, Sat.–Sun. 9:30–5.*

Fodor'sChoice
★ **Sunset Cliffs.** As the name suggests, the 60-foot-high bluffs on the western side of Point Loma south of Ocean Beach are a perfect place to watch the sun set over the sea. To view the tide pools along the shore, use the staircase off Sunset Cliffs Boulevard at the foot of Ladera Street.

The dramatic coastline here seems to have been carved out of ancient rock. The impact of the waves is very clear: each year more sections of the cliffs are posted with caution signs. Don't ignore these warnings— it's easy to slip in the crumbling sandstone, and the surf can be extremely rough. The small coves and beaches that dot the coastline are popular with surfers drawn to the pounding waves. The homes along the boulevard—pink stucco mansions beside shingled Cape Cod–style cottages—are fine examples of Southern California luxury. ⊠ *Sunset Cliffs Blvd., Point Loma.*

WORTH NOTING

Scott Street. Running along Point Loma's waterfront from Shelter Island to the old Naval Training Center on Harbor Drive, this thoroughfare is lined with deep-sea fishing charters and whale-watching boats. It's a good spot to watch fishermen (and women) haul marlin, tuna, and puny mackerel off their boats. ☒ *1 block from America's Cup Harbor, Point Loma.*

OCEAN BEACH

At the northern end of Point Loma lies the chilled-out, hippyesque town of Ocean Beach, commonly referred to as "OB." The main thoroughfare of this funky neighborhood is dotted with dive bars, coffeehouses, surf shops, and 1960s diners. OB is a magnet for everyone from surfers to musicians and artists. Newport Avenue, generally known for its boisterous bars, is also home to San Diego's largest antiques district. Fans of OB applaud its resistance to "selling out" to upscale development, whereas detractors lament its somewhat scruffy edges.

TOP ATTRACTIONS

Ocean Beach Pier. This T-shape pier is a popular fishing spot and home to the Ocean Beach Pier Café and a small tackle shop. Constructed in 1966, it is the longest concrete pier on the West Coast and a perfect place to take in views of the harbor, ocean, and Point Loma peninsula. Surfers flock to the waves that break just below. ☒ *1950 Abbott St., Ocean Beach.*

SHELTER ISLAND

In 1950 San Diego's port director decided to raise the shoal that lay off the eastern shore of Point Loma above sea level with the sand and mud dredged up during the course of deepening a ship channel in the 1930s and '40s. The resulting peninsula, **Shelter Island,** became home to several marinas and resorts, many with Polynesian details that still exist today, giving them a retro flair.

Shelter Island. This reclaimed peninsula now supports towering palms and resorts, restaurants, and side-by-side marinas. Shelter Island is the center of San Diego's yacht-building industry, and so boats in every stage of construction are visible in its yacht yards. A long sidewalk runs past boat brokerages to the hotels and marinas that line the inner shore, facing Point Loma. On the bay side, fishermen launch their boats and families relax at picnic tables along the grass, where there are fire rings and permanent barbeque grills. Within walking distance is the huge Friendship Bell, given to San Diegans by the people of Yokohama, Japan, in 1960 and the Tunaman's Memorial, a statue commemorating San Diego's once-flourishing fishing industry. ☒ *Shelter Island Dr., Shelter Island.*

HARBOR ISLAND

Following the successful creation of Shelter Island, in 1961 the U.S. Navy used the residue from digging berths deep enough to accommodate aircraft carriers to build **Harbor Island.** Restaurants and high-rise hotels dot the inner shore of this 1½-mile-long man-made peninsula adjacent to the airport. The bay's shore is lined with pathways, gardens, and scenic picnic spots. On the east end point, **Island Prime and C-level Lounge** (⇨ *Where to Eat*) has killer views of the downtown skyline.

Harbor Island. Restaurants and high-rise hotels dot the inner shore of this 1½-mile-long man-made peninsula adjacent to the airport. The bay's shore is lined with pathways, gardens, and scenic picnic spots. On the east end point, **Island Prime and C-level Lounge** (☎ *880 Harbor Island Dr.*, ☎ *619/298–6802*, ⊕ *www.cohnrestaurants.com*) offers a killer view of the downtown skyline. On the west point, the restaurant **Tom Ham's Lighthouse** (☎ *2150 Harbor Island Dr.*, ☎ *619/291–9110*, ⊕ *www.tomhamslighthouse.com*) has a U.S. Coast Guard–approved beacon shining from its tower and a sweeping view of San Diego's bayfront. ⊠ *Harbor Island Dr., Harbor Island.*

CORONADO

As if freeze-framed in the 1950s, Coronado's quaint appeal is captured in its old-fashioned storefronts, well-manicured gardens, and charming **Ferry Landing Marketplace.** The streets of Coronado are wide, quiet, and friendly, and many of today's residents live in grand Victorian homes handed down for generations. Naval Air Station North Island was established in 1911 on Coronado's north end, across from Point Loma, and was the site of Charles Lindbergh's departure on the transcontinental flight that preceded his famous solo flight across the Atlantic. Coronado's long relationship with the U.S. Navy have made it an enclave for military personnel; it's said to have more retired admirals per capita than anywhere else in the United States.

TOP ATTRACTIONS

FAMILY **Coronado Ferry Landing.** This collection of shops at Ferry Landing is on a smaller scale than the Embarcadero's Seaport Village, but you do get a great view of the downtown San Diego skyline. The little bayside shops and restaurants resemble the gingerbread domes of the Hotel Del Coronado. **Bikes and Beyond** (☎ *619/435–7180* ⊕ *http://hollandsbicycles.com*) rents bikes and surreys, perfect for riding through town and along Coronado's scenic bike path. ⊠ *1201 1st St., at B Ave., Coronado* ☎ *619/435–8895* ⊕ *www.coronadoferrylandingshops.com.*

Fodor'sChoice **Hotel Del Coronado.** The Del's distinctive red-tile roofs and Victorian ★ gingerbread architecture have served as a set for many movies, political meetings, and extravagant social happenings. It's speculated that the Duke of Windsor may have first met the Duchess of Windsor Wallis Simpson here. Eleven presidents have been guests of the Del, and the film *Some Like It Hot*—starring Marilyn Monroe, Jack Lemmon, and Tony Curtis—used the hotel as a backdrop.

The Hotel Del, as locals call it, was the brainchild of financiers Elisha Spurr Babcock Jr. and H. L. Story, who saw the potential of Coronado's virgin beaches and its view of San Diego's emerging harbor. It opened in 1888 and has been a National Historic Landmark since 1977. The History Gallery displays photos from the Del's early days, and books elaborating on its history are sold, along with logo apparel and gifts, in the hotel's 15-plus shops.

FERRY TO CORONADO

Coronado Ferry. Fifteen-minute ferries connect two locations along the downtown San Diego waterfront with the Coronado Ferry Landing. Boats depart on the hour from the Broadway Pier on the Embarcadero and on the half-hour from Coronado Ferry Landing to the Embarcado during operating hours. Between the San Diego Convention Center and the Coronado Ferry Landing, service departs every half-hour during operating hours. Buy tickets at the Broadway Pier, 5th Avenue Landing, or Coronado Ferry Landing. Water taxi service (it comes on request) is also available Friday through Sunday from noon to 10 pm. To reach the heart of downtown Coronado from the Ferry Landing, you can rent a bike at the landing (or bring one with you), or catch the 904 shuttle bus that runs along Orange Avenue. Ferry service is operated by Flagship Cruises (previously SD Harbor Excursion). ⊠ *Broadway Pier on the Embarcadero, 990 N. Harbor Dr.* ☎ *619/234–4111, 800/442–7847, 619/235–8294 water taxi* ⊕ *www. flagshipsd.com* 🖃 *Ferry $4.25 each way; water taxi $8 per person per ride* ☉ *Sun.–Thurs. 9–9, Fri. and Sat. 9–10.*

Although the pool area is reserved for hotel guests, several surrounding dining patios make great places to sit back and imagine the scene during the 1920s, when the hotel rocked with good times. Behind the pool area, an attractive shopping arcade features a classic candy shop as well as several fine clothing and accessories stores. A lavish Sunday brunch is served in the Crown Room. During the holidays, the hotel hosts Skating by the Sea, an outdoor beachfront ice-skating rink open to the public. Tours of the Del are $15 per person and take place on Monday, Wednesday, and Friday at 10:30, and weekends at 2; reservations are required. ⊠ *1500 Orange Ave., at Glorietta Blvd., Coronado* ☎ *619/435–6611, 619/437–8788 tour reservations (through Coronado Visitor Center)* ⊕ *www.hoteldel.com.*

Fodor's Choice **Orange Avenue.** Comprising Coronado's business district and its village-
★   like heart, this avenue is surely one of the most charming spots in Southern California. Slow-paced and very "local" (the city fights against chain stores), it's a blast from the past, although entirely up to date in other respects. The military presence—Coronado is home to the U.S. Navy Sea, Air and Land (SEAL) forces—is reflected in shops selling military gear and places like **McP's Irish Pub,** at No. 1107. A family-friendly stop for a good, all-American meal, it's the unofficial SEALs headquarters. Many clothing boutiques, home-furnishings stores, and upscale restaurants cater to visitors with deep pockets, but you can buy plumbing supplies, too, or get a genuine military haircut at **Crown Barber Shop,** at No. 947. If you need a break, stop for a latte at the sidewalk café of **Bay Books,** San Diego's largest independent bookstore, at No. 1029. ⊠ *Orange Ave., near 9th St., Coronado.*

WHERE TO EAT

Updated by Ron and Mary James

San Diego is an up-and-coming culinary destination, thanks to its stunning Pacific Ocean setting, proximity to Mexico, diverse population and the area's extraordinary farming community. Increasingly the city's veteran top chefs are being joined by a new generation of talented chefs and restaurateurs who are adding stylish restaurants with innovative food and drink programs to the dining scene at a record pace. Yes, visitors still are drawn to the San Diego Zoo and miles of beaches, but now they come for memorable dining experiences as well.

The city's culinary scene got a significant boost when San Diego emerged as one of the world's top craft beer destinations, with artisan breweries and gastropubs now in almost every neighborhood. San Diego also was on the cutting edge of the farm-to-table, slow-food movement. Local sourcing is possible for everything from seafood to just-picked produce from a host of nationally recognized producers like Chino Farms and Carlsbad Aquafarm. The city's ethnically diverse neighborhoods with their modest eateries offering affordable authentic international cuisines add spice to the dining mix.

San Diego's distinct neighborhoods have their own dining personalities with friendly restaurants and bistros catering to every craving in this sun blessed city. The trendy Gaslamp Quarter delights visitors looking for a broad range of innovative dining and nightlife, while bustling Little Italy is a center for affordable Italian fare. Modern restaurants and cafés thrive in the East Village, amid the luxury condos near PETCO Park, and Bankers Hill, just west of Balboa Park, is one of the hottest food destinations in the city.

The Uptown neighborhoods centered on Hillcrest—an urbane district with San Francisco flavor—are a mix of bars and independent restaurants. North Park, in particular, has a happening restaurant scene, with

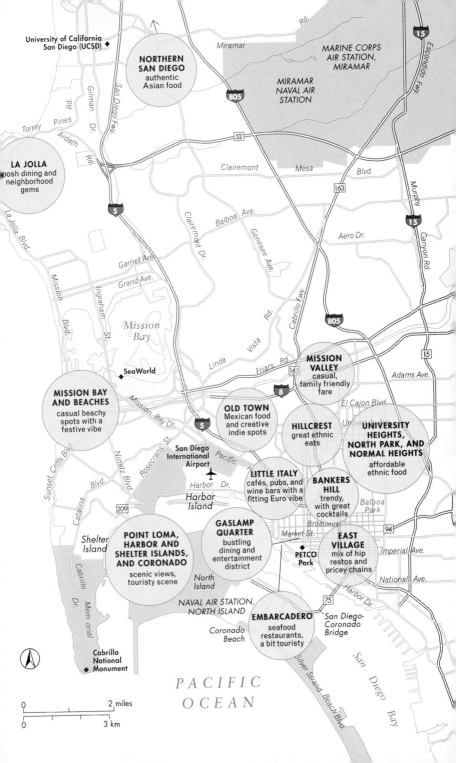

University of California
San Diego (UCSD) ◆

**NORTHERN
SAN DIEGO**
authentic
Asian food

Miramar Rd.

MARINE CORPS
AIR STATION,
MIRAMAR

MIRAMAR
NAVAL AIR
STATION

LA JOLLA
posh dining and
neighborhood
gems

Torrey Pines

Ardath Rd.

Gilman Dr.

San Diego Fwy.

Escondido Fwy.

Clairemont Mesa Blvd.

Balboa Ave.

Clairemont Dr.

Genesee Ave.

Aero Dr.

Murphy Canyon Rd.

La Jolla Blvd.

Mission Blvd.

Ingraham St.

Garnet Ave.

Grand Ave.

*Mission
Bay*

Cabrillo Fwy.

Vista Rd.

Linda Vista Rd.

Friars Rd.

**MISSION
VALLEY**
casual,
family friendly
fare

Adams Ave.

◆ SeaWorld

Mission Bay Dr.

**MISSION BAY
AND BEACHES**
casual beachy
spots with a
festive vibe

OLD TOWN
Mexican food
and creative
indie spots

HILLCREST
great ethnic
eats

El Cajon Blvd.

University

**UNIVERSITY
HEIGHTS,
NORTH PARK, AND
NORMAL HEIGHTS**
affordable
ethnic food

Sunset Cliffs Blvd.

Nimitz Blvd.

Rosecrans St.

San Diego
International
Airport

Pacific

Harbor Dr.

LITTLE ITALY
cafés, pubs, and
wine bars with a
fitting Euro vibe

**BANKERS
HILL**
trendy,
with great
cocktails

*Balboa
Park*

Catalina Blvd.

*Harbor
Island*

**GASLAMP
QUARTER**
bustling
dining and
entertainment
district

Broadway

Market St.

94

**EAST
VILLAGE**
mix of hip
restos and
pricey chains

Imperial Ave.

*Shelter
Island*

**POINT LOMA,
HARBOR AND
SHELTER ISLANDS,
AND CORONADO**
scenic views,
touristy scene

*North
Island*

◆ PETCO
Park

National Ave.

Cabrillo Mem orial Dr.

NAVAL AIR STATION,
NORTH ISLAND

75

Harbor Dr.

EMBARCADERO
seafood
restaurants,
a bit touristy

San Diego–
Coronado
Bridge

Silver Strand Beach Blvd.

*Coronado
Beach*

San Diego Bay

Cabrillo
National
Monument

**PACIFIC
OCEAN**

0 ———— 2 miles

0 ———— 3 km

just about every kind of cuisine you can think of, and laid-back prices to boot. And scenic La Jolla offers some of the best fine dining in the city.

Ethnic cuisine remains popular in the Gaslamp Quarter, Hillcrest, and Convoy Street in Kearney Mesa, which is a hub for Chinese, Korean, and Vietnamese fare. In Chula Vista you'll find authentic Mexican food, while Coronado—the peninsula city across San Diego Bay—has beachy neighborhood eateries and extravagant hotel dining rooms with dramatic water views.

SAN DIEGO DINING PLANNER

DINING HOURS

Unless otherwise noted, the restaurants listed in this guide are open daily for lunch and dinner. Lunch is typically served 11:30 am to 2:30 pm, and dinner service in most restaurants begins at 5:30 pm and ends at 10 pm, though a number of establishments serve until 11 pm or later on Friday and Saturday night.

RESERVATIONS

We mention reservations in reviews only when they're essential or not accepted. But reservations are usually a very good idea especially for popular dining spots — reserve as far ahead as you can, and reconfirm when you arrive in town.

WHAT TO WEAR

In San Diego restaurants, generally a "come-as-you-are" attitude prevails. It's a casual city for men and women alike, but going-out dress is generally fashionable and fun, especially for celebratory or upscale dining. Very few dress-up places remain.

CHILDREN

Most San Diego restaurants welcome children and many have special kid's menus with food offerings targeted to younger palates and parent's pocketbooks. Some high-end and bar-oriented establishments may not be appropriate for children—if unsure, call the establishment for confirmation. The restaurants we recommend for families with children are marked with a ☾ symbol.

PARKING

With the boom of new apartments and condominiums downtown and in Little Italy, street parking near many restaurants can be frustrating, especially in the evenings and on weekends. Valet ($5–$15) parking in front of many major restaurants is easy and convenient. Some valet parking is subsidized by restaurants; call ahead for parking offers and suggestions. There are several parking garages and lots throughout downtown with prices that fluctuate depending on events. Savvy locals use the limited free parking with validation at downtown's Horton Plaza. For major downtown events where parking is impossible, consider parking for free at the Old Town transit center and get a quick San Diego Trolley ride to stops in Little Italy, East Village and the Gaslamp Quarter.

SMOKING

Smoking is banned in restaurants in California. The city of San Diego permits smoking on patios, but many restaurants don't allow it. Check before you go.

PRICES

Meals in San Diego popular dining spots can be pricey, especially in areas like La Jolla, the Gaslamp Quarter, and Coronado. Many other restaurants are very affordable or offer extra value with fixed-price menus, early-dining specials and early and late happy hours.

Prices in the reviews are the average cost of a main course at dinner or, if dinner is not served, at lunch.

WHAT IT COSTS				
	$	$$	$$$	$$$$
Restaurants	under $18	$18–$27	$28–$35	over $35

Prices are per person for a main course or equivalent combination of smaller plates (e.g., tapas, sushi), excluding 8.75% sales tax.

RESTAURANT REVIEWS

Listed alphabetically within neighborhoods. Use the coordinate (⊕ 1: B2) at the end of each listing to locate a site on the San Diego Dining and Lodging Atlas following this chapter.

DOWNTOWN

Downtown San Diego with its gleaming skyscrapers hugs the bayside Embarcadero and embraces some of the city's trendiest neighborhoods including East Village, the Gaslamp Quarter and Little Italy. It's known around the world for a lively mix of nightlife, fine and casual dining, and ethnic specialty restaurants that reflect the city's multicultural heritage and growing culinary sophistication.

GASLAMP QUARTER

The historic heart of downtown spread across 4th, 5th, and 6th avenues, the Gaslamp Quarter satisfies foodies, conventioneers, and nightclubbers with a wide choice of eateries and nightlife. Many are pricey, upscale chains and tourist-driven concepts, while others are stylish restaurants or casual gastropubs with local roots, featuring everything from sushi to authentic Mexican and aged steaks.

$$$ ✕ **BiCE Ristorante.** Well-heeled regulars and conventioneers consistently
ITALIAN laud this sleek downtown Italian restaurant. So do its peers in the California Restaurant Association, which in 2014 named it the best Italian fine-dining restaurant in the Gaslamp. "Bee-Chay" is known for its cheese bar, a robust collection of formaggi italiani personally curated by the chef. The menu's trademark is modern Italian cuisine with dishes like lobster pizza, mint-scented paparadelle with lamb ragu and cedar plank-cooked sea bass. Waiters are professional and informed on the extensive Italian wine list, while the bar features local artisanal and

BEST BETS FOR SAN DIEGO DINING

With hundreds of restaurants from which to choose, how will you decide where to eat? We've selected our favorite restaurants by price, cuisine, and experience in the Best Bets list below. In the first column, Fodor's Choice properties represent the "best of the best" in every price category. Bon appétit!

Fodor's Choice ★

A. R. Valentien $$$$, p. 136

Bankers Hill bar and grill $$, p. 123

The Blind Burro $, p. 117

Buona Forchetta $, p. 132

Croce's Park West $$$, p. 124

Cucina Urbana $$, p. 124

Eddie V's Prime Seafood $$$, p. 121

George's at the Cove $$$$, p. 138

Ironside Fish & Oyster $$, p. 120

Island Prime and C Level $$$$, p. 148

Karen Krasne's Extraordinary Desserts $, p. 120

Ortega's Bistro $$, p. 129

Piatti Ristorante and Bar $$, p. 139

Point Loma Seafood's $, p. 145

Prepkitchen $$, p. 120

Puesto $, p. 122

Red Door $$, p. 130

Taka $$, p. 116

Wa Dining Okan $, p. 143

Whisknladle $$, p. 141

By Price

$

Buona Forchetta, p. 132

Carnitas' Snack Shack, p. 132

Puesto, p. 122

Wa Dining Okan, p. 143

$$

Bankers Hill bar and grill, p. 123

Bencotto, p. 118

Busalacchi's A Modo Mio, p. 128

Cucina Urbana, p. 124

Ironside Fish & Oyster, p. 120

Ortega's Bistro, p. 129

Prepkitchen, p. 120

Red Door, p. 130

Whisknladle, p. 141

$$$

Cowboy Star, p. 117

Croce's Park West, p. 124

Eddie V's, p. 121

Searsucker, p. 116

Sushi Ota, p. 136

$$$$

A. R. Valentien, p. 136

George's at the Cove, p. 138

Morton's, The Steakhouse, p. 116

By Cuisine

AMERICAN

A. R. Valentien, p. 136

Bankers Hill, p. 123

Craft & Commerce, p. 119

Croce's Park West, p. 124

Jimmy's Famous American Tavern, p. 144

Morton's, p. 116

Searsucker, p. 116

Urban Solace, p. 133

ASIAN

Harney Sushi, p. 127

Lucky Liu's, p. 114

Sushi Ota, p. 136

Taka, p. 116

Wa Dining Okan, p. 143

CHINESE

China Max, p. 142

Dumpling Inn, p. 142

Lucky Liu's, p. 114

FRENCH

Bertrand at Mister A's, p. 124

Bistro Bijou, p. 137

Tapenade, p. 140

GASTROPUBS

Craft & Commerce, p. 119

Neighborhood, p. 118

Slater's 50/50, p. 145

Stone Brewing World Bistro & Gardens, p. 145

Waypoint Public, p. 133

ITALIAN

Bencotto, p. 118

Buona Forchetta, p. 132

Busalacchi's A Modo Mio, p. 128

Cucina Urbana, p. 124

Davanti Enoteca Little Italy, p. 119

Piatti Ristorante and Bar, p. 139

JAPANESE

Hane Sushi, p. 125

Sushi Ota, p. 136

Taka, p. 116
Wa Dining Okan, p. 143

LATIN/MEXICAN

The Blind Burro, p. 117
Carnitas' Snack
Shack, p. 132
El Zarape, p. 131
Isabel's Cantina,
p. 134
Ortega's Bistro, p. 129
Puesto, p. 122

MEDITERRANEAN

The Kebab Shop, p.
118
Mama's Bakery &
Lebanese Deli, p. 132

SEAFOOD

Eddie V's, p. 121
George's at the Cove,
p. 138
Ironside Fish &
Oyster, p. 120
Point Loma Seafood's,
p. 145
Top of the Market,
p. 122

STEAKHOUSES

Cowboy Star, p. 117
Fogo de Chao, p. 114
Island Prime and C
Level, p. 148
Morton's, p. 116
Puerto La Boca, p. 121

By Experience

BRUNCH

Café Chloe, p. 117

Hash House A Go Go,
p. 128
Isabel's Cantina,
p. 134
The Mission, p. 118
Patio on Lamont,
p. 135
Snooze, p. 130
Tom Ham's Light-
house, p. 149

COCKTAILS

Bankers Hill bar and
grill, p. 123
Craft & Commerce,
p. 119
Indigo Grill, p. 119
Juniper & Ivy, p. 120
Prepkitchen, p. 120
Searsucker, p. 116

DINING WITH KIDS

The Blind Burro, p. 117
Hodad's, p. 147
Ortega's Bistro, p. 129
Pizzeria Arrivederci,
p. 129
Project Pie, p. 129
Puesto, p. 122
Slater's 50/50, p. 145
Stone Brewing World
Bistro & Gardens,
p. 145
Tender Greens, p. 146
Waypoint Public, p. 133

GOOD FOR GROUPS

A. R. Valentien, p. 136
Bistro Bijou, p. 137
Busalacchi's A Modo
Mio, p. 128
Piatti Ristorante and
Bar, p. 139

Stone Brewing World
Bistro & Gardens,
p. 145
URBN Coal-Fired
Pizza, p. 133

OUTDOOR DINING

1500 Ocean, p. 149
BO-Beau kitchen +
garden, p. 144
Café Chloe, p. 117
George's at the Cove,
p. 138
Jimmy's Famous
American Tavern,
p. 144
Piatti Ristorante and
Bar, p. 139
The Prado, p. 123
Sea180, p. 145

ROMANTIC

A. R. Valentien, p. 136
Bertrand at Mister A's,
p. 124
BO-Beau kitchen +
bar, p. 143
Chez Loma, p. 149
Eddie V's, p. 121
George's at the Cove,
p. 138
Marine Room, p. 138
Red Door, p. 130
Whisknladle, p. 141

SINGLES SCENE

Bankers Hill bar and
grill, p. 123
George's at the Cove,
p. 138
JRDN at Tower 23,
p. 134
Juniper & Ivy, p. 120
Searsucker, p. 116

TRENDY

Bankers Hill, p. 123
Craft & Commerce,
p. 119
Ironside Fish &
Oyster, p. 120
Juniper & Ivy, p. 120
Neighborhood, p. 118
Prepkitchen, p. 120
Searsucker, p. 116
Stone Brewing World
Bistro & Gardens,
p. 145

WATER VIEWS

Bali Hai, p. 148
Eddie V's, p. 121
George's at the Cove,
p. 138
Island Prime and C
Level, p. 148
JRDN, p. 134
Marine Room, p. 138
Sea180, p. 145
Tom Ham's Light-
house, p. 149
Top of the Market,
p. 122

WINE LISTS

3rd Corner Wine Shop
and Bistro, p. 146
100 Wines, p. 127
1500 Ocean, p. 149
Cucina Urbana, p. 124
George's at the Cove,
p. 138
Patio on Lamont,
p. 135
Village Vino, p. 131

8

imported beers and appropriate cocktails like the Il Rutino, with Aperol and prosecco. [$] *Average main: $34* ✉ *425 Island Ave., Gaslamp Quarter* ☎ *619/239–2423* 🌐 *www.bicesandiego.com* ⊙ *No lunch* ✥ *1:D5.*

$ IRISH 🍴 **The Field.** Get your Irish on at this family-run pub imported piece-by-piece from Ireland and reassembled in the Gaslamp Quarter. Home-style meals, traditional brews, and Irish music draw diners here from around the world. Menu classics include corned beef croquettes, Irish stew, fish-and-chips, corned beef and cabbage, lamb sliders, and—best of all—the burrito-like boxty, a thin, crisp potato pancake stuffed with savory fillings like Irish bacon and cheese. As the evening wears on, the crowd grows younger, livelier, louder, and sometimes rowdier. A traditional Irish breakfast is served on weekends, and there's dancing and live music many nights of the week. [$] *Average main: $15* ✉ *544 5th Ave., Gaslamp Quarter* ☎ *619/232–9840* 🌐 *www.thefield.com* ⊙ *No breakfast weekdays* ✥ *1:D5.*

$$$$ BRAZILIAN 🍴 **Fogo de Chao.** It's a Brazilian-style meat lover's paradise featuring 16 cuts of savory fire roasted meats and cuts. The restaurant is beautiful, comfortable, and lively. It's also fun and interactive; this San Diego newcomer is almost like a culinary game show. Patrons flip a disk to signal the table-roaming, meat-cleaving gauchos (servers) that they are ready for another slice of flavorful beef, lamb, pork, or chicken. Seafood lovers are offered Mango Chilean Sea Bass or a jumbo shrimp cocktail with malagueta pepper sauce. Meals begin with a trip around the extensive salad bar and meats are accompanied by tasty sides including caramelized bananas, crispy polenta, and caipirinhas. [$] *Average main: $50* ✉ *668 6th Ave., Downtown* ☎ *619/338–0500* 🌐 *www.fogodechao.com* ✥ *1:E4.*

$$ AMERICAN 🍴 **Jsix.** The recently remodeled room with distressed brick walls, rustic wood tables, and vintage waterfront photos suits the restaurant's commitment to modern all-natural coastal cuisine. Start with the refreshing "Local" cocktail—one of several named for regions of the country, and pair it with sharable starters like the citrus-chili-flavored panfried baby artichokes or spicy black chicken wings and house-made kimchi cucumbers. Locals as well as guests at the adjacent boutique Hotel Solamar savor comfort-food entrées like the brown-butter-basted pork chop and grits or bacon-wrapped monk fish. One of the city's top pastry chefs contributes meal-ending sweets ranging from yogurt gelato to Nutella-flavored pudding. ■ **TIP→ The open-air rooftop lounge upstairs serves up skyline views.** [$] *Average main: $26* ✉ *616 J St., Gaslamp Quarter* ☎ *619/531–8744* 🌐 *www.jsixrestaurant.com* ✥ *1:E5.*

$ CHINESE 🍴 **Lucky Liu's.** No Asian fusion here; instead this red-walled Gaslamp restaurant guarded by two bright-eyed dragons cooks up authentic Chinese comfort food to eat in or take out. The veteran chef, who often takes orders in Chinese from non-English speaking customers, shops daily for seafood, meat, and vegetables for the Cantonese and Szechuan dishes. Start with tender pot stickers bursting with shrimp and pork, the popular lettuce wraps, or a bowl of hot-and-sour soup. In addition to kung pao, Mongolian beef, honey-glazed walnut shrimp, and scrumptious orange chicken, entrées include black-pepper filet mignon, oolong sea bass, and other chef specialties on "Grandma's Secret Menu."

$ *Average main: $15* ⊠ *332 J St., Gaslamp* ☎ *619/255–5487* ⊕ *www. luckyliuschinese.com* ✛ *1:D5.*

$$$$ ✕ **Morton's, The Steakhouse.** Convenient to the San Diego Convention
STEAKHOUSE   Center and Gaslamp Quarter, this traditional steak house teems with celebrating local couples, as well as visitors and conventioneers seeking a fun night on the town. Happy hour at the bar and adjacent dog-friendly patio offers original cocktails and high-end appetizers like filet mignon sliders. In the clubby main dining room, the restaurant excels with superb classic steak-house fare: hefty bone-in rib eye, New York strip steak, and mixed grills such as filet mignon with shrimp and scallops. The extensive wine list includes some excellent vintages that won't break the bank. Expert friendly service caps this indulgent dining experience. $ *Average main: $40* ⊠ *Harbor Club, 285 J St., Downtown* ☎ *619/696–3369* ⊕ *www.mortons.com* ⊘ *No lunch* ✛ *1:D5.*

$$$ ✕ **Nobu.** The San Diego outpost of this fusion trendsetter, located in the
JAPANESE   Hard Rock Hotel, serves inventive sushi and hot dishes with Japanese-Peruvian flair. The sexy if rather noisy room with scorched ash-wood treatments and jade-green walls is a cool space to enjoy founding chef Nobu Matuhisa's classics like sashimi tacos, lobster with yuzu dressing, or black cod with miso. When feeling adventurous, let the sushi chef's whims guide you through an omakase, or tasting menu, that begins at $100. A nightly happy hour is a good introduction, with tapas-size nibbles, specialty cocktails, sake and beers at $12 and under. $ *Average main: $34* ⊠ *Hard Rock Hotel, 207 5th Ave., Gaslamp Quarter* ☎ *619/814–4124* ⊕ *www.noburestaurants.com* ⊘ *No lunch, except during major conventions* ✛ *1:E5.*

$$$ ✕ **Searsucker.** Since opened by celebrity chef Brian Malarkey a few years
AMERICAN   ago, this high-energy flag-ship restaurant has become the Gaslamp's best for food and energetic atmosphere. Foodies from near and far savor Malarkey's up-scale down-home fare like small plates of mac and cheese with fried chicken skins, duck fat fries, and shrimp and grits. He is masterful with locally caught seafood like opah sauced with chipotle. The open kitchen serves a full range of poultry and meat dishes, while specialty cocktails from the bar keep things lively in the sofa-furnished lounge. If you prefer a quiet place to chat and dine, this isn't for you. $ *Average main: $30* ⊠ *611 5th Ave., Gaslamp Quarter* ☎ *619/233–7327* ⊕ *www.searsucker.com* ⟆ *Reservations essential* ✛ *1:E4.*

$$ ✕ **Taka.** Pristine fish imported from around the world and presented
JAPANESE   creatively attracts crowds nightly to this intimate Gaslamp restaurant. Take a seat at bar and watch one of the sushi chefs preparing appetizers, perhaps the monkfish liver with ponzu or some slices of tender hamachi sashimi. Table service is available inside and outside where an omakaze (tasting menu) or eight-piece rolls range from spicy tuna to eel and vegetable can be shared and savored. Hot dishes include salmon teriyaki and an East-meets-West-style New York steak. The restaurant is a favorite with Japanese visitors and conventioneers. $ *Average main: $18* ⊠ *555 5th Ave., Gaslamp Quarter* ☎ *619/338–0555* ⊕ *www.takasushi.com* ⊘ *No lunch* ✛ *1:E5.*

$ ✕ **The Tin Fish.** This casual walk-up seafood eatery always packed with
SEAFOOD   baseball fans and conventioneers is only 100 yards from the PETCO

Park baseball stadium and a couple of blocks from the convention center. Downtown office workers also lunch on the umbrella-shaded patio. Musicians entertain some evenings and weekends, making this a lively and festive spot to enjoy grilled and fried fish, seafood burritos, and fish and shrimp tacos. The extra large 32-ounce beer for $8 is a great value downtown and a perfect pairing with baseball fan-favorite salmon fish and chips. Hours are subject to change, depending on Convention Center and PETCO Park activities. [$] *Average main: $10* ✉ *170 6th Ave., Gaslamp Quarter* ☎ *619/238–8100* 🌐 *www.tinfishgaslamp.com* ✍ *Reservations not accepted* ✣ *1:E5.*

EAST VILLAGE

Revived with the opening of the San Diego Padres stadium, PETCO Park, this trendy high-rise residential area is an eclectic mix of hip gastropubs, wine bars, and cafés serving everything from French bistro fare to Baja-Mexican, burgers, and artisan-baked bread.

$$ | MODERN MEXICAN | FAMILY | Fodor's Choice ★

🍴 **The Blind Burro.** East Village families, baseball fans heading to or from PETCO Park and happy-hour bound singles flock to this airy restaurant with Baja-inspired food and drink with an Asian twist. Traditional margaritas get a fresh kick from fruit juices or jalapeño peppers; other libations include sangrias and Mexican beers, all perfect pairings for house-made guacamole, ceviche, or salsas with chips. For variety, try the grilled yellowtail fish collar glazed with orange-chipotle BBQ sauce. No enchiladas or burritos are served here, but the taco, torta entrée, and side choices are extensive and innovative. Don't miss the spicy off-the-cob corn and save room for warm cinnamon-sugared churros. [$] *Average main: $18* ✉ *639 J St., East Village* ☎ *619/795–7880* 🌐 *www.theblindburro.com* ✣ *1:E5.*

$$ | FRENCH

🍴 **Café Chloe.** Parisian stylish, jewel-box cozy, and welcoming describe this neighborhood favorite on a busy street in artsy East Village. Surrounded by residential high-rises, hotels, and boutiques, this pretty spot offers French bistro-inspired breakfast, lunch, dinner, and brunch to residents, baseball fans, and courting couples. Poached eggs with wild mushrooms are an excellent way to start the day; lunch might mean a truffle-scented smoked trout and wild mushroom crepe. Dinner highlights include duck confit, steak frites, or melt-in-your mouth gnocchi. Expect frequent menu changes to reflect the chef's finds at local farms. Enjoy carefully selected wines by the glass, imported teas and coffee with desserts like seasonal fruit tarts or chocolate pot de crème. [$] *Average main: $24* ✉ *721 9th Ave., East Village* ☎ *619/232–3242* 🌐 *www.cafechloe.com* ✣ *1:E4.*

$$$$ | STEAKHOUSE

🍴 **Cowboy Star.** Special-occasion diners, conventioneers on expense accounts, and meat-loving locals haunt this surprisingly intimate dining room for great beef expertly prepared. The wood-and-brick interior has leather accents, Western landscapes, and vintage Old West photos, and servers wear stylish plaid shirts, all creating a relaxed urban-cowboy ambience. Here, prime 35-day dry-aged beef is king. Savor choice cuts with everyone's favorite side, mashed potatoes and cheese with chunks of smoked bacon, and a paired artisan brew. Non–steak options include Dungeness crab cakes and pan-roasted salmon. High-back booths are comfy, as is the chef's counter and the bar, where mixologists shake

8

up strong bourbon cocktails. $ *Average main: $44* ✉ *640 10th Ave., East Village* ☎ *619/450–5880* ⊕ *www.thecowboystar.com* ⊗ *No lunch Sat.–Mon.* ✛ *1:E4.*

$

GREEK

✕**The Kebab Shop.** At its four San Diego locations—downtown, Little Italy, Mira Mesa, and Mission Valley—this fast-food Mediterranean eatery offers a mix of slowly cooked rotisserie meats, grilled to-order seafood, and crispy falafel served on plates of saffron rice or wrapped in grilled flatbread. Fresh tabouli, 11 Mediterranean salads and baklava desserts round out the meals. For a meal on the go, order the döner box: a choice of spiced lamb, marinated chicken, or falafel accompanied by fries or rice, fresh veggies, and creamy garlic yogurt sauce. $ *Average main: $8* ✉ *630 9th Ave., East Village* ☎ *619/525–0055* ⊕ *www. thekebabshop.com* ⚘ *Reservations not accepted* ✛ *1:E4.*

$

AMERICAN

✕**The Mission.** Healthy, creative dishes and a friendly staff make this art-filled East Village café a local favorite for breakfast and lunch. Hungry San Diegans wait 30 minutes or more to enjoy fluffy scrambled eggs with chicken apple sausage or strawberry banana pancakes with a side of eggs and bacon. Also popular are Mexican-inspired dishes like chilaquiles, breakfast burritos, and quesadillas. Outstanding rosemary, cinnamon, brown, and gluten-free breads are house-made and the Mission Mocha coffee and Mexican hot chocolate are like liquid desserts. Lunch favorites include border-inspired chicken pesto quesadillas, tamales verdes, and grilled chicken tacos. Locations also in Mission Beach and North Park. $ *Average main: $10* ✉ *1250 J St., East Village* ☎ *619/232–7662* ⊕ *www.themissionsd.com* ⊗ *No dinner* ✛ *1:F5.*

$

AMERICAN

✕**Neighborhood.** Hip and happening, this East Village gastropub buzzes with crowds drawn to a beer selection many say is second to none locally. Twenty-six craft brews are on tap, with dozens more available by the bottle. Whiskey flights from the extensive spirit list are around $20. There's no ketchup in the house—the young owners don't want anything to mar the flavor of their burgers topped with pickled daikon or spicy Cajun sauce. Fries are dipped in garlicky aioli and onion rings in mustard-seed mayo. Also highly recommended are the smoked, porter-braised beef ribs, the bacon-wrapped mini-dogs and butter-poached mussels. $ *Average main: $10* ✉ *777 G St., East Village* ☎ *619/446–0002* ⊕ *www.neighborhoodsd.com* ⚘ *Reservations not accepted* ✛ *1:E4.*

LITTLE ITALY

One of San Diego's oldest and liveliest neighborhoods steeped in the city's Italian and Portuguese fishing culture, Little Italy is known for its bustling nightlife and Italian fine and casual dining mixed with trendy new eateries, dessert destinations, sidewalk cafés and a few late-night bars.

$$

ITALIAN

✕**Bencotto.** The new ultramodern Italian eatery with young Milanese owners is getting cheers for its design and cuisine from hip Little Italy residents and visitors alike. Diners linger over drinks and house-made pasta at the friendly long bar and more intimate upstairs dining room. Small plates designed for sharing include fried saffron risotto balls and meatballs with a spicy tomato dipping sauce. Pasta Your Way offers full and half-portion pastas with one of 10 sauces, plus chicken, shrimp, or meatballs if desired. Traditional soups, salads, and meat and seafood dishes pair well with one of the many Italian wines available by glass or bottle. **■ TIP→ Parking can be challenging but the Little Italy valet service is available after 6 pm.** [$] *Average main: $20* ✉ *750 W. Fir St., Little Italy* ☎ *619/450–4786* 🌐 *www.lovebencotto.com* 🕑 *Closed Mon. except June to Sept.* ✣ *1:C2.*

$$ ITALIAN ✕ **Buon Appetito.** This charmer serves old world–style cooking in a casual cozy environment in vibrant Little Italy. For a more relaxed meal, choose a table on the sidewalk; inside, the dining room is livelier, and jammed with local art and fellow diners. Baked eggplant in a mozzarella-topped tomato sauce is a dream of a dish—tomato sauce doesn't get better than this. Other favorite options include the linguine with fresh clams, mussels, scallops, and shrimp; a hearty cioppino; and an expert osso bucco. The wine list is affordable and the young Italian waiters' good humor makes this a fun experience. [$] *Average main: $19* ✉ *1609 India St., Little Italy* ☎ *619/238–9880* 🌐 *www.buonappetito.signonsandiego.com* ✣ *1:C2.*

$ MODERN AMERICAN ✕ **Craft & Commerce.** C&C, as locals know this Little Italy lounge, oozes slightly surreal cool. Crammed bookshelves line the walls, banquettes and mirrors are scrawled with sayings, and taxidermy appears in odd settings, like the lion-skin rug on the ceiling. The management's no-fear mind-set extends to the menu; ketchup and vodka have been outlawed here. But young fans and neighborhood residents who gather here after work find plenty to savor among the craft cocktails and snacks served by bearded bartenders in plaid shirts and suspenders. Dinner brings typical gastropub fare like fried chicken, mussels, and thick burgers and a not-so-typical dessert—the bacon ice-cream sandwich. [$] *Average main: $12* ✉ *675 W. Beech St., Little Italy* ☎ *619/269–2202* 🌐 *www.craft-commerce.com* ✍ *Reservations not accepted* ✣ *1:C2.*

$$ ITALIAN ✕ **Davanti Enoteca Little Italy.** With its innovative, affordable Italian food, polished service, bustling bar scene and olive tree–shaded patio, this Chicago transplant is right at home in Little Italy. Sip the Davanti Spritz (Aperol, prosecco, and soda) while nibbling on warm cheesy focaccia sweetened with honey or antipasti cheeses, meats, and olives. Dine family-style, sharing slices of thin-crust pizza, plates of classic pastas like cacao e pepe or a steaming bowl of mascarpone polenta topped with the ragu of the day. Craving a sweet but bored with gelato or tiramisu? Then indulge in the Purple Pig Panino, toasted bread slathered with Nutella and marshmallow fluff. **■ TIP→ Build your own Bloody Mary during weekend brunch.** [$] *Average main: $18* ✉ *1655 India St., Little Italy* ☎ *619/237–9606* 🌐 *www.davantienoteca.com/sandiego* 🕑 *No lunch weekends* ✣ *1:C2.*

$$ SOUTHWESTERN ✕ **Indigo Grill.** This pioneer Little Italy restaurant dramatically refreshed its look and menu, adding to its appeal to hip neighborhood residents, long-time fans, and first-time visitors. Urban-industrial decor infuses fire pits on the expanded patio and a sunken communal cocktail table ideal for people-watching. Favorites from chef-partner Deborah Scott—pipian-crusted brie, squid-ink pasta—star alongside executive chef Jason Maitland's global Latin plates to share ranging from Peruvian-style street food and ceviche to exotic offerings like Flaming Hot

Cheetosans, crispy pigs-ear strips with lime zest and cotijia. Desserts are south-of-the-border favorites, too, like warm churros for dipping in Mexican hot chocolate. Expanded hours make room for lively early and late happy hours. A dog-friendly patio area help make this a favoite destination for the locals. $ *Average main: $26* ⊠ *1536 India St., Little Italy* 🕾 *619/234–6802* ⊕ *www.indigogrill.com* ☉ *No lunch* ✛ *1:C2.*

$$
SEAFOOD
Fodor's Choice
★

✕ **Ironside Fish & Oyster.** Hundreds of piranhas cover one wall of this soaring, nautically themed dining room dedicated to fresh seafood in all its guises. At the raw bar with its refrigerated metal top, a half dozen or more varieties of oysters are available for slurping, along with drinks from the notebook size cocktail menu. (During the weekday 3–6 happy hour, oysters are just $1 each). Platters for sampling and sharing—a mix of oysters, shrimp, mussels, and lobster—can be ordered for up to eight people. For entrées, day-catch fish and lobsters just plucked from a tank can be savored grilled or à la plancha. Fresh whole fish with simple sides are a bargain at less than $25. Other specialties range from zesty mussels with andouille sausage to a hefty lobster roll slathered with brown butter mayo. $ *Average main: $24* ⊠ *1654 India St., Little Italy* 🕾 *619/269–3033* ⊕ *www.ironsidefishandoyster.com* ✛ *1:C2.*

$$$
MODERN
AMERICAN

✕ **Juniper & Ivy.** Celebrity chef Richard Blais's hot new addition to San Diego's restaurant scene fills an open-beamed former packing house with seating for 250 and an open stainless-steel dream kitchen where diners can watch the chef and team in action. Blais sources local farm fresh ingredients for his "left coast cookery" with a molecular gastronomy twist. Oysters on the half shell are dotted with liquid nitrogen-frozen "pearls" of horseradish cream and a gazpacho is topped with buttermilk "snow." Even familiar carne asada surprises as spicy steak tartar on toast. The comfort-food crowd might want to order from the "secret menu" with its "In & Haute" double-patty burger served with fries. ∎TIP→ Restaurant valet parking is only $5. $ *Average main: $28* ⊠ *2228 Kettner Blvd., Little Italy* 🕾 *619/269–9036* ⊕ *www.juniperandivy.com* ☉ *Closed for lunch* ✛ *1:B1.*

$
CAFÉ
Fodor's Choice
★

✕ **Karen Krasne Extraordinary Desserts.** For Paris-perfect cakes and tarts embellished California-style with fresh flowers, head to this sleek, serene branch of Karen Krasne's pastry shop and café, a few blocks east from the heart of Little Italy. The converted commercial space with soaring ceilings hosts breakfasts, lunches, and light dinners, accompanied by a wide selection of private-blend loose teas, coffee drinks, organic wines, and craft beers. For those who don't want to start with dessert, there are sandwiches, soups, salads, and artisanal cheeses. Then it's time to satisfy sweet cravings with a slice of passion fruit ricotta cake, a mini banana cream pie or helping of croissant bread pudding. The original shop near Balboa Park, at 2929 5th Avenue, serves only desserts, coffees, and teas. $ *Average main: $13* ⊠ *1430 Union St., Little Italy* 🕾 *619/294–7001* ⊕ *www.extraordinarydesserts.com* ⌫ *Reservations not accepted* ✛ *1:C2.*

$$
MODERN
AMERICAN
Fodor's Choice
★

✕ **Prepkitchen Little Italy.** Urbanites craving a hip casual setting and gourmet menu pack architectural salvage-styled Prepkitchen Little Italy, tucked upstairs above a busy corner in this thriving neighborhood. With first-date cocktails, after-work brews or birthday champagne, diners relish familiar choices like catch-of-the day, chops, and roast chicken paired with seasonal fruits and vegetables with flare and daring. Generously sized dishes like spicy Carlsbad mussels or zesty tagliatelle bolognese could serve as dinner for two. Farmers' market flatbreads, changed daily, are made for sharing, too, while the hefty WNL Burger topped with bacon and egg is a staple lunch, brunch, and dinner. ■TIP→ For cheap treats, fill up on $5 tapas during the daily happy hour. $ *Average main: $24* ⊠ *1660 India St., Little Italy* ☎ *619/398–8383* ⊗ *No lunch weekends* ✛ *1:C2.*

$$$
ITALIAN
╳ **Po Pazzo Bar & Grille.** Po Pazzo earns its name, which means "a little crazy," by mixing a lively bar scene with a restaurant that serves steaks, chops, and Italian fare. The bar is a favorite watering hole for many locals in the Little Italy neighborhood. Don't expect hip and chic here; the scene is more retro steak house with an Italian accent, offering attractive salads and pasta dishes, as well as the signature bone-in rib eye, served Scilian-style (with mushrooms, tomatoes, and onions). Live music Friday–Sunday turns up the volume, so head elsewhere for intimate conversations. $ *Average main: $31* ⊠ *1917 India St., Little Italy* ☎ *619/238–1917* ⊕ *www.popazzo.com* ✛ *1:C2.*

$$
ARGENTINE
╳ **Puerto La Boca.** Located on the fringe of Little Italy's bustling restaurant scene, this intimate Argentine steak house is named for a Buenos Aires waterfront neighborhood home to generations of Italian immigrants. The dimly lighted spot may not be as trendy as other dining venues here, but is still a romantic and comfortable destination for visitors and neighborhood regulars. Patio seating is perfect for happy-hour munching on popular empanadas or tender marinated octopus in olive oil and garlic. The many Argentinean-style steaks, including the signature skirt steak, get a flavor boost from the tangy chimichurri sauce. An extensive wine list includes some delicious malbecs from Mendoza. $ *Average main: $27* ⊠ *2060 India St., Little Italy* ☎ *619/234–4900* ⊕ *www.puertolaboca.com* ⊗ *No lunch on Sun.* ✛ *1:C1.*

EMBARCADERO AND MARINA DISTRICT

This walkable downtown bay-front strip between the iconic County Administration building and the convention center offers visitors access to historic maritime destinations and a wide range of dining served up with spectacular views.

$$$
SEAFOOD
Fodor's Choice
★
╳ **Eddie V's Prime Seafood.** Don't be put off by the name, or that it is part of a small chain. This fine-dining restaurant in the Headquarters downtown has won a devoted following for innovative seafood, casual but sophisticated settings, and nightly live jazz. Chilled oysters and other shellfish compete with Maine lobster tacos and kung pao–style calamari to start the meal. The polished staff helps with informed descriptions of almost two dozen entrées starring fish flown in fresh daily and prime steaks. Sea bass in a savory soy broth and parmesan-crusted sole are favorites, while the seafood chopped salad is light and sharable. Garlicky fries and truffled mac and cheese are not-to-be-missed sides. Nightly happy hours in the V Lounge offer $10 wines, cocktails, and appetizers. ■TIP→ A second location in La Jolla has wonderful ocean views and the same dinner menu, but different happy-hour specials. It also serves lunch on weekends. $ *Average main: $34* ⊠ *789 W. Harbor Dr., Embarcadero* ☎ *619/615-0281* ⊕ *www.eddiev.com* ✛ *1:B5.*

8

$ ✕ **Pizzeria Mozza.** This pizzeria by acclaimed chefs Nancy Silverton and
PIZZA   Mario Batali, already a huge success in Los Angeles and Orange County,
finally found a San Diego home in the new Headquarters downtown.
Residents and visiting foodies gather indoors in a long room warmed by
wood or outdoors on the small patio to enjoy the upscale Italian fare.
Silverton's small thin-crust pizzas crisped to perfection in a wood-burn-
ing oven include the classic Margherita, her famed fennel sausage with
red onions, and a meat-lover's pie with bacon, sausage, and pancetta.
Begin the meal with antipasti, salads or bruschetta, but be sure to end
with signature silky butterscotch budino. $ *Average main: $17* ✉ *789
W. Harbor Dr., Downtown* ☎ *619/376–4353* ⊕ *www.pizzeriamozza.
com* ✛ *1:B5.*

$ ✕ **Puesto.** Bold graffiti graphics, chandeliers with tangled telephone
MEXICAN   wires, and beat-heavy music energize this downtown eatery that cel-
Fodor'sChoice   ebrates Mexican street food with a modern twist. Settle into one of the
★   interior rooms or the sunny patio under orange umbrellas to sip margaritas and other specialty cocktails, Baja wines, or fruity aguas frescas
made daily. Guacamole, ceviche, seafood tostadas, and a festive stack of
chili-and-salt-spiced fresh fruit whet appetites for tasty street tacos—11
varieties including lobster, filet mignon, and carnitas that can be mixed
and matched for plates of three. Chicken moles, BBQ short ribs, and
classic cochinita pibil with slow-roasted pork round out the menu.
The original (and smaller) Puesto is in downtown La Jolla. $ *Average
main: $13* ✉ *789 W. Harbor Dr., Downtown* ☎ *619/233–8880* ⊕ *www.
eatpuesto.com* ✛ *1:B5.*

$$ ✕ **Roy's San Diego Waterfront.** The modern and inviting space that is
ECLECTIC   Roy's Restaurant overlooks the marina from inside the downtown Mar-
riott Hotel and showcases chef Roy Yamaguchi's version of Hawaiian
cuisine, with an additional chef's menu from local chef-partner Jessie
Glessner. Inventive sushi such as a delicious surf-and-turf roll draped in
Kobe beef and Roy's signature blackened island ahi give way to delicate
lobster pot stickers and Szechuan baby back ribs. Entrées run from the
original macadamia-crusted mahimahi in lobster-studded beurre blanc
sauce to a spicy seafood hot pot and salt-crusted rib eye. Desserts, like
a hot chocolate soufflé, are served with island-style warmth. $ *Aver-
age main: $27* ✉ *333 W. Harbor Dr., Embarcadero* ☎ *619/239–7697*
⊕ *www.roysrestaurant.com* ✛ *1:C5.*

$$$$ ✕ **Top of the Market.** With its bay views from Point Loma to the Coro-
SEAFOOD   nado Bridge, this upscale seafood house is just right for a memorable
evening. The romantic teak-paneled dining room and a deck that sits
over the water are popular spots for visitor splurges and locals cel-
ebrating special occasions. Starters include smoked fish samplers or
a chilled seafood platter with a half Maine lobster, Dungeness crab,
clams, prawns, and oysters, shared with sips of champagne. The star
among salad offerings is the Oregon Dungeness crab Louie. For mains,
choose from mesquite-grilled Pacific Coast fresh fish or specialties like
the Dover sole, zesty cioppino, or ink linguini with prawns and scallops.
$ *Average main: $38* ✉ *750 N. Harbor Dr., Embarcadero* ☎ *619/234–
4867 Top of the Market* ⊕ *www.thefishmarket.com* ✛ *1:A4.*

BALBOA PARK AND BANKERS HILL

This area is defined by the sprawling world-famous park bursting with museums and gardens, but increasingly it is known for an exceptional contemporary dining scene, mostly located in the adjacent neighborhood of Bankers Hill. Choices range from delis, bistros, and trendy ethnic eateries to one of the city's top fine-dining restaurants.

BALBOA PARK

The culinary heart of this museum-filled urban park is the Prado, a stylish sit-down restaurant with a sunny patio. Other dining is limited to museum and zoo food stands, cafés, and food carts.

> ### WORD OF MOUTH
>
> "If you go to the Prado (which I love), try their tres leches cake for dessert…. It is the best version I've ever had. I would try to do it for happy hour after the zoo."
> —ncounty

$$ \times **The Prado at Balboa Park.** Striking Spanish-Moorish details like painted
ECLECTIC ceilings and wrought-iron chandeliers are only part of the appeal of this lovely restaurant in the historic House of Hospitality. It also makes contemporary fare, friendly service and patio dining available to legions of museum and theatergoers who come to Balboa Park. The bar is a fashionable destination for creative drinks and light nibbles spiced with Latin, Italian, and Asian flavors. In the dining room, lunch specialties range from fish tacos and panini to risotto and paella, for dinner opt for one of the unusual surf 'n' turf combos. Late evening happy hours are ideal for posttheater snacks and drinks. ■TIP➔ **Parking in Balboa Park can be daunting; take advantage of the valet parking at the entrance of the restaurant.** $ *Average main: $27* ⌧ *1549 El Prado, Balboa Park* ☎ *619/557-9441* ⊕ *www.pradobalboa.com* ⊗ *No dinner Mon.* ✢ *2:F6.*

BANKERS HILL

The recent influx of upscale condo dwellers in this neighborhood west of Balboa Park has been matched by the arrival of notable restaurants, creating one of the city's most exciting new dining destinations. Once the fine-dining turf of the legendary Mr. A's (now Bertrand at Mister A's), the area now boasts standout French, Asian, and Italian food mixed in with divey bars and sandwich shops.

$$ $$ \times **Bankers Hill bar and grill.** The living wall of succulents, hip ware-
MODERN house interior, and wine bottle chandeliers suit this vibrant restaurant
AMERICAN where good times and great eats meet. An after-work crowd joins resi-
Fodor's Choice dents of this quiet stretch of Bankers Hill for happy-hour cocktails,
★ craft beers, and well-curated wines served from the zinc bar. Don't be surprised when the sommelier, also a cicerone (beer expert), suggests unusual brews to pair with everything from appetizers to dessert. Dinner standbys—mostly sophisticated comfort food often with Southwest flair—include the crispy BBQ pork tacos, Mexican-style red snapper, a juicy burger, seasonal bruschettas, and truffled french fries. Always save room for the silky butterscotch pudding topped with brittle and whipped cream. $ *Average main: $21* ⌧ *2202 4th Ave., Bankers Hill* ☎ *619/231-0222* ⊕ *www.bankershillsd.com* ⊗ *No lunch* ✢ *2:D6.*

8

$ MEXICAN 🍴 **Barrio Star.** At this colorful neighborhood cantina in Bankers Hill, classic Mexican "soul food" gets a refined spin. Everything is fresh here; the tortillas are hand-pressed from freshly ground corn and the salsas and margaritas are made from scratch. Mexican favorites, including chicken, steak, and carnitas tacos, chili rellenos, tamales, and guacamole, are served, but the menu gets interesting with dishes like shoestring plantains, salmon tacos, or soy chorizo tacos, and red pozole. Sweet endings include creamy coconut flan or flourless chocolate chipotle cake; both are muy bueno. On weekends starting at 9 am breakfasts of scrambled-egg burritos, avocado scramble, and blackberry pancakes are served. [$] *Average main: $16* ✉ *2706 5th Ave., Bankers Hill* ☎ *619/501–7827* 🌐 *www.barriostar.com* ✥ *2:D6.*

$$$$ FRENCH 🍴 **Bertrand at Mister A's.** For decades, this venerable 12th-floor dining room with panoramic city and bay views has reigned as a celebratory fine-dining destination. Rejuvenated decor and cuisine, plus a popular happy hour, now draw after-work and pretheater crowds for cocktails and bites. Chef Stephane Voitzwinkler creates California-luxe seasonal dishes that span paella and cassoulet, grilled duck and veal, and Maine lobster and Dover sole. Fries and mac and cheese are scented with truffles for a continental touch, while one popular dessert, the popcorn-topped caramel and chocolate bar, is deliciously playful. The professional staff, led by the restaurant's namesake Betrand Hug, is polished and attentive. **■ TIP→ Park for free on the street after 6 pm; there's no validation for the underground garage.** [$] *Average main: $38* ✉ *2550 5th Ave., 12th fl., Bankers Hill* ☎ *619/239–1377* 🌐 *www.bertrandatmisteras.com* ✍ *Reservations essential* ⊙ *No lunch on weekends* ✥ *2:D6.*

$$$ MODERN AMERICAN Fodor's Choice ★ 🍴 **Croce's Park West.** The pioneer Gaslamp restaurant has new digs near Balboa Park, bringing supper-club glam to an upscale neighborhood eager for such grown-up fare. Rich woods, mood lighting, and comfy seating indoors and on the patio make it easy to linger while enjoying oysters from the raw bar and wines-by-the-glass from a *Wine Spectator*–lauded list. An Italian-accented menu offers whole and half portions of cherry-splashed duck confit, scallops with squash blossom risotto, or truffle-scented meatball linguini. Jazz bands perform Wednesday to Sunday at the far end of the dining room where owner Ingrid Croce pays homage to her late husband Jim Croce with a display of gold records and other memorabilia. [$] *Average main: $28* ✉ *2760 5th Ave., Bankers Hill* ☎ *619/233–4355* 🌐 *www.crocesparkwest.com* ⊙ *No lunch. Brunch weekends* ✥ *2:D6.*

$$ ITALIAN Fodor's Choice ★ 🍴 **Cucina Urbana.** Twentysomethings mingle with boomers in this convivial Bankers Hill dining room and bar, one of the most popular restaurants in town. Country-farmhouse decor that mixes rolling pins with modern art looks and feels festive. The open kitchen turns out innovative Italian food with a California sensibility to enjoy traditionally or at communal tables. Many dishes are under $20, including crowd-pleasing short-rib pappardelle, fried stuffed squash blossoms, ricotta gnudi and thin-crust pizzas. At the in-house Wine Shop, purchase reasonably priced bottles from "the Americas and Mediterranean," opened tableside for an $8 corkage fee. End the meal with espresso sipped between

bites of gelato, tiramisu, or cannoli. $ *Average main: $21* ⊠ *505 Laurel St., Bankers Hill* ☎ *619/239–2222* ⊕ *www.cucinaurbana.com* ⚃ *Reservations essential* ⊗ *No lunch Sat.–Mon.* ⊹ *2:E6.*

$$ ✕ **Hane Sushi.** An airy room with a sleek red-and-black Japanese aes-
JAPANESE thetic is the setting for pristine, contemporary sushi by Roger Naka-
mura, who spent years learning his craft from Yukito Ota of San Diego's
beloved Sushi Ota restaurant. Though Hane (pronounced "hah-nay")
is trendier than Ota and offers nonsushi options like kobe beef car-
pacco, sushi purists will be happy with the toro, golden eye snapper,
octopus carpaccio, and special delicacies imported from Japan. The
sweet shrimp and buttery uni are local. Modernists will like the cre-
ative rolls, specialty cocktails and sake selections. Lunch specials for
under $15 including a combined sushi and California roll with miso
or noodle soup. $ *Average main: $25* ⊠ *2760 5th Ave., Bankers Hill*
☎ *619/260–1411* ⊗ *Closed Mon. No lunch weekends* ⊹ *2:D6.*

$ ✕ **Marketplace Deli.** San Diego is perfect for picnics and this popular
AMERICAN deli just a block from Balboa Park helps turn these outdoor affairs into
memorable feasts. Fans, including workers from nearby offices, rave
about the ample and affordable hot and cold sandwiches, home-made
soups, chili, and pizza by the slice or pie. Some favorites include the Cal-
ifornia sandwich with turkey, avocado, bacon, and sprouts; a chopped
chicken salad with chipotle ranch dressing; and the albondigas soup.
Don't be put off by the retro sign out front; inside there's a surprisingly
modern and well-stocked grocery, wine shop, and liquor store, too.
$ *Average main: $6* ⊠ *2601 5th Ave., Bankers Hill* ☎ *619/239–8361*
⊕ *www.marketplacedeli.menutoeat.com* ⊹ *2:E6.*

8

OLD TOWN AND UPTOWN

With some notable exceptions, historic Old Town celebrates Mexican
dining. Nearby, Uptown's diverse communities offers many bars, bistros
and gastropubs, along with ethnic restaurants ranging from Afghan and
Indian to Russian and Vietnamese.

OLD TOWN

Touristy, but fun Mexican food reigns here with giant margaritas and
heaping dishes of enchiladas, tacos, and carnitas (slow-cooked pork),
and you'll also find a few gourmet gems celebrating other cuisines
mixed in.

$ ✕ **Blue Water Seafood Market & Grill.** Blame a television segment by Guy
SEAFOOD Fieri on "Diners, Drive-ins and Dives" for the long lines of fans from
FAMILY around the globe. But it's the fresh seafood cooked to order that keeps
them coming back to this no-frills fish market and restaurant. Have
the fish, including wild salmon, ahi, halibut, yellowtail, your way—
grilled with a choice of marinades and served with a side or on a salad,
tortilla, or sandwich bread. Other favorites include fish-and-chips, ahi
poke, lobster bisque, and cioppino. Beer lovers will enjoy local craft
brews on tap. On the kids' menu is grilled cheddar cheese for seafood-
adverse little ones. $ *Average main: $11* ⊠ *3667 India St., Old Town*
☎ *619/497–0914* ⊕ *www.bluewaterseafoodsandiego.com* ⚃ *Reserva-
tions not accepted* ⊹ *2:C5.*

CLOSE UP

Where to Refuel Around Town

San Diego has a number of homegrown restaurant chains that won't break the bank.

Burger Lounge (⊕ www.burgerlounge.com) specializes in juicy burgers made from grass-fed beef—besides skipping grain, the cows were also raised without growth hormones or antibiotics. Eight locations around the county (see burgerlounge.com for details) share a retro-mod decor and hearty side dishes like onion rings and house-made french fries, sodas, and malts.

A homegrown chain specializing in seafood is the **Brigantine**, which offers a cozy atmosphere in seven cities around the county (see brigantine.com for details) and a menu that ranges from fish tacos to fresh oysters, grilled swordfish with avocado butter, and wok-charred ahi tuna. The happy hours at any of the Brigantine (aka "The Brig" to locals) restaurants are popular for the oysters and fish tacos. There's also a bargain First Catch three-course menu for early diners.

The Mission, a local minichain open only for breakfast and lunch (there's no service after 3 pm), has three locations: Mission Beach (⊠ 3795 Mission Blvd. ☎ 858/488–9060), North Park (⊠ 2801 University Ave. ☎ 619/220–8992), and the East Village (⊠ 1250 J St. ☎ 619/232–7662). The menu runs the gamut from banana-blackberry pancakes to a Zen breakfast with tofu and brown rice and creative Chino-Latino rollups and brown rice and veggie bowls.

Or if you're in the mood for excellent Mexican-style comfort fare, head to **Achiote** (⊕ www.achioterestaurants.com) in San Ysidro (⊠ 4119 Camino de la Plaza ☎ 619/690–1494) and Otay Mesa (⊠ 2110 Birch Rd. ☎ 619/482–0307)—the omelet with chipotle cream sauce is muy rico.

Family-run Lolita's Mexican Food, with five county locations (details at lolitasmexicanfood.com) has satisfied cravings for tacos and burritos for 30 years. Daily lunch specials served with beans rice and a drink start at $7.

Sushi lovers should head to **Harney Sushi** in Old Town (⊠ 3964 Harney St. ☎ 619/295–3272) and Oceanside (⊠ 301 Mission Ave. ☎ 760/967–1820 ⊕ www.harneysushi.com) for California-style sushi and superfresh fish with a rocking atmosphere and a sexy modern Asian design.

San Diego's enormously popular **Sammy's Woodfired Pizza** (multiple locations; see ⊕ www.sammyspizza.com) chain has outlets in La Jolla, Mission Valley, and the Gaslamp Quarter. Sammy's makes oversize salads, pizzas and pastas.

Finger-licking sauce on Southern-style barbecue drawn long lines of fans to **Phil's BBQ**, a local chain with a new outlet at Lindbergh Field as well as in Point Loma (⊠ 3750 Sports Arena Blvd. ☎ 619/226–6333), Santee (⊠ 9816 Mission Gorge Rd. P619/449–7700) and San Marcos (⊠ 579 Grand Ave. ☎ 760/759–1400).

Hodad's (⊠ 5010 Newport Ave. ☎ 619/224–4623) is great for great giant hamburgers and now downtown (⊠ 945 Broadway ☎ 619/ 234–6323) and in PETCO Park. Try the new Guido burger inspired by chef Guy Fieri of "Diners, Drive-ins and Dives."

$$ JAPANESE 🍴 **Harney Sushi.** One of San Diego's most popular sushi restaurants is set in a sea of touristy Mexican dining spots in the heart of Old Town. Fans young and old flock here for refreshing sangrias, sustainable California-style sushi and modern Asian cuisine served up in a soft-lighted room enlivened with DJ-driven R&B music. For a bit more tranquil and intimate experience, settle into the outdoor patio seating to sample inventive sushi rolls like the Bomb, James Bomb—tempura, cream cheese, spicy scallop, and spicy mayo. Festivities are enhanced by craft cocktails and good selections of local artisan beers and sake. ■ **TIP→ Find ample free parking within walking distance at the Old Town Transportation Center off Pacific Highway.** [$] *Average main: $20* ✉ *3964 Harney St., Old Town* ☎ *619/295–3272* 🌐 *www.harneysushi.com* 🕒 *No lunch on weekends* ✣ *2:A4.*

OLD VINES

Napa and Sonoma counties in Northern California might get all the publicity when it comes to wine, but California viticulture got its start in San Diego—in Old Town to be exact. There are no vines there anymore, but Wine Cabana (✉ *2539 Congress St.* ☎ *619/574–9463*) offers cozy cabanas for sneaking away from the tourist trail and relaxing with a glass of California Chardonnay.

HILLCREST AND MISSION HILLS

Gay-friendly Hillcrest and the affluent enclave of Mission Hills are meccas for affordable and diverse dining experiences that may begin with hearty breakfasts and span lunches and dinners at trendy neighborhood dining spots before ending at nightclubs and late-night eateries in the wee hours of the morning.

$$ WINE BAR 🍴 **100 Wines.** Locals of every stripe share good times at this relaxed Hillcrest bistro, so expect much laughter and toasting during meals in the cozy bar, dining room, and comfortable patio warmed by a fireplace. The value-packed wine list is the focus here, with unusual varietals and blends from around the world. Crisp cauliflower with pancetta and a trio of lamb meatball sliders easily make a meal and are bargain-priced during happy hour. Pastas and flatbreads are entrée options along with scallops and risotto, oven-roasted chicken and crispy duck. Topping the short but sweet dessert list is a popular warm iced cinnamon bun and Ménage A Trois, a triple chocolate extravagance. [$] *Average main: $20* ✉ *1027 University Ave, Hillcrest* ☎ *619/491–0100* 🌐 *www.cohnrestaurants.com/100wines* ✣ *2:E4.*

$ CAFÉ 🍴 **Bread & Cie.** San Diego's love affair with artisanal bread began when this artsy urban bakery and café opened its doors two decades ago. Owner Charles Kaufman, a former New Yorker and a filmmaker, gave Bread & Cie a sense of theater by putting bread ovens imported from France center stage. Inhale irresistible aromas as you choose among classic baguettes and focaccia, crusty black olive and bacon breads, or glazed bear claws and cinnamon rolls. Can't decide? A sample plate serves up three warm slices with butter, preserves, and cream cheese. Lunchtime adds options like house-made salads, panini, and sandwiches, including vegetarian options, and for kids, a gooey peanut butter sandwich. ■ **TIP→ Be prepared for lines and limited parking**

8

at peak hours. $ *Average main: $8* ✉ *350 University Ave., Hillcrest* ☎ *619/683–9322* ⊕ *www.breadandcie.com* ⊘ *No dinner* ✥ *2:D4.*

$$ ✕**Brooklyn Girl.** Residents of Mission Hills have made this friendly

MODERN
AMERICAN
restaurant their neighborhood dining pick, but so have transplanted and visiting Brooklynites who flock here for a hometown fix. Owner and native Brooklyn girl, Victoria McGeath, and her husband Michael welcome customers like old friends to the bright high-ceiling room with its trove of Brooklyn memorabilia like subway signs and vintage public school chairs. The menu is Brooklyn-inspired, too, in that it ranges across that borough's many ethnic neighborhoods. Try fried oyster tacos, Vietnamese meatballs, Thai-flavored mussels, or wood-oven baked pizzas. Or opt for a roasted whole fish or shellfish from the seafood bar. Many wines-by-the-glass and cocktails are value-priced at $10 or less. $ *Average main: $24* ✉ *4033 Goldfinch St., Mission Hills* ☎ *619/296–4600* ⊕ *www.brooklyngirleatery.com* ⊘ *No lunch on weekends* ✥ *2:C4.*

$$ ✕**Busalacchi's A Modo Mio.** Diners feel transported to Italy at this styl-

ITALIAN
ish but cozy restaurant operated by the food-loving Busalacchi family for 25 years. Their pastas made in-house daily are topped with sauces created from recipes handed down from one generation to the next. Dinner favorites include authentic "my way" classics like meatballs and spaghetti by patriarch-chef Joe Busalacchi. Among the newer menu additions is spaghettini with an unforgettable Dungeness crab cream sauce spiced with serrano chili and saffron. Popular happy hours and weekly specials like half-priced bottles of wine or martinis pack in patrons. On Friday and Saturday evenings live jazz plays on the delightful patio; arrive early to get a seat. $ *Average main: $24* ✉ *3707 5th Ave., Hillcrest* ☎ *619/298–0119* ⊕ *www.busalacchis.com* ⊘ *No lunch weekends* ✥ *2:D5.*

$$ ✕**Hash House A Go Go.** Big caloric portions and long lines are hallmarks

AMERICAN
FAMILY
of this comfort food destination. During prime weekend brunch hours, hungry regulars from near and far wait an hour or more for an indulgent meal in the crowded (and sometimes noisy) dining room decorated with farm machinery photos. Typical of the Southern-accented breakfast fare is Andy's Sage Fried Chicken Benedict served with eggs, bacon mashed potatoes, and a biscuit. At lunch and dinner customers favor overflowing chicken pot pies and the cedar planked bourbon rib eye. Bring an appetite and a friend; sharing plates is a necessity here. $ *Average main: $24* ✉ *3628 5th Ave., Hillcrest* ☎ *619/298–4646* ⊕ *www.hashhouseagogo.com* ⊘ *Closed Mon. night* ✥ *2:D5.*

$$ ✕**Kous Kous Moroccan Bistro.** With one sip of the bubbly "Moroccan

MOROCCAN
Kiss" cocktail in this room lit with lanterns and draped in desert-hued fabrics, diners are transported to the exotic land of chef-owner Moumen Nouri's birth. The culinary journey continues with tapas like the B'stila roll stuffed with orange water-scented chicken and cinnamon almonds or classic zaalouk of roasted eggplant flavored with preserved lemons. Traditional tagines with chicken, lamb, or veggies top the dinner menu that also includes ground beef (Kefta), merguez sausage, and chicken kebabs, all served with traditional couscous. Moroccan feasts served family-style start at $24 per person, and on Mondays meatless

dishes are discounted 25%. $ *Average main: $18* ✉ *3940 4th Ave., Hillcrest* ☎ *619/295–5560* ⊕ *www.kouskousrestaurant.com* ◷ *No lunch* ✛ *2:D4.*

$ ✕ **La Pizzeria Arrivederci.** Reasonable prices and authentic Naples-style

ITALIAN thin-crust pizzas with fresh toppings make this a favorite pizzeria of choosy Hillcrest locals. The broad and sometimes quirky pizza selection includes the Boscaiola with forest mushrooms and smoky scamorza cheese and the Messicana, a Mexican-inspired pie topped with beans, pork sausage, cilantro, and crushed red peppers. Though primarily a pizza joint, the restaurant serves antipasti, soups, and a few classic pasta dishes like linguine with clams and penne pasta in vodka with salmon. Start with a well-priced glass or bottle of wine and a plate of roasted peppers with anchovies. $ *Average main: $13* ✉ *3789 4th Ave., Hillcrest* ☎ *619/542–0293* ⊕ *www.arrivederciristorante.com* ◷ *No lunch Mon.–Thurs.* ✛ *2:D4.*

$ ✕ **Lucha Libre Gourmet Taco Shop.** Named for a form of Mexican wres-

MEXICAN tling, this taco shop with its hot-pink walls and shiny booths was famous mostly for its lack of parking until it appeared on the Travel Channel's "Man v. Food." Then long lines of burrito-crazed fans began forming outside the walkup window for lunch. Most say the array of gourmet tacos and burritos is worth the wait. The Surfin' California burrito packed with grilled steak, shrimp, french fries, avocado, and chipotle sauce is a favorite. So are the nachos smothered in cheese and guacamole. There are also many meatless options. ■ **TIP**➜ **Don't park in the gas station next door; they watch and will tow.** $ *Average main: $7* ✉ *1810 W. Washington St., Mission Hills* ☎ *619/296–8226* ⊕ *www.tacosmackdown.com* ✛ *2:B5.*

$$ ✕ **Ortega's Bistro.** Seafood lovers have long flocked to Puerto Nuevo, the

MEXICAN "lobster village" just south of San Diego in Baja California, Mexico.

FAMILY When a family that operates several Puerto Nuevo restaurants opened

Fodor'sChoice Ortega's in Hillcrest, it quickly became a top draw for authentic Baja

★ coastal cuisine, minus the long lines to cross the border. The delicious house-made, Mexican fare stars succulent, sweet Baja-style lobster (steamed then grilled) served with beans, rice and made-to-order tortillas. At market price, it can top $35 a serving; but there are many less-pricey menu options, too, including two versions of tortilla soup, melt-in-your-mouth carnitas (slow-cooked pork), made-at-the-table guacamole, and Ensenada-style battered fish tacos. The pomegranate margaritas are a must, as is the special red salsa for authentic spice. $ *Average main: $19* ✉ *141 University Ave., Hillcrest* ☎ *619/692–4200* ⊕ *www.ortegasbistro.com* ✛ *2:D4.*

$ ✕ **Project Pie.** Walls covered in quotable sayings keep the conversation

PIZZA flowing between bites of these "build your own" or "order by num-

FAMILY ber" thin-crust pizzas baked in minutes in the on-site oven. Seven red- and white-sauced pizzas are creative classics like the four cheese with fresh basil or three meats with mozzarella. Or choose from more than two-dozen toppings for a one-of-a-kind pie. Three salads, including one on a pizza crust, and Boylan's sodas with free refills round out the simple menu. Expect to see tables of hungry families, singles grabbing a late-night nosh, and the occasional firefighter—they and other civil

8

servants get a discount. Project Pie shops also are in Chula Vista and Eastlake in South County. $ *Average main: $10* ⊠ *3888 4th Ave., Hillcrest* ☎ *619/241–2881* ⊕ *www.projectpie.com* ✛ *2:D4.*

$$
MODERN
AMERICAN
Fodor's Choice
★

✕ **The Red Door.** Farm-to-table at this cottage-comfy Mission Hills restaurant starts at owners Trish and Tom Watlington's extensive home garden that supplies half the needed produce and herbs. Local organic growers and ranchers add everything else showcased on the constantly changing menu. In the hands of chef Karrie Hills, these ingredients are expertly cooked and creatively paired. Residents from around the county have discovered her fried green tomatoes topped with stuffed squash blossoms and lasagna with chard and kale pasta. Hills also turns out satisfying desserts like crème brûlée "of the moment" and light-as-a-feather sherry poppy-seed cakes. Ask the affable staff for help matching dishes with wines offered by the glass. $ *Average main: $24* ⊠ *741 W. Washington St., Mission Hills* ☎ *619/295–6000* ⊕ *www.thereddoorsd. com/* ⊘ *No lunch weekends* ✛ *2:C4.*

$
VIETNAMESE

✕ **Saigon on Fifth.** This upscale Vietnamese restaurant, open until 3 am, is a favorite for special family gatherings, date nights, and Asian dining adventure. It's also where the hipsters go for a steaming hot bowl of pho soup after bar-hopping in Hillcrest. A tall white Buddha stands at the entrance to the spacious, art-filled dining room, known for its attentive service and fresh authentic dishes. Beside the traditional pho, fans rave about spicy crab fried rice, seafood-stuffed imperial rolls, and clay pot-cooked fish. Original dishes include the Saigon Love Boat, seafood wrapped in a banana leaf and grilled. The restaurant validates parking at the nearby Union Bank Garage. ■TIP→ **The entrance is around the corner on University Avenue, rather than 5th Avenue, as the name and address suggests.** $ *Average main: $15* ⊠ *3900 5th Ave., Hillcrest* ☎ *619/220–8828* ✛ *2:D4.*

$
AMERICAN

✕ **Snooze.** Bright "Brady Bunch" decor, plus plenty of sunshine and fresh air pouring through windows and skylights are cheery wake-ups for diners at this hip neighborhood haunt for pancakes and lattes. Expect long waits for a table, especially on weekends; free coffee helps the time pass. Then indulge in made-from-scratch breakfast bliss with a sausage-gravy pot pie, eggs "benny" Mexican or Italian style, or OMG French toast stuffed with mascarpone. A pancake flight samples three flavors like the sinful pineapple upside-down pancakes sweetened with cinnamon butter. Inventive mimosas or spicy Bloody Marys toast this fine start to the day. $ *Average main: $10* ⊠ *3940 5th Ave., Hillcrest* ☎ *619/500–3344* ⊕ *www.snoozeeatery.com* ✍ *Reservations not accepted* ✛ *2:D4.*

MISSION VALLEY

Mission Valley, home to Hotel Circle and the area's massive malls, isn't known for groundbreaking cuisine, but it has lots of satisfying chain and casual eateries.

$$
SEAFOOD
FAMILY

✕ **King's Fish House.** This brick-warehouse-size restaurant featuring seafood, steaks, and salads is a popular gathering place for business people and shoppers from Mission Valley malls. Inside the wood-beamed dining room are display tanks filled with Maine lobsters ready for steaming. An extensive menu that changes daily with the catch includes cold plates of freshly shucked oysters, hand-cut sushi rolls and shrimp and crab cocktails. Seasonal fish and shellfish are char-grilled, deep-fried, sautéed, steamed, or skewered, and meat eaters can choose from cheeseburgers, roasted chicken, and grilled sirloin. Jack Daniels bread pudding and key lime pie are favorite endings. The large patio is the place to be on warm days and evenings. [$] *Average main: $23* ✉ *825 Camino de la Reina N, Mission Valley* ☎ *619/574–1230* 🌐 *www.kingsfishhouse.com* ⊕ *2:E2.*

SAN DIEGO'S BOUNTY

Sunny San Diego is one of the premier agricultural areas in the country. Visit a farmers' market and have a taste: spring is the season for cherimoyas and strawberries, summer brings peaches and boysenberries, autumn is the time for apples and pears, and winter is abundant with tangerines and grapefruit. There's a different market every day of the week; check the list of farmers' markets around the county at 🌐 *www.sdfarmbureau.org.*

UNIVERSITY HEIGHTS, NORMAL HEIGHTS, AND KENSINGTON

On the mesas overlooking Mission Valley, these historic neighborhoods are experiencing a culinary renaissance with new casual ethnic dining and an array of wine bars and brew pubs, many with nightly entertainment.

$ MEXICAN 🍴 **El Zarape.** Don't be fooled by the humble facade. This tiny Mexican taqueria serves up some of the best seafood-focused border food in town. There's almost always a crowd of Uptown locals and savvy travelers here, but orders for burritos, tacos, and combination plates almost fly out of the kitchen. The expansive menu and list of intriguing daily specials can make ordering a challenge, but newcomers can't go wrong with fish, calamari, or seared scallop tacos and burritos or burritos stuffed with chili rellenos or shrimp and carne asada. For an affordable snack, try the famous 99-cent fish tacos. House-made salsas offer heat and flavor for every palate. [$] *Average main: $6* ✉ *4642 Park Blvd., University Heights* ☎ *619/692–1652* 🌐 *www.elzarape.menutoeat.com* ⊕ *2:F3.*

$ WINE BAR 🍴 **Village Vino.** Wine lovers rejoice at this unpretentious neighborhood wine bar that caters to enthusiasts and novices, offering hundreds of hard-to-find wines that appeal to most palates and pocketbooks. Vintages are personally selected by proprietor Rita Pirkl (aka Chief Wino), a savvy wine industry veteran, who searches out wine gems from small family producers around the world. The menu of handcrafted gourmet flatbreads, salads, and cheese and charcuterie plates pair perfectly with the wine selections and can be enjoyed in the cozy dining room or on the patio. The late-afternoon special—salad and flatbread and two glasses of wine for $30—makes a great light dinner. [$] *Average main: $12* ✉ *4095 Adams Ave., Kensington* ☎ *619/437–7969* 🌐 *www.villagevino.com* 🕓 *Closed Mon.* ⊕ *2:H2.*

8

NORTH PARK AND SOUTH PARK

Hip gastropubs, community bistros, health-conscious eateries, and soul-satisfying Mexican fare—all often served with the city's acclaimed craft beers—thrive in these artsy, eclectic, and rejuvenated neighborhoods adjacent to Balboa Park.

$ ╳ **Buona Forchetta.** A golden-domed pizza oven, named Sofia after the
ITALIAN   owner's daughter, delivers authentic Neapolitan-style pizza to fans
FAMILY   who often line up for patio tables at this dog- and kid-friendly Ital-
Fodor'sChoice   ian café in South Park. Slices of classic margherita or truffle-flavored
★   mozzarella and mushroom pizzas make a meal or can be shared, but
don't miss the equally delicious appetizers like the tender calamari or
succulent artichokes, heaping fresh salads or fresh pastas, including a
hearty lasagna, delicate ravioli, or gnocchi with wild boar sauce. Enjoy
house sangrias and wines by the carafe, a craft beer, or a glass of reasonably priced Italian wine. Save room for dolci, too—cannoli, gelato,
tiramisu, and other Italian desserts. $ *Average main: $15* ⊠ *3001
Beech St., Hillcrest* ⊕ *www.buonaforchettasd.com* ☉ *No lunch Mon.
and Tues.* ✣ *2:H6.*

$ ╳ **Carnitas' Snack Shack.** Midday and evening, long lines snake down
MODERN   the block outside this quintessential San Diego dining spot where chef-
MEXICAN   owner Hanis Cavin serves up fast-casual cuisine based on the humble
hog. He's so pork-focused that he sports a hog tattoo on his arm and
plays with a pet mini-pig named Carnitas. The taco-shop's tiny "shack'
has a walk-up window where hungry fans order favorites like carnitas
tacos, bacon-wrapped corn dogs, and the "Triple Threat," a large bun
stuffed with schnitzel, bacon, and pulled pork. More bacon seasons
the ketchup served with fries. Enjoy your order and a craft beer or
wine from the bar under shaded tables on the rustic patio. $ *Aver-
age main: $8* ⊠ *2632 University Ave., North Park* ☏ *619/294–7675*
⊕ *www.carnitassnackshack.com* ✣ *2:G4.*

$ ╳ **Mama's Bakery & Lebanese Deli.** This small converted house with
MIDDLE EASTERN   about 10 tables in North Park serves some of the best authentic Leba-
FAMILY   nese fare in San Diego County. It's not fancy dining. Shawarma, baba
ghanoush, and baklava fans line up at one small window to order,
pick up at another, and enjoy large portions of Mediterranean fare
under a covered patio. Sajj, a superheated oven, cooks the flat bread
mostly used for wraps like garlicky marinated chicken, hummus, and
eggplant. The hearty seasoned ground beef "kafta" plate includes
hummus, rice, salad, and pita bread. The ultimate ending is the but-
tery pistachio and cashew baklava. There is a special kid's menu that
includes a pita cheese melt and a Nutella hazelnut chocolate wrap.
$ *Average main: $10* ⊠ *4237 Alabama St., North Park* ☏ *619/688–
0717* ⊕ *www.mamasbakery.net* ⌕ *Reservations not accepted* ☉ *No
dinner weekends* ✣ *2:F3.*

$$ ╳ **Urban Solace.** Comforts abound at this popular casual North Park
AMERICAN   eatery with its long bar, communal tables, and covered patio. Regulars
who live in this revived neighborhood bustling with galleries, bars, and

trendy restaurants flock to chef-owner Matt Gordon's modern comfort food with a Southern accent, all created with all-natural, sustainably sourced ingredients. "Not Your Mama's Meatloaf" mixes lamb and pork with figs, almonds, and feta, while pulled chicken is served with buttermilk dumplings and gravy. Thursday night features a prix-fixe vegetarian menu and Sunday, a blue-grass brunch with cheesy "egga-roni" and kitchen-sink biscuits and gravy. Affordable wines and cocktails share the spotlight with dozens of craft beers by the bottle or on tap. $ *Average main: $24* ✉ *3823 30th St., North Park* ☎ *619/295–6464* ⊕ *urbansolace.net* ✛ *2:H4.*

$$
PIZZA
✕ **URBN Coal-Fired Pizza.** A 5,000-square-foot brick-and-wood industrial-style dining room and bar suits the North Park restaurants specialty pizzas scorched in a red-hot coal-fired oven. The casually chic spot attracts hip young locals who chow down on thin-crust New Haven–style pies, fresh salads, cheese boards, and chicken wings. The odd-sounding mashed potato pizza topped with pancetta, mozzarella, and Parmesan has been a favorite since day one. The coal-fired oven even cooks desserts like the gooey S'More pizza. It can get loud and crowded at times, but is always festive for groups—first dates, not so much. A sister restaurant is now open in El Cajon. $ *Average main: $20* ✉ *3085 University Ave., North Park* ☎ *619/255–7300* ⊕ *www. urbnnorthpark.com* ✛ *2:H4.*

$
CAFÉ
FAMILY
✕ **Viva Pops.** Inspired by Mexico's palettas, owner Liza Altmann elevates frozen treats to an art form at her colorful shop in Normal Heights. Viva Pops' sassy flavors are a mix of organic seasonal fruits, herbs, and spices. Cool down on a hot day with a Thai lime lemongrass pop; in cooler weather, flavors like pineapple chili or mango chili add a welcome hint of heat. The popular Mexican chocolate and lavender-lemon-ade are available year-round. $ *Average main: $3* ✉ *3330 Adams Ave., Normal Heights* ☎ *619/795–1080* ⊕ *www.ilovevivapops.com* ⊘ *Closed Mon. and Tues.* ✛ *2:H2*

$
MODERN
AMERICAN
FAMILY
✕ **Waypoint Public.** Kids romp in their own picket fence-enclosed play area while parents join fellow neighborhood residents in sophisticated meals in this beer-centric casual restaurant. A unique 28-tap system serves up West Coast craft brews; hundreds more from around the world can be had by the bottle. Many are suggested as pairings with the seasonal value-priced menu of healthy salads, sandwiches, and grilled fish and meats from the kitchen of "Top Chef" veteran Amanda Baumgarten. For the adventurous, she offers po'boy tacos, charred Spanish octopus, and her signature blood sausage crostini. S'mores, tarts, and cobblers end the evening on a sweet note. As might be expected, brunch highlights include "breakfast in a bottle" beers. $ *Average main: $17* ✉ *3794 30th St., North Park* ☎ *619/255–8778* ⊕ *www.waypointpublic.com* ✛ *2:H4.*

8

MISSION BEACH AND PACIFIC BEACH

This sprawling area is all about great views of the water, sandy beaches, and relaxation. Most of the restaurants here are casual spots that diners can visit in T-shirts, shorts, and flip-flops. Food is similarly laid-back. Burgers and tacos are easy to find, but so are sushi, Mexican, and Thai food. Many of the restaurants here are bars at heart.

MISSION BEACH

Home to beach lovers and Arizona heat escapees, this beach community on a man-made sandy strip of land between the ocean and bay bustles with walkers and bicyclists who frequent the dozens of laid-back beach bars and eateries along ocean-side boardwalk.

PACIFIC BEACH

Streets closest to the ocean in San Diego's largest beach community can be party central for visitors and locals who jam-pack a wide range of restaurants and bars reflecting the casual surf and beach culture.

$ ECLECTIC 🍴 **Isabel's Cantina.** The dragon above the rustic door announces that this is no typical cantina. Instead chef and cookbook author Isabel Cruz has blended Asian and Latin fare with a healthy outlook that suits her youthful Pacific Beach clientele. Start the day with refreshing pineapple-orange-kale juice and a good-for-you egg white scramble. Or indulge Mexican cravings with a bowl piled high with carnitas, crisp potatoes, black beans, and spicy sauces. Lunch options include tortas, tacos, and the "Buddha Bowl" of vegetables in a coconut milk and lemongrass broth. For dinner, there's a vegetarian Asian grill, along with house-made tamales and grilled salmon. Calorie counting stops though for desserts like the decadent flourless chocolate cake and rich coconut flan. [$] *Average main: $17* ✉ *966 Felspar St., Pacific Beach* ☎ *858/272–8400* 🌐 *www.isabelscantina.com* ✥ *3:C5.*

$$$$ AMERICAN 🍴 **JRDN.** Seating in this chic ocean-facing restaurant (pronounced Jordan), in the boutique Tower23 Hotel, is divided between a long, narrow outdoor terrace and a series of relatively intimate indoor rooms. Chef Nick Shinton prepares modern steak-house fare including chops and steaks with sauces of the diner's choosing, lightened with lots of seasonal produce and a raw bar menu. Lunch and weekend brunch have a similar appeal, with dishes like eggs Benedict with citrus hollandaise, a blackened mahimahi sandwich, and hamachi sashimi salad. On Friday and Saturday the bar is jammed with under-thirty types eager to see and be seen. [$] *Average main: $37* ✉ *Tower 23 Hotel, 723 Felspar St., Pacific Beach* ☎ *858/270–5736* 🌐 *www.jrdn.com* ✥ *3:B5.*

$ AMERICAN FAMILY 🍴 **Kono's Surf Club Café.** Surfers, bicyclists, and sun worshipers visiting or living in Pacific Beach line up at the counter of this casual seaside café for hearty breakfasts and lunches. Some chow down inside surrounded by surfing decor, while others watch waves crash from the outdoor patio. The "Little Breakfast" (two eggs, potatoes, and toast) pales when compared to four different egg burritos, pancakes, French toast, and the "Big Breakfast" (eggs, bacon, English muffins, potatoes, and pancakes). Burgers are the lunch crowd's favorite but there are lower calorie salads and sandwiches, plus a "Kiddo Dog" for youngsters.

CLOSE UP

Talking Tacos

Even though terms like taco, burrito, enchilada, and tostada are as common as macaroni and cheese to San Diegans, don't count on any residents to agree on where to find the best ones. That's because tacos are as individual as spaghetti sauce and come in endless variations from small, authentic Mexico City–style tacos to Cal-Mex versions in crunchy shells topped with cheddar cheese.

The most traditional style of taco features a small soft corn tortilla pressed from corn masa dough and filled with shredded beef, carne asada (roasted beef), braised tongue in green sauce, spicy marinated pork, or deep-fried fish or seafood. Tortillas made from white flour are out there, too, but they're not nearly as tasty.

Garnishes usually include a drizzle of salsa and a squeeze of tart Mexican lime (a small citrus similar to the Key lime that's juicier than the large lime commonly found in the United States), along with chopped cilantro and onion. Whole radishes topped with lime juice and a sprinkle of salt are served on the side.

[$] *Average main: $6* ✉ *704 Garnet Ave., Pacific Beach* ☎ *858/483–1669* ⏲ *No dinner* ✣ *3:B5.*

$ THAI

🍴 **Lanna.** Recipes passed down for generations yield the fresh, vibrant dishes from various regions served at this flower-filled Thai restaurant tucked in a strip mall on the eastern edge of Pacific Beach. Among the house specialties are "Talay Thai," a batter-fried fish fillet topped with a green-apple salad, onions, and cashews; spice-braised duck in a deep, dark, wonderfully fragrant red curry sauce; and "Spicilicious Seafood," a mix of shrimp, squid, mussels, and scallops stir-fried in a chili-garlic sauce. The expansive menu also features appetizer platters, hearty soups, lime-dressed salads and desserts like home-made ice-creams and delicious mango sticky rice. Service is prompt and gracious; parking can be challenging. [$] *Average main: $12* ✉ *4501 Mission Bay Dr., Pacific Beach* ☎ *858/274–8424* 🌐 *www.lannathaicuisine.com* ✣ *3:D4.*

$$ MODERN AMERICAN FAMILY

🍴 **The Patio on Lamont.** Soft breezes blow through the stylish patio of this modern California bistro that straddles a quiet side street in Pacific Beach. Seated beneath a "green wall" of tropical plants, tourists join locals, many with pets in tow, for breakfast, lunch, and dinner, the popular weekday 11 to 6 happy hour and weekend brunch. Menus feature signature flatbreads like the truffle-scented beef and bleu, small plates like the grilled-pear salad and ahi poke tacos, and full-size entrées like the braised port shank offered since the restaurant opened. A breakfast flatbread with ham, bacon, and eggs and tomatillo-sauced chilaquiles are among the breakfast and brunch highlights. A second location, the Patio on Goldfinch, is in Mission Hills. [$] *Average main: $26* ✉ *4445 Lamont St., Pacific Beach* ☎ *858/412–4648* 🌐 *www.thepatiosd.com* ✣ *3:D5.*

8

$$$
SUSHI
Fodor's Choice
★

✕ **Sushi Ota.** One fan called it "a notch above amazing"—an accolade not expected for a Japanese eatery wedged in a strip mall in Pacific Beach. But it's a destination for lovers of high-quality, superfresh raw fish from around San Diego and abroad. Japanese visitors frequently call for reservations before leaving home. Besides the usual California roll and tuna and shrimp sushi, there are daily such as sea urchin or surf clam sushi, soft-shell crab roll, or the omakase tasting menu. Reservations are strongly encouraged. ■TIP➔ The front parking lot is very small, but there's additional parking behind the mall. $ *Average main: $30* ✉ *4529 Mission Bay Dr., Pacific Beach* ☎ *858/270–5670* ⊕ *www.sushiota.com/* ☽ *No lunch Sat.–Mon.* ✛ *3:D4.*

LA JOLLA, CLAIREMONT MESA AND KEARNY MESA

La Jolla is one of the most scenic and prosperous coastal communities in the county, so it's no surprise that it has some of the area's top culinary gems. Kearny Mesa and Clairemont Mesa, in contrast, are inland older neighborhoods where small, independent, and mostly Asian restaurants thrive, often jammed into strip malls.

LA JOLLA

This tony enclave that hugs the ocean from the Bird Rock area to Torrey Pines draws diners from around the world to experience an amazing collection of relaxed fine and casual dining establishments, ranging from classic French bistro fare to California modern cuisine. Ocean-view restaurants along Prospect Street are very popular, but there are many affordable neighborhood favorites that serve tasty food in attractive settings like La Jolla Cove.

$$$$
AMERICAN
Fodor's Choice
★

✕ **A. R. Valentien.** Champions of in-season, fresh-today produce and seafood, executive chef Jeff Jackson and Chef de Cuisine Kelli Crosson have made this cozy room in the luxurious, Craftsman-style Lodge at Torrey Pines one of San Diego's top fine dining destinations. Their food combinations are simultaneously simple and delightfully inventive—pork belly with strawberry, kale and quinoa salad; halibut with roasted eggplant and curried cucumbers; or oak fire-cooked pork loin with chard, red walnuts, and roasted apricots. Lunch and dinner tasting menus ($75) are like a walk through a farmers' market. Still there are menu perennials like the silky chicken liver pate. In good weather, enjoy meals plus ocean views from the terrace. $ *Average main: $38* ✉ *11480 N. Torrey Pines Rd., La Jolla* ☎ *858/777–6635* ⊕ *www.arvalentien.com* ✛ *3:B1.*

$$
ITALIAN

✕ **Barbarella Restaurant & Bar.** A sunny patio brightened by year-round blooms and menu of casual Cal-Italian fare has made Barbarella a perennial favorite for locals and visitors alike. The warm, woodsy room is accented with original work by local artists and a pizza oven decorated with mosaic tile by the late French sculptor, Niki de Saint Phalle. The seasonal menu ranges from crispy wild-mushroom pizzas, black mussels, and roasted half chicken, to the oversize Barbarella Burger topped with grilled red onions and cheddar cheese, and a whole stone-roasted fish of the day. Brunchgoers rave about the huevos rancheros with two salsas and the citrus hollandaise-topped eggs Benedict.

[$] *Average main: $23* ✉ *2171 Ave. de la Playa, La Jolla* ☎ *858/454–7373* ⊕ *www.barbarellarestaurant.com* ✛ *3:B2.*

$ ✕ **Bernini's Bistro.** The restaurant's motto is "where the locals eat," but
INTERNATIONAL lots of visitors frequent this bright art-filled La Jolla bistro and bar with its European-style dog-friendly sidewalk patio dining. The friendly international staff is professional and owner Hamdi Gumustekin regularly greets patrons from morning until closing. Menu items are made fresh in-house; the wine list is well-priced and live music fills the room four nights a week. Breakfast favorites, served until 5 pm, include lemon ricotta pancakes and Bernini's Benedict with its decadent avocado hollandaise. The French dip sandwich and fries often are rated the best in town and for dinner, pastas, steaks, and seafood choices are extensive. [$] *Average main: $12* ✉ *7550 Fay Ave., La Jolla* ☎ *858/454–5013* ⊕ *www.berninisbistro.com* ⊙ *Breakfast served until 5 pm* ✛ *3:A2.*

$$$ ✕ **Bistro Bijou.** Chef William Bradley, who helms Addison, the county's
BISTRO top fine-dining restaurant, now has this casual offshoot in the heart of La Jolla. Bistro Bijou harkens back to 1930s Paris with a wine-hued dining room, lively lounge, Edith Piaf soundtrack, and menu of deftly prepared French classics. Bradley worked with Chef de Cuisine Shaun Gethin to polish small plates like salmon rillettes, oeufs mayonnaise, and expertly dressed salads. Entrées, some days in the making, range from coq au vin and steak frites to French-style gnocchi and rainbow trout on a bed of pistou-flavored lentils. A refined list of French and West Coast vintages makes wine parings an adventure. Warm beignets or Parsian macarons for dessert are très bon. [$] *Average main: $30* ✉ *1205 Prospect St., La Jolla* ☎ *858/750–3695* ⊕ *www.bijoufrenchbistro.com* ✛ *3:B2.*

$$ ✕ **Brockton Villa.** One of the few restaurants with a view that's also worth
AMERICAN eating at, Brockton Villa is tucked in an historic cottage on a hillside above La Jolla cove. Food is served all day, but this dining spot excels at brunch and lunch when ocean views are best. Snag a seat by the fireplace and start the day with the soufflé-like orange-scented Coast French Toast, breakfast tacos, or the popular blue crab-cake eggs Benedict. For lunch enjoy the crab cakes as sliders, a lobster roll, or chopped Mediterranean salad. During the late-afternoon social hour, a bottle of wine and artisan cheese board are only $30. [$] *Average main: $20* ✉ *1235 Coast Blvd., La Jolla* ☎ *858/454–7393* ⊕ *www.brocktonvilla.com* ✛ *3:B2.*

$ ✕ **Cody's La Jolla.** This cozy dining spot in a converted house a block
AMERICAN from beautiful La Jolla Cove and Park serves up ocean views and tasty contemporary American fare for well-heeled La Jollans and tourists alike. The atmosphere is laid-back and beach-festive, especially on the front porch patio cooled by sea breezes. Servers buzz about with favorite dishes like fish-and-chips, crab cakes Benedict, and lobster chowder. Breakfast fare like the French toast topped with candied walnuts, fresh strawberries, and mascarpone honey butter is served all day. ■ **TIP→ Parking can be tough, but there are a number of nearby parking structures that charge around $10 for the day.** [$] *Average main: $13* ✉ *8030 Girard Ave., La Jolla* ☎ *858/459–0040* ⊕ *www.codyslj.com* ⊙ *No dinner* ✛ *3:A2.*

8

$
SEAFOOD

X **El Pescador Fish Market.** This small, bustling fish market and café in the heart of La Jolla village has been popular with locals for its super-fresh fish for more than 30 years. Order the char-grilled, locally caught halibut, swordfish, or yellowtail on a toasted torta roll to enjoy in-house or to-go for an oceanfront picnic at nearby La Jolla Cove. Other delicious choices include seafood cocktails, ceviche, Dungeness crab and shrimp salad, and fish and shrimp tacos. Seating is limited during the lunch hours, and tables often are shared, but the food is worth the wait. Check the website for the current address; a move is planned across the street to a larger location. $ *Average main: $15* ⊠ *627 Pearl St., La Jolla* ☎ *858/456–2526* ⊕ *www. elpescadorfishmarket.com* ⌂ *Reservations not accepted* ✛ *3:A2.*

$$$$
AMERICAN
Fodor's Choice
★

X **George's at the Cove.** La Jolla's ocean-view destination restaurant includes three dining areas: California Modern on the bottom floor, George's Bar in the middle, and Ocean Terrace on the roof. Hollywood types and other visiting celebrities can be spotted at California Modern, the sleek main dining room with its wall of windows. Elegant preparations of fresh seafood, tender beef, and California lamb reign, which star-chef Trey Foshee enlivens with amazing local produce. Give special consideration to the legendary fish tacos. Two levels of tasting menus are available; but the four-course offering generally is perfect for pocketbook and palate. For a more casual and inexpensive experience, go to the indoor/outdoor George's Bar, where you can enjoy pastas and grilled fish while watching a game, or head upstairs to the outdoor-only Ocean Terrace for spectacular views of La Jolla Cove. $ *Average main: $36* ⊠ *1250 Prospect St., La Jolla* ☎ *858/454–4244* ⊕ *www. georgesatthecove.com* ⌂ *Reservations essential* ✛ *3:B2.*

$$$
MODERN
AMERICAN

X **The Marine Room.** It's hard to dine closer to the Pacific than here at this venerable La Jolla Shores mainstay. Two-story-tall windows capture beachgoers, kayakers, snorkelers, and swooping gulls. If the tide is high, waves race across the sand and crash against the glass. Longtime executive chef Bernard Guillas easily distracts patrons from the sea show with a fine-dining menu that's seasonally fresh, internationally sophisticated, and deliciously playful. A prawn cocktail is served with tabbouleh, crusted ahi with avocado beignets, and lobster with bourbon vanilla butter. Afternoon happy hours in the lounge every day but Saturday are a comfortable way to sample the atmosphere and gourmet fare without breaking the bank. $ *Average main: $35* ⊠ *2000 Spindrift Dr., La Jolla* ☎ *866/644–2351* ⊕ *www.marineroom.com* ⌂ *Reservations essential* ✛ *3:B2.*

$ CAFÉ FAMILY 🍴 **Michele Coulon Dessertier.** The desserts are magnificent at this small, charming shop in the heart of La Jolla, where dessertier Michele Coulon confects wonders, using organic produce and imported chocolate. Snack on cookies, cupcakes, brownies, chocolate-dipped strawberries, and mini-desserts. Other irresistible treats found here are a chocolate-lovers' Torte Lion Belge, pear-frangipane tart, and Marjolaine Torte with layers of meringue, chocolate ganache and buttercreams. Several gluten-free items usually are available, too. This is not just a place for dessert, however. Lunch is served Monday through Saturday (the store is open 9 am to 4 pm), and the simple menu includes quiche Lorraine and salads. [$] *Average main: $11* ✉ *7556 Fay Ave., Suite D, La Jolla* ☎ *858/456–5098* 🌐 *www.dessertier.com* ✍ *Reservations not accepted* 🕒 *Closed Sun. No dinner* ✥ *3:A2.*

$$$ AMERICAN 🍴 **Nine-Ten.** Accolades continue to roll in for executive chef Jason Knibb—most recently crowned chef of the year by peers in the local restaurant association. His exciting seasonal menus for breakfast, lunch, and dinner at La Jolla's Grande Colonial Hotel are magnets for travelers and San Diegans seeking a memorable meal in the cozy ground-floor dining room, bar, or ocean-glimpse covered patio. At night deftly executed appetizers may include Jamaican jerk pork belly with plantains and black-eyed peas or a salad of jewel-toned beets dusted with cocoa. Mains range from halibut with fava beans and fiddlehead ferns to steaks, lamb or short ribs paired with baby vegetables. Comfort-food desserts always include a twist, like the smoked cherry sorbet with almond rice pudding. A three-course market menu or five-course "Mercy of the Chef" menu, both prix-fixe, are available for the whole table. [$] *Average main: $33* ✉ *Grande Colonial Hotel, 910 Prospect St., La Jolla* ☎ *858/964–5400* 🌐 *www.nine-ten.com* ✥ *3:A2.*

8

$ ITALIAN 🍴 **Osteria Romantica.** Two guys who grew up in Italy founded this cozy La Jolla Shores eatery a decade ago to bring authentic Italian food to residents and visitors of the walkable neighborhood and its nearby beaches. Italian opera plays in the dining room where friendly servers deliver house-made breads, pastas, and sauces. Pasta choices include pappardelle with braised lamb and wild mushrooms and bucatini sauced with baby octopus, capers, and olives. Pork osso buco in port wine sauce is a popular main course that can be enjoyed alfresco on warm summer nights on the dog-friendly sidewalk patio. On Tuesday, wines from the Italian-centric list are half-price. [$] *Average main: $17* ✉ *2151 Ave. de la Playa, La Jolla* ☎ *858/551–1221* 🌐 *www.osteriaromantica.com* ✥ *3:B2.*

$$ MODERN ITALIAN FAMILY Fodor's Choice ★ 🍴 **Piatti Ristorante and Bar.** Blocks from the beach in La Jolla Shores, this comfortably modern dining room and shaded patio hits all the right notes—affordable, polished, and family-friendly. From lunch through close, it bustles with regulars from the neighborhood and visitors from around the world who are guided through the extensive Italian menu by the professional staff, some of whom have worked here for decades. Warm bread and spicy dipping sauce are hard to resist, but save room for favorites like grilled romaine hearts wrapped in crisp prosciutto, saffron shrimp pappardelle, and veal scaloppini with mushroom risotto cakes. Kids love their special menu, while parents relish the

value-packed wine list with excellent selections by the glass. Ⓢ *Average main: $18* ✉ *2182 Avenida de la Playa, La Jolla* ☎ *858/454–1589* ⊕ *www.piatti.com* ⊹ *3:B2.*

$ ✕ **Prepkitchen La Jolla.** Like its sister PK in Little Italy, this homey desti-
AMERICAN nation dining spot draws locals and visitors looking to relax with good food at reasonable prices. The seasonal menu of soups, sandwiches, and mains is studded with customer favorites like local yellowtail in pozole broth, house-made tagliatelle with pork sausage ragu and boneless stuffed quail. At weekend brunch, try chilaquiles, a delicious dish of tortilla strips, chipotle chicken, fried eggs, and queso fresco. If you'd rather picnic than dine in, family meals for four to five people are available for takeout after 5. Ⓢ *Average main: $17* ✉ *7556 Fay Ave., La Jolla* ☎ *858/875–7737* ⊕ *www.prepkitchen.com* ⌂ *Reservations not accepted* ⊹ *3:A2.*

$$ ✕ **Roppongi Restaurant and Sushi Bar.** The wood-toned dining room
ASIAN accented with a tropical fish tank, Buddhas, and other statuary sets the mood at this popular Asian-fusion dining spot inspired by Tokyo's nightlife district. Rows of comfortable booths inside are perfect for small groups, while an outdoor patio is great for people-watching. The extensive menu features tapas like the tofu lettuce wrap, duck quesadillas, hamachi tacos, and ahi poke, perfect for a small-plates meal combined with sake or a refreshing ginger mojito. For more filling fare try the Kobe beef sliders, crab-crusted mahimahi, or Mongolian shrimp. An extensive list of sashimi and sushi rolls also is available, along with a gluten-free menu. Ⓢ *Average main: $22* ✉ *875 Prospect St., La Jolla* ☎ *858/551–5252* ⊕ *www.roppongiusa.com* ⊹ *3:A2.*

$ ✕ **Shorehouse Kitchen.** This casual indoor-outdoor eatery in La Jolla
AMERICAN Shores has a sprawling outdoor patio perfect for leisurely lunches with friends and family. Surfers and well-heeled locals populate the 50-seat patio while enjoying made-to-order organic smoothies and fresh salads. The black cherry almond smoothie is addictive, while the tarragon chicken salad with lemon aioli, green apple, avocado, pistachios and dried cranberries over mixed greens with a citrus vinaigrette is a tantalizing mix of flavors. Shorehouse also serves a scrumptious breakfast and creative dinner entrees that include locally caught fish. The 1200-square-foot, beachy space was started by Angela Montion and John Freis of San Diego's Pizza Nova restaurants. (Freis also sits on the board of The Fish Market in San Diego.) Ⓢ *Average main: $15* ✉ *2236 Avenida de la PlayaLa Jolla* ☎ *858/459–3300* ⊕ *www.shorehousekitchen.com* ☾ *No dinner Mon.–Tues.* ⊹ *3:B2.*

$$$ ✕ **Tapenade.** Sunny Provençal flavors reign at this unpretentious restau-
MODERN FRENCH rant, a La Jolla fixture since 1998. The light and airy dining room, lined with 1960s French movie posters, is comfortable, if not romantic, an ideal setting for acclaimed chef Jean Michel Diot's ever-changing menu that emphasizes fresh ingredients, delicate sauces, and seafood. Classics like Coq au Vin and scallops Saint Jacques vie with more unusual fare like wild boar stewed in red wine, lobster with white corn sauce flavored with Tahitian vanilla, and huckleberry-and-wine-sauced venison with spätzle. Among the desserts are crêpes Suzette gilded with mandarin caramel. The daily two-course lunch special at $21.95 is a

steal. **TIP→ The restaurant is moving in early 2015; check the website for the new La Jolla location.** [$] *Average main: $32* ✉ *7612 Fay Ave., La Jolla* ☎ *858/551–7500* 🌐 *www.tapenaderestaurant.com* ⏲ *No lunch Sat.–Tues.* ⊕ *3:A2.*

$$$ SEAFOOD 🍴 **Truluck's Seafood, Steak and Crab House.** This Southern-style restaurant is known for gracious service and fresh seafood sourced from its own fisheries. Extras like black napkins for black-attired guests, adjustable lighting at each table and warm moist towels offered after meals add to the memorable experience. Miso-glazed sea bass is a menu classic, along with Alaskan king crab and a New Orleans–inspired blackened swordfish. The crab fried rice is so popular and plentiful that some guests order it as an entrée. On Monday, fill up with all-you-can-eat stone crab claws. For dessert, share the carrot cake or coconut cream pie. Live piano music and happy hour half-price cocktails can be enjoyed nightly in the Stone Crab Lounge. [$] *Average main: $30* ✉ *8990 University Center La., La Jolla* ☎ *858/453–2583* 🌐 *www.trulucks.com* ⊕ *3:D1.*

$$ SEAFOOD Fodor's Choice ★ 🍴 **Whisknladle.** This hip, popular eatery has won national acclaim for its combination of casual comfort and a menu of ever-changing local fare. In nice weather, request a patio table to enjoy the people-watching along with original or classic cocktails like the cucumber honey mimosa or house sangria. Executive chef Ryan Johnston's commitment to farm-fresh, from scratch cooking shines in the sharable charcuterie board with house-made salumi, pate, pickles, and condiments served with grilled crusty bread. Ask servers about salads, pastas, flatbreads, and entrées with that day's seasonal ingredients that can range from tree-ripened peaches to radish greens and new potatoes. Desserts change, too, but one timeless favorite is the decadent meringue topped with peanut butter ice cream and fudge sauce. [$] *Average main: $26* ✉ *1044 Wall St., La Jolla* ☎ *858/551–7575* 🌐 *www.whisknladle.com* ✍ *Reservations essential* ⊕ *3:A2.*

CLAIREMONT MESA

This postwar bedroom community offers adventurous diners numerous affordable and authentic mom-and-pop ethnic restaurants and grocery stores. The setting may be simple, and the service minimal, but the food can be unforgettable.

$ SUSHI 🍴 **Sushi Diner.** With Rastafari flags, surfer videos on loop, and Bob Marley–inspired sushi rolls, chef/owner Daisuke makes it clear that this is a place to chill. The tiny and always bustling restaurant has a loyal following of locals who don't mind waiting for tables because of the friendly service, inexpensive sushi, and tasty island-inspired extras like Spam fried rice. Vegetarians won't have a problem here; there are several veggie rolls, tofu dishes, and meatless appetizers. **TIP→ During the 4–7 pm happy hour, many appetizers and hand rolls are 99¢ with the purchase of a beer.** [$] *Average main: $10* ✉ *7530 Mesa College Dr., Clairemont* ☎ *858/565–1179* 🌐 *www.sushidiner1.com* ✍ *Reservations not accepted* ⏲ *Closed Sun. No lunch Sat.* ⊕ *3:G4.*

KEARNY MESA

Kearny Mesa, considered the city's "Asian Restaurant Row," is definitely off the tourist radar but offers a host of small family-owned eateries serving superb authentic Japanese, Chinese, Korean, and Vietnamese food.

$ CHINESE 🍴 **China Max.** Convoy Street is San Diego's hub for Asian eateries, but this Chinese dim sum restaurant stands out, winning multitudes of loyal fans from around Southern California. Instead of the traditional rolling carts, there's a menu with pictures to help novices choose among dim sum standards like har gow (shrimp wrapped in rice paper), sieumai (wanton-wrapped pork and shrimp), and cha sieu bao (BBQ pork bun). Dishes not to be missed include lettuce "tacos" stuffed with stir-fried shrimp, Peking duck and tangerine pork chops. Service is hit and miss, but most just go for the food. A late supper menu is offered nightly from 9 to 11 pm. [$] *Average main: $17* ✉ *4698 Convoy St., Kearny Mesa* ☎ *858/650–3333* 🌐 *www.chinamaxsandiego.com* ✥ *3:G3.*

$$ KOREAN 🍴 **Dae Jang Keum Korean BBQ.** Once parked in the small lot of this strip mall, follow the scent of smoky BBQ to this casual, family-run Korean spot, a block off Convoy Street. Korean foodie fans, who swear it's the best in San Diego, gather around tabletop charcoal grills to cook seasoned duck, marinated chicken, short ribs, pork belly, and beef brisket for $15–$28 per person. Diners also can order from the plentiful menu of authentic Korean dishes prepared in the kitchen. Beer, wine, and soju (vodka-like Korean liquor) are available. Service can be inconsistent and slow but the leisurely Korean feast is stellar. [$] *Average main: $22* ✉ *7905 Engineer Rd., Kearny Mesa* ☎ *858/573–2585* 🌐 *www.daejangkeumkoreanbbq.menutoeat.com/* ✥ *3:H3.*

$ CHINESE 🍴 **Dumpling Inn.** Lovers of traditional Northern Chinese food flock here to sample this value-packed menu, overlooking frequent long waits outside, crowded seating, and lack of in-house restrooms. The tiny establishment loads its 10 or so tables with bottles of aromatic and spicy condiments for the boiled, steamed, and fried dumplings that are the house specialty—the pork and chive are particularly good. After dumplings, move on to house specialties like sea bass with black bean sauce, salt-and-pepper calamari, and pork shank Shanghai-style. Ask about daily specials. Only tea and soft drinks are served. [$] *Average main: $9* ✉ *4619 Convoy St., #F, Kearny Mesa* ☎ *858/268–9638* 🌐 *www.dumplinginn.menutoeat.com/* 🕒 *Closed Mon.* ✥ *3:G3.*

$ VIETNAMESE 🍴 **Phuong Trang.** This much-praised, popular Vietnamese restaurant offers such a mind-numbing selection of dishes that choosing a meal here can be difficult. Waiters steer diners to familiar tasty offerings like traditional pho soups, kung pao chicken, garlic butter–fried chicken wings, and fresh pork or shrimp spring rolls. For the adventurous, more exotic options abound, like the broken rice dishes, bird's nest soup with seafood and vegetables, and bo luc lac, sizzling cubes of beef served with a chunk of butter melting on top. The large, relatively spare dining room gets packed, especially on weekends, but service is usually prompt, if sometimes curt, typical of almost all Convoy Street dining spots. [$] *Average main: $10* ✉ *4170 Convoy St., Kearny Mesa* ☎ *858/565–6750* *www.phuongtrangrestaurant.com/ Reservations not accepted ⊕ 3:G3.*

$ JAPANESE Fodor's Choice ★ 🍴 **Wa Dining Okan.** "Okan," Western Japanese slang for Mom, suits this tiny but warm and homey Japanese restaurant in a Convoy Street strip mall. There's even a woman the staff calls "Mama" in the kitchen. Visiting businesspeople and regulars from around the county come early to get one of eight tables or a chair around the bilevel dining bar. During lunch, grilled fish, noodle dishes, and daily specials paired with miso, rice, and sides selected by the kitchen are served on trays. Evenings, handsome bowls lining the bar hold seasonal casseroles, vegetables, and salads. An extensive à la carte Grand Menu is also available, along with a good selection of Japanese beers and sakes. [$] *Average main: $8 ✉ 3860 Convoy St., Kearny Mesa ☎ 858/279–0941 www.okanus.com ⊕ 3:G4.*

WHEN THE GRUNIONS RUN

A generations-old San Diego tradition is heading to the beach during certain high tides—preferably when the moon is full—to hunt grunion. These small, barely edible fish come ashore during mating periods and "run" on the beach, causing great excitement among spectators. As the fish flop across the sand in search of adventure (as it were), bold individuals chase them down and scoop up a few with their hands—catching them by any other means is illegal. Beach-area businesses and eateries often know the date of the next run.

POINT LOMA, OCEAN BEACH, SHELTER AND HARBOR ISLANDS, AND CORONADO

Bays and beaches are stars in these diverse coastal communities that include Harbor and Shelter Islands. Although there's some fine dining here, most eateries are casual and cater to laid-back locals, sun-loving tourists, and sailing enthusiasts.

POINT LOMA

Once a neighborhood of tuna-fishing families, this famous peninsula is now a wealthy enclave where residents enjoy charming neighborhood restaurants, and new upscale dining spots clustered in walkable Liberty Station, and Harbor and Shelter Islands.

$$ BISTRO 🍴 **Bo-Beau kitchen + bar.** Ocean Beach is a slightly eccentric beach town, not a place diners would expect to find this warm, romantic bistro that evokes a French farmhouse. Executive chef Katherine Humphus, who refined her skills at French Laundry and New York's wd-50, has crafted a satisfying French-inspired menu of soups, woodstone oven flatbreads, mussels, and other bistro classics served in cozy dining rooms and a rustic outdoor patio. Go traditional with boeuf bourguignon or chicken fricassee or spice it up with a flatbread topped with butternut squash, leeks, Italian cheeses, and pumpkin seeds. Don't leave without a side of the popular crispy Brussels sprouts. Tuesday's "Cheep Date Night" special offers two entrées and bottle of wine for $39. [$] *Average main: $19 ✉ 4996 W. Point Loma Blvd., Ocean Beach ☎ 619/224–2884 www.bobeaukitchen.com ⌚ No lunch ⊕ 4:B1.*

8

$$ MODERN AMERICAN 🍴 **BO-beau kitchen + garden.** Related to BO-Beau Ocean Beach, this bistro nestled among antique stores in La Mesa village looks dramatically different even as it serves up a menu similar in spirit. Here, industrial chic decorates the dining room and bar, both lined streetside by open windows. A large open-air patio heated by tall free-standing fireplaces is a favorite of East County residents who flock there on hot summer nights. BO-Beau classics like the roasted Brussels sprouts, mussels, and crisp flatbreads share the menu with casual mains like steak and frites, burgers and fried chicken. A new Sunday brunch adds coffee-rubbed steak, strawberry buttermilk waffles, and crab cake Benedict. [$] *Average main: $21* ✉ *8384 La Mesa Blvd., La Mesa* ☎ *619/337–3445* 🌐 *www.cohnrestaurants.com/bobeaukitchengarden* 🕒 *Closed Mon.* ✥ *4:H2.*

$ CAFÉ 🍴 **Con Pane Rustic Breads & Cafe.** The scent of fresh-baked bread whets the appetite of customers at this Liberty Station bakery and café seeking rustic scones or raisin brioche cinnamon rolls for breakfast or one of the hearty lunch sandwiches like almost grilled cheese with melted brie and gorgonzola on warm rosemary olive oil bread. All can be enjoyed inside or on the sunny patio with hot or cold drinks including the house-made lemonade. The bakery turns out 24 different loaves; among them are the popular Point Loma sourdough, gruyère, and chive, and the Pane Cioccolata with Belgian and Swiss chocolate (only available weekends). Box lunches with a sandwich, chips, and cookie, a perfect accompaniment to picnics or other outings, are $9 to $12 each. [$] *Average main: $7* ✉ *2750 Dewey Rd., Point Loma* ☎ *619/224–4344* 🕒 *Closed Wed.* ✥ *4:C1.*

$ AMERICAN 🍴 **Jimmy's Famous American Tavern.** Tucked bay-side between Harbor and Shelter islands, Jimmy's (JFAT for short) draws hungry boaters and sea-lovers with its marina views and satisfying all-American comfort food. A standout in the wave of recent gastropubs, it blends lots of varnished wood with industrial-chic I-beams and garage-style doors. There's even a nod to the beach with a patio fire pit. The menu elevates backyard BBQ faves; the Jimmy burger is typical with unusual toppings like pimento cheese, applewood smoked bacon, and jalapeño jelly. Bottles of the company's zesty chipotle ketchup now can be purchased to take home. Evening happy hours around the bar can be loud, regardless of where you're seated. [$] *Average main: $17* ✉ *4990 N. Harbor Dr., Point Loma* ☎ *619/226–2103* 🌐 *www.j-fat.com* ✥ *4:B1.*

$ BARBECUE 🍴 **Phil's BBQ.** During peak hours at San Diego's most popular BBQ, lines can be long for diners craving heaping portions of fall-off-the-bone baby-back ribs, moist pulled pork, or huge, crispy onion rings. The Toro tri-tip sandwich made the 2012 list of America's best sandwiches compiled by Travel Channel celebrity Adam Richman. The hand-cut fries and other traditional sides at this friendly dining spot are favorites and BBQ fans love the sauce, but don't bother asking—the recipe is secret. Don't be discouraged by the line, it moves quickly. Carry out is great for picnics at the nearby Mission Bay beaches and parks. There are Phil's branches inside PETCO Park and in Santee as well. [$] *Average main: $14* ✉ *3750 Sports Arena Blvd., Point Loma* ☎ *619/226–6333* 🌐 *www.philsbbq.net* ✍ *Reservations not accepted* 🕒 *Closed Mon.* ✥ *4:B1.*

$ ✕ Point Loma Seafood's. When fishing boats unload their catch there, a
SEAFOOD seafood restaurant and market earns the right to boast that they offer
FAMILY "The Freshest Thing in Town." At first, mostly sport fishermen came
Fodor'sChoice here for tasty just-caught grilled fish on San Francisco–style sourdough
★ bread. But the word got out and now locals and visitors come to enjoy
bay views, sunshine, and a greatly expanded menu of seafood dishes. A
friendly, efficient crew takes orders for food and drinks at the counter
keeping the wait down even on the busiest days. In addition to sandwiches, favorites include fish tacos, seafood cocktails, sushi, salads, and
fried platters of fish, shrimp, and scallops. $ *Average main: $12* ✉ *2805
Emerson St., Point Loma* ☎ *619/223–1109* ⊕ *www.pointlomaseafoods.
com* ✛ *4:B2.*

$$ ✕ Sea180 Coastal Tavern. It's hard to dine any closer to sea and sand
MODERN than on the spacious patio at this modern casual restaurant at Pier
AMERICAN South Resort in Imperial Beach. Tables steps from the sand offer views
of the rustic IB pier, Coronado Bay Bridge, and city skyline, as well as
diving seabirds and colorful sunsets. South Bay families join military
contractors, hotel guests, and beachgoers to nosh on fish-and-chips,
tuna tacos, crab cakes, and duck quesadillas. Entrées range from grilled
whole fish to lamb osso buco and bison and pork meatballs. Monday
to Thursday specials include "Date Night" with shared plates with a
bottle of wine for two for $39. $ *Average main: $22* ✉ *800 Seacoast
Dr., Beach, Imperial Beach* ☎ *619/631–4949* ✛ *4:G6.*

$ ✕ Sessions Public. From the pork belly sliders, pastrami sandwich, and
MODERN fried chicken, it's clear this is no vegetarian joint. This eclectic neigh-
AMERICAN borhood gastropub with stuffed ducks on the walls draws a young
crowd more hipster than hippie with its menu featuring farm-to-table
fare and 20 craft beers on tap daily. Highlights include the mussels, a
gouda-topped Angus beef burger, and duck-fat fries with garlic aioli.
While quaffing a craft brew, try bacon lollipops or braised pork belly
on a stick. Sunday brunch is fun and casual with $5 drink specials
and comfort food offerings like biscuits and gravy and shaved bacon
Benedict. So is happy hour when select craft beers are $3. $ *Average
main: $14* ✉ *4204 Voltaire St., Ocean Beach* ☎ *619/756–7715* ⊕ *www.
sessionspublic.com* ☾ *No lunch Mon.–Thurs.* ✛ *4:B1*

$ ✕ Slater's 50/50. Bacon is king at this lively burger, beer, and sports bar
BURGER in Liberty Station. Founder Scott Slater's signature "designer" patty,
FAMILY half beef and half ground bacon, is topped with a fried egg, cheese, and
sauced with baconaise or bacon island dressing. Or design your own
burger from a menu with toppings like bacon turkey chili or bacon
American cheese. Even french fries get a lift from bacon ketchup. While
kids munch sliders from the kid's menu, parents quaff one of the 100
craft and local beers on tap and join military from nearby bases and
other sports fans following games on the room's many flat screen TVs.
And for dessert? What else but a bacon brownie à la mode. $ *Average
main: $10* ✉ *2750 Dewey Rd., Point Loma* ☎ *619/398–2600* ⊕ *www.
slaters5050.com* ✛ *4:C1.*

$$ ✕ Stone Brewing World Bistro and Gardens. Judging by the lines out the
ECLECTIC door, this 23,000-square-foot monument to beer and good food in
FAMILY Liberty Station is a crowd-pleaser, especially for fans of San Diego's

8

nationally known craft beer scene. BBQ duck tacos, chicken tikka masala, and other dishes on the global menu are perfect pairings with on-tap and bottled beers from around the world and Stone's own artisan brews like Arrogant Bastard Ale. Dine indoors in high-ceiling rooms guarded by etched-metal gargoyles and lit by beer-bottle chandeliers. Or, relax outdoors where parents often unwind as their kids enjoy the park-like grounds. Before leaving, browse the company store for hip logo-wear like hats, hoodies, and even a onesie for babies. [$] *Average main: $20* ✉ *2816 Historic Decatur Rd., Suite 116, Liberty Station* ☎ *619/269–2100* 🌐 *www.stonelibertystation.com* ✍ *Reservations essential* ✣ *4:C1.*

A FISH TALE

From the 1930s to the early '70s, San Diego was the capitol of the American tuna-fishing industry. Visit Point Loma to see the remnants of the fishing industry or stop by Whole Foods for a sample of this favorite fish canned by American Tuna, a company formed by six local fishing families who only use poles—not nets—to catch premium albacore tuna in a sustainable way.

$ AMERICAN FAMILY 🍴 **Tender Greens.** "Farm-fresh ingredients served up with little fuss" is the ethos behind this casual cafeteria-style spot, now in Liberty Station, La Jolla, and downtown San Diego. All are very popular at lunch but the lines move quickly. Expect big salads like seared tuna Niçoise with quail egg, P. Balistreri salumi with kale, or grilled Thai octopus with green papaya. Naturally raised beef and chicken are roasted or grilled and then tucked into sandwiches or served as a dinner plate with vegetables. Wine and house-made soups and desserts round out the menu. [$] *Average main: $12* ✉ *2400 Historic Decatur Rd., Point Loma* ☎ *619/226–6254* 🌐 *tendergreens.com* ✣ *4:C1.*

$$ ITALIAN FAMILY 🍴 **The Venetian Point Loma.** Two sons carry on the tradition of Italian home cooking begun by their father almost 50 years ago at this neighborhood favorite. The spacious back room of this casual restaurant is actually a sheltered garden that can be enjoyed in any weather. House specialties like shrimp puttanesca, and bow-tie pasta tossed with prosciutto, peas, and mushrooms in a rose-tinted cream sauce reflect the family's origins in Southern Italy The well-priced selection of veal, chicken, and seafood dishes is excellent, but many regulars settle for the lavishly garnished antipasto salad and one of the tender-crusted signature pizzas. [$] *Average main: $18* ✉ *3663 Voltaire St., Point Loma* ☎ *619/223–8197* 🌐 *www.venetian1965.com* ⏲ *No lunch Fri.–Sun.* ✣ *4:B1.*

OCEAN BEACH

One of the last "real" California beach towns, OB, as locals know it, has one foot in its hippy past and another in gentrified coastal living, which explains why it's one of the area's up-and-coming culinary communities, home to scores of fun and eclectic bars and restaurants.

$$ MODERN HAWAIIAN 🍴 **3rd Corner Wine Shop and Bistro.** Enthusiasts from around the world laud this combined wine shop, bar, and cozy California bistro. An amazing array of nicely discounted wines can be purchased to go or enjoy on premises (with a $5 corkage fee). Available from lunch until after midnight Tuesday to Saturday, the tasty wine-friendly American

bistro fare starts with baked brie in puff pastry or chicken liver mouse, moves on to savory short rib sliders and seafood risotto, and ends with apple-almond galette or goat's milk cheesecake. On Sunday, the popular bottomless mimosa brunch is followed in the evenings by a three-course prix-fixe dinner for $19.95 with optional paired wine flights. ■ **TIP→ Ask the friendly wine buyers to help select a bottle that suits your palate and meal.** [$] *Average main: $18* ✉ *2265 Bacon St., Ocean Beach* ☎ *619/223–2700* 🌐 *www.the3rdcorneroceanbeach.com/* ⏲ *Closed Mon.* ✥ *4:B1.*

$ CUBAN 🍴 **Azucar.** For a taste of Cuba in San Diego, head to this casual Ocean Beach bakery. Owner Vivian Hernandez Jackson combines her Cuban heritage, Miami childhood, and London culinary training for breakfast and lunch offerings at her friendly café, an ideal stop for a quick bite before shopping or hitting the beach. Morning specialties like raspberry scones with passion fruit icing, tea cakes, and ham and Spanish cheese quiche can be savored with café con leche, sweet Cuban espresso with hot milk. For lunch, try the Cubano slow-roasted pork sandwich with plantain chips, followed by a classic flan or slice of key lime pie. [$] *Average main: $7* ✉ *4820 Newport Ave., Ocean Beach* ☎ *619/523–2020* 🌐 *www.iloveazucar.com* ⏲ *No dinner* ✥ *4:B1.*

$ AMERICAN FAMILY 🍴 **Hodad's.** Like a little sass with your burger? This funky joint in Ocean Beach delivers plenty along with world-famous bacon-cheese burgers, fries, onion rings, and shakes. Don't be put off by lines out the door, they move quickly and the wait is worth it. Once inside, marvel at the hippy-beach decor of beat-up surf boards and license plates from almost every state, and at surfers with big appetites chowing down huge, messy burgers. A miniburger is a less-filling option for customers from around the world making a pilgrimage to this, the original Hodad's.Newer outposts—as family-friendly as the original—are downtown and at PETCO Park. [$] *Average main: $9* ✉ *5010 Newport Ave., Ocean Beach* ☎ *619/224–4623* 🌐 *hodadies.com* ✥ *4:B1.*

$ PIZZA 🍴 **Pizza Port.** Rows of picnic tables, surf-board decor and beer-brewing on-site have made this funky, friendly brewpub a block from the beach a locals' favorite. Beers on tap number in the dozens and include the Pizza Port and other craft beers that have made San Diego a beer-drinkers destination. Between sips, nosh on munchies like garlic beer buddies or seasoned bits of pizza crust. Surfers, families, and others with big appetites order one of 11 signature pizzas slathered with toppings, available whole or by the slice. Got a sweet tooth? Try a stout or porter float. Crowds can make it hard to get a seat or find parking, especially on warm summer days. [$] *Average main: $17* ✉ *1956 Bacon St., La Jolla* ☎ *619/224–4700* 🌐 *www.pizzaport.com* ✥ *4:B1.*

$ AMERICAN 🍴 **Shades.** With great views of the shore, surfers and the Ocean Beach pier, this pet-friendly casual dining spot welcomes hungry beachgoers with generous portions of meat loaf, fish-and-chips, shepherd's pie, flat-bread pizza, burgers, and other comfort food. Breakfast favorites include eggs Benedict with crab cakes or filet mignon. Dogs of all sizes happily dine from the fido menu with chopped K9-favorites like boneless grilled chicken or lean roast beef. There's also a full bar with wine and craft beer. ■ **TIP→ Daily happy-hour bargains include $5 well drinks** and on Tuesday bottles of wine are half-price. $\boxed{\text{s}}$ *Average main: $10* ✉ *5083 Santa Monica Ave., Ocean Beach* ☎ *619/222–0501* ⊕ *www. shadesob.com* ✛ *4:B1.*

SHELTER ISLAND

Countless yachts and sailboats are berthed at marinas and hotels along this bayfront spit of land where visitors and locals come to picnic, enjoy concerts, and dine at a variety of casual bayside restaurants specializing in fresh seafood.

$$

HAWAIIAN

✗ **Bali Hai.** For more than 50 years, generations of San Diegans and visitors have enjoyed this Polynesian-theme icon with its stunning bay and city skyline views. Much of the kitsch has been replaced by more contemporary decor, but you'll still spot tikis here and there. The menu is a fusion of Hawaiian, Asian, and California cuisines with an emphasis on seafood. Standouts include the Hawaiian tuna poke, Mongolian lamb with pad Thai, and pan-seared barramundi with coconut lobster sauce. Vegetarian and gluten-free menus also are offered. A visit won't be complete without a world-famous Bali Hai Mai Tai topped with a little umbrella. $\boxed{\text{s}}$ *Average main: $23* ✉ *2230 Shelter Island Dr., Shelter Island* ☎ *619/222–1181* ⊕ *www.balihairestaurant.com* ✛ *4:C2.*

$$

MODERN
AMERICAN
FAMILY

✗ **Humphreys Restaurant.** Step inside this view restaurant, part of a tropic-style hotel complex and concert venue on Shelter Island, and discover a dining room that's contemporary in look and outlook. Muted colors, comfortable chairs and mood lighting enhance vistas of bobbing sailboats, seabirds, and sunsets. Hotel guests, concertgoers, yachties and a few locals enjoy long-time chef Paul Murphy's contemporary menu that changes every couple of weeks. Seafood dishes with a twist shine in appetizers like sriracha-honey shrimp or entrées like swordfish Oscar or macadamia-crusted sea bass. After sharing an in-house dessert, stop by the bar next door to work off the calories dancing to live music. ■**TIP**➔ Reservations are needed during concert nights; check the website for schedule. $\boxed{\text{s}}$ *Average main: $26* ✉ *2241 Shelter Island Dr, Shelter Island* ☎ *619/224-3577* ⊕ *www.humphreysbythebay.com* ✛ *4:C2.*

HARBOR ISLAND

The man-made peninsula across from the airport, with its bayside parks, marinas, and hotels, is a popular dining destination for lunches and dinners served with stunning views of San Diego Bay and the city skyline.

$$$$

MODERN
AMERICAN
Fodor's Choice
★

✗ **Island Prime and C Level.** Two restaurants in one share this enviable spot on the shore of Harbor Island: the splurge-worthy Island Prime steak house and the relaxed C Level with a choice terrace fanned by sea breezes. Both venues tempt with unrivaled views of downtown San Diego's impressive skyline. Island Prime's surf-and-turf dinner menu offers a trio of fillets topped with blue cheese, wild mushrooms, and blue crab along with Alaskan king crab legs and lobster. At C Level, sharable plates are often Asian fusion-inspired, like the ahi stack with mango salsa and taro chips, or comfort food like the bacon-lobster sandwich. Chef Deborah Scott also offers a tasty "fuel" menu with lighter fare. The not-to-be-missed dessert is a decadent sundae—warm brownie, peanut-butter ice cream, whipped cream, and a maraschino cherry. $ *Average main: $36* ✉ *880 Harbor Island Dr., Harbor Island* ☎ *619/298–6802* ⊕ *www.islandprime.com* ✛ *4:F1.*

$$$ ✕ **Tom Ham's Lighthouse.** It's hard to
SEAFOOD top this longtime Harbor Island restaurant's incredible views across San Diego Bay to the downtown skyline and Coronado Bridge. Now a new alfresco dining deck and a contemporary seafood-focused menu ensure the dining experience doesn't take a back seat to the scenery. Sample the

iced shellfish platter before moving on to traditional lobster bouillabaisse and paella or an adventuresome squid-ink risotto. The family-owned institution also serves a popular Sunday brunch that stars crab legs, peel-and-eat shrimp, smoked salmon and oysters along with bottomless orange or pineapple mimosas. Prefer beer? Choose from a long list of on-tap and bottled craft brews. $ *Average main: $30* ✉ *2150 Harbor Island Dr., Harbor Island* ☎ *619/291–9110* ⊕ *www.tomhamslighthouse. com* ⊗ *No lunch Sun.* ✛ *4:D1.*

CORONADO

The home of charming, but pricey, vintage houses, the famous Hotel Del Coronado, and historic North Island Naval Station offers visitors a great variety of tourist-oriented bars and eateries—a few of them very good.

$$$$ ✕ **1500 Ocean.** The world-famous Hotel Del Coronado's top dining
AMERICAN room is steps from the beach where Marilyn Monroe, Tony Curtis, and Jack Lemmon frolicked in "Some Like it Hot." Its elegant interior dining rooms evoke posh poolside cabanas while the wide terrace embraces ocean views—all ideal settings for special occasions. Seafood, much of it local, shines in starters like the yellowtail crudo with chili-flecked avocado mousse and succulent poached white prawns. Sharable entrées like rack of lamb and duck two ways are easily paired with wines from the extensive list. The lobster mashed potato side is deliciously decadent. Unusual desserts like chocolate chipotle cake cap a sweet seaside experience. $ *Average main: $38* ✉ *Hotel Del Coronado, 1500 Orange Ave., Coronado* ☎ *619/522–8490* ⊕ *www.hoteldel.com/1500-ocean* ◬ *Reservations essential* ⊗ *Closed. Sun. and Mon. No lunch* ✛ *4:G6.*

$$ ✕ **Chez Loma.** French meets Southern Californian cuisine at this charm-
FRENCH ing historic Victorian home in the heart of Coronado. A favorite of locals and guests at nearby Hotel Del Coronado, the romantic bistro offers French favorites like boeuf bourguignon and mussels à la marinière as well as California standbys like rockfish ceviche in tomatillo sauce. On cool evenings try the winter fish stew that combines chunks of halibut, shrimp, and scallops in a rich stock. The solid dessert selection includes gingerbread with orange-caramel sauce and chocolate pot de crème. Sunday brunch is equally eclectic, featuring both croque monsieur and madame and the Mexican-inspired chilaquiles. $ *Average*

8

main: $25 ✉ 1132 Loma Ave., Coronado ☎ 619/435–0661 ⏲ No lunch ✥ 4:G6.

OFF THE BEATEN PATH

EAST SAN DIEGO

Bedroom communities, some of them upscale enclaves, dominate this area of the county, home to La Mesa, Mt. Helix, El Cajon, and Alpine. The dining scene is changing, as ethnic eateries and fast-casual chains are being joined by newcomers opening stylish dining spots in league with their coastal counterparts.

SOUTH BAY

Called the gateway to Baja California, this rapidly developing area that stretches from the Mexican border to the Coronado Bridge encompasses the cities and communities of Chula Vista, Bonita, National City, San Ysidro, and Imperial Beach. Dominated by national chains, traditional mom-and-pop restaurants and taco shops, the area is beginning to attract restaurateurs who feel the area is ready for fresh culinary ideas.

$$ MEXICAN FUSION 🍴 **Romesco Mexiterranean Bistro.** Mediterranean bistro meets Baja California ingredients at this restaurant by Javier Plascencia and family, Tijuana's renowned restaurateurs. The varied menu starts with salmon carpaccio or tapas like the spicy shrimp dish *cazuelita de gambas* and ahi tuna tostadas. On Tuesday, tapas dishes are half-price. Exquisitely flavored entrées include lobster ravioli in brandy cream sauce and mesquite-grilled duck breast, while desserts run to crepes in tangy *cajeta* goat milk caramel. Romesco offers a full bar and the rare chance to taste some of the fine wines made in Baja California Norte, Mexico's premier wine country. Service can be leisurely so you might want to request the check when you're close to finishing your meal. [$] *Average main: $25 ✉ 4346 Bonita Rd., Chula Vista ☎ 619/475–8627 🌐 www.romescobajamed.com ⏲ Closed Mon. ✥ 4:H3.*

$ MEXICAN 🍴 **Tacos El Gordo.** At the Chula Vista and National City branches of this well-known Tijuana taco franchise, carne asada and seasoned pork adobada tacos on small freshly made tortillas are considered by many to be the best on this side of the boarder. Adventurous diners might want to try more exotic fillings like sesos (brain) or tripa (intestines). The authentic menu also includes tostadas, sopes, and quesadillas. Look for their distinctive red-and-white sign, because there are imitators. [$] *Average main: $10 ✉ 689 H St., Chula Vista ☎ 619/691–8848 🌐 www.tacoselgordobc.com/ ✍ Reservations not accepted ⏲ No dinner ✥ 4:B6.*

WHERE TO EAT AND STAY IN SAN DIEGO

KEY

- ☐ Hotels
- ■ Restaurants
- ▦ Restaurant in Hotel
- following dining and lodging reviews indicates a map-grid coordinate

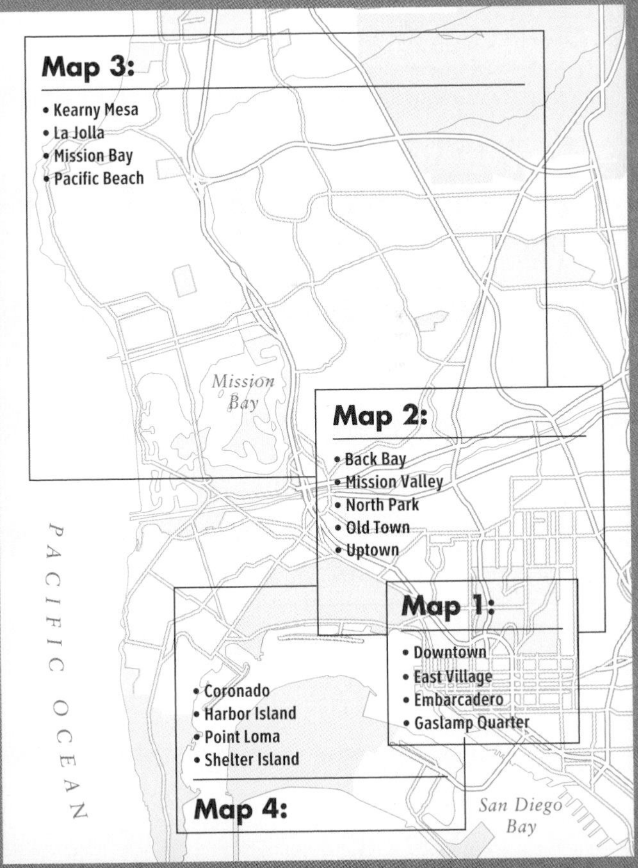

Map 3:

- Kearny Mesa
- La Jolla
- Mission Bay
- Pacific Beach

Mission Bay

Map 2:

- Back Bay
- Mission Valley
- North Park
- Old Town
- Uptown

Map 1:

- Downtown
- East Village
- Embarcadero
- Gaslamp Quarter

PACIFIC OCEAN

- Coronado
- Harbor Island
- Point Loma
- Shelter Island

Map 4:

San Diego Bay

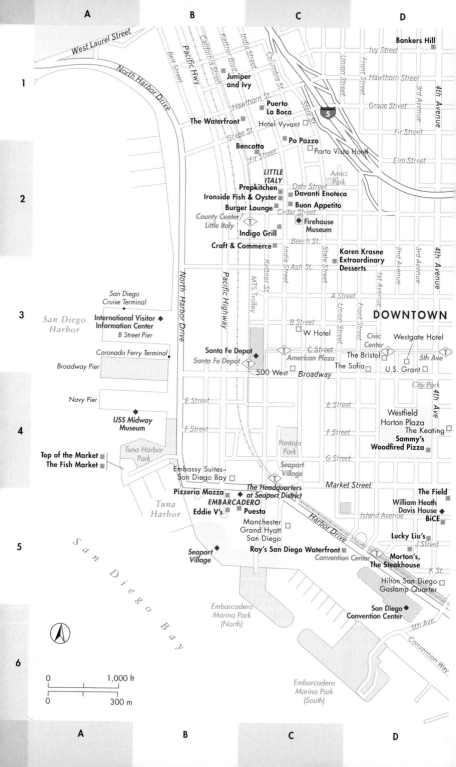

A

B

C

D

West Laurel Street

North Harbor Drive

Pacific Hwy

Belt Street

California Street

Kettner Blvd.

India Street

Columbia St.

State St.

Union Street

Front Street

3rd Avenue

4th Avenue

Bankers Hill ■

Ivy Street

Hawthorn Street

1

Hawthorn St.

Grape Street

Juniper and Ivy ■

Puerto La Boca ■

Fir Street

The Waterfront ■

Hotel Vyvant □

Grape St.

Po Pazzo □

Elm Street

Bencotto □

Fir Street

Porto Vista Hotel □

San Diego Harbor

LITTLE ITALY

Amici Park

Date Street

Prepkitchen ■

Davanti Enoteca ■

2

Ironside Fish & Oyster ■

Buon Appetito ■

Burger Lounge ■

Cedar Street

County Center/ Little Italy

Indigo Grill ■

Firehouse Museum ◆

Beech St.

Craft & Commerce ■

Kettner St.

MTS Trolley

India Street

Ash St.

State Street

1st Avenue

2nd Avenue

3rd Avenue

4th Avenue

Karen Krasne Extraordinary Desserts ■

A Street

San Diego Cruise Terminal

North Harbor Drive

Pacific Highway

Union Street

Front Street

DOWNTOWN

3

International Visitor Information Center ◆

B Street Pier

B Street

W Hotel □

Civic Center

Westgate Hotel

Coronado Ferry Terminal

C Street

American Plaza

The Bristol □

5th Ave □

Broadway Pier

Santa Fe Depot ◆

Santa Fe Depot □

The Sofia □

U.S. Grant □

500 West □

Broadway

City Park

Navy Pier

E Street

E Street

4th Ave

USS Midway Museum ◆

F Street

F Street

Westfield Horton Plaza

The Keating

4

Top of the Market ■

The Fish Market ■

Tuna Harbor Park

Pantoja Park

G Street

Sammy's Woodfired Pizza ■

Embassy Suites– San Diego Bay □

Seaport Village

Market Street

Pizzeria Mozza ◆

EMBARCADERO

The Headquarters at Seaport District ◆

The Field ■

Eddie V's ■

Puesto ■

Manchester Grand Hyatt San Diego

William Heath Davis House ◆

Island Avenue

BiCE ■

Tuna Harbor

Lucky Liu's ■

J Street

5

Seaport Village ◆

Roy's San Diego Waterfront ■

Convention Center

Morton's, The Steakhouse ■

Harbor Drive

K St.

S a n   D i e g o   B a y

Hilton San Diego Gaslamp Quarter □

Embarcadero Marina Park (North)

San Diego Convention Center ◆

5th Ave

Convention Way

6

0   1,000 ft

0   300 m

Embarcadero Marina Park (South)

A

B

C

D

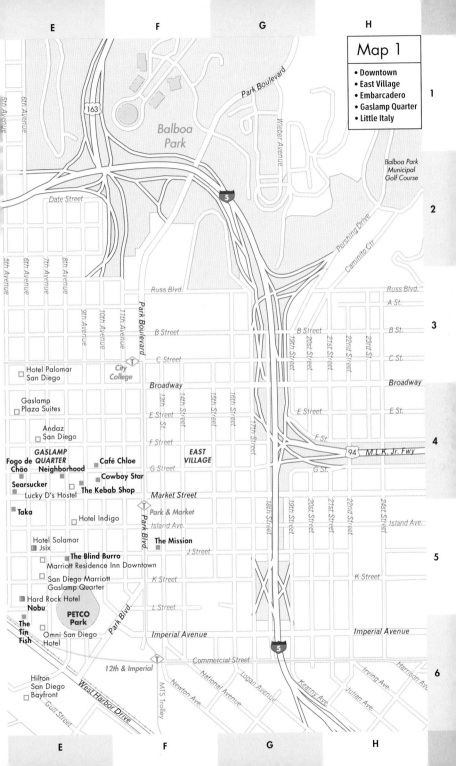

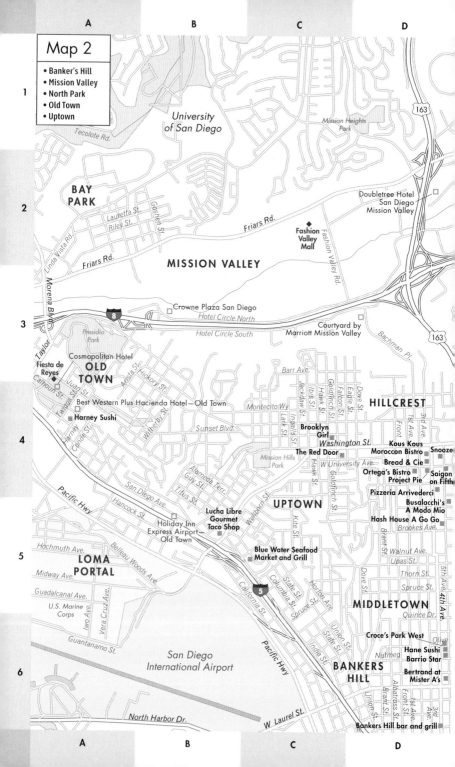

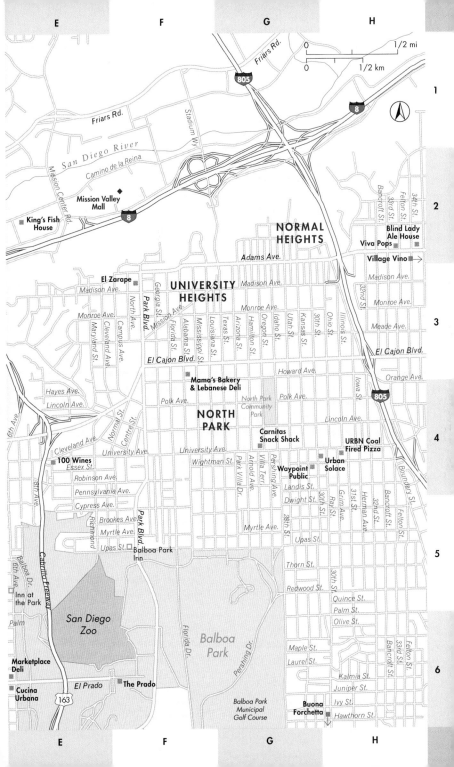

E   F   G   H

Friars Rd.

805

8

1

Friars Rd.

San Diego River

Camino de la Reina

Stadium Wy.

Mission Center Rd.

♦ Mission Valley Mall

8

■ King's Fish House

2

Bancroft St.
33rd St.
34th St.
Felton St.

NORMAL HEIGHTS

■ Blind Lady Ale House

Viva Pops ■ ■

■ Village Vino ■ →

Adams Ave.

El Zarape ■

Madison Ave.

UNIVERSITY HEIGHTS

Madison Ave.

Madison Ave.

North Ave.

Park Blvd.

Georgia St.

Mission Ave.

Monroe Ave.

Monroe Ave.

Maryland St.

Cleveland Ave.

Campus Ave.

Florida St.

Alabama St.

Mississippi St.

Louisiana St.

Texas St.

Arizona St.

Hamilton St.

Oregon St.

Idaho St.

Utah St.

Kansas St.

30th St.

Ohio St.

Illinois St.

Monroe Ave.

Meade Ave.

3

El Cajon Blvd.

El Cajon Blvd.

Orange Ave.

805

Howard Ave.

Hayes Ave.

Lincoln Ave.

Mama's Bakery & Lebanese Deli ■

Polk Ave.

North Park Community Park

Polk Ave.

NORTH PARK

Lincoln Ave.

Iowa St.

4

6th Ave.

Cleveland Ave.

Normal St.

Centre St.

University Ave.

■ 100 Wines

Essex St.

Robinson Ave.

Pennsylvania Ave.

Cypress Ave.

University Ave.

Wightman St.

Park Villa Dr.

Arnold Ave.

Villa Terr.

Pershing Ave.

Carnitas Snack Shack ■

Waypoint Public ■

Urban Solace ■

URBN Coal Fired Pizza ■

30th St.

Ray St.

Grim Ave.

31st St.

Herman Ave.

32nd St.

Bancroft St.

Felton St.

Boundary St.

Landis St.

Dwight St.

28th St.

Myrtle Ave.

Brookes Ave.

Myrtle Ave.

Upas St.

Upas St. □ Balboa Park Inn

Park Blvd.

Richmond

8th Ave.

Cabrillo Freeway

Balboa Dr.

6th Ave.

□ Inn at the Park

Palm

Thorn St.

30th St.

5

San Diego Zoo

Florida Dr.

Balboa Park

Redwood St.

Quince St.

Palm St.

Olive St.

Bancroft St.

33rd St.

Felton St.

■ Marketplace Deli

■ Cucina Urbana

El Prado

163

■ The Prado

Pershing Dr.

Maple St.

Laurel St.

Kalmia St.

Juniper St.

Ivy St.

Buona Forchetta ■

Hawthorn St.

6

Balboa Park Municipal Golf Course

↓

E   F   G   H

0   1/2 mi

0   1/2 km

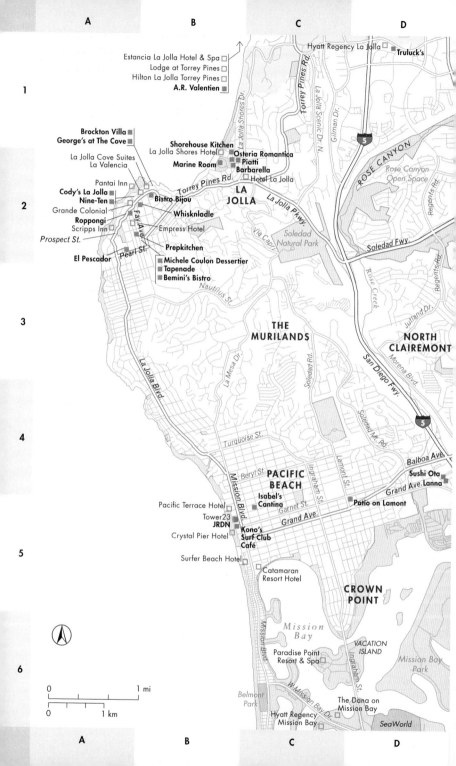

A   **B**   **C**   **D**

Hyatt Regency La Jolla
Truluck's

Estancia La Jolla Hotel & Spa
Lodge at Torrey Pines
Hilton La Jolla Torrey Pines
A.R. Valentien

1

ROSE CANYON

Rose Canyon
Open Space

Brockton Villa
George's at The Cove

Shorehouse Kitchen
La Jolla Shores Hotel
Osteria Romantica
Piatti
Barbarella

La Jolla Cove Suites
La Valencia

Marine Room
Hotel La Jolla

Soledad Fwy.

Pantai Inn
Cody's La Jolla
Nine-Ten
Grande Colonial
Roppongi
Scripps Inn
Prospect St.

Bistro Bijou

LA
JOLLA

Whisknladle

Empress Hotel

Soledad
Natural Park

2

Rose Creek

El Pescador

Prepkitchen

Michele Coulon Dessertier
Tapenade
Bemini's Bistro

Nautilus St.

3

THE
MURILANDS

NORTH
CLAIREMONT

4

Turquoise St.

Balboa Ave.

Sushi Ota
Grand Ave. **Lanna**

Beryl St.

PACIFIC
BEACH

Isabel's
Cantina

Garnet St.

Patio on Lamont

Pacific Terrace Hotel
Tower23
JRDN
Crystal Pier Hotel

Grand Ave.

Kono's
Surf Club
Café

5

Surfer Beach Hotel

Catamaran
Resort Hotel

CROWN
POINT

Mission
Bay

VACATION
ISLAND

Mission Bay
Park

6

0   1 mi

0   1 km

Paradise Point
Resort & Spa

Belmont
Park

The Dana on
Mission Bay

Hyatt Regency
Mission Bay

SeaWorld

A   **B**   **C**   **D**

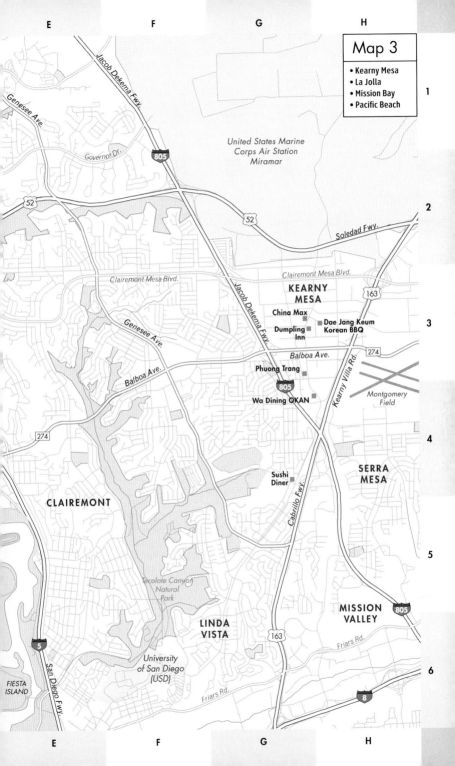

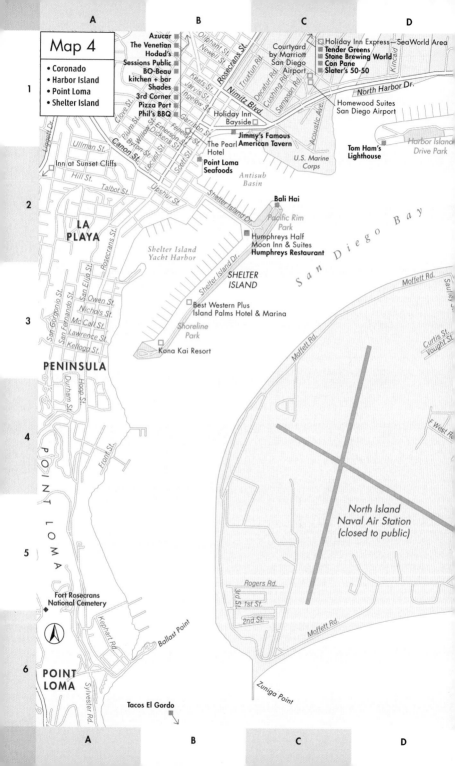

Map 4

- Coronado
- Harbor Island
- Point Loma
- Shelter Island

A **B** **C** **D**

Azucar
The Venetian
Hodad's
Sessions Public
kitchen + bar
BO-Beau
Shades
3rd Corner
Pizza Port
Phil's BBQ

Oliphant St.
Newell St.
Rosecrans St.
Truxtun Rd.
Decatur Rd.
Cushing Rd.
Sampson Rd.
Nimitz Blvd.
Keats St.
Jarvis St.
Ingelow St.
Garrison St.
Fenelon St.
Emerson St.
Scott St.
Dickens St.
Byron St.
Locust St.
Willow St.
Plum St.
Clove St.
Canon St.

Leggett Dr.
Ullman St.
Hill St.
Talbot St.
Upshur St.

Inn at Sunset Cliffs

Holiday Inn
Bayside

The Pearl
Hotel

**Point Loma
Seafoods**

Kincaid
North Harbor Dr.

☐ Holiday Inn Express—SeaWorld Area
■ **Tender Greens**
■ **Stone Brewing World**
■ **Con Pane**
■ **Slater's 50-50**

Courtyard
by Marriott
San Diego
Airport

Acoustic Ave.

Homewood Suites
San Diego Airport

Harbor Island
Drive Park

**Jimmy's Famous
American Tavern**

U.S. Marine
Corps

Antisub
Basin

**Tom Ham's
Lighthouse**

1

2

**LA
PLAYA**

Shelter Island Dr.

Shelter Island
Yacht Harbor

Bali Hai

Pacific Rim
Park

**Humphreys Half
Moon Inn & Suites
Humphreys Restaurant**

**SHELTER
ISLAND**

San Diego Bay

Moffett Rd.

Sealley Dr.

Curtis St.
Vought St.

3

PENINSULA

San Gorgonio St.
San Fernando St.
San Elijo St.
Owen St.
Nichols St.
McCall St.
Lawrence St.
Kellogg St.
Rosecrans St.

☐ Best Western Plus
Island Palms Hotel & Marina

Shoreline
Park

☐ Kona Kai Resort

Moffett Rd.

4

**POINT
LOMA**

Durham St.
Hoop St.
Front St.

F West Rd.

*North Island
Naval Air Station
(closed to public)*

5

Fort Rosecrans
National Cemetery

Kephart Rd.

Ballast Point

Rogers Rd.
3rd St.
1st St.
2nd St.

Moffett Rd.

6

**POINT
LOMA**

Sylvester Rd.

Tacos El Gordo

Zuniga Point

A **B** **C** **D**

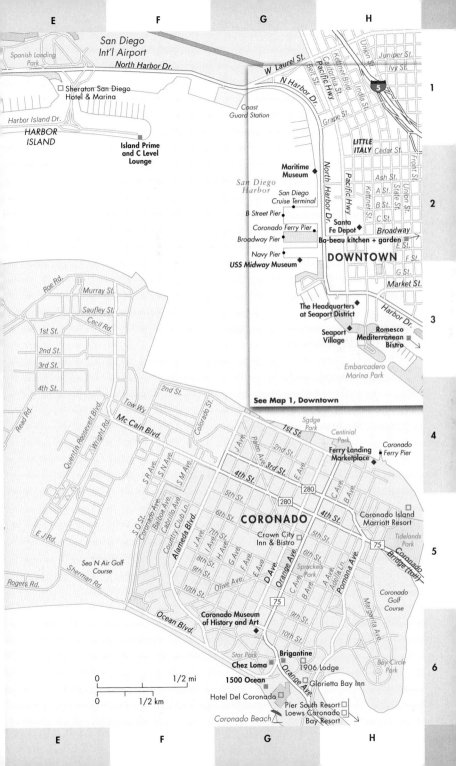

E   F   G   H

San Diego Int'l Airport

Spanish Landing Park

North Harbor Dr.

1

☐ Sheraton San Diego Hotel & Marina

W Laurel St.

Coast Guard Station

N Harbor Dr.

Pacific Hwy

Kettner Blvd.

California St.

India St.

Union St.

Juniper St.

Ivy St.

5

Harbor Island Dr.

HARBOR ISLAND

Island Prime and C Level Lounge

Grape St.

LITTLE ITALY   Cedar St.

Front St.

2

Maritime Museum ◆

San Diego Harbor

North Harbor Dr.

San Diego Cruise Terminal

Ash St.

Pacific Hwy

A St.

Kettner St.

State St.

Union St.

B Street Pier ●

Coronado Ferry Pier

Santa Fe Depot ◆

B St.

C St.

Broadway ●

Broadway Pier ●

Ba-beau kitchen + garden ■

DOWNTOWN

E St.

Navy Pier ●

F St.

USS Midway Museum ◆

G St.

Market St.

Roe Rd.

Murray St.

Saufley St.

Cecil Rd.

The Headquarters at Seaport District ●

Harbor Dr.

3

1st St.

2nd St.

3rd St.

4th St.

Seaport Village ●

Romesco Mediterranean Bistro ■

2nd St.

Colorado St.

Embarcadero Marina Park

See Map 1, Downtown

Tow Wy

Mc Cain Blvd.

Sgdge Park

Centinial Park

4

Quentin Roosevelt Blvd.

J Wright Rd.

Read Rd.

1st St.

J Ave.

Palm Ave.

2nd St.

3rd St.

E Ave.

Ferry Landing Marketplace ●

Coronado Ferry Pier

S R Ave.

S N Ave.

S M Ave.

4th St.

280

C Ave.

B Ave.

Coronado Ave.

Balboa Ave.

Cabrillo Ave.

Country Club Ln.

5th St.

280

4th St.

Coronado Island Marriott Resort ☐

S O St.

6th St.

CORONADO

5th St.

75

Tidelands Park

5

Alameda Blvd.

Sea N Air Golf Course

E J Rd.

7th St.

I Ave.

H Ave.

G Ave.

F Ave.

Crown City Inn & Bistro ☐

6th St.

A Ave.

Adella Ln.

Pomona Ave.

Coronado Bridge (toll)

8th St.

9th St.

D Ave.

Orange Ave.

Spreckels Park

B Ave.

Margarita Ave.

Rogers Rd.

Sherman Rd.

Olive Ave.

10th St.

E Ave.

C Ave.

Coronado Golf Course

Ocean Blvd.

Coronado Museum of History and Art ◆

75

9th St.

10th St.

Bay Circle Park

6

0   1/2 mi

0   1/2 km

Star Park

Chez Loma ■

Brigantine ■

1906 Lodge ☐

1500 Ocean ■

Glorietta Bay Inn ☐

Orange Ave.

Hotel Del Coronado ☐

Pier South Resort ☐

Coronado Beach ⚓

Loews Coronado Bay Resort ☐

E   F   G   H

Dining

100 Wines, 2:E4

1500 Ocean, 4:G6

3rd Corner Wine Shop and Bistro, 4:B1

A. R. Valentien, 3:B1

Azucar, 4:B1

Bali Hai, 4:C2

Bankers Hill bar and grill, 1:D5

Barbarella, 3:B2

Barrio Star, 2:D6

Bencotto, 1:C2

Bertrand at Mister A's, 2:D6

BiCE Ristorante, 1:D5

Bistro Bijou, 3:B2

The Blind Burro, 1:E5

Blue Water Seafood Market & Grill, 2:C5

BO-Beau kitchen + bar, 4:B1

Bo-beau kitchen + garden, 4:H2

Bread & Cie, 2:D4

Brooklyn Girl, 2:C4

Buon Appetito, 1:C2

Buona Forchetta, 2:H6

Busalacchi's A Modo Mio, 2:D5

Café Chloe, 1:E4

Carnitas' Snack Shack, 2:G4

Chez Loma, 4:G6

China Max, 3:G3

Con Pane Rustic Breads & Café, 4:C1

Cowboy Star, 1:E4

Craft & Commerce, 1:C2

Croce's Park West, 2:D6

Cucina Urbana, 2:E6

Dae Jang Keum Korean BBQ, 3:H3

Davanti Enoteca Little Italy, 1:C2

Dumpling Inn, 3:G3

Eddie V's Prime Seafood, 1:B5

El Pescador, 3:A2

El Zarape, 2:F3

The Field, 1:D5

Fish Market, 1:A4

Fogo de Chão, 1:E4

George's at the Cove, 3:B2

Hane Sushi, 2:D6

Harney Sushi, 2:A4

Hash House A Go Go, 2:D5

Hodad's, 4:B1

Humphreys Restaurant, 4:B2

Indigo Grill, 1:C2

Ironside Fish & Oyster, 1:C2

Isabel's Cantina, 3:C5

Island Prime and C Level, 4:F1

Jimmy's Famous American Tavern, 4:B1

JRDN, 3:B5

Jsix, 1:E5

Juniper and Ivy, 1:B1

Karen Krasne Extraordinary Desserts, 1:C2

The Kebab Shop, 1:E4

King's Fish House, 2:E2

Kono's Surf Club Café, 3:B5

Kous Kous Moroccan Bistro, 2:D4

La Pizzeria Arrivederci, 2:D4

Lanna, 3:D4

Lucha Libre Gourmet Taco Shop, 2:B5

Lucky Liu's, 1:D5

Mama's Bakery & Lebanese Deli, 2:F3

Marine Room, 3:B2

Marketplace Deli, 2:E6

Michele Coulon Dessertier, 3:A2

Morton's, The Steakhouse, 1:D5

Neighborhood, 1:E4

Nine-Ten, 3:A2

Nobu, 1:E5

Ortega's Bistro, 2:D4

Osteria Romantica, 3:B2

Phil's BBQ, 4:B1

Phuong Trang, 3:G3

Piatti, 3:B2

Pizza Port, 4:B1

Pizzeria Mozza, 1:B5

Po Pazzo Bar and Grille, 1:C2

Point Loma Seafoods, 4:B2

The Prado at Balboa Park, 2:F6

Prepkitchen Little Italy, 1:C2

Prepkitchen, 3:A2

Project Pie, 2:D4

Puerto La Boca, 1:C1

Puesto, 1:B5

The Red Door, 2:C4

Romesco Mediterranean Bistro, 4:H3

Roppongi Restaurant and Sushi Bar, 3:A2

Roy's San Diego Waterfront, 1:C5

Saigon on Fifth, 2:D4

Searsucker, 1:E4

Sessions Public, 4:B1

Shades, 4:B1

Shorehouse Kitchen, 3:B2

Slater's 50/50, 4:C1

Snooze, 2:D4

Stone Brewing World Bistro and Gardens, 4:C1

Sushi Diner, 3:G4

Sushi Ota, 3:D4

Tacos El Gordo, 4:B6

Taka, 1:E5

Tapenade, 3:B2

Tender Greens, 4:C1

The Tin Fish, 1:E5

Tom Ham's Lighthouse, 4:D1

Top of the Market, 1:A4

Truluck's, 3:D1

Urban Solace, 2:G4

URBN Coal Fired Pizza, 2:H4

The Venetian Point Loma, 4:B1

Village Vino, 2:H2

Viva Pops, 2:H2

Waypoint Public, 2:G4

Whisknladle, 3:A2

Lodging

1906 Lodge, 4:G6

500 West, 1:C3

Andaz San Diego, 1:E4

Balboa Park Inn, 2:F5

Best Western Plus Hacienda Hotel–Old Town, 2:A4

Best Western Plus Island Palms Hotel & Marina, 4:B3

The Bristol, 1:D3

Catamaran Resort Hotel, 3:C5

Coronado Island Marriott Resort, 4:H5

The Cosmopolitan Hotel, 2:A4

Courtyard by Marriott Mission Valley, 2:D3

Courtyard by Marriott San Diego Airport, 4:C1

Crown City Inn & Bistro, 4:G5

Crowne Plaza San Diego, 2:B3

Crystal Pier Hotel and Cottages, 3:B5

The Dana on Mission Bay, 3:C6

Doubletree Hotel San Diego Mission Valley, 2:D2

Embassy Suites–San Diego Bay, 1:B4

Empress Hotel, 3:A2

Estancia La Jolla Hotel & Spa, 3:B1

Gaslamp Plaza Suites, 1:E4

Glorietta Bay Inn, 4:G6

Grande Colonial, 3:A2

Hard Rock Hotel, 1:E5

Hilton La Jolla Torrey Pines, 3:B1

Hilton San Diego Bayfront, 1:E6

Hilton San Diego Gaslamp Quarter, 1:D5

Holiday Inn Bayside, 4:C1

Holiday Inn Express Airport–Old Town, 2:B5

Holiday Inn Express–SeaWorld Area, 4:C1

Homewood Suites San Diego Airport, 4:C1

Hotel Del Coronado, 4:G6

Hotel Indigo, 1:E5

Hotel La Jolla, 3:C2

Hotel Palomar San Diego, 1:E3

Hotel Solamar, 1:E5

Hotel Vyvant, 1:C1

Humphreys Half Moon Inn & Suites, 4:B2

Hyatt Regency La Jolla, 3:D1

Hyatt Regency Mission Bay Spa & Marina, 3:C6

Inn at Sunset Cliffs, 4:A2

Inn at the Park, 2:E5

The Keating Hotel, 1:D4

Kona Kai Resort, 4:B3

La Jolla Cove Suites, 3:B2

La Jolla Shores Hotel, 3:B2

La Valencia, 3:B2

Lodge at Torrey Pines, 3:B1

Loews Coronado Bay Resort, 4:H6

Lucky D's Hostel, 1:E4

Manchester Grand Hyatt San Diego, 1:C5

Marriott Residence Inn Downtown, 1:E5

Omni San Diego Hotel, 1:E6

Pacific Terrace Hotel, 3:B5

Pantai Inn, 3:A2

Paradise Point Resort & Spa, 3:C6

The Pearl Hotel, 4:B1

Pier South Resort, 4:H6

Porto Vista Hotel & Suites, 1:C2

San Diego Marriott Gaslamp Quarter, 1:E5

Scripps Inn, 3:A2

Sheraton San Diego Hotel & Marina, 4:E1

The Sofia Hotel, 1:D3

Surfer Beach Hotel, 3:C5

Tower23, 3:B5

U.S. Grant, 1:D3

W Hotel, 1:C3

Westgate Hotel, 1:D3

WHERE TO STAY

Updated
by Maren
Dougherty

In San Diego, you could plan a luxurious vacation at the beach, staying at a resort with panoramic ocean views, private balconies, and a full-service spa. Or you could stay downtown, steps from the bustling Gaslamp Quarter, in a hotel featuring swanky rooftop pools, complimentary wine receptions, and high-tech entertainment systems. But with some flexibility—maybe opting for a partial-view room a quick drive from the action—it's possible to experience San Diego at half the price.

Sharing the city's postcard-perfect sunny skies are neighborhoods and coastal communities that offer great diversity; San Diego is no longer the sleepy beach town it once was. In action-packed downtown, luxury hotels cater to solo business travelers and young couples with trendy restaurants and cabana-encircled pools. There are also hostels and some budget-friendly options in and near Little Italy.

You'll need a car if you stay outside downtown, but the beach communities are rich with lodging options. Across the bridge, Coronado's hotels and resorts offer access to a stretch of glistening white sand that's often recognized as one of the best beaches in the country. La Jolla offers many romantic, upscale ocean-view hotels and some of the area's best restaurants and specialty shopping. But it's easy to find a water view in any price range: surfers make themselves at home at the casual inns and budget stays of Pacific Beach and Mission Bay. If you're planning to fish, check out hotels located near the marinas in Shelter Island, Point Loma, or Coronado.

For families, Uptown, Mission Valley, and Old Town are close to SeaWorld and the San Diego Zoo, offering good-value accommodations with extras like sleeper sofas and video games. Mission Valley is ideal for business travelers; there are plenty of well-known chain hotels with conference space, modern business centers, and kitchenettes for extended stays.

WHERE SHOULD I STAY?

	Neighborhood Vibe	Pros	Cons
Downtown	Downtown's hub is the Gaslamp Quarter, an action-packed area with many hotels, boutiques, restaurants, and clubs. Little Italy and Embarcadero areas are quieter.	Close to food and nightlife options for every age and taste. Quick walk or trolley ride to convention center. Won't need a car to get to many attractions.	Streets can be congested and noisy at night, particularly in the Gaslamp Quarter and East Village. Overnight parking is expensive.
Uptown and Old Town	Quieter area north of downtown with more budget-friendly hotels. Old Town has a busy stretch of Mexican restaurants and historic sites.	Central location that's close to Balboa Park and major freeways. Good for business travelers. More inexpensive dining options.	Limited nightlife options. Feels more removed from San Diego's beachy vibe. Mission Valley area lacks character; it's filled with malls and car lots.
Mission Bay, Beaches, and SeaWorld	Relaxed and casual beachside area with many resorts, golf courses, and parks. Largest man-made aquatic park in the country.	Right on the water. Can splurge on Jet Skis and other water sports or stick to BBQs and public playgrounds. Close to SeaWorld.	Resorts are spaced far apart, and area is somewhat removed from central San Diego. Watch for high resort fees and other not-so-obvious charges.
La Jolla	The "jewel" of San Diego, an affluent coastal area with a small-town atmosphere. Has a range of luxury hotels and a few value choices.	Gorgeous views. Close to or right on the beach. Some of the best seafood restaurants and high-end shopping in the state. Safe area for walking.	Often congested, and parking can be nearly impossible in summer. Very expensive area. Has few hotels that cater to children.
Point Loma and Coronado with Harbor and Shelter Islands	Areas by the bay have historic and resort hotels, beaches, and tourist-oriented restaurants. Coronado and Point Loma are more residential, home to many military families.	Great views of the city, bay, and beaches. Near the airport. Convenient for boaters. Hotels tend to be family-friendly, with large rooms and pools.	Isolated from the rest of the city; you'll spend significant time commuting to other parts of San Diego, such as La Jolla and Balboa Park.

When your work (or sightseeing) is done, join the trendsetters flocking to downtown's Gaslamp Quarter for its eateries, lounges, and multilevel clubs that rival L.A.'s stylish scenes.

PLANNING

LODGING STRATEGY

Where should I stay? With hundreds of San Diego hotels in dozens of neighborhoods, it may seem like a daunting question. But fret not—our expert writers and editors have done most of the legwork. The selections here represent the best this sunny paradise has to offer—from the best budget motels to the sleekest boutique hotels. Scan "Best Bets" for our top recommendations by price and experience.

BEST BETS FOR
SAN DIEGO LODGING

Fodor's offers a selective listing of quality lodging experiences. Here we've compiled our top recommendations. The very best properties—in other words, those that provide a particularly remarkable experience in their price range—are designated in the listings with a Fodor's Choice logo.

Fodor's Choice ★

1906 Lodge $$$$, p. 177

Andaz San Diego $$$$, p. 166

Courtyard by Marriott Mission Valley $, p. 170

Grande Colonial $$$$, p. 173

Hard Rock Hotel $$$, p. 166

Homewood Suites San Diego Airport $$$, p. 176

Hotel Del Coronado $$$$, p. 178

Hotel Solamar $$$, p. 167

Lodge at Torrey Pines $$$$, p. 175

The Pearl Hotel $, p. 176

The Sofia Hotel $$$, p. 168

Westgate Hotel $$$, p. 168

By Price

$

Best Western Plus Hacienda Hotel–Old Town, p. 170

Courtyard by Marriott Mission Valley, p. 170

Crown City Inn & Bistro, p. 177

Hotel Vyvant, p. 169

The Pearl Hotel, p. 176

$$

The Dana on Mission Bay, p. 171

Hotel Indigo, p. 168

$$$

Catamaran Resort Hotel, p. 172

Grande Colonial, p. 173

Hard Rock Hotel, p. 166

Homewood Suites San Diego Airport, p. 176

Hotel Solamar, p. 167

Paradise Point Resort & Spa, p. 172

The Sofia Hotel, p. 168

$$$$

Andaz San Diego, p. 166

Hotel Del Coronado, p. 178

La Valencia, p. 175

Lodge at Torrey Pines, p. 175

Pacific Terrace Hotel, p. 172

By Experience

BEST BEACH

Catamaran Resort Hotel, p. 172

Hotel Del Coronado, p. 178

La Jolla Shores Hotel, p. 175

Paradise Point Resort & Spa, p. 172

Tower23, p. 172

BEST POOL

Andaz San Diego, p. 166

Hotel Solamar, p. 167

Hyatt Regency Mission Bay Spa & Marina, p. 171

Loews Coronado Bay Resort, p. 178

Manchester Grand Hyatt San Diego, p. 169

BEST FOR ROMANCE

1906 Lodge, p. 177

Hotel Del Coronado, p. 178

Hotel Solamar, p. 167

La Valencia, p. 175

Lodge at Torrey Pines, p. 175

BEST SPA

Catamaran Resort Hotel, p. 172

Estancia La Jolla Hotel & Spa, p. 173

Loews Coronado Bay Resort, p. 178

BEST VIEWS

Crystal Pier Hotel and Cottages, p. 172

Hilton San Diego Bayfront, p. 167

Hyatt Regency Mission Bay Spa & Marina, p. 171

Inn at Sunset Cliffs, p. 176

Pacific Terrace Hotel, p. 172

MOST TRENDY

Andaz San Diego, p. 166

Hotel La Jolla, p. 173

The Keating Hotel, p. 167

The Pearl Hotel, p. 176

Tower23, p. 172

PARKING

Given the distances between attractions and limited public transportation routes, a car is almost a necessity for visitors to San Diego. That being said, a vehicle can significantly add to your expenses if you stay in the ritzier areas. Overnight parking in Coronado, La Jolla, and downtown's Gaslamp Quarter can be as high as $40 per night; in Uptown and Mission Bay it usually runs $10 to $20.

NEED A RESERVATION?

Book well in advance, especially if you plan to visit in summer, which is the busy season for most hotels. In spring and fall, conventions and sports events can fill every downtown hotel room. When you make reservations, ask about specials. Several properties in the Hotel Circle area of Mission Valley offer reduced rates and even free tickets to the San Diego Zoo and other attractions. You can save on hotels and attractions by visiting the San Diego Tourism Authority website (⊕ *www.sandiego. org*) for special seasonal offers.

STAYING WITH KIDS

The area is full of hotels suited to a family's budget and/or recreational needs, and many allow kids under 18 to stay free with their parents. You'll find the most choices and diversity in and around Mission Bay, which is close to SeaWorld, beaches, parks, and Old Town.

SERVICES

Downtown hotels once catered primarily to business travelers, though the new boutique hotels are attracting hip leisure travelers to the area, while those at Mission Bay, in coastal locations such as Carlsbad and Encinitas, and at inland resort areas offer golf and other sports facilities, spa services, children's activities, and more. If you're traveling with pets, note that pet policies do change and some hotels require substantial cleaning fees of $50 to $100. At many San Diego hotels, even smoking outdoors is frowned on or prohibited.

PRICES

Note that even in the most expensive areas, you can find affordable rooms. High season is summer, and rates are lowest in fall. If an ocean view is important, request it when booking, but it will cost you.

Prices in the reviews are the lowest cost of a standard double room in high season. For expanded hotel reviews, facilities, and current deals, visit Fodors.com.

WHAT IT COSTS			
$	$$	$$$	$$$$
Hotels	under $150	$150–$225	$226–$300	over $300

Prices are for a standard double room in high (summer) season, excluding 10.5% tax.

HOTEL REVIEWS

Listed alphabetically within neighborhoods. Use the coordinates (✥ 2:F3) after property names or reviews to locate the property on the San Diego Dining and Lodging Atlas. The first number after the ✥ symbol indicates the map number. Following that is the property's coordinate on the map grid.

DOWNTOWN

Lively downtown is San Diego's hotel hub, with everything from budget chains to boutique and business hotels. Here's a part of Southern California where you won't need a car; you can walk or take the trolley to Seaport Village, the Embarcadero, PETCO Park, the convention center, galleries and coffeehouses, and the Horton Plaza shopping center. Smack in the middle of downtown is the Gaslamp Quarter where you'll find nightlife options for every night of the week, ranging from gastropubs to clubs with celebrity DJs.

GASLAMP QUARTER

$ HOTEL **500 West.** The historic Armed Services YMCA Building houses this no-frills hostel suitable for backpackers and other budget-minded travelers. **Pros:** near shops and restaurants; good value; kitchen. **Cons:** small and dated rooms; no air-conditioning. [$] *Rooms from: $59* ✉ *500 W. Broadway, Gaslamp Quarter* ☎ *619/234–5252, 866/500–7533* 🌐 *www.500westhotelsd.com* 🛏 *259 rooms* 🍴 *No meals* ✥ *1:C3.*

$$$$ HOTEL Fodor's Choice ★ **Andaz San Diego.** The lobby of the luxury, Hyatt-managed Andaz—with its sexy vibe, tall columns wrapped in braided leather, buckets of chilled wine awaiting guests, and welcoming service—pretty much sums up the experience here: high-style stay without the attitude. **Pros:** luxurious rooms; romantic vibe; friendly service. **Cons:** noisy on weekends; not a good choice for families. [$] *Rooms from: $315* ✉ *600 F St., Gaslamp Quarter* ☎ *619/849–1234* 🌐 *www.sandiego.andaz.hyatt.com* 🛏 *142 rooms, 17 suites* 🍴 *No meals* ✥ *1:E4.*

$$ HOTEL **The Bristol.** Pop art by Peter Max and Andy Warhol sets a mod 1960s tone at this casual boutique hotel. **Pros:** modern rooms; centrally located; good value. **Cons:** few amenities, somewhat seedy area. [$] *Rooms from: $159* ✉ *1055 1st Ave., Gaslamp Quarter* ☎ *619/232–6141, 888/745–4393* 🌐 *www.thebristolsandiego.com* 🛏 *102 rooms* 🍴 *No meals* ✥ *1:D3.*

$ HOTEL **Gaslamp Plaza Suites.** One of San Diego's first "skyscrapers," this 11-story structure has a central location and a vintage feel. **Pros:** historic building; good location a block from Horton Plaza; well priced. **Cons:** books up early; smallish rooms. [$] *Rooms from: $130* ✉ *520 E St., Gaslamp Quarter* ☎ *619/232–9500, 800/874–8770* 🌐 *www.gaslampplaza.com* 🛏 *12 rooms, 52 suites* 🍴 *Breakfast* ✥ *1:E4.*

$$$ HOTEL Fodor's Choice ★ **Hard Rock Hotel.** Self-billed as a hip playground for rock stars and people who want to party like them, the Hard Rock is near PETCO Park overlooking glimmering San Diego Bay. **Pros:** central location; energetic scene; luxurious rooms. **Cons:** pricey drinks; some attitude. [$] *Rooms from: $276* ✉ *207 5th Ave., Gaslamp Quarter* ☎ *619/702–3000,*

866/751–7625 ⊕ *www.hardrockhotelsd.com* ↬ *244 rooms, 176 suites* ⦿ *No meals* ✛ *1:E5.*

$$
HOTEL
FAMILY

⌂ **Hilton San Diego Bayfront.** Not your typical Hilton, this modern 30-story hotel overlooking San Diego Bay strives for a boutique feel. **Pros:** close to the convention center and PETCO Park; new rooms. **Cons:** pricey dining options; not as family-friendly as other area hotels. ⓢ *Rooms from: $209* ✉ *1 Park Blvd., Gaslamp Quarter* ☎ *619/564–3333* ⊕ *www.hiltonsandiegobayfront.com* ↬ *1,159 rooms, 31 suites* ⦿ *No meals* ✛ *1:E6.*

$$
HOTEL

⌂ **Hilton San Diego Gaslamp Quarter.** The moment you experience the cozy lounge spaces and wood accents of the Hilton's modern and sophisticated lobby, you realize this isn't your run-of-the-mill chain hotel. **Pros:** nice decor; upscale lofts; near restaurants and shops. **Cons:** noisy area; pricey parking. ⓢ *Rooms from: $219* ✉ *401 K St., Gaslamp Quarter* ☎ *619/231–4040, 800/445–8667* ⊕ *www.hiltongaslamp.com* ↬ *240 rooms, 13 suites, 30 lofts* ⦿ *No meals* ✛ *1:D5.*

$$
HOTEL
FAMILY

⌂ **Hotel Palomar San Diego.** A few blocks from the heart of the Gaslamp Quarter, this swanky Kimpton-operated hotel features luxurious guestrooms and a popular rooftop lounge. **Pros:** new rooms; centrally located; luxury amenities. **Cons:** expensive parking; Saltbox restaurant is pricey and needs improvement; can hear street noise. ⓢ *Rooms from: $208* ✉ *1047 5th Ave., Gaslamp Quarter* ☎ *619/515–3000* ⊕ *www.hotelpalomar-sandiego.com* ↬ *146 rooms, 37 suites* ⦿ *No meals* ✛ *1:E3.*

$$$
HOTEL
FAMILY
Fodor's Choice
★

⌂ **Hotel Solamar.** The hip Solamar is best known for its pool-side rooftop bar, LoungeSix, and stylish lobby decor. **Pros:** great restaurant; attentive service; upscale rooms. **Cons:** busy valet parking; bars are crowded and noisy on weekends. ⓢ *Rooms from: $265* ✉ *435 6th Ave., Gaslamp Quarter* ☎ *619/819–9500, 877/230–0300* ⊕ *www.hotelsolamar.com* ↬ *217 rooms, 16 suites* ⦿ *No meals* ✛ *1:E5.*

$$
HOTEL

⌂ **The Keating Hotel.** At this boutique hotel in the heart of San Diego's downtown nightlife scene, guests are greeted with a sports car–red lobby that leads to 35 rooms designed by Pininfarina, the Italian company that makes Ferraris and Maseratis. **Pros:** great location; modern style. **Cons:** street noise; industrial-feeling rooms; small lobby. ⓢ *Rooms from: $196* ✉ *432 F St., Gaslamp Quarter* ☎ *619/814–5700, 877/753–2846* ⊕ *www.thekeating.com* ↬ *26 rooms, 9 suites* ⦿ *Breakfast* ✛ *1:D4.*

$$
HOTEL

⌂ **Marriott Residence Inn Downtown.** A home away from home for urbanites, the all-suites hotel is the best option for extended stays in downtown San Diego. **Pros:** spacious rooms; central location; pet-friendly. **Cons:** no room service; pricey valet-only parking will add up quickly during an extended stay. ⓢ *Rooms from: $219* ✉ *356 6th Ave., Gaslamp Quarter* ☎ *619/487–1200* ⊕ *www.marriott.com/sanrg* ↬ *240 suites* ⦿ *Breakfast* ✛ *1:E5.*

$$
HOTEL

⌂ **Omni San Diego Hotel.** Business travelers who also want to catch a baseball game flock to this modern masterpiece that occupies the first 21 floors of a 32-story high-rise overlooking PETCO Park. **Pros:** great views; good location; modern setting. **Cons:** busy; crowded during baseball season. ⓢ *Rooms from: $224* ✉ *675 L St., Gaslamp Quarter*

9

☎ 619/231–6664, 800/843–6664 🌐 www.omnihotels.com 🛏 478 rooms, 33 suites 🍴 No meals ✥ 1:E6.

$$$ HOTEL 🏨 **San Diego Marriott Gaslamp Quarter.** The 22-story Marriott sits amid the Gaslamp's restaurants and boutiques, near a trolley station, the convention center, and PETCO Park. **Pros:** good views; modern decor; central location. **Cons:** rooftop bar can get rowdy; no pool. [$] *Rooms from: $249 ✉ 660 K St., Gaslamp Quarter ☎ 619/696–0234 🌐 www.sandiegogaslamphotel.com 🛏 291 rooms, 15 suites 🍴 No meals ✥ 1:E5.*

$$$ HOTEL Fodor's Choice ★ 🏨 **The Sofia Hotel.** This stylish and centrally located boutique hotel may have small rooms, but it more than compensates with pampering extras like motion-sensor temperature controls, a Zen-like 24-hour yoga studio, and in-suite spa services. **Pros:** upscale amenities; historic building; near shops and restaurants. **Cons:** busy area; small rooms. [$] *Rooms from: $259 ✉ 150 W. Broadway, Gaslamp Quarter ☎ 619/234–9200, 800/826–0009 🌐 www.thesofiahotel.com 🛏 183 rooms, 28 suites 🍴 No meals ✥ 1:D3.*

$$ HOTEL 🏨 **U.S. Grant.** Stepping into the regal U.S. Grant not only places you in the lap of luxury but also transports you back in time. **Pros:** modern rooms; great location; near shopping and restaurants. **Cons:** small elevators; some reports of trouble with a/c units. [$] *Rooms from: $199 ✉ 326 Broadway, Gaslamp Quarter ☎ 619/232–3121, 800/325–3589 🌐 www.usgrant.net 🛏 223 rooms, 47 suites 🍴 No meals ✥ 1:D3.*

$$$ HOTEL 🏨 **W Hotel.** Come here for the trendy decor, upscale rooms, and central location between Gaslamp and Little Italy. **Pros:** large lobby that's fun for people-watching; modern rooms; friendly staff. **Cons:** expensive parking; not centrally located. [$] *Rooms from: $235 ✉ 421 W. B St., Gaslamp Quarter ☎ 619/398–3100 🌐 www.thewsandiegohotel.com 🛏 253 rooms, 5 suites 🍴 No meals ✥ 1:C3.*

$$$ HOTEL Fodor's Choice ★ 🏨 **Westgate Hotel.** A modern high-rise near Horton Plaza hides San Diego's most opulent old-world-style hotel, featuring a lobby outfitted with bronze sculptures and Baccarat chandeliers. **Pros:** elegant rooms; grand lobby, near shopping. **Cons:** formal atmosphere; mandatory facility fee. [$] *Rooms from: $239 ✉ 1055 2nd Ave., Gaslamp Quarter ☎ 619/238–1818, 800/522–1564 🌐 www.westgatehotel.com 🛏 216 rooms, 7 suites 🍴 No meals ✥ 1:D3.*

EAST VILLAGE

$$ HOTEL 🏨 **Hotel Indigo.** Smart-looking spaces and great service for the business traveler are the hallmarks of the Indigo chain of modern hotels. **Pros:** close to restaurants and bars; new rooms; friendly staff. **Cons:** no pool; somewhat noisy neighborhood. [$] *Rooms from: $172 ✉ 509 9th Ave., East Village ☎ 619/727–4000 🌐 www.hotelinsd.com 🛏 210 rooms, 5 suites 🍴 No meals ✥ 1:E5.*

$ B&B/INN 🏨 **Lucky D's Hostel.** A quick walk from PETCO Park and downtown bars, this hostel is a good fit for travelers content with shared bathrooms and the sounds of late-night partiers stumbling home. **Pros:** solo travelers can easily find friends here; central location; free dinner on some nights. **Cons:** can get very hot in summer; noisy; no on-site parking. [$] *Rooms from: $50 ✉ 615 8th Ave., East Village ☎ 619/595–0000*

🌐 *www.luckydshostel.com* 🛏 *35 dorms, 5 private rooms* 🍴 *Some meals* ✣ *1:E4.*

LITTLE ITALY

$ B&B/INN 🏨 **Hotel Vyvant.** You'll find more amenities at other downtown hotels but it's hard to beat this property's value and charm. **Pros:** good location; historic property; welcoming staff. **Cons:** some shared baths; no parking. [$] *Rooms from: $139* ✉ *505 W. Grape St., Little Italy* ☎ *619/230–1600, 800/518–9930* 🌐 *www.hotelvyvant.com* 🛏 *21 rooms, 2 suites* 🍴 *Breakfast* ✣ *1:C1.*

$ HOTEL 🏨 **Porto Vista Hotel & Suites.** This former budget motel has transformed into a contemporary hotel-motel with updated furnishings, a stylish restaurant and lounge, and a fitness center. **Pros:** new decor in common areas, some guest rooms, and the fitness center; airport shuttle. **Cons:** spotty service; small rooms, some still in need of updating. [$] *Rooms from: $149* ✉ *1835 Columbia St., Little Italy* ☎ *619/544–0164* 🌐 *www.portovistasd.com* 🛏 *198 rooms, 6 suites* 🍴 *No meals* ✣ *1:C2.*

EMBARCADERO

$$ HOTEL 🏨 **Embassy Suites–San Diego Bay.** The front door of each spacious, contemporary suite here opens out onto a 12-story atrium. **Pros:** harbor-facing rooms have spectacular views; spacious accommodations; good location. **Cons:** busy area; wildly varying rates. [$] *Rooms from: $200* ✉ *601 Pacific Hwy., Embarcadero* ☎ *619/239–2400, 800/362–2779* 🌐 *www.sandiegobay.embassysuites.com* 🛏 *341 suites* 🍴 *Breakfast* ✣ *1:B4.*

$$$ HOTEL FAMILY 🏨 **Manchester Grand Hyatt San Diego.** Primarily for business travelers, this hotel between Seaport Village and the convention center is San Diego's largest, and its 33- and 40-story towers make it the West Coast's tallest waterfront hotel. **Pros:** great views; conference facilities; good location; spacious rooms. **Cons:** very busy; some trolley noise. [$] *Rooms from: $239* ✉ *1 Market Pl., Embarcadero* ☎ *619/232–1234, 800/233–1234* 🌐 *www.manchestergrand.hyatt.com* 🛏 *1,552 rooms, 76 suites* 🍴 *No meals* ✣ *1:C5.*

BALBOA PARK AND BANKERS HILL

Balboa Park is the nation's largest urban cultural park; among locals, it's the "Soul of San Diego." Home to museums, theaters, gardens, and the San Diego Zoo, the 1,200-acre park is an attraction for locals and tourists alike. Located just across Balboa Park's Cabrillo Bridge, neighboring Bankers Hill has few lodging options but it has a thriving dining scene and can serve as a centrally located home base for sightseeing around the city.

BANKERS HILL

$$ HOTEL 🏨 **Inn at the Park.** The original 1926 ceiling graces the lobby of this historic hotel within walking distance of Balboa Park and the San Diego Zoo. **Pros:** spacious rooms; full kitchens; free Wi-Fi. **Cons:** valet parking only; two-night minimum stay; no on-site restaurants. [$] *Rooms from: $159* ✉ *525 Spruce St., Bankers Hill* ☎ *619/291–0999* 🌐 *www.shellhospitality.com/Inn-at-the-Park* 🛏 *82 suites* 🍴 *No meals* ✣ *2:E5.*

OLD TOWN, MISSION VALLEY, AND NORTH PARK

San Diego's Uptown area is close to the San Diego Zoo and Balboa Park, and includes the neighborhoods of Hillcrest, Mission Hills, Bankers Hill, North Park, and University Heights. There are few hotels, but the area offers pedestrian-friendly shopping and many of San Diego's venerable craft beer bars and breweries.

Dense with Mexican eateries, Old Town is the place to be for quick and easy access to house-made tortillas. The neighborhood is also home to historic adobe shops and museums. East of Old Town is Mission Valley, a suburban maze of freeways, shopping centers, and Hotel Circle, where many spacious and inexpensive lodging options are located.

OLD TOWN

$ HOTEL FAMILY **Best Western Plus Hacienda Hotel–Old Town.** Perched on a hill in the heart of Old Town, this hotel is known for its expansive courtyards, outdoor fountains, and maze of stairs that connect eight buildings of guest rooms. **Pros:** airport shuttle; well-maintained outdoor areas. **Cons:** some rooms need renovating; spotty service; complicated layout. [$] *Rooms from: $129* ✉ *4041 Harney St., Old Town* ☎ *619/298–4707* 🌐 *www.haciendahotel-oldtown.com* 🛏 *178 rooms, 20 suites* 🍴 *No meals* ✥ *2:A4.*

$$ B&B/INN **The Cosmopolitan Hotel.** With antique furniture, pull-chain toilets, and a veranda overlooking Old Town State Historic Park, the Cosmo offers guests a taste of Victorian-era living. **Pros:** historic charm; huge suites; romantic. **Cons:** no TVs; limited on-site parking. [$] *Rooms from: $159* ✉ *2660 Calhoun St., Old Town* ☎ *619/297–1874* 🌐 *www.oldtowncosmopolitan.com* 🛏 *6 rooms, 4 suites* 🍴 *Breakfast* ✥ *2:A4.*

$ HOTEL **Holiday Inn Express Airport–Old Town.** Already an excellent value for Old Town, this cheerful property throws in such perks as a free breakfast buffet. **Pros:** good location; hot continental breakfast; few add-on fees. **Cons:** some freeway noise; few nightlife options. [$] *Rooms from: $110* ✉ *1955 San Diego Ave., Old Town* ☎ *619/543–1130, 877/834–3613* 🌐 *www.hiexpress.com* 🛏 *116 rooms, 7 suites* 🍴 *Breakfast* ✥ *2:B5.*

MISSION VALLEY

$ HOTEL FAMILY Fodor's Choice ★ **Courtyard by Marriott Mission Valley.** Amenities abound for families seeking a fun and casual base for trips to SeaWorld and the zoo. **Pros:** easy freeway access to area attractions; good value; nice perks for families and business travelers. **Cons:** few stores and restaurants in walking distance; halls can be noisy with kids. [$] *Rooms from: $149* ✉ *595 Hotel Circle S, Mission Valley* ☎ *619/291–5720, 800/321–2211* 🌐 *www.courtyardsd.com* 🛏 *309 rooms, 8 suites* 🍴 *No meals* ✥ *2:D3.*

$$ HOTEL **Doubletree Hotel San Diego Mission Valley.** Near the Fashion Valley shopping mall and adjacent to the Hazard Center—which has a seven-screen movie theater, four major restaurants, and more than 20 shops—the Doubletree is also convenient to Route 163 and I–8. **Pros:** stellar service; large rooms; good for fitness buffs. **Cons:** dated bathrooms; unimpressive views. [$] *Rooms from: $199* ✉ *7450 Hazard Center Dr.* ☎ *619/297–5466, 800/222–8733* 🌐 *www.doubletree.com* 🛏 *300 rooms, 3 suites* 🍴 *No meals* ✥ *2:D2.*

$ 🏨 **Crowne Plaza San Diego.** Clean
HOTEL and comfortable, the Crowne Plaza may not have the frills of downtown hotels and coastal resorts, but it's a reliable pick for budget-minded families. **Pros:** near shopping; free shuttles; lush grounds. **Cons:** near freeway; dated public areas. $ *Rooms from: $137* ⊠ *2270 Hotel Circle N, Mission Valley* ☎ *619/297–1101* ⊕ *www.cp-sandiego.com* ➥ *405 rooms, 11 suites* ⦿ *No meals* ✢ *2:B3.*

WORD OF MOUTH

"One of the great things to enjoy about San Diego is its ocean and bay views. Shelter Island, Harbor Island, and Mission Bay fit the bill. They would be central so you can get to sites quickly and they provide a location where you can get the kids outside for those few minutes." —travelbuggie

NORTH PARK

$ 🏨 **Balboa Park Inn.** Located on the edge of Balboa Park between the Hill-
B&B/INN crest and North Park neighborhoods, this budget guesthouse occupies four Spanish colonial–style 1915 residences connected by courtyards. **Pros:** good value; convenient location; continental breakfast. **Cons:** no parking; no on-site services; busy area. $ *Rooms from: $99* ⊠ *3402 Park Blvd., North Park* ☎ *619/298–0823, 800/938–8181* ⊕ *www.balboaparkinn.com* ➥ *26 suites* ⦿ *Breakfast* ✢ *2:F5.*

MISSION BAY, BEACHES, AND SEAWORLD

Mission Bay Park, with its beaches, bike trails, boat-launching ramps, golf course, and grassy parks—not to mention SeaWorld—is a haven of hotels and resorts. Smaller hotels, motels, and hostels can be found nearby in Mission Beach and Pacific Beach. These coastal communities are popular among local twentysomethings for the many inexpensive dining and nightlife possibilities. The streets are also filled with surf shops and boutiques for picking up flip-flops, sundresses, and other beachy souvenirs. You can't go wrong with any of these beachfront areas, as long as the frenzied crowds at play don't bother you.

9

MISSION BAY

$$ 🏨 **The Dana on Mission Bay.** This waterfront resort down the road from
RESORT SeaWorld has an ideal location for active leisure travelers. **Pros:** water
FAMILY views; many outdoor activities. **Cons:** some rooms need renovation; many children in common areas. $ *Rooms from: $159* ⊠ *1710 W. Mission Bay Dr., Mission Bay* ☎ *619/222–6440, 800/445–3339* ⊕ *www.thedana.com* ➥ *259 rooms, 12 suites* ⦿ *No meals* ✢ *3:C6.*

$$$ 🏨 **Hyatt Regency Mission Bay Spa & Marina.** This modern property has
RESORT many desirable amenities, including balconies with excellent views of
FAMILY the garden, bay, ocean, or swimming pool courtyard. **Pros:** close proximity to water sports; 120-foot waterslides in pools, plus kiddie slide. **Cons:** slightly hard to navigate surrounding roads; thin walls; not centrally located. $ *Rooms from: $299* ⊠ *1441 Quivira Rd., Mission Bay* ☎ *619/224–1234, 800/233–1234* ⊕ *www.missionbay.hyatt.com* ➥ *300 rooms, 129 suites* ⦿ *No meals* ✢ *3:C6.*

$$$ ⊤ **Paradise Point Resort & Spa.** Minutes from SeaWorld but hidden in a
RESORT   quiet part of Mission Bay, the beautiful landscape of this 44-acre resort
FAMILY   offers plenty of space for families to play and relax. **Pros:** water views;
pools; good service. **Cons:** not centrally located; motel-thin walls; park-
ing and resort fees. $ *Rooms from: $279* ⊠ *1404 Vacation Rd., Mis-
sion Bay* ☎ *858/274–4630, 800/344–2626* ⊕ *www.paradisepoint.com*
↪ *462 cottages* ⊙| *No meals* ⊹ *3:C6.*

MISSION BEACH

$$$ ⊤ **Catamaran Resort Hotel.** Tiki torches light the way through grounds
RESORT   thick with tropical foliage to the six two-story buildings and the 14-story
FAMILY   high-rise on Mission Bay. **Pros:** spa; bay views; many activities for kids.
Cons: common areas need renovating; dated room decor. $ *Rooms
from: $249* ⊠ *3999 Mission Blvd., Mission Beach* ☎ *858/488–1081,
800/422–8386* ⊕ *www.catamaranresort.com* ↪ *262 rooms, 50 suites*
⊙| *No meals* ⊹ *3:C5.*

PACIFIC BEACH

$$ ⊤ **Crystal Pier Hotel and Cottages.** Rustic little oases with a charm all their
HOTEL   own, the beachy cottages may lack some of the amenities of compara-
bly priced hotels, but you're paying for character and proximity to the
ocean—these lodgings are literally on the pier. **Pros:** ocean view; historic
lodgings; free parking. **Cons:** few amenities; no air-conditioning in most;
reservations fill up fast. $ *Rooms from: $175* ⊠ *4500 Ocean Blvd.,
Pacific Beach* ☎ *800/748–5894, 858/483–6983* ⊕ *www.crystalpier.com*
↪ *23 cottages, 6 suites* ⊙| *No meals* ⊹ *3:B5.*

$$$$ ⊤ **Pacific Terrace Hotel.** Travelers love this terrific beachfront hotel and
RESORT   the ocean views from most rooms; it's a perfect place for watching sun-
sets over the Pacific. **Pros:** beach views; large rooms; friendly service.
Cons: busy and sometimes noisy area; lots of traffic. $ *Rooms from:
$428* ⊠ *610 Diamond St., Pacific Beach* ☎ *858/581–3500, 800/344–
3370* ⊕ *www.pacificterrace.com* ↪ *61 rooms, 12 suites* ⊙| *No meals*
⊹ *3:B5.*

$$ ⊤ **Surfer Beach Hotel.** Choose this place for its great location—right on
HOTEL   bustling Pacific Beach. **Pros:** beach location; ocean-view rooms; pool.
Cons: dated rooms; no air-conditioning. $ *Rooms from: $219* ⊠ *711
Pacific Beach Dr., Pacific Beach* ☎ *858/483–7070, 800/787–3373*
⊕ *www.surferbeachhotel.com* ↪ *53 rooms, 16 suites* ⊙| *No meals*
⊹ *3:C5.*

$$$ ⊤ **Tower23.** A neomodern masterpiece with a beachy vibe, this boutique
HOTEL   hotel is a favorite of the young and young-at-heart. **Pros:** beach views;
central location; hip decor. **Cons:** no pool; busy area. $ *Rooms from:
$259* ⊠ *723 Felspar St., Pacific Beach* ☎ *866/869–3723, 858/270–2323*
⊕ *www.t23hotel.com* ↪ *38 rooms, 6 suites* ⊙| *No meals* ⊹ *3:B5.*

LA JOLLA

Multimillion-dollar homes line the beaches and hillsides of beauti-
ful and prestigious La Jolla, a community about 20 minutes north
of downtown. La Jolla Shores is a mile-long sandy beach that gets
crowded in summer with kayakers, sunbathers, and students in scuba-
diving classes. The village—the heart of La Jolla—is chockablock with

expensive boutiques, art galleries, restaurants, and a grassy beachfront park that's popular for picnics and weddings.

$$ HOTEL **Empress Hotel.** Less glitzy than neighboring lodging options in La Jolla, the five-story Empress attracts business travelers and couples looking for a basic but comfortable place to stay. **Pros:** well-trained staff; near shops and restaurants; quiet street. **Cons:** not exciting for kids; some travelers report that noise carries between the thin walls. [$] *Rooms from: $159* ✉ *7766 Fay Ave., La Jolla* ☎ *858/454–3001, 888/369–9900* 🌐 *www.empress-hotel.com* 🛏 *69 rooms, 4 suites* 🍴 *Breakfast* ✥ *3:A2.*

$$ RESORT **Estancia La Jolla Hotel & Spa.** With its rambling California mission–style architecture and brilliant gardens, this resort on what once was a famous equestrian ranch exudes rustic elegance. **Pros:** upscale rooms; nice spa; landscaped grounds. **Cons:** mandatory resort fees; not centrally located. [$] *Rooms from: $219* ✉ *9700 N. Torrey Pines Rd., La Jolla* ☎ *858/550–1000, 877/437–8262* 🌐 *www.estancialajolla.com* 🛏 *200 rooms, 10 suites* 🍴 *No meals* ✥ *3:B1.*

$$$$ HOTEL Fodor's Choice ★ **Grande Colonial.** This white wedding cake–style hotel in the heart of La Jolla village has ocean views and charming European details that include chandeliers, mahogany railings, and French doors. **Pros:** near shopping; near beach; superb restaurant. **Cons:** somewhat busy street; no fitness center. [$] *Rooms from: $319* ✉ *910 Prospect St., La Jolla* ☎ *858/454–2181, 877/792–8053* 🌐 *www.thegrandecolonial.com* 🛏 *52 rooms, 41 suites* 🍴 *No meals* ✥ *3:A2.*

$$ HOTEL **Hilton La Jolla Torrey Pines.** Blending discreetly into the Torrey Pines cliff top, the hotel overlooks the Pacific Ocean and the 18th hole of the Torrey Pines Golf Course, the future site of the 2021 U.S. Open. **Pros:** ocean view; near golf; large rooms. **Cons:** not centrally located; restaurant could be improved. [$] *Rooms from: $202* ✉ *10950 N. Torrey Pines Rd., La Jolla* ☎ *800/774–1500, 858/558–1500* 🌐 *www.hiltonlajollatorreypines.com* 🛏 *382 rooms, 12 suites* 🍴 *No meals* ✥ *3:B1.*

$$ HOTEL **Hotel La Jolla.** This coastal-chic hotel boasts sparkling views of the Pacific and an excellent 11th-floor restaurant, Cusp Dining & Drinks. **Pros:** new rooms; stunning views from the higher floors. **Cons:** tiny gym; valet parking only. [$] *Rooms from: $209* ✉ *7955 La Jolla Shores Dr., La Jolla* ☎ *858/459–0261, 800/941–1149* 🌐 *www.hotellajolla.com* 🛏 *106 rooms, 4 suites* 🍴 *No meals* ✥ *3:C2.*

$$ HOTEL **Hyatt Regency La Jolla.** Popular among business travelers, this Hyatt is in the Golden Triangle area, about 10 minutes from the beach and the village of La Jolla. **Pros:** many restaurants; modern rooms; upscale amenities. **Cons:** busy hotel; not centrally located. [$] *Rooms from: $209* ✉ *Aventine Center, 3777 La Jolla Village Dr., La Jolla* ☎ *800/233–1234, 858/552–1234* 🌐 *www.hyattregencylajolla.com* 🛏 *395 rooms, 24 suites* 🍴 *No meals* ✥ *3:D1.*

$$ HOTEL **La Jolla Cove Suites.** It may lack the charm of some properties in this exclusive area, but this motel with studios and suites (some with spacious oceanfront balconies) gives its guests the same first-class views of La Jolla Cove at lower rates. **Pros:** good value; ocean views; some large rooms. **Cons:** dated rooms; busy street. [$] *Rooms from: $179*

9

LODGING ALTERNATIVES

APARTMENT RENTALS

Travelers planning on more than a weekend with Shamu can find a variety of apartment and hotel options suitable for extended stays. Some of these properties also work well for larger families and groups looking for shared accommodations with full kitchens and eating areas.

If you're sticking to hotels, many properties with suites offer special weekly and monthly rates, especially during the off-season. Downtown's **Marriott Residence Inn** has studios and one-bedroom suites with full-size refrigerators and two-burner stoves. **Homewood Suites San Diego Airport** offers a similar setup; the hotel also has two-bedroom suites and offers complimentary grocery shopping service and light dinner receptions on weeknights. Less expensive options include **500 West**, a no-frills property offering a shared kitchen, laundry facilities, and social hostel-like common areas, and **Lucky D's Hostel**, a casual home away from home for international students and young travelers looking for an inexpensive place to stay for a week or two.

Oakwood Apartments rents comfortable furnished apartments in several popular neighborhoods with housekeeping services and linens; there's a one-week to 30-day minimum stay depending on locations. Parking can be difficult in some of these areas, so be sure to ask about private parking and any associated fees.

Many travelers recommend the online **Vacation Rentals by Owner** (VRBO) and **Airbnb** directories for condos and beach houses that owners rent directly to individuals.

Renting directly from an owner can be the most cost-effective option but there are risks involved. To avoid a dud, ask owners for referrals from previous renters and be sure to review the sites' cancellation and refund policies.

Oakwood Apartments (☎ 877/902–0832 ⊕ www.oakwood. com). **Vacation Rentals by Owner** (⊕ www.vrbo.com). **Airbnb** (⊕ www. airbnb.com)

BED-AND-BREAKFASTS

San Diego is known more for its resorts and chain properties, but the city has several bed-and-breakfasts, most of which are in private homes and are well maintained and accommodating. Travelers hoping to stay in the Uptown neighborhoods near Balboa Park may find that bed-and-breakfasts are their best bet because there are few recommendable hotels but many activities and restaurants are within walking distance. The website for the San Diego Bed & Breakfast Guild lists a number of high-quality inns, including several historic sites. The California Association of Boutique and Breakfast Inns also maintains a website with listings for small boutique properties.

San Diego Bed & Breakfast Guild (☎ 619/523–1300 ⊕ www. bandbguildsandiego.org). **California Association of Boutique and Breakfast Inns** (☎ 800/373–9251 ⊕ www.cabbi.com).

✉ *1155 Coast Blvd., La Jolla* ☎ *858/459–2621, 888/525–6552* ⊕ *www.lajollacove.com* ⌨ *25 rooms, 90 suites* ⏸ *Breakfast* ✛ *3:B2.*

$$$ ⌂ **La Jolla Shores Hotel.** One of San Diego's few hotels actually on the
HOTEL beach, this property is part of La Jolla Beach and Tennis Club. **Pros:**
FAMILY on beach; great views; quiet area. **Cons:** not centrally located; pool
can be noisy. $ *Rooms from: $279* ✉ *8110 Camino del Oro, La Jolla*
☎ *858/459–8271, 877/346–6714* ⊕ *www.ljshoreshotel.com* ⌨ *127
rooms, 1 suite* ⏸ *No meals* ✛ *3:B2.*

$$$$ ⌂ **La Valencia.** This pink Spanish-Mediterranean confection drew Hol-
HOTEL lywood film stars in the 1930s and '40s with its setting and views of
La Jolla Cove; now it draws the Kardashians. **Pros:** upscale rooms;
views; near beach. **Cons:** standard rooms are tiny; lots of traffic outside.
$ *Rooms from: $380* ✉ *1132 Prospect St., La Jolla* ☎ *858/454–0771,
800/451–0772* ⊕ *www.lavalencia.com* ⌨ *82 rooms, 15 villas, 15 suites*
⏸ *No meals* ✛ *3:B2.*

$$$$ ⌂ **Lodge at Torrey Pines.** This beautiful Craftsman-style lodge sits on
RESORT a bluff between La Jolla and Del Mar and commands a coastal view.
Fodor's Choice **Pros:** spacious upscale rooms; good service; adjacent the famed Torrey
★ Pines Golf Course. **Cons:** not centrally located; expensive. $ *Rooms
from: $450* ✉ *11480 N. Torrey Pines Rd., La Jolla* ☎ *858/453–4420,
888/826–0224* ⊕ *www.lodgetorreypines.com* ⌨ *169 rooms, 8 suites*
⏸ *No meals* ✛ *3:B1.*

$$$$ ⌂ **Pantai Inn.** Located along La Jolla coastline with ocean views from
HOTEL almost every corner, this sophisticated, Bali-inspired inn offers a mix
of studios, one- and two-bedroom suites, cottages, and townhomes.
Pros: spacious rooms; ocean views; free parking. **Cons:** no pool; no
fitness center. $ *Rooms from: $350* ✉ *1003 Coast Blvd., La Jolla*
☎ *858/224–7600, 855/287–2682* ⊕ *www.pantai.com* ⌨ *7 rooms, 24
suites* ⏸ *Breakfast* ✛ *3:A2.*

$$$ ⌂ **Scripps Inn.** You'd be wise to make reservations well in advance for
B&B/INN this small, quiet inn tucked away on Coast Boulevard; its popularity
with repeat visitors ensures that it's booked year-round. **Pros:** beach
access; intimate feel; inexpensive parking. **Cons:** thin walls; motel layout; busy area. $ *Rooms from: $230* ✉ *555 S. Coast Blvd., La Jolla*
☎ *858/454–3391, 888/976–2912* ⊕ *www.scrippsinn.com* ⌨ *7 rooms,
7 suites* ⏸ *Breakfast* ✛ *3:A2.*

POINT LOMA AND CORONADO WITH HARBOR AND SHELTER ISLANDS

Coronado feels like something out of an earlier, more gracious era, making it a great getaway. The clean white beaches are some of the best in
the state, and they're rarely crowded. But if you plan to see many of
San Diego's attractions, you'll spend significant time commuting across
the bridge or riding the ferry.

Harbor Island and Shelter Island, two man-made peninsulas between
downtown and Point Loma, have grassy parks, tree-lined paths, and
views of the downtown skyline. Closer to downtown, Harbor Island is
less than five minutes from the airport. Shelter Island is next to Point
Loma, a hilly community that's home to Cabrillo National Monument,

a naval base, and a growing destination for shopping and dining called NTC Liberty Station.

POINT LOMA

$$ **Courtyard by Marriott San Diego Airport.** Close to the restaurants and
HOTEL   shops of Liberty Station, this family-friendly hotel spares travelers the
FAMILY   extra fees charged by most downtown and coastal lodgings. **Pros:** modern rooms; near airport; friendly service; free parking. **Cons:** unimpressive views. $ *Rooms from: $200* ⊠ *2592 Laning Rd., Point Loma* ☎ *619/221–1900, 888/236–2427* ⊕ *www.marriott.com/sanal* ⟿ *197 rooms, 3 suites* ¶⊙¶ *No meals* ✛ *4:C1.*

$$ **Holiday Inn Bayside.** If SeaWorld and the San Diego Zoo aren't enough
HOTEL   to sap kids of their energy, the outdoor activities at this hotel across
FAMILY   from San Diego Bay fishing docks should do the trick. **Pros:** great for kids; close to airport. **Cons:** some dated rooms; confusing layout; not centrally located. $ *Rooms from: $170* ⊠ *4875 N. Harbor Dr., Point Loma* ☎ *619/224–3621, 800/662–8899* ⊕ *www.holinnbayside.com* ⟿ *275 rooms, 16 suites* ¶⊙¶ *No meals* ✛ *4:C1.*

$$ **Holiday Inn Express–SeaWorld Area.** In Point Loma near the West Mis-
HOTEL   sion Bay exit off I–8, this is a surprisingly cute and quiet lodging option
FAMILY   despite proximity to bustling traffic. **Pros:** near SeaWorld; free parking; good service. **Cons:** not a scenic area; somewhat hard to find. $ *Rooms from: $160* ⊠ *3950 Jupiter St., Point Loma* ☎ *619/226–8000, 877/834–3613* ⊕ *www.seaworldhi.com* ⟿ *68 rooms, 2 suites* ¶⊙¶ *Breakfast* ✛ *4:C1.*

$$$ **Homewood Suites San Diego Airport.** Families and business travelers
HOTEL   on long trips will benefit from the space and amenities at this all-suites
FAMILY   hotel. **Pros:** complimentary grocery shopping service; free parking; close
Fodor's Choice   to paths for joggers and bikers. **Cons:** often crowded dining room; far
★   from nightlife. $ *Rooms from: $289* ⊠ *2576 Laning Rd., Point Loma* ☎ *619/222–0500* ⊕ *www.homewoodsuites.com* ⟿ *150 suites* ¶⊙¶ *Multiple meal plans* ✛ *4:C1.*

$$ **Inn at Sunset Cliffs.** At this beachfront property, you really do hear
HOTEL   the sound of waves crashing against the shore. **Pros:** romantic; breathtaking views; friendly staff. **Cons:** standard rooms are tiny; no elevator. $ *Rooms from: $175* ⊠ *1370 Sunset Cliffs Blvd., Point Loma* ☎ *619/222–7901, 866/786–2543* ⊕ *www.missionbay.hyatt.com* ⟿ *7 rooms, 17 suites* ¶⊙¶ *No meals* ✛ *4:A2.*

$ **The Pearl Hotel.** This previously vintage motel received a makeover,
HOTEL   turning it into a retro-chic hangout decorated with kitschy lamps and
Fodor's Choice   original, in-room art by local children. **Pros:** near marina; hip bar/res-
★   taurant on-site (dinner only, except for seasonal specials). **Cons:** not centrally located; one bed in rooms. $ *Rooms from: $139* ⊠ *1410 Rosecrans St., Point Loma* ☎ *619/226–6100* ⊕ *www.thepearlsd.com* ⟿ *23 rooms* ¶⊙¶ *No meals* ✛ *4:B1.*

SHELTER ISLAND

$$ **Best Western Plus Island Palms Hotel & Marina.** With tennis courts, two
HOTEL   pools, jogging paths, and complimentary bike rentals, this waterfront
FAMILY   hotel is a natural fit for fitness enthusiasts. **Pros:** near water; great room views; free tennis; private marina. **Cons:** somewhat confusing area; can be noisy. $ *Rooms from: $159* ⊠ *2051 Shelter Island Dr.,*

Shelter Island ☎ *619/222–0561, 800/922–2336* 🌐 *www.islandpalms.com* 🛏 *167 rooms, 60 suites* 🍴 *No meals* ✚ *4:B3.*

$$ RESORT 🏨 **Humphreys Half Moon Inn & Suites.** This sprawling South Seas–style resort has grassy open areas with palms and tiki torches; many of the rooms have water views. **Pros:** water views; near marina; free admission to Backstage Live music club. **Cons:** resort fee; vast property; not centrally located. [$] *Rooms from: $219* ✉ *2303 Shelter Island Dr., Shelter Island* ☎ *619/224–3411, 800/542–7400* 🌐 *www.halfmooninn.com* 🛏 *128 rooms, 54 suites* 🍴 *No meals* ✚ *4:B2.*

$$ RESORT 🏨 **Kona Kai Resort.** In 2014, a $22 multimillion renovation introduced a beachy chic vibe throughout this 11-acre property at the tip of Shelter Island. **Pros:** quiet area; near marina; water views. **Cons:** not centrally located; resort fees. [$] *Rooms from: $189* ✉ *1551 Shelter Island Dr., Shelter Island* ☎ *619/221–8000, 800/566–2524* 🌐 *www.resortkonakai.com* 🛏 *124 rooms, 5 suites* 🍴 *No meals* ✚ *4:B3.*

HARBOR ISLAND

$$ HOTEL 🏨 **Sheraton San Diego Hotel & Marina.** Of this property's two high-rises, the smaller, more intimate Bay Tower has larger rooms, with separate areas suitable for business entertaining; the more recently renovated Marina Tower has better sports facilities. **Pros:** water views; near marina and airport; free airport shuttle. **Cons:** not centrally located; some rooms show wear. [$] *Rooms from: $209* ✉ *1380 Harbor Island Dr., Harbor Island* ☎ *619/291–2900, 888/625–5144* 🌐 *www.sheratonsandiegohotel.com* 🛏 *1,001 rooms, 52 suites* 🍴 *No meals* ✚ *4:E1.*

CORONADO

$$$$ B&B/INN Fodor's Choice ★ 🏨 **1906 Lodge at Coronado Beach.** Smaller but no less luxurious than the sprawling beach resorts of Coronado, this lodge welcomes couples for romantic retreats two blocks from the ocean. **Pros:** most suites feature Jacuzzi tubs, fireplaces, and porches; historic property; free underground parking. **Cons:** too quiet for families; no pool. [$] *Rooms from: $309* ✉ *1060 Adella Ave., Coronado* ☎ *619/437–1900, 866/435–1906* 🌐 *www.1906lodge.com* 🛏 *6 rooms, 11 suites* 🍴 *Some meals* ✚ *4:G6.*

$$$ RESORT FAMILY 🏨 **Coronado Island Marriott Resort.** Near San Diego Bay, this snazzy hotel has rooms with great downtown skyline views. **Pros:** spectacular views; on-site spa; close to water taxis. **Cons:** not in downtown Coronado; difficult to find. [$] *Rooms from: $249* ✉ *2000 2nd St., Coronado* ☎ *619/435–3000, 800/228–9290* 🌐 *www.marriotthotels.com/sanci* 🛏 *273 rooms, 27 suites* 🍴 *No meals* ✚ *4:H5.*

$ B&B/INN 🏨 **Crown City Inn & Bistro.** On Coronado's main drag close to shops, restaurants, and the beach, this two-story motor inn is one of the island's best deals. **Pros:** affordable; on-site restaurant; complimentary bikes; public park across street. **Cons:** few amenities; somewhat dated rooms; a hike from downtown. [$] *Rooms from: $109* ✉ *520 Orange Ave., Coronado* ☎ *619/435–3116, 800/422–1173* 🌐 *www.crowncityinn.com* 🛏 *35 rooms* 🍴 *No meals* ✚ *4:G5.*

$$ HOTEL 🏨 **Glorietta Bay Inn.** The main building on this property is an Edwardian-style mansion built in 1908 for sugar baron John D. Spreckels, who once owned much of downtown San Diego.**Pros:** great views; friendly staff; close to beach. **Cons:** mansion rooms are small; lots of

traffic nearby. $ *Rooms from: $189* ⌧ *1630 Glorietta Blvd., Coronado* ☎ *619/435–3101, 800/283–9383* ⊕ *www.gloriettabayinn.com* ↝ *100 rooms* �‖*Breakfast* ✛ *4:G6.*

$$$$
RESORT
FAMILY
Fodor's Choice
★

⌓ **Hotel Del Coronado.** As much of a draw today as it was when it opened in 1888, the Victorian-style "Hotel Del" is always alive with activity, as guests—including U.S. presidents and celebrities—and tourists marvel at the fanciful architecture and ocean views. **Pros:** romantic; on the beach; hotel spa. **Cons:** some rooms are small; expensive dining; hectic public areas. $ *Rooms from: $329* ⌧ *1500 Orange Ave., Coronado* ☎ *800/468–3533, 619/435–6611* ⊕ *www.hoteldel.com* ↝ *679 rooms, 78 cottages and villas* �‖*No meals* ✛ *4:G6.*

$$$
RESORT
FAMILY

⌓ **Loews Coronado Bay Resort.** You can park your boat at the 80-slip marina of this romantic retreat set on a secluded 15-acre peninsula on the Silver Strand. **Pros:** great restaurants; lots of activities; all rooms have furnished balconies with water views. **Cons:** far from anything; confusing layout. $ *Rooms from: $259* ⌧ *4000 Coronado Bay Rd., Coronado* ☎ *619/424–4000, 800/815–6397* ⊕ *www.loewshotels.com/ CoronadoBay* ↝ *402 rooms, 37 suites* �‖*No meals* ✛ *4:H6.*

IMPERIAL BEACH

$$$
RESORT

⌓ **Pier South Resort.** This Marriott-affiliated resort opened in 2014 as the first and only luxury lodging option in Imperial Beach, a quiet seaside community about 12 miles south of downtown San Diego. **Pros:** steps from the sand; new rooms; contemporary design. **Cons:** tiny fitness center; not centrally located. $ *Rooms from: $229* ⌧ *800 Seacoast Dr., Imperial Beach* ☎ *619/621–5900, 888/236–2427* ⊕ *www. piersouthresort.com* ↝ *78 suites* �‖*No meals* ✛ *4:H6.*

NIGHTLIFE

Updated by
Jeff Terich

The San Diego nightlife scene has exploded in the last few years. Just a little over a decade ago, options were limited to the pricey singles-heavy dance clubs downtown, the party-hearty atmosphere of Pacific Beach, and a handful of charmingly musty neighborhood dive bars popular with locals. Since then, options in San Diego have expanded dramatically, boasting more than 90 craft breweries throughout the county, not to mention several stylish cocktail lounges.

The Gaslamp Quarter is still one of the most popular areas to go for a night on the town. Named for actual gaslights that once provided illumination along its once-seedy streets (it housed a number of gambling halls and brothels), the neighborhood bears only a trace of its debauched roots. Between the Gaslamp and nearby East Village, downtown San Diego mostly comprises chic nightclubs, tourist-heavy pubs, and a handful of live music venues. Even most of the hotels downtown have a street-level or rooftop bar—so plan on making it a late night if that's where you intend to bunk. On weekends, parking can be tricky; most lots run about $20, and though there is metered parking (free after 6 pm and all day Sunday), motorists don't give up those coveted spots so easily. Some restaurants and clubs offer valet, though that can get pricey.

Hillcrest, and to a lesser extent University Heights are both popular areas for LGBT nightlife and culture, whereas just a little bit east of Hillcrest, ever-expanding North Park features a diverse range of bars and lounges that cater to a twenty- and thirtysomething crowd, bolstering its reputation as the city's hipster capital. Nearby Normal Heights is a slightly less pretentious alternative, though whichever of these neighborhoods strikes your fancy, a cab from downtown will run about the same price: $15

Nightlife along the beaches is more of a mixed bag. Where the scene in Pacific Beach might feel like every week is Spring break, La Jolla veers toward being more cost-prohibitive. And although Point Loma is often

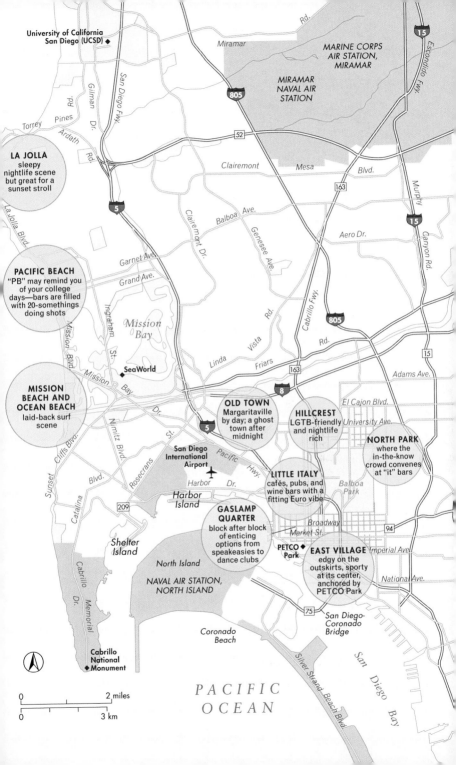

University of California
San Diego (UCSD) ◆

Rd.

Miramar

MARINE CORPS
AIR STATION,
MIRAMAR

15

Escondito Fwy.

MIRAMAR
NAVAL AIR
STATION

805

Torrey Pines

Ardath Rd.

52

Gilman Dr.

San Diego Fwy.

Clairemont   Mesa   Blvd.

LA JOLLA
sleepy
nightlife scene
but great for a
sunset stroll

163

La Jolla Blvd.

5

Clairemont Dr.

Balboa   Ave.

Genesee Ave.

Aero Dr.

15

Murphy Canyon Rd.

PACIFIC BEACH
"PB" may remind you
of your college
days—bars are filled
with 20-somethings
doing shots

Garnet Ave.

Grand Ave.

Ingraham St.

**Mission
Bay**

Vista   Rd.

Cabrillo Fwy.

Linda   Friars   Rd.

805

Mission Blvd.

Mission Bay Dr.

◆ SeaWorld

163

**MISSION
BEACH AND
OCEAN BEACH**
laid-back surf
scene

Sunset Cliffs Blvd.

Nimitz Blvd.

5

8

OLD TOWN
Margaritaville
by day; a ghost
town after
midnight

HILLCREST
LGTB-friendly
and nightlife
rich

El Cajon Blvd.

University Ave.

Adams Ave.

NORTH PARK
where the
in-the-know
crowd convenes
at "it" bars

Catalina   Blvd.

Rosecrans St.

San Diego
International
Airport ✈

Pacific   Hwy.

LITTLE ITALY
cafés, pubs, and
wine bars with a
fitting Euro vibe

Balboa
Park

209

Harbor Dr.

Harbor
Island

**GASLAMP
QUARTER**
block after block
of enticing
options from
speakeasies to
dance clubs

Broadway

Market St.

94

Cabrillo Memorial Dr.

Shelter
Island

PETCO ◆
Park

EAST VILLAGE
edgy on the
outskirts, sporty
at its center,
anchored by
PETCO Park

Imperial Ave.

National Ave.

North Island

NAVAL AIR STATION,
NORTH ISLAND

75

San Diego-
Coronado
Bridge

San Diego Bay

◆ Cabrillo
National
Monument

Coronado
Beach

Silver Strand Beach Blvd.

0 ———— 2 miles
0 ———— 3 km

PACIFIC
OCEAN

seen as a sleeper neighborhood in terms of nightlife, it's coming into its own with some select destinations.

If your drink involves caffeine and not alcohol, there's no shortage of coffeehouses in San Diego, and some of the better ones in Hillcrest and North Park stay open past midnight. Many of them also serve beer and wine, if the caffeine buzz isn't enough.

And if you're up for a drive, head to North County for seaside drinks or live music, including the Belly Up Tavern, which has one of the best sound systems in the county, and an impressive line-up of talent on its calendar. *(For more info look in the North County destination listings.)*

PLANNING

THE LOWDOWN

Dolled up and set to paint the town red? Remember these important tips before your night out:

Step outside to smoke. Many clubs and bars allow e-cigarettes or vaporizer pens, however, as is true everywhere these days, avoid puffing real smoke indoors.

What to wear. In the Gaslamp, East Village and some of North Park's more upscale spots, dress code is strictly enforced: no flip-flops, ball-caps, jerseys, or shorts at any of the city's swankier bars.

Last call for alcohol. The last chance for nightcaps is theoretically 2 am, but most bars stop serving around 1:30. Listen for the bartender's announcement.

WHAT'S GOING ON?

Do your homework before you hit the town. Scour local resources for nightly entertainment to get the scoop on what's happening that night.

The city's daily paper, *U-T San Diego* (⊕ *www.utsandiego.com*), has up-to-date entertainment listings, as well as the paper's more nightlife-heavy sister site *DiscoverSD* (⊕ *www.discoversd.com*), which provides event listings and editorial suggestions. San Diego has two alt-weeklies, of which *The Reader* (⊕ *www.sandiegoreader.com*) boasts more extensive online listings, from tiny shows to huge festivals. *San Diego City-Beat* (⊕ *sdcitybeat.com*) is more selective with its recommendations, highlighting the edgier and more innovative cultural events.

San Diego magazine (⊕ *www.sandiegomagazine.com*) is a mainstream read for all walks of life; *Riviera* (⊕ *sandiego.modernluxury.com*) is younger, more upscale, and au courant. Both glossy monthlies have calendar sections and tips on topics such as haute nightlife attire and the hottest DJs.

Head to SDDialedIn (⊕ *sddialedin.com*) for concert and music listings.

NIGHTLIFE BY NEIGHBORHOOD

DOWNTOWN

GASLAMP QUARTER

Partygoers line up behind velvet ropes to dance inside downtown's most exclusive clubs.

BARS

Altitude Sky Lounge. Location is everything at this sophisticated lounge on the roof of the 22-floor San Diego Marriott Gaslamp Quarter. The views of the downtown skyline and PETCO Park will give you a natural high. ✉ *660 K St., Gaslamp Quarter* ☎ *619/446–6086* ⊕ *www.altitudeskylounge.com.*

barleymash. A gigantic newcomer to the Gaslamp can resemble either a raucous club or a sports bar, depending on what night you're there. But the drinks are strong and reasonably priced, and the reclaimed wood decor makes for an intimate atmosphere, even when the DJs are spinning mostly Top 40. ✉ *600 5th Ave., Gaslamp Quarter* ☎ *619/255–7373* ⊕ *www.barleymash.com.*

Hard Rock Hotel. A-list wannabes (and a few real celebs) gather in two bars, the loungey 207 off the lobby and the rooftop Float. The latter's Intervention and Wintervention daytime parties feature some of the world's biggest DJ names, or if you prefer a rock show, head to Maryjane's Underground or Third Thursdays at 207. Maybe you can't be a rock star, but you might as well party like one. Just be prepared to spend like one, too. ✉ *207 5th Ave., Gaslamp Quarter* ☎ *619/764–6924* ⊕ *hardrockhotelsd.com.*

La Puerta. This Mexican-theme bar and restaurant is great for late-night eats (the kitchen is open until 1 am), but also has DJs seven nights a week and some of the best margaritas in the city. If you're looking for an unrivaled tequila selection, there are literally hundreds to choose from. ✉ *560 4th Ave., Gaslamp Quarter* ☎ *619/696–3466* ⊕ *www.lapuertasd.com.*

LOUNGEsix. The trendy poolside bar on the fourth floor of the swank Hotel Solamar is a sexy spot to people-watch while sipping sangria or chili–mango margaritas and noshing on snacks from the "slow food" menu. On cool evenings, reserve a cabana or warm up next to one of the roaring fire pits. ✉ *435 6th Ave., Gaslamp Quarter* ☎ *619/531–8744* ⊕ *www.jsixrestaurant.com.*

Patrick's II. Patrons enjoy live jazz, blues, soul, and rock in this intimate Irish-theme setting, although actual Irish music is—ironically—somewhat rare. ✉ *428 F St., Gaslamp Quarter* ☎ *619/233–3077* ⊕ *patricksgaslamppub.com/.*

Prohibition. This underground jazz lounge lives up to its name with a slinky speakeasy style. Red lighting, dark wood, and leather tufted couches provide a cozy 1920s–'30s-inspired backdrop to the live jazz on weekends. ✉ *548 5th Ave., Gaslamp Quarter* ☎ *619/663–5485* ⊕ *prohibitionsd.com.*

10

Altitude Sky Lounge, atop the Marriott Gaslamp Quarter, keeps things hot with fire pits on chilly nights.

Quality Social. It's been open several years, but this large, industrial-designed space recently got a shot in its proverbial after-dark arm thanks to a new booker who's been bringing in the best local DJs to spin a mix of house and electro remixes. What you won't hear? The sign on the side of the DJ booth says it all: "No Hip-Hop. No Dubstep. No LMFAO." ⊠ *789 6th Ave., Gaslamp Quarter* ☎ *619/501–7675* ⊕ *www.qualitysocial.com.*

Fodor's Choice ★ **Rooftop 600 @Andaz.** At this rooftop bar and lounge atop the Andaz hotel, a fashionable crowd sips cocktails poolside while gazing at gorgeous views of the city. Thursday through Saturday, the scene heats up with a DJ spinning dance music, while velvet ropes and VIP bottle service please the A-listers (like Prince Harry) in the crowd. ⊠ *600 F St., Gaslamp Quarter* ☎ *619/849–1234* ⊕ *www.rooftop600.com.*

Side Bar. One of San Diego's premier clubs has a "more is more" decor and an attitude to match. Painted birdcages hang from the loft ceiling and DJs spin from inside a giant cage, which also provides sturdy scaffolding for female go-go dancers on weekends. The black-clad chandeliers and mismatched velvet couches (including one that once belonged to Paris Hilton) get an additional visual pop from the nudie paintings lining the walls. Fancy martinis are a must, and if you get hungry after last call, step next door to get some NYC-style pizza at Ciro's, open till 3 am. ⊠ *536 Market St., Gaslamp Quarter* ☎ *619/696–0946* ⊕ *www.sidebarsd.com.*

SummerSalt Rooftop Lounge @ Hotel Palomar. The fourth-floor rooftop of the Hotel Palomar remains a go-to spot for posh party people who don't mind dropping big money for a poolside cabana. Note, though, that the music shuts down after midnight. Those looking for a more nuanced and romantic setting should seek out the plush leather couches and craft cocktails at the lobby-side Saltbox bar. ✉ *1047 5th Ave., Gaslamp Quarter* ☎ *619/515–3000* ⊕ *www. hotelpalomar-sandiego.com.*

Tivoli. Rumor has it that Wyatt Earp himself threw back a whiskey or two at the oldest bar in the Gaslamp, way before the walls were lined with neon beer signs. Perhaps old age accounts for the grungy veneer, but that doesn't stop locals from hitting this dive for $9 pitchers of PBR and hot dogs. The jukebox and pool table keep the unruly in check. Is that a spittoon in the corner? ✉ *505 6th Ave., Gaslamp Quarter* ☎ *619/232–6754* ⊕ *www. tivolibargrill.com.*

COCKTAILS WITH A VIEW

Take in the sun and San Diego skyline while having a drink at the city's best rooftop bars.

ROOFTOP BARS

Altitude Skybar (Gaslamp Quarter)

Cannonball (Mission Beach)

Level 9 @ Hotel Indigo (East Village)

LOUNGEsix (Gaslamp Quarter)

Rooftop 600 @ Andaz (Gaslamp Quarter)

Stingaree (Gaslamp Quarter)

Top of the Park (Hillcrest)

Whiskey Girl. A major stop on the bachelorette party circuit sports a spiffy karaoke and photo booth, a Pop Art–inspired interior, and DJs spinning '80s and Top 40 almost every night. This is also a solid choice for grabbing some bar grub and watching a game. ✉ *702 5th Ave., Gaslamp Quarter* ☎ *619/236–1616* ⊕ *www.whiskeygirl.com.*

Yard House. It's a chain, yes, but you can't really go wrong with more than 100 beers on tap—billed as the world's largest selection of draft beer. With a backdrop of classic rock and an unbeatable downtown location, Yard House goes the distance. ✉ *1023 4th Ave., Gaslamp Quarter* ☎ *619/233–9273* ⊕ *www.yardhouse.com.*

COFFEEHOUSES

Fumari Hookah Lounge. This relaxed café is a dark and cozy spot for smoking from a water pipe—the richly flavored tobaccos are worth the exorbitant price tag (around $20 for a bowl, except during the nightly happy hour from 7 to 8). The chill ambience makes it easy to hang out and blow smoke rings all night, and desserts, coffee, and beer are also on offer. ✉ *330 G St., Gaslamp Quarter* ☎ *619/501–0613* ⊕ *www. fumari.com.*

COMEDY AND CABARET

American Comedy Co. At this underground space modeled after the legendary comedy clubs in New York, there's not a bad seat in the house—which is especially great since the venue pulls in some of the hugest names in stand-up comedy. ✉ *818 B 6th Ave., Gaslamp Quarter* ☎ *619/795–3858* ⊕ *www.americancomedyco.com.*

10

DANCE CLUBS

Fluxx. Arguably the hottest club in the Gaslamp, this Vegas-style, multitheme space is packed to the gills on weekends with pretty people dancing to house and electro music and dropping major cash at the bar. ■TIP→ Get here early for a lower cover and to avoid the epic lines that snake around the block. ✉ *500 4th Ave., Gaslamp Quarter* ☎ *619/232–8100* ⊕ *www.fluxxsd.com.*

Sevilla. For more than two decades, Cafe Sevilla and the Sevilla nightclub have brought a Latin flavor to the Gaslamp Quarter through a mix of contemporary and traditional Spanish and Latin American music. Get fueled up at the tapas bar before venturing downstairs for dancing. Salsa lessons during the week provide an especially memorable experience. ✉ *353 5th Ave., Gaslamp Quarter* ☎ *619/233–5979* ⊕ *sevillanightclub.com.*

Stingaree. One could argue that Stingaree was the Gaslamp's first megaclub and, almost a decade later, it's still going strong. Guests can enjoy electro and Top 40 in the main nightclub, a smashing three-story space with translucent "floating" staircases and floor-to-ceiling water walls. Dress nicely. The air of exclusivity at this hangout is palpable, and to reinforce the point, the drink prices are steep. ✉ *454 6th Ave., at Island St., Gaslamp Quarter* ☎ *619/544–9500* ⊕ *www.stingsandiego.com.*

OFF THE BEATEN PATH **Kava Lounge.** This free-spirited underground dance club a short trek from downtown, near the airport, is a favorite of the nightlife-lovin' counterculture. You're likely see the next big thing in electronic music here, and DJs spin everything from downtempo to breakbeat. Organic cocktails keep sweaty bodies cool when the dance floor heats up. ✉ *2812 Kettner Blvd., Middletown* ☎ *619/543–0933* ⊕ *www.kavalounge.com.*

PIANO BARS

The Shout! House. Dueling pianos and interactive, rock-and-roll sing-alongs make for a festive, even boisterous, evening here, but be sure to make reservations or come early to snag the best seats. ✉ *655 4th Ave., Gaslamp Quarter* ☎ *619/231–6700* ⊕ *www.theshouthouse.com.*

Fodor's Choice ★ **Westgate Hotel Plaza Bar.** The old-money surroundings, including leather-upholstered seats, marble tabletops, and a grand piano, supply one of the most elegant and romantic settings for a drink in San Diego. ✉ *1055 2nd Ave., Gaslamp Quarter* ☎ *619/557–3650* ⊕ *www.westgatehotel.com.*

ROCK, POP, HIP-HOP, FOLK, AND BLUES CLUBS

House of Blues. The local branch of the renowned music chain is decorated floor to ceiling with colorful folk art and features three different areas to hear music. There's something going on here just about every night of the week, and the gospel brunch on select Sundays is one of the most praiseworthy events in town. Can we get a hallelujah? ✉ *1055 5th Ave., Gaslamp Quarter* ☎ *619/299–2583* ⊕ *www.houseofblues.com.*

OFF THE BEATEN PATH **The Casbah.** This small club near the airport, the unofficial headquarters of the city's indie music scene, has a national reputation for showcasing up-and-coming acts of all genres. Nirvana, Smashing Pumpkins, and the White Stripes all played here on the way to stardom. ✉ *2501 Kettner Blvd., Middletown* ☎ *619/232–4355* ⊕ *www.casbahmusic.com.*

WINE BARS

Vin de Syrah. This "spirit and wine cellar" sends you down a rabbit hole (or at least down some stairs) to a whimsical spot straight out of Alice in Wonderland. Behind a hidden door (look for a handle in the grass wall), you'll find visual delights (grapevines suspended from the ceiling, vintage jars with flittering "fireflies," cozy chairs nestled around a faux fireplace and pastoral vista) that rival the culinary ones—the wine list is approachable and the charcuterie boards are exquisitely curated. ■ TIP➔ More than just a wine bar, the cocktails are also worth a try. ✉ *901 5th Ave., Gaslamp Quarter* ☎ *619/234–4166* ⊕ *www.syrahwineparlor.com.*

EAST VILLAGE

Upscale style mashed up with hip, underground dives in this up-and-coming urban hood.

BARS

Bar Basic. This spot is always bustling, in part because it's *the* place to be seen for Padres fans or anyone else attending events at PETCO Park. True to its name, Basic reliably dishes up simple pleasures: strong drinks and hot, coal-fired pizza. The garage-style doors roll up and keep the industrial-chic former warehouse ventilated during the balmy summer. ✉ *410 10th Ave., East Village* ☎ *619/531–8869* ⊕ *www.barbasic.com.*

Cat Eye Club. Separated from the hectic hustle of East Village by just a short and dimly lit foyer, Cat Eye Club might as well be in an entirely different world. More specifically, it's a trip back to the 1960s, with mid-century modern furnishings, a Wurlitzer jukebox and Rat Pack flicks on regular rotation. Their menu of tiki cocktails ranges from simple sips to punchbowls, or for those who prefer their drinks flashier, the Cradle of Life, garnished with a flaming lime wedge. ✉ *370 7th Ave., East Village* ⊕ *cateyeclubsd.com/.*

East Village Tavern & Bowl. Twelve bowling lanes means no more hauls to the suburbs to channel one's inner Lebowski. Lane rental is pricey during prime times, but reasonable if you consider that some nearby clubs charge a Jackson just for admission, though reservations are definitely recommended. From the expansive bar area you can watch sports on 33 flat screens, and the satellite radio plays an assortment of alt- and classic rock. ✉ *930 Market St., East Village* ☎ *619/677–2695* ⊕ *www.tavernbowl.com.*

El Dorado. El Dorado means "The Gold," and that's exactly what this hip hangout—part trendy club, part sophisticated speakeasy—has brought to a dodgy strip of downtown. The Western saloon–theme comes with creative drinks, cute bartenders, and local DJs on Friday and Saturday. Save your own gold with a $5 happy hour that runs from 7 till 9 pm. ✉ *1030 Broadway, East Village* ☎ *619/237–0550* ⊕ *eldoradobar.com.*

Monkey Paw. What was once a notorious dive bar attracts hipsters and grizzled locals alike for a vast selection of craft beers (some brewed on-site), shuffleboard, and cheesesteaks that hit the spot no matter the hour. ✉ *805 16th St., East Village* ☎ *619/358–9901* ⊕ *www.monkeypawbrewing.com.*

10

PIANO BARS

Fodor's Choice ★ **Noble Experiment.** There are a handful of speakeasy-style bars in San Diego, though none deliver so far above and beyond the novelty quite like this cozy-yet-swank cocktail lounge hidden in the back of a burger restaurant. Seek out the hidden door (hint: look for the stack of kegs), tuck into a plush leather booth next to the wall of golden skulls, and sip on the best craft cocktails in the city. ■TIP→ Reservations are almost always a must, so be sure to call ahead. ✉ 777 G St., East Village ☎ 619/888–4713 ⊕ nobleexperimentsd.com.

LITTLE ITALY

Amid its arty galleries and boutiques, Little Italy houses several popular open-air beer bars.

BARS

Fodor's Choice ★ **The Waterfront Bar & Grill.** It isn't really on the waterfront, but San Diego's oldest bar was once the hangout of Italian fishermen. Most of the collars are now white, and patrons enjoy an excellent selection of beers, along with chili, burgers, fish-and-chips, and other great-tasting grub, including fish tacos. Get here early, as there's almost always a crowd. ✉ 2044 Kettner Blvd., Little Italy ☎ 619/232–9656 ⊕ www.waterfrontbarandgrill.com.

BREWPUBS

Karl Strauss' Brewing Company. San Diego's first microbrewery now has multiple locations, but the original one remains a staple. This locale draws an after-work crowd for pints of Red Trolley Ale and later fills with beer connoisseurs from all walks of life to try Karl's latest concoctions. Beer-to-go in half-gallon "growlers" is very popular, and the German-inspired pub food is above average. ✉ 1157 Columbia St., Little Italy ☎ 619/234–2739 ⊕ www.karlstrauss.com.

JAZZ CLUBS
NIGHT BAY CRUISES

Flagship Cruises and Events. Flagship Cruises welcomes guests aboard with a glass of champagne as a prelude to nightly dinner-dance and holiday cruises. ✉ 990 N. Harbor Dr., Little Italy ☎ 619/522–6155 ⊕ www.flagshipsd.com.

Hornblower Cruises. Take a dinner-dance cruise aboard the Lord Hornblower—the trip comes with fabulous views of the San Diego skyline. ✉ 1066 N. Harbor Dr., Little Italy ⊕ hornblower.com.

EMBARCADERO

Scenic drinking spots and higher bar tabs overlooking tall ships and naval history.

BARS

The Lion's Share. Hemingway would have loved this exquisitely designed brick-and-wood bar that serves up equally exquisite craft cocktails that, while pricey, are definitely made for sipping. The place attracts a sophisticated crowd and is highly recommended for those looking to impress a special someone. ✉ 629 Kettner Blvd., Embarcadero ☎ 619/564–6924 ⊕ lionssharesd.com.

For a bit of history, check out the Waterfront in Little Italy, San Diego's oldest bar.

Top of the Hyatt. This lounge at the Manchester Grand Hyatt crowns the tallest waterfront building in California, affording great views of San Diego Bay, including Coronado to the west, Mexico to the south, and Point Loma and La Jolla to the north. It's pricey and pretentious (don't you dare wear flip-flops), but this champagne-centric bar is great for catching a sunset or celebrating an anniversary. ⊠ *1 Market Pl., Embarcadero* ☎ *619/232–1234* ⊕ *manchestergrand.hyatt.com.*

COFFEEHOUSES
Upstart Crow. A bookstore and coffeehouse in one is tucked into downtown's charming Seaport Village. The secluded upstairs space is ideal for chatting or flipping through the book you just bought. Irreverent gifts are sold, too. ⊠ *835C W. Harbor Dr., Embarcadero* ☎ *619/232–4855* ⊕ *upstartcrowtrading.com.*

BALBOA PARK AND BANKERS HILL

BANKERS HILL
Duck into a cozy jazz lounge or sip a mocha just outside of downtown's hectic environs.

BARS
Croce's Park West. Ingrid Croce books superb acoustic-jazz musicians, among others, in this newly reopened update of the intimate dinner joint and jazz lounge, formerly located in the Gaslamp Quarter. Her son, A.J. Croce, frequently performs here. ⊠ *2760 5th Ave., Bankers Hill* ⊕ *crocesparkwest.com.*

OLD TOWN AND UPTOWN

OLD TOWN

Old-timey saloons lure tourists with margaritas, mezcal, and mariachis.

BARS

The Cosmopolitan. The bar at the Cosmopolitan Hotel in Old Town maintains the old-timey aesthetic of the tourist-heavy neighborhood, complete with servers in period garb and game trophies on the walls. The quality of the cocktails and the friendly atmosphere make this a gem among the rest of the old west kitsch. ⊠ *2660 Calhoun St., Old Town* ☎ *619/297–1874* ⊕ *www.oldtowncosmopolitan.com/.*

> ### HEY, BIG SPENDER
>
> You can dress to impress and bat your eyelashes, but unless you're a supermodel or a pro athlete, at the most exclusive of San Diego's clubs and lounges just about the only way to bypass a long queue or nab a corner booth is to arrange for bottle service. Just be forewarned: a lowly bottle of Jack Daniels will run you about $250.

El Agave Tequileria. The bar of this restaurant named for the cactus whose sap is distilled into tequila stocks hundreds of top-shelf brands that are as sip-worthy as the finest cognac. ⊠ *2304 San Diego Ave., Old Town* ☎ *619/220–0692* ⊕ *www.elagave.com.*

HILLCREST

San Diego's most active area for LGBT nightlife.

BARS

Nunu's. This retro-cool hangout with stiff cocktails might be one of the most popular bars in très gay Hillcrest, but don't expect a glitzy facade. The intentionally dated decor sits within the tatty walls of a white-brick box that probably hasn't had a face-lift since the LBJ administration. ⊠ *3537 5th Ave., Hillcrest* ☎ *619/295–2878* ⊕ *nunuscocktails.com.*

COFFEEHOUSES

Fodor'sChoice ★ **Extraordinary Desserts.** This café lives up to its name, which explains why there's often a line, despite the ample seating. Paris-trained Karen Krasne turns out award-winning cakes, tortes, and pastries of exceptional beauty. The Japanese-theme patio invites you to linger over yet another coffee drink. A second location is in Little Italy. ⊠ *2929 5th Ave., Hillcrest* ☎ *619/294–2132* ⊕ *www.extraordinarydesserts.com.*

Filter Coffee House. A colorful cast of Hillcrest locals crowds this place, open until 3 am on weekends, to get their caffeine buzz going before heading to the clubs. The comfy couches and relaxed atmosphere certainly help, not to mention the fact that they also serve beer and wine. ⊠ *1295 University Ave., Hillcrest* ☎ *619/299–0145.*

GAY NIGHTLIFE

Fodor'sChoice ★ **Baja Betty's.** Although it draws plenty of gay customers, the festive and friendly atmosphere is popular with just about everyone in the Hillcrest area (and their pets are welcome, too). The bar staff stocks more than 100 brands of tequila and mixes plenty of fancy cocktails. ⊠ *1421 University Ave., Hillcrest* ☎ *619/269–8510* ⊕ *www.bajabettyssd.com.*

CLOSE UP

San Diego On Tap

San Diego is home to more than 90 breweries, with more opening every year. But the city's beer culture expands well beyond the breweries; along 30th Street in North Park, on up to Adams Avenue in Normal Heights, there's a sprawl of craft-beer bars and brewpubs. While you can find all styles of beer in San Diego, many local brewers contend that the specialty is Double IPA, an India Pale Ale with attitude. Every brewery has its own version.

Bars with the best microbrew selection: Blind Lady Ale House, Hamilton's Tavern, Live Wire, O'Brien's, Toronado.

Best fests: Try Winter Brew Fest in February, Rhythm and Brews in May, Heroes Brew Fest in July, during Comic-Con ⊕ www.heroesbrewfest. com), the San Diego Festival of Beers in September ⊕ www.sdbeerfest. org, San Diego Beer Week (November ⊕ www.sdbw.org), and the Strong Ale Fest (December). ⊕ www. sandiegobrewersguild.org has more listings.

Best way to sample it all: Sign up for Brewery Tours of San Diego (⊕ www.brewerytoursofsandiego.com) to sample the best craft beers.

SAN DIEGO'S BEST BREWERIES Head to the source, where beer is brewed. These are worth the trek for beer aficionados.

AleSmith Brewing Co. This artisanal microbrewery offers tastings at its out-of-the-way locale. How artisanal is it? The "Kopi Luwak" special edition of AleSmith's Speedway Stout is brewed with Civet coffee from Indonesia, made from rare coffee berries that have been eaten—and passed,

undigested—by the Asian Palm Civet. Tours take place Saturdays at 2 pm. ✉ 9368 Cabot Dr., Scripps Ranch ☎ 858/549–9888 ⊕ www.alesmith. com.

Fodor'sChoice★ Alpine Brewing Co. Well worth the mountain drive, this operation run by brewmaster Pat McIlhenney, a former fire captain, has won international kudos for its hopped-up creations. Tasters are only a buck each, or fill a growler, which holds a half gallon. Don't pass up Duet, Pure Hoppiness, or Exponential Hoppiness. Alpine also opened a pub a few doors down. ✉ 2351 Alpine Blvd., Alpine ☎ 619/445–2337 ⊕ www.alpinebeerco.com.

Ballast Point Brewing Co. With one location in Miramar/Scripps Ranch, this craft brewery just opened a local taproom in Little Italy. The Sculpin IPA is outstanding, and for more adventurous drinkers, there's the Habanero sculpin, brewed with Habanero peppers. ✉ 10051 Old Grove Rd., Scripps Ranch ☎ 858/695–2739 ⊕ www.ballastpoint.com.

Stone Brewing World Gardens and Bistro. The Big Daddy of San Diego craft brewing was founded by a few basement beer tinkerers in 1996; the company now exports nationwide. Stone's monumental HQ is off the beaten path, but worth a visit for its tours ($3 includes souvenir tasting glass), vast on-tap selection (not just Stone beers), and hard-to-beat bistro eats. ✉ 1999 Citracado Pkwy., Escondido ☎ 760/294–7866 ⊕ www. stonebrew.com.

10

Martinis Above Fourth. This swank lounge presents live piano, comedy, and cabaret on weekends to a friendly crowd. Swill cocktails inside or on the patio, and consider a meal afterward in the restaurant serving contemporary American fare. ⊠ *3940 4th Ave., 2nd fl., Hillcrest* ☎ *619/400–4500* ⊕ *www.martinisabovefourth.com.*

Rich's. The dancing and music here are some of the best in the city, making Rich's popular not only with gay men but also plenty of lesbians and straight revelers. ⊠ *1051 University Ave., Hillcrest* ☎ *619/295–2195* ⊕ *www.richssandiego.com.*

Urban Mo's Bar and Grill. Cowboys gather for line dancing and two-stepping on the wooden dance floor—but be forewarned, yee-hawers, it can get pretty wild on Western nights. There are also Latin, hip-hop, and drag revues but the real allure is in the creative drinks ("Gone Fishing"—served in a fishbowl, for example) and the breezy patio where love (or something like it) is usually in the air. ⊠ *308 University Ave., Hillcrest* ☎ *619/491–0400* ⊕ *www.urbanmos.com.*

WINE BARS

Wine Steals. This room crackles with excitement on busy nights—you can actually hear the din of conversation from half a block away. A wide assortment of reasonably priced wines draws patrons in, and the freshly baked pizza keeps them in top form for imbibing. Check out the other locations in the East Village, Point Loma, and Cardiff. ⊠ *1243 University Ave., Hillcrest* ☎ *619/295–1188* ⊕ *www.winestealssd.com.*

MISSION HILLS

Take your pick between unpretentious pubs or ultrastylish cocktail grottos.

BARS

Aero Club. Named for its proximity to the airport, this watering hole draws in twenty- and thirty-somethings with its pool tables, dominoes, and 20 beers on tap (including a few local brews). Drinks are cheap, which makes this a popular place to fuel up before heading downtown. Don't miss the cool fighting warplanes mural. ⊠ *3365 India St., Mission Hills* ☎ *619/297–7211* ⊕ *www.aeroclubbar.com.*

Shakespeare Pub & Grille. This Mission Hills hangout captures all the warmth and camaraderie of a traditional British pub—except here you can enjoy consistently sunny weather on the sprawling patio. The bar hands pour from a long list of imported ales and stouts, and the early hours for big matches make this *the* place to watch soccer. ⊠ *3701 India St., Mission Hills* ☎ *619/299–0230* ⊕ *www.shakespearepub.com.*

COFFEEHOUSES

Gelato Vero Caffe. A youthful crowd gathers here for authentic Italian ice cream, espresso, and a second-floor view of the downtown skyline. The place is usually occupied by regulars who stay for hours at a time. ⊠ *3753 India St., Mission Hills* ☎ *619/295–9269.*

PIANO BARS

Fodor's Choice
★

Starlite. Bar-goers are dazzled by Starlite's award-winning interior design, which includes rock walls, luxe leather booths, and a massive mirror-mounted chandelier. A hexagonal wood-plank entryway leads to a sunken white bar, where sexy tattooed guys and girls mix creative cocktails, such as the signature Starlite Mule, served in a copper mug. An iPod plays eclectic playlists ranging from old-timey jazz and blues to obscure vintage rock (and DJs are on hand on certain evenings). During warmer months, procuring a spot on the outside wood-decked patio is an art form. ⊠ *3175 India St., Mission Hills* ☎ *619/358–9766* ⊕ *www.starlitesandiego.com.*

UNIVERSITY HEIGHTS

A low-key uptown corner by day, and San Diego's next gay neighborhood scene by night.

BARS

Small Bar. True to its name, this University Heights pub is, well, pint-sized, but the beer selection is huge. This means that on any given night the place is packed with aficionados and novices alike vying to try old favorites and new additions. ⊠ *4628 Park Blvd., University Heights* ☎ *619/795–7998* ⊕ *www.smallbarsd.com.*

BREWPUBS

Blind Lady Ale House. There's almost no combination on earth as satisfying as pizza and beer—which just happen to be Blind Lady's specialties. The old world–style pizzas are topped with organic ingredients, like house-made chorizo and avocado, which offer an excellent complement to their extensive beer selection, which is updated on their chalkboard daily. Just be patient waiting for a seat at the popular neighborhood spot, which is decorated in resourced materials such as reclaimed wood floors and glass cases of vintage beer cans. ⊠ *3416 Adams Ave., University Heights* ☎ *619/255–2491* ⊕ *www.blindladyalehouse.com.*

NORTH PARK AND SOUTH PARK

Where young, hip artist types gather to sip craft beer along the 30th street corridor.

BARS

Bar Pink. Cheap drinks, loud music, and a hip crowd explain the line that's usually waiting outside this divey bar co-owned by Rocket From the Crypt frontman John "Speedo" Reis. Stop by on Tiki Tuesday for $5 drinks like their signature Sneaky Tiki, and DJs spinning vintage lounge and exotica tunes. ⊠ *3829 30th St., North Park* ☎ *619/564–7194* ⊕ *www.barpink.com.*

Fodor'sChoice ★ **Hamilton's Tavern.** Affectionately known to its loyal crowd of locals as Hammy's, this bar has one of the best beer lists in town. On the ceiling, lights strung between old beer taps twinkle as bright as the eyes of the suds-lovers who flock here. In between pours, grab something from Hammy's kitchen—people come from all over for the wings and burgers. ⊠ *1521 30th St., South Park* ☎ *619/238–5460* ⊕ *hamiltonstavern.com.*

Live Wire. A tried-and-true authentic dive just on the border of the trendy North Park neighborhood lures pierced and tattooed kids in their twenties. A wide-ranging (and very loud) jukebox and TVs screening movies or music videos are the main entertainment, unless you count the people-watching. The cocktails as well as the excellent beers come

10

in pint glasses, so pace yourself; the police lie in wait on nearby side streets. ⊠ *2103 El Cajon Blvd., North Park* ☎ *619/291–7450* ⊕ *www. livewirebar.com.*

Fodor's Choice **Seven Grand.** This whiskey lounge is a swanky addition to an already
★ thriving North Park nightlife scene and a welcome alternative to the neighboring dives and dance clubs. Live jazz, a tranquil atmosphere, and a bourbon-loving craft cocktail list keep locals flocking. ⊠ *3054 University Ave., North Park* ☎ *619/269–8820* ⊕ *www.sevengrandbars. com/sd.*

Toronado. One of San Diego's favorite gathering spots for hop-heads is named in honor of the San Francisco beer bar of the same name. The beer list—both on tap and by the bottle—is hard to beat. The place can get noisy, but the food—a mix of burgers and American-style comfort food—more than makes up for it. ⊠ *4026 30th St., North Park* ☎ *619/282–0456* ⊕ *www.toronadosd.com.*

BREWPUBS

Tiger! Tiger!. A communal vibe prevails at this wood, metal, and brick gastropub, where patrons sit at picnic tables to schmooze and sip from one of the dozens of carefully selected craft and micro brews on tap. ⊠ *3025 El Cajon Blvd., North Park* ☎ *619/487–0401* ⊕ *www. tigertigertavern.com.*

COFFEEHOUSES

Claire de Lune. High ceilings and huge arched windows give the redesigned, historic Odd Fellows building in North Park a funky charm. There are sofas and armchairs for lounging as well as tables for studying. Local musicians and poets take the stage on various nights. ⊠ *2906 University Ave., North Park* ☎ *619/688–9845* ⊕ *www.clairedelune. com.*

DANCE CLUBS

Whistle Stop Bar. Here's a place to get your groove on to indie, electro, and hip-hop, plus live bands on Friday. This tiny-but-banging locals' favorite just a few minutes from downtown gets hot and crowded, and the dance floor is always happening on Saturday. Plus, the cover's usually five bucks. ⊠ *2236 Fern St., South Park* ☎ *619/284–6784* ⊕ *whistlestopbar.com/.*

GAY NIGHTLIFE

Red Fox Steak House. Referred to as Red Fox Room by those in the know, this dimly lit lounge is dearly loved by locals, and not just the seniors who flock here to sing Sinatra tunes to tickled ivories and the occasional impromptu horn section. ⊠ *2223 El Cajon Blvd., North Park* ☎ *619/297–1313* ⊕ *www.redfoxsd.com.*

NORMAL HEIGHTS

Where beer snobs share barstools with urban hippies, bourbon yuppies, and surly locals.

BARS

The Hideout. True to its name, the Hideout offers refreshment and respite from the urban congestion of El Cajon Boulevard. The still-young cocktail lounge's marketing slogan is "Grains, Hops and Music," and though it's a fine place to see live rock music, there's a reason the grains and hops come first. Their craft cocktail menu offers a lot more than typical dive bar fare—not that you don't have the option for an American pilsner if that's what you seek. ✉ *3519, El Cajon Blvd., City Heights* ☎ *619/501–6540* ⊕ *thehideoutsd.com/.*

Polite Provisions. The look of this cocktail lounge on the border of North Park and Normal Heights is drugstore chic, but the drinks themselves—none of which contain vodka—are much more sophisticated fare, shaken or stirred with house-made bitters and sodas. If you're looking to nosh, the adjoining Soda & Swine serves meatballs right to your table, and the six-hour Monday–Thursday happy hour is a must for those seeking mixology on a budget. ✉ *4696 30th St., Normal Heights* ☎ *619/677–3784* ⊕ *politeprovisions.com/.*

Soda Bar. Don't be fooled by the name. Soda is in short supply at this off-the-beaten-path music venue that has earned a reputation as the place to see up-and-coming bands or grab a potent cocktail. ✉ *3615 El Cajon Blvd., Normal Heights* ☎ *619/255–7224* ⊕ *www.sodabarmusic.com.*

COFFEEHOUSES

Lestat's Coffee Shop. One of the few San Diego coffee shops that's open 24 hours a day, this Normal Heights mainstay also has a great selection of baked goods and a neighboring music venue that stages acoustic and comedy acts seven days a week. ✉ *3343 Adams Ave., Normal Heights* ☎ *619/282–0437* ⊕ *www.lestats.com.*

MISSION BAY AND THE BEACHES

MISSION BAY

A seaside spot to glug some suds by the boardwalk after a splash in the Pacific.

Draft. Patrons can have their seaside views and craft beer too at this spacious Belmont Park bar and restaurant. The relaxed, boardwalk atmosphere—and giant wall-size television screen—makes it a perfect spot for lounging after riding some waves at Mission Beach, or to cool down after soaking in some sun. ✉ *3105 Ocean Front Walk, Mission Beach* ☎ *858/228–9305* ⊕ *www.belmontpark.com/restaurants/draft/.*

10

NIGHT BAY CRUISES

Bahia Belle. This Mississippi-style stern-wheeler offers relaxing evening cruises along Mission Bay that include cocktails, dancing, karaoke, and live music. Cruises run from Wednesday through Sunday in early summer, daily in July and August, and Friday and Saturday in winter (there are no cruises in December). The $10 fare is less than most nightclub covers, but if you are choosey about the company you keep, remember, these floating bars are known as "booze cruises" for a reason. ✉ *998 W. Mission Bay Dr., Mission Bay* ☎ *858/539–7779* ⊕ *www.bahiahotel.com.*

PACIFIC BEACH

Where surfers meet for happy hour and college students converge to spend their lost weekends.

BARS

Amplified Ale Works. Pacific Beach often veers between the trendy and the tawdry, so it's refreshing to see a genuine craft brewhouse open up to offer a more casual middle ground. Amplified serves more than a dozen in-house-brewed beers at its scenic outdoor beer garden, with breathtaking ocean views. ⊠ *4150 Mission Blvd., #208, Pacific Beach* ☎ *858/270–5222* ⊕ *www.amplifiedales.com/.*

Bar West. Bar West brings downtown flavor to style-starved PB. Though clean-lined and attractive, the bar is packed with the usual suspects (collegiates and beach crowd), and the dance floor is a sweaty meat market on weekends. ⊠ *959 Hornblend St., Pacific Beach* ☎ *858/273–9378* ⊕ *barwestsd.com.*

JRDN. This contemporary lounge (pronounced "Jordan") occupies the ground floor of Pacific Beach's chicest boutique hotel, Tower23, and offers a more sophisticated vibe in what is a very party-happy neighborhood. Sleek walls of windows and an expansive patio overlook the boardwalk. ⊠ *723 Felspar St., Pacific Beach* ☎ *858/270–5736* ⊕ *www.t23hotel.com.*

Pacific Beach Bar & Grill. Only a block away from the beach, this popular nightspot has a huge outdoor patio, so you can enjoy star-filled skies as you party. The lines here on weekends are generally the longest of any club in Pacific Beach. There's plenty to see and do, from billiards and satellite TV sports to an interactive trivia game. The grill takes orders until 1 am, so this is a great place for a late-night snack. ⊠ *860 Garnet Ave., Pacific Beach* ☎ *858/272–4745* ⊕ *pbbarandgrill.com.*

BREWPUBS

Tap Room. Beachside locals have been clamoring for an authentic beer bar and certainly got one with this place. Hoppy choices are in the hundreds and the food is better than average bar food. ⊠ *1269 Garnet Ave., Pacific Beach* ☎ *858/274–1010* ⊕ *www.sdtaproom.com.*

COFFEEHOUSES

Zanzibar Café. This cozy, dimly lighted spot along Pacific Beach's main strip is a great place to mellow out and eavesdrop, or just to watch the club-hopping singles make their way down the street. ⊠ *976 Garnet Ave., Pacific Beach* ☎ *858/272–4762* ⊕ *www.zanzibarcafe.com.*

LA JOLLA AND KEARNY MESA

A healthy mixture of laid-back beach bars and upper crust craft-cocktail couture.

BARS

Cusp. The stone walls and modern metal accents along the bar give the impression of Cusp being a dark, intimate lounge, but the panoramic views of La Jolla shores brighten up this chic spot on the 11th floor of Hotel La Jolla. Drop in for live acoustic or jazz music on weekends, or simply sip on one of their signature cocktails during their daily happy hour from 4 to 7. ⊠ *7955 La Jolla Shores Dr., La Jolla* ☎ *858/551–3620* ⊕ *www.cusprestaurant.com/.*

George's Bar. Upstairs from the upscale George's At the Cove is this hip, casual, and somewhat more affordable hangout, which is always buzzing with activity—especially on weekends. Stop in for drinks or bar snacks that rank among La Jolla's best, and with gorgeous ocean views to boot. ⊠ *1250 Prospect St., La Jolla* ☎ *858/454–4244* ⊕ *www.georgesatthecove.com/georges-bar.*

COFFEEHOUSES

Living Room Coffee. La Jolla's outpost of this local coffee chain is open until midnight and sports a full bar, which means that customers can spend a pleasant evening sipping a true-blue Irish coffee complete with whiskey at one of the many tables or couches. ⊠ *1010 Prospect St., La Jolla* ☎ *858/459–1187* ⊕ *www.livingroomcafe.com.*

COMEDY AND CABARET

Comedy Store La Jolla. Like its sister establishment in Hollywood, this club hosts some of the best national touring and local talent. Cover charges range from nothing on open-mike nights to $20 or more for national acts. Seating is at bistro-style tables, and a two-drink minimum applies for all shows. ⊠ *916 Pearl St., La Jolla* ☎ *858/454–9176* ⊕ *lajolla.thecomedystore.com.*

KEARNY MESA

Beer snob heaven, situated between ramen houses and car dealerships.

BARS

O'Brien's. The self-proclaimed "Hoppiest Place on Earth" makes up for its tacky interior (pleather executive chairs?) with a world-class beer list. This must-visit mecca for hardcore beer lovers is hidden among the Asian-oriented strip malls of Kearny Mesa, about 15 minutes north of downtown. ⊠ *4646 Convoy St., Kearny Mesa* ☎ *858/715–1745* ⊕ *obrienspub.net.*

POINT LOMA, OCEAN BEACH, AND CORONADO

POINT LOMA

A diverse range of unique watering holes amid a sleepy, residential burg.

10

BARS

Modern Times Beer. Point Loma's funky and unique entry into the craft beer game, Modern Times lives up to its name with innovative design—including a mural made entirely of Post-It notes—simple and stylish take-home six-packs, and a rotating cast of beers on tap with the diversity to please every type of palate. ⊠ *3725 Greenwood St., Point Loma* ☎ *619/546–9694* ⊕ *moderntimesbeer.com/.*

The Pearl Hotel. Step into late '60s Palm Springs, with shag carpet, clean lines, and lots of wood accents. The lobby bar is almost as fabulous as the outdoor pool area, where inflatable balls bob in illuminated water and vintage flicks show on a huge screen. And feel free to drink to excess. After 10 pm, when the bar closes, you can stay over at a discounted $79 "play and stay" rate if there are any rooms available. ⊠ *1410 Rosecrans St., Point Loma* ☎ *619/226–6100* ⊕ *www.thepearlsd.com.*

COFFEEHOUSES

Living Room. This coffeeshop in an old house has creaky wooden floors and plenty of cubbyholes for the college students who are regulars here. Not far from the water, it's a great place to catch a caffeine buzz before walking along Shelter Island. There are several other locations, including popular branches in Old Town and La Jolla. ⊠ *3636 Rosecrans St., Point Loma* ☎ *619/222–6852* ⊕ *www.livingroomcafe.com.*

OCEAN BEACH

Hippie hangouts, campy cocktail lounges, and not a dress code in sight.

BARS

Pacific Shores. This bar isn't going for classy with its acid-trip mermaid mural, but hey, it's OB—a surf town populated by leftovers from the '60s, man. A laid-back but see-and-be-seen crowd congregates here for relatively inexpensive drinks (no beers on tap, though), pool games, and pop and rock tunes on the jukebox. ⊠ *4927 Newport Ave., Ocean Beach* ☎ *619/223–7549.*

ROCK, POP, HIP-HOP, FOLK, AND BLUES CLUBS

Winston's. This Ocean Beach rock club in a former bowling alley hosts local bands, reggae groups, and, occasionally, 1960s-style bands. The crowd, mostly locals, is typically mellow but can get rowdy. ⊠ *1921 Bacon St., Ocean Beach* ☎ *619/222–6822* ⊕ *www.winstonsob.com.*

SHELTER ISLAND

Tiki kitsch and mid-century charm, with one of the city's best concert destinations.

ROCK, POP, HIP-HOP, FOLK, AND BLUES CLUBS

Humphrey's by the Bay. From June through September this dining and drinking oasis surrounded by water hosts the city's best outdoor jazz, folk, and light-rock concert series and is the stomping ground of such musicians as the Cowboy Junkies and Chris Isaak. The rest of the year the music moves indoors for first-rate jazz, blues, and more. ⊠ *2241 Shelter Island Dr., Shelter Island* ☎ *619/224–3577* ⊕ *www. humphreysconcerts.com.*

THE ARTS

Updated by
Jeff Terich

A diverse and sophisticated arts scene probably isn't the first thing that visitors—or even locals—associate with San Diego. It's a destination for those who seek out its perennial sunshine, gorgeous beaches, and beautiful scenery. Even those within the arts scene readily admit their fiercest competition is the beach! But just a little to the right of the Pacific Ocean, there are some amazing and diverse artistic offerings to prove that San Diego can hold its own.

The theater scene in San Diego may not have the commercial appeal that Broadway does, but it more than makes up for it with talent. In fact, a long list of Broadway-bound productions started right here, including *Jersey Boys*, The Who's *Tommy, Dirty Rotten Scoundrels*, and *Memphis*.

Balboa Park's Old Globe Theatre is modeled after the Shakespearian Globe Theatre in England, and hosts both an annual Shakespeare Festival as well as contemporary plays. A little bit north is La Jolla Playhouse, which was founded by Gregory Peck in 1947, and has hosted dozens of world-premiere productions, in addition to star actors like Laura Linney and Neil Patrick Harris. The Playhouse has also launched the Without Walls initiative, which places theater in a new context by removing the theater entirely.

Music also has a major presence in San Diego, courtesy of the world-class San Diego Opera, which performs major works by Puccini and Mozart, and the San Diego Symphony, which caters to a diverse audience thanks to both its classical concerts and its more accessible Summer Pops series.

There's always something new and exciting happening with visual arts in San Diego. No longer limited to a collector's market, younger urban artists are making in-roads with warehouse gallery spaces in Barrio Logan, while galleries in La Jolla and Little Italy showcase bold works of contemporary art on their walls. The annual San Diego Art Prize

TOP ARTS EXPERIENCES

Arts free-for-all: Summertime means free concerts, movies, and theater throughout the county.

Puppet strings: Your kids might not care for Shakespeare at the Old Globe, but you can introduce them to great acting at Balboa Park's Marie Hitchcock Puppet Theatre.

Gallery gathering: Before you visit, scour gallery websites or places like www.sdcitybeat.com for upcoming openings, which usually include a spread of sips and snacks—and art, of course.

San Diego Film Festival: This five-day festival in September is a must for film lovers and celebrity spotters—a day pass will get you into some of San Diego's most glamorous parties.

highlights rising figures in the visual arts realm, and in the field of architecture, Orchids and Onions honors the best and worst in structural design—and with a sense of humor at that.

THE ARTS PLANNER

TICKETS

Plan ahead and buy tickets early—ideally around the same time that you book your hotel. Not that you can't find an outlet that sells day-of-show tickets, but you'll run the risk of paying a grossly inflated price, and might not end up with good seats.

Arts Tix. You can buy advance tickets, many at half price, to theater, music, and dance events at Arts Tix. ✉ *28 Horton Plaza, 3rd Ave. and Broadway, Gaslamp Quarter* ☎ *858/381–5595* ⊕ *www.sdartstix.com.*

Ticketmaster. Ticketmaster sells tickets to many performances, as well as to select museum exhibitions. Service charges vary according to the event, and most tickets are nonrefundable. ☎ *800/745–3000* ⊕ *www.ticketmaster.com.*

GALLERY AND MUSEUM NIGHTS

The art gallery and museum experience in San Diego isn't limited to the daytime—at night, a number of different museums and venues host after-business-hours events that attract a younger, cosmopolitan crowd.

Four times a year, the San Diego Museum of Art hosts a seasonal sundown series called **Culture & Cocktails** (☎ *619/232–7931* ⊕ *www.sdmart.org*), which coincides with major new exhibitions, including its annual floral-themed Art Alive event. For a $15 admission, visitors can enjoy cocktails and nibbles, DJs and live entertainment, and a cool artsy twenty- and thirtysomething crowd.

The San Diego Museum of Contemporary Art Downtown (⊕ *www.mcasd.org*) ups the artsy ante with its long-running Thursday Night Thing—aka **TNT**—a boisterous three-times-a-year happening with drinks, performances by some of the better local bands, and thematically related activities.

The Spreckels Organ Pavilion in Balboa Park hosts free Monday night concerts in the summer.

Up in North County, Encinitas' Lux Art Institute (⊕ www.luxartinstitute.org) has launched a periodic event called **Creative Nights**, which features live music, food, drinks, and on-site art-making for a $15 admission.

North Park, meanwhile, hosts a monthly event every second Saturday called **Ray at Night** (⊕ www.rayatnight.com), where the galleries on Ray Street stay open late, and patrons are treated to tasty offerings from food trucks, and street performers.

DANCE

Whether you fancy *rond de jambes* or something a bit more modern, San Diego's scene is *en pointe* for dance fans.

California Ballet Company. The company performs high-quality contemporary and classical works September–May at the **Civic Theatre**. The *Nutcracker* is staged annually around the holiday season. ⊠ *1100 3rd Ave., Downtown* ☎ *619/570–1100* ⊕ *www.californiaballet.org.*

Balboa Theatre. This historic landmark hosts ballet, music, plays, and even stand-up comedy performances. ⊠ *868 4th Ave., Downtown* ☎ *619/570–1100* ⊕ *www.sandiegotheatres.org*

City Ballet. The ballet holds performances at the **Spreckels Theatre** and a few other area venues from November through May. At Christmastime, they dance a mean *Nutcracker*. ⊠ *Spreckels Theatre, 121 Broadway, Downtown* ☎ *858/272–8663* ⊕ *www.cityballet.org.*

Jean Isaacs San Diego Dance Theater. The company has earned serious kudos for its diverse company and provocative programming, including

Mexican waltzes and its annual "Trolley Dances," which take place at various trolley stops throughout San Diego. Other performances are held at venues around the city. ✉ *2650 Truxtun Rd., Suite 108* ☎ *619/225–1803* ⊕ *www.sandiegodancetheater.org.*

FILM

Cinephiles won't be left reeling by the unexpectedly diverse cinematic riches in San Diego, from indoor and outdoor theaters to a variety of seasonal film festivals.

Digital Gym. Operated by Media Arts Center San Diego—the organization behind the San Diego Latino Film Festival—Digital Gym provides an alternative to mainstream cinema with a one-screen theater showing foreign and art films, as well as compelling documentaries. Make sure to spend some time in the gift shop, which has everything from kitschy memorabilia to DVD collections of contemporary filmmakers. ✉ *2921 El Cajon Blvd., North Park* ☎ *619/230–1938* ⊕ *digitalgym.org/.*

Landmark Theatres. Known for first-run foreign, art, American independent, and documentary offerings, Landmark operates three theaters in the San Diego area. **La Jolla Village Cinemas** is a modern multiplex set in a shopping center. **Hillcrest Cinemas** (✉ *3965 5th Ave., Hillcrest*) is a posh multiplex right in the middle of Uptown's action. **Ken Cinema** (✉ *4061 Adams Ave., Kensington*) is considered by many to be the last bastion of true avant-garde film in San Diego. It plays a roster of art and revival films that changes regularly (many programs are double bills). ☎ *619/298–2904* ⊕ *www.landmarktheatres.com.*

Museum of Photographic Arts. In its 226-seat theater, the museum runs a regular film program that includes classic American and international cinema by prominent filmmakers, as well as the occasional late-night screenings of cult classics. Each MoPA screening is preceded by an informative introduction from the museum staff. ✉ *1649 El Prado, Balboa Park* ☎ *619/238–7559* ⊕ *www.mopa.org.*

Reuben H. Fleet Science Center. Movies about space, science, and nature are shown on the gigantic IMAX screen here. ✉ *1875 El Prado, Balboa Park* ☎ *619/238–1233* ⊕ *www.rhfleet.org.*

San Diego Film Festival. Usually held in late September, this festival screens local, national, and international entries at the **Gaslamp Theater** (✉ *701 5th Ave., Gaslamp Quarter*), as well as the **Museum of Contemporary Art-La Jolla** (✉ *700 Prospect St., La Jolla*). The city's glitterati—as well as a few Hollywood celebs—love to rub shoulders at the fest's films, panels, and finale fête. ✉ *2683 Via de la Valle, #G210, Del Mar* ☎ *619/818–2221* ⊕ *sdfilmfest.com.*

GALLERIES

The gallery scene in San Diego comprises a broad canvas, ranging from certified works of fine art to more accessible pieces by contemporary up-and-comers.

FAMILY **Barracks 15 & 16 at NTC Liberty Station.** The former Naval Training Center at Liberty Station has been transformed into an eclectic and family-friendly alternative to the more avant garde arts scene in San Diego. Galleries include the Mexican-theme works at **Casa Valencia Baja** and innovative photography at **Outside the Lens**—just look for the giant Polaroid camera replica. ⊠ *2750 Historic Decatur Rd., Point Loma* ☎ *619/573–9300* ⊕ *www.NTCLibertyStation.com.*

Le Blank Art. An up-and-coming gallery in the La Jolla art community, Le Blank features modern and cutting-edge works by local artists in a minimalist, albeit comfortable setting. ⊠ *7920 Herschel Ave., La Jolla* ☎ *858/729–9880* ⊕ *leblankart.com.*

Quint Contemporary Art. For more than 30 years, art lovers and museum directors have snagged new pieces from established locals as well as international contemporary artists at this La Jolla mainstay. If you're in town at the time of one of the gallery's openings, you can schmooze with San Diego art royalty. ⊠ *7547 Girard Ave., La Jolla* ☎ *858/454–3409* ⊕ *quintgallery.com.*

The Stuart Collection @ UCSD. Less a gallery than an open-air scavenger hunt for some of the city's most impressive works of visual art, the Stuart Collection—located on campus at UCSD—boasts a number of must-see, and sometimes massive, pieces by some of the biggest names in contemporary art, including Jenny Holzer, John Baldessari, and Robert Irwin. ⊠ *UCSD, 9500 Gilman Dr., La Jolla* ⊕ *stuartcollection.ucsd.edu/.*

Thumbprint Gallery. This quaint little gallery brings a little edge to otherwise sleepy La Jolla, showing off some of the best lowbrow and street artists in the city. This is a great place to purchase something truly unique for a low price. ⊠ *920 Kline St., La Jolla* ☎ *858/354–6294* ⊕ *www.thumbprintgallerysd.com.*

MUSIC

From its world-class symphony and opera to the sharp array of theaters that host live music, San Diego's musical offerings will have you returning for an encore performance.

Balboa Theatre. This renovated theater offers a variety of performances including ballet, music, plays, and even stand-up comedy. In addition to architectural splendor, the space offers unsurpassed sound. ⊠ *868 4th Ave., Gaslamp Quarter* ☎ *619/570–1100* ⊕ *www.sandiegotheatres.org.*

Fodor's Choice
★ **Copley Symphony Hall.** The great acoustics here are surpassed only by the incredible Spanish baroque interior. Not just the home of the San Diego Symphony Orchestra, the renovated 2,200-seat 1920s-era theater has also hosted major stars like Elvis Costello, Leonard Cohen, and Sting. ⊠ *750 B St., Downtown* ☎ *619/235–0804* ⊕ *www.sandiegosymphony.org.*

Sleep Train Amphitheatre. The largest concert venue in town, the amphitheater can accommodate 20,000 concertgoers with reserved seats and lawn seating. It presents top-selling national and international acts during its late-spring to late-summer season. ⊠ *2050 Entertainment Circle,*

BALBOA

WWW. SDBALBOA. ORG

DID YOU KNOW?

Before reopening in 2008, the Balboa Theatre had many lives. Originally built in 1924, it screened films from Mexico as Teatro Balboa, then housed sailors during World War II.

Chula Vista ☎ 619/671–3500 ⊕ *www.sleeptrain.com/about-sleep-train-amphitheatre-chula-vista.html.*

Humphreys Concerts by the Bay. This waterfront, outdoor venue stages intimate shows from big-name national acts from April into October. There's not a bad seat in the house, but those who don't want to pay the sometimes big ticket prices can catch the concert by renting a canoe or boat and parking it in the adjacent bay for a one-of-a-kind view. ☒ *2241 Shelter Island Dr., Point Loma* ☎ 800/745–3000 ⊕ *humphreys concerts.com.*

La Jolla Athenaeum Music & Arts Library. The Athenaeum is a membership-supported, nonprofit library with an exceptional collection of books, periodicals, CDs, and other media related to arts and music. It also hosts intimate jazz, chamber music, and the occasional folk concert throughout the year. ☒ *1008 Wall St., La Jolla* ☎ 858/454–5872 ⊕ *ljathenaeum.org.*

North Park Theatre. The North Park Theatre has 85 years of history inside its ornate and beautiful walls, even though it was closed for quite a few of them. But in its newly renovated state, it's a top-tier destination for touring musical acts, ranging from comedians like Rita Rudner and bands like the New Pornographers. ☒ *2891 University Ave., North Park* ☎ 619/239–8836 ⊕ *www.thenorthparktheatre.com/.*

Open-Air Theatre. Top-name rock, reggae, and popular artists give summer concerts under the stars at this theater in the middle of the San Diego State University campus. ☒ *San Diego State University, 5500 Campanile Dr., College Area* ☎ 619/594–6947.

San Diego Opera. Drawing international performers, the opera's season runs January–April. Past performances have included *Die Fledermaus, Faust, Idomeneo,* and *La Bohème,* plus solo concerts by such talents as Renee Fleming. ☒ *Civic Theatre, 3rd Ave. and B St., Downtown* ☎ 619/533–7000 ⊕ *www.sdopera.com.*

San Diego Symphony Orchestra. The orchestra's events include classical concerts and summer and winter pops, nearly all of them at Copley Symphony Hall. The outdoor Summer Pops series is held on the Embarcadero, on North Harbor Drive beyond the convention center. ☒ *Box office, 750 B. St., Downtown* ☎ 619/235–0804 ⊕ *www. sandiegosymphony.org.*

Spreckels Theatre. A landmark theater erected in 1912, the Spreckels hosts comedy, dance, theater, and concerts. Good acoustics and old-time elegance make this a favorite local venue. ☒ *121 Broadway, Downtown* ☎ 619/235–9500 ⊕ *www.spreckels.net.*

Valley View Casino Center. Big-name concerts are held at this historic arena with room for 13,000-plus fans. ☒ *3500 Sports Arena Blvd., Sports Arena* ☎ 619/224–4171 ⊕ *valleyviewcasinocenter.com.*

Viejas Arena. Located on the San Diego State campus, the Viejas Arena attracts big-name musical and comedy acts to its 12,500-person facility. ☒ *San Diego State University, 5500 Canyon Crest Dr., College Area* ☎ 619/594–0234.

The Lamb's Players Theater presented Tim Slover's *Joyful Noise*, about the creation of Handel's *Messiah*.

THEATER

More than a few Tony-winning Broadway productions have been launched at San Diego theaters; the Old Globe and La Jolla Playhouse are just two stars in the city's large ensemble.

Coronado Playhouse. This cabaret-type theater near the Hotel Del Coronado stages regular dramatic and musical performances. ✉ *1835 Strand Way, Coronado* ☎ *619/435–4856* ⊕ *www.coronadoplayhouse.com.*

Cygnet's Old Town Theatre. A 248-seat theater operated by Cygnet Theatre Company, this is one of the more interesting small San Diego theater groups. Catch local takes on edgy classics like *Sweeney Todd* and *Little Shop of Horrors.* ✉ *4040 Twiggs St., Old Town* ☎ *619/337–1525* ⊕ *www.cygnettheatre.com.*

Diversionary Theatre. San Diego's premier gay and lesbian company presents a range of original works that focus on LGBT themes. ✉ *4545 Park Blvd., Suite 101, University Heights* ☎ *619/220–0097* ⊕ *www. diversionary.org.*

Ion Theatre Company. The little theater company that could, most of Ion's unique and sometimes controversial productions now take place in the quaint BLKBOX Theatre in Hillcrest and have included productions of *Gypsy* and *Topdog/Underdog.* ✉ *3704 6th Ave., Hillcrest* ☎ *619/600–5020* ⊕ *iontheatre.com.*

Fodor'sChoice
★
La Jolla Playhouse. Under the artistic direction of Christopher Ashley, the playhouse presents exciting and innovative plays and musicals on three stages. Many Broadway shows—among them *Memphis, Tommy,* and *Jersey Boys*—have previewed here before their East Coast premieres.

Its Without Walls program also ensures that the productions aren't limited to the playhouse, having put on site-specific shows in places like outdoor art spaces, cars, and even the ocean. ⊠ *University of California at San Diego, 2910 La Jolla Village Dr., La Jolla* ☎ *858/550–1010* ⊕ *www.lajollaplayhouse.org.*

Lamb's Players Theatre. The theater's regular season of five mostly uplifting productions runs from February through November. It also stages an original musical, *Festival of Christmas,* in December. The company has two performance spaces, the one used for most productions in Coronado, and the Horton Grand Theatre in the Gaslamp Quarter. ⊠ *1142 Orange Ave., Coronado* ☎ *619/437–6000* ⊕ *www.lambsplayers.org.*

Marie Hitchcock Puppet Theater. Amateur and professional puppeteers and ventriloquists entertain here five days a week. The cost is just a few dollars for adults and children alike. If you feel cramped in the 200-seat theater, don't worry; the shows rarely run longer than a half hour. ⊠ *2130 Pan American Rd., Balboa Park* ☎ *619/544–9203* ⊕ *www.balboaparkpuppets.com.*

Mo'olelo Performing Arts Company. Staging three productions over the year at the 10th Avenue Theatre in downtown, this company is committed to performances by newer playwrights as well as more obscure works by old masters. ⊠ *930 10th Ave., Downtown* ☎ *619/342–7395* ⊕ *moolelo.net.*

North Coast Repertory Theatre. A diverse mix of comic and dramatic works is shown in the 194-seat space. The emphasis is on contemporary productions, but the theater has been known to stage some classics, too. ⊠ *987 Lomas Santa Fe Dr., Suite D, Solana Beach* ☎ *858/481–1055* ⊕ *www.northcoastrep.org.*

Fodor's Choice ★ **The Old Globe.** This complex, comprising the Sheryl and Harvey White Theatre, the Lowell Davies Festival Theatre, and the Old Globe Theatre, offers some of the finest theatrical productions in Southern California. Theater classics such as *The Full Monty* and *Dirty Rotten Scoundrels,* both of which went on to Broadway, premiered on these famed stages. The Old Globe presents the family-friendly *How the Grinch Stole Christmas* around the holidays, as well as a renowned summer Shakespeare Festival with three to four plays in repertory. ⊠ *1363 Old Globe Way, Balboa Park* ☎ *619/234–5623* ⊕ *www.oldglobe.org.*

San Diego Civic Theatre. In addition to being the home of the San Diego Opera, the theater presents musicals and other major Broadway-style touring productions throughout the year. ⊠ *1100 3rd Ave., Downtown* ☎ *619/570–1100* ⊕ *www.sandiegotheatres.org.*

Sledgehammer Theatre. This theater company offers postmodern productions of contemporary works in an intimate, 40-seat theater. ⊠ *Tenth Avenue Arts Center, 930 10th Ave., Downtown* ☎ *619/354–5888* ⊕ *www.sledgehammer.org/.*

BEACHES

SAN DIEGO'S BEST BEACHES

In San Diego you're never far from a coastal breeze, the sting of saltwater on your face, or the feeling of soft sand squishing between your toes.

(above) Pacific Beach is the place to party. (lower right) Sea lions at the Children's Pool. (upper right) The U.S. Open Sandcastle Competition at Imperial Beach takes place annually in July or August.

This unique Southern California city, known for its easygoing charm, has 70-plus miles of pristine coastline, and the beaches here can rival any in Hawaii or the Mediterranean in terms of beauty and variety. There are beaches backed by dramatic, sheer cliffs, wide, straight stretches, and exotic coves with palm trees and shimmering blue water. Surfing and surf culture dominate some beaches, but nonsurfers can appreciate the delights of snorkeling or stand-up paddling in calmer waters. Each beach charms in a different way. Most beaches are family-friendly, but some attract more specific crowds. **Ocean Beach** has a bohemian feel, while **Pacific Beach** is a magnet for partiers. The North County lays claim to some of the choicest surfing spots, and **Black's Beach** attracts a smattering of nudists.

BEACH BONFIRE

Just because the sun went down doesn't mean it's time to go home. Nothing compares to sitting around a crackling fire as the evening breeze ushers in whiffs of the sea. Fires are allowed only in fire rings, which you can find at **Ocean Beach, Mission Beach, Pacific Beach,** and **Coronado Beach.** Revelers snap up ring slots quickly in summer; stake your claim early by filling one with wood and setting your gear nearby.

12

BEST BEACHES FOR . . .

OCEAN VIEWS

The view at **Sunset Cliffs** in Point Loma is dramatic and heart-achingly beautiful. Look for the few picnic tables that are positioned near the edge of the cliffs. **Torrey Pines State Natural Reserve** also provides fantastic views from its 300-foot-high cliffs.

ROMANCE

For a beautiful secluded spot, head to the lone shacklike hut that's nestled among the rocks at La Jolla's **Windansea Beach**. At **Fletcher Cove** in Solana Beach, look for the single bench overlooking the sea at the beach entrance.

KIDS

Despite its name, the **Children's Pool** isn't a great spot to take your kids to swim, but they'll love watching the seals and sea lions that populate its waters. **La Jolla Shores** is popular for the gentle waves in its swimmer's section, and **Mission Bay**'s serene inlets make for shallow swimming pools.

OCEAN WALK

The Hotel Del Coronado on **Coronado Beach** makes the perfect backdrop to a walk along silky sand stretching toward the horizon. **Silver Strand** and **Imperial Beach** are also lovely.

AFTER-BEACH DRINKS

Pacific Beach's Garnet Street is home to the neighborhood's liveliest bars. College students head to Garnet on Friday and Saturday nights; at other times, it's more laid-back. **Pacific Beach Bar and Grill** attracts a younger crowd, the **Silver Fox** is the quintessential dive bar, and **JRDN** at the Tower23 Hotel draws stylish locals for mojitos and small bites.

BEST BEACH EATS

The Baked Bear. This ice cream–sandwich shop a block from Pacific Beach is a local favorite. ⊠ *4516 Mission Blvd., Suite C, Pacific Beach* ☎ *858/886–7433* ⊕ *thebakedbear.com.*
Bull Taco. This taco shop perched above San Elijo State Beach is worth seeking out for its gourmet tacos like lobster, bacon, and chorizo. ■TIP➔ Parking in the campground isn't allowed for noncampers, so park along Highway 101 and walk in. ⊠ *2050 S. Coast Hwy. 101, Pacific Beach* ☎ *760/635–3595* ⊕ *www.bulltaco.com.*
Ki's Restaurant. This organic café across the street from Cardiff State Beach offers an array of healthy breakfast and lunch items. ⊠ *2591 S. Coast Hwy. 101, North County* ☎ *760/436–5236* ⊕ *www.kisrestaurant.com.*
South Beach Bar & Grill. The kitchen here makes what many consider the best fish tacos in San Diego. You must be 21 to enter. ⊠ *5059 Newport Ave. #104, Ocean Beach* ☎ *619/226–4577* ⊕ *www.southbeachob.com.*

LA JOLLA'S BEACHES AND BEYOND

La Jolla (pronounced La Hoya) means "the jewel" in Spanish and appropriately describes this small, affluent village and its beaches. Some beautiful coastline can be found here, as well as an elegant upscale atmosphere.

(above) La Jolla is synonymous with beautiful vistas. (lower right) The view from Coast Highway 101 in Carlsbad is spectacular. (upper right) Hike down to the beach from Torrey Pines.

Between North County and the Mission and South bays, La Jolla is easily accessible from downtown San Diego and North County. It's worth it to rent a car so you can sample the different beaches along the coast. The town's trademark million-dollar homes won't disappoint either—their cliff-side locations make them an attractive backdrop to the brilliant views of the sea below. Downtown La Jolla is more commercialized, with high-end stores great for browsing. La Jolla Shores, a mile-long beach, lies in the more residential area to the north. Above all, the beach and cove are La Jolla's prime charms—the cove's seals and underwater kelp beds are big draws for kayakers and nature lovers.

IN THE BUFF

Some people just don't like tan lines. Black's Beach is one of the largest clothing-optional beaches in the United States. The chances of running into naked beachgoers of all ages are higher at the north end, and Black's is properly secluded and difficult to get to. The members of Black's Beach Bares (⊕ *www.blacksbeach.org*) chronicle the beach's brand of free-spirited nudism on its website.

COAST HIGHWAY 101

The portion of Coast Highway 101 that runs south from North County into La Jolla is one of San Diego's best drives. Start at South Carlsbad beach at Tamarack Avenue and continue through Leucadia, Encinitas, Cardiff-by-the-Sea, Solana Beach, Del Mar, and, finally, La Jolla. Any turn west will take you toward the beach. The drive offers intermittent glimpses of the sea; views from Carlsbad and Cardiff are especially beautiful. The grand finale is at Torrey Pines, where the waves roll into the misty, high-bluffed beach.

THE CLIFFS AT TORREY PINES

The ocean views from the 300-foot-high sandstone cliffs atop Torrey Pines State Natural Reserve are vast and exquisite. To reach the cliffs, hike one of the short trails that lead from the visitor center. Perch along the sandy edge, and let your legs dangle. You may even see dolphins swimming along the shore or surfers riding a break.

SEALS AT THE CHILDREN'S POOL

This small protected beach has become one of San Diego's most contentious issues. Originally constructed to provide children a safe place to swim, over the last two decades much of La Jolla's harbor seal population has made itself at home on the sandy beach protected by a seawall. In the late '90s swimmers were told to avoid the pools due to concerns about water contamination and out of concern for the animals; in 2004, one irked swimmer took legal action, claiming that the pool is for children and snorkelers—not for the seals. Animal rights groups argued that the seals should be protected in their chosen habitat. In 2014 the San Diego City Council voted to close the beach entirely to beachgoers during the five-month pupping season; legal battles continue.

LA JOLLA COVE WALK AND SHOP

If you're not keen on dipping your toes in the water (or even the sand, for that matter), head over to La Jolla Cove, an ideal spot for strolling and shopping with a view. Park at any of the available metered spaces on Girard Avenue in downtown La Jolla and browse the Arcade Building, built in the Spanish Mission style. Make your way toward the cove by following the signs, or simply walk toward any patches of ocean you see.

WATER SPORTS

One of the most popular water activities is kayaking along the caves and snorkeling among the kelp beds near the cove at the Underwater Ecological Reserve. Kayak rental shops offer special outings that include midnight moonlight kayaking and the chance to dive among the leopard sharks that roam La Jolla's waters. Don't worry; the sharks are harmless.

Updated
by Casey
Hatfield-Chiotti

California's entire coastline enchants, but the state's southernmost region stands apart when it comes to sand, surf, and sea. Step out of the car and onto the beach to immediately savor its allure: smell the fresh salty air, feel the plush sand at your feet, hear waves breaking from the shore, and take in breathtaking vistas.

San Diego's sandstone bluffs offer spectacular views of the Pacific as a palette of blues and greens: there are distant indigo depths, emerald coves closer to shore, and finally, the mint-green swirls of the foamy surf.

San Diego's beaches have a different vibe from their northern counterparts in Orange County and glitzy Los Angeles. San Diego is more laid-back and less of a scene. Cyclists whiz by as surfers saunter toward the waves and sunbathers relax in the sun, be it July or November.

Whether you're seeking a safe place to take the kids or a hot spot to work on your tan, there's a beach here that's just right for you. La Jolla Shores and Mission Bay both have gentle waves and shallow waters that provide safer swimming for kids; whereas the high swells at Black's and Swami's attract surfers worldwide. If you're looking for dramatic ocean views, Torrey Pines State Beach and Sunset Cliffs provide a desertlike chaparral backdrop, with craggy cliffs overlooking the ocean below. Beaches farther south in Coronado and Silver Strand have longer stretches of sand that are perfect for a contemplative stroll or a brisk jog. Then there are those secluded, sandy enclaves that you may happen upon on a scenic drive down Highway 101.

⇨ *Beach reviews are listed geographically from south to north.*

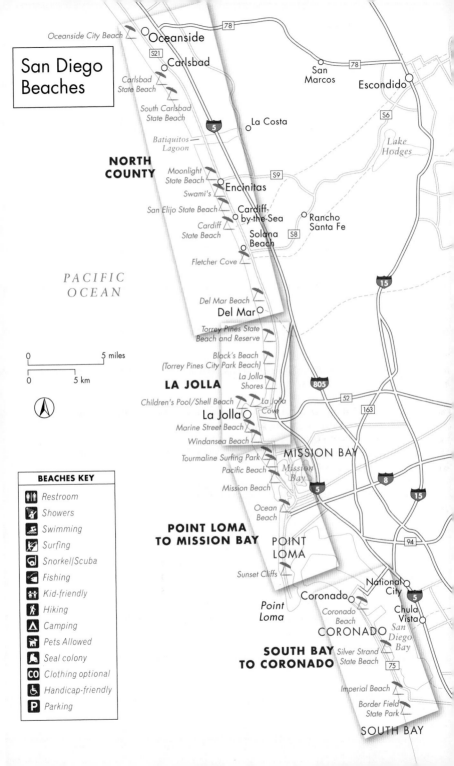

San Diego Beaches

Oceanside City Beach

Oceanside

78

S21

Carlsbad

San Marcos

78

Escondido

Carlsbad State Beach

South Carlsbad State Beach

5

La Costa

S6

Lake Hodges

Batiquitos Lagoon

NORTH COUNTY

Moonlight State Beach

Encinitas

S9

Swami's

San Elijo State Beach

Cardiff-by-the-Sea

Rancho Santa Fe

Cardiff State Beach

Solana Beach

S8

PACIFIC OCEAN

Fletcher Cove

Del Mar Beach

Del Mar

15

Torrey Pines State Beach and Reserve

0   5 miles
0   5 km

Black's Beach (Torrey Pines City Park Beach)

La Jolla Shores

LA JOLLA

52

805

163

Children's Pool/Shell Beach

La Jolla Cove

La Jolla

Marine Street Beach

Windansea Beach

Tourmaline Surfing Park

MISSION BAY

Pacific Beach

Mission Bay

8

15

Mission Beach

Ocean Beach

POINT LOMA TO MISSION BAY

POINT LOMA

94

Sunset Cliffs

National City

5

Coronado

Point Loma

Coronado Beach

Chula Vista

CORONADO

San Diego Bay

SOUTH BAY TO CORONADO

Silver Strand State Beach

75

Imperial Beach

Border Field State Park

SOUTH BAY

BEACHES KEY

- Restroom
- Showers
- Swimming
- Surfing
- Snorkel/Scuba
- Fishing
- Kid-friendly
- Hiking
- Camping
- Pets Allowed
- Seal colony
- **CO** Clothing optional
- Handicap-friendly
- **P** Parking

BEACH PLANNER

WATER TEMPERATURE

Even at summer's hottest peak, San Diego's beaches are cool and breezy. Ocean waves are large, and the water is colder than what it is at tropical beaches. Temperatures range from 55°F to 65°F from October through June, and 65°F to 73°F from July through September.

SURF FORECAST

For a surf and weather report, call San Diego's Lifeguard Services at ☎619/221–8824. These websites also provide live webcams on surf conditions and water temperature forecasts: ⊕ *www.surfingsandiego. com* and ⊕ *www.surfline.com.*

THE GREEN FLASH

Some people think it's a phony phenomenon, but the fleeting "green flash" is real, if rare. On a clear day and under certain atmospheric conditions, higher-frequency green light causes a brief green flash at the moment when the sun sinks into the sea. For a chance at seeing it, head to **Lahaina Beach House** in Pacific Beach. The bar has a large patio right on the sand and is great place to grab a pitcher at sunset.

WHAT TO BRING

In addition to beach essentials like sunscreen, many beachgoers bring boogie boards to ride the waves, blankets to lie on, buckets for the kids to make sand castles, and a beach umbrella for shade. Many beaches do not have shoreline concessions, so bring your own bottles of water and snacks. Surfers and bodysurfers often wear wet suits, which are available for purchase or rental in the shops in beach towns.

Despite Southern California's famous balminess, fog and a marine layer may creep in unexpectedly at various parts of the day. This happens often in early summer, and is referred to as "May Gray" and "June Gloom." Bring a light sweater in case the fine mist rolls in, or if you plan on staying at the beach until dark, when temperatures get cooler.

GETTING TO THE BEACH

San Diego Transit buses (⊕ *www.sdcommute.com*) stop a short walk from the beaches, but it's better to rent a car to explore on your own. Driving the scenic coastal routes is fun in itself. County Highway S21 runs along the coast between Torrey Pines State Beach and Reserve and Oceanside, although its local names (Old Highway 101 or Coast Highway 101, for example) vary by community.

PARKING

Parking is usually near the beaches, but in a few cases, such as Black's Beach, a bit of a hike is required. Finding a parking spot near the ocean can be hard in summer, but for the time being, unmetered parking is available at all San Diego city beaches. Del Mar has a pay lot and metered street parking around the 15th Street Beach. La Jolla Shores, Mission Beach, and other large beaches have visitor parking lots, but space can be limited. Your best bet is to arrive early.

12

BEACH RULES

Pay attention to signs listing illegal activities; undercover police often patrol the beaches. Smoking and alcoholic beverages are completely banned on city beaches. Drinking in beach parking lots, on boardwalks, and in landscaped areas is also illegal. Glass containers are not permitted on beaches, cliffs, and walkways, or in park areas and adjacent parking lots. Littering is not tolerated, and skateboarding is prohibited at some beaches. Fires are allowed only in fire rings or elevated barbecue grills. Although it may be tempting to take a sea creature from a tide pool as a souvenir, it may upset the delicate ecological balance, and it's illegal, too.

SAFETY

Lifeguards are stationed at city beaches from Sunset Cliffs up to Black's Beach in the summertime, but coverage in winter is provided by roving patrols only. When swimming in the ocean be aware of rip currents, which are common in California shores. If you are caught in one, don't panic. Swim parallel to the shore until you can reach land without resistance. To be safe, go swimming near lifeguard posts where you will be visible.

Few beaches have lockers to keep your belongings secure. If you're going to the beach solo and plan on going in the water, leave your wallet out of sight in your car.

POLLUTION

San Diego's beaches are well maintained and very clean during summertime, when rainfall is infrequent. Beaches along San Diego County's northern cities are typically cleaner than ones farther south. Pollution is generally worse near river mouths and storm-drain outlets, especially after heavy rainfall. Call San Diego's Lifeguard Services at ☎ *619/221–8824* for a recorded message that includes pollution reports along with surfing and diving conditions. The Heal the Bay organization (⊕ *www.healthebay.org*) monitors and grades California coastal water conditions yearly.

BEACH CAMPING

Overnight camping is not allowed on any San Diego city beach, but there are campgrounds at some state beaches (☎ *800/444–7275 for reservations* ⊕ *www.reserveamerica.com*) throughout the county.

DOG BEACHES

Leashed dogs are permitted on most San Diego beaches and adjacent parks from 6 pm to 9 am; they can run unleashed anytime at Dog Beach at the north end of Ocean Beach and, from the day after Labor Day through June 14, at Dog Beach at the rivermouth in Del Mar. It's rarely a problem, however, to take your pet to isolated beaches in winter.

RED TIDE

When sporadic algae blooms turn coastal waters a reddish-brown hue, San Diegans know the "red tide" has arrived. Environmentalists may see it as a bane to healthy ocean life, but the phenomenon is welcomed as a chance to witness ocean phosphorescence. The phytoplankton that causes the discoloration is unsightly only until nightfall. After dark,

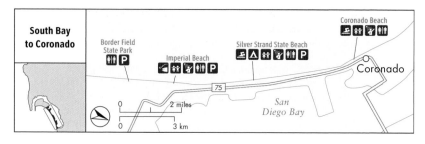

the algae-rich waters crash against the sand, inciting bioluminescent plankton to emit a bluish-green neon light. The result is a marvelous display of glow-in-the-dark waves.

BEACHES BY NEIGHBORHOOD

SOUTH BAY TO CORONADO

SOUTH BAY

Border Field State Park. San Diego's southernmost beach lies within Border Field State Park, an area with sand dunes and salt marshes favored by horseback riders and hikers. The Tijuana River Estuary, designated as a Wetland of National Importance, is a haven for endangered birds. The beach has soft sand, but due to the amount of debris and seaweed that washes up on the shore, it's not a particularly good place for sunbathing. You're better off going for a long walk or picnicking at one of the Monument Mesa sites, which offer scenic ocean views, barbecue grills, and shaded areas. Flooding in winter often restricts access, but normally the park is open to pedestrians, hikers, and equestrians on weekdays. Motorized vehicles are permitted only on weekends and holidays. ⚠ Beware: Swimming and wading are discouraged due to inshore holes and rip currents, and because no lifeguards are on duty. **Amenities:** parking (fee), toilets. **Best for:** solitude, walking. ⊠ *Monument Rd., 15 miles south of San Diego, South Bay ⊹ Exit I–5 at Dairy Mart Rd. and head west along Monument Rd. for about 5 miles* ⊕ *www.parks. ca.gov* ✉ *$5 per vehicle.*

FAMILY **Imperial Beach.** More and more people from around the country are discovering this once sleepy stretch of sand thanks to a new Marriott Autograph Collection hotel right on the beach. The 3.5-mile-long beach is a great place for long walks and bird-watching—more than 370 species can be spotted here. The Boca Rio beach break is excellent; there are year-round lifeguards, two parks with covered picnic areas, two playgrounds, and volleyball and basketball courts. Sea 180, the restaurant at the new Pier South Resort, serves Baja-Med cuisine steps from the surf. The fishing pier has views of Mexico to the south and Point Loma to the north. In July the beach is the site of the U.S. Open Sandcastle Competition. **Amenities:** lifeguards, food and drink, parking (fee), showers, toilets. **Best for:** surfing, swimming, walking. ⊠ *Seacoast Dr. at Evergreen Ave., Beach extends from Carnation Ave. to Imperial*

Beach Blvd., parking at Seacoast Dr. and Palm Ave., South Bay ✛ From I–5, take Palm Ave. west until it hits beach ☎ *619/595–3954* ⊕ *www. parks.ca.gov* 🅿 *Parking $2 a day.*

CORONADO

FAMILY

Fodor's Choice

★

Coronado Beach. This wide beach is one of San Diego's most picturesque thanks to its soft white sand and sparkly blue water. The historic Hotel Del Coronado serves as a backdrop, and it's perfect for sunbathing, people-watching, and Frisbee tossing. The beach has limited surf, but it's great for boogie-boarding and swimming. Exercisers might include Navy SEAL teams or other military units that conduct training runs on beaches in and around Coronado. There are picnic tables, grills, and popular fire rings, but don't bring laquered wood or pallets. Only natural wood is allowed for burning. There's also a dog beach on the north end. There's free parking along Ocean Boulevard, though it's often hard to snag a space. **Amenities:** food and drink, lifeguards, showers, toilets. **Best for:** walking, swimming. ⊠ *Ocean Blvd., Between S. O St. and Orange Ave., Coronado ✛ From the San Diego–Coronado bridge, turn left on Orange Ave. and follow signs.*

FAMILY

Silver Strand State Beach. This quiet beach on a narrow sand-spit allows visitors a unique opportunity to experience both the Pacific Ocean and the San Diego Bay. The 2.5 miles of ocean side is great for surfing and other water sports while the bay side, accessible via foot tunnel under Highway 75, has calmer, warmer water and great views of the San Diego skyline. Lifeguards and rangers are on duty year-round, and there are places for biking, volleyball, and fishing. Picnic tables, grills, and fire pits are available in summer, and the Silver Strand Beach Cafe is open Memorial Day through Labor Day. The beach is close to Loews Coronado Bay Resort and the Coronado Cays, an exclusive community popular with yacht owners and celebrities. You can reserve RV sites ($65 beach; $50 inland) online (⊕ *www.reserveamerica.com*). Three day-use parking lots provide room for 800 cars. **Amenities:** food and drink, lifeguards, parking (fee), showers, toilets. **Best for:** walking, swimming, surfing. ⊠ *5000 Hwy. 75, 4.5 miles south of city of Coronado, Coronado* ☎ *619/435–5184* ⊕ *www.parks.ca.gov/silverstrand* 🅿 *Parking $10, $30 motorhome.*

POINT LOMA, MISSION BAY, AND LA JOLLA

POINT LOMA

Ocean Beach. This mile-long beach south of Mission Bay's channel is the place to get a slice of vintage SoCal beach culture. It's likely you'll see VW vans in the parking lot near the Ocean Beach Pier. The wide beach is popular with volleyball players, sunbathers, and surfers. The municipal pier at the southern end extends a ½ mile out to sea and is one of the only places you can fish in San Diego without a valid California fishing license. There's a café about halfway out, and bars and restaurants can be found on the streets near the beach. Swimmers should beware of strong rip currents around the main lifeguard tower. One of Ocean Beach's most popular features is the dog beach at the northern end, where canines can run freely and splash in the waves 24 hours a day.

The grassy palm-lined park above La Jolla Cove is great for picnics.

For shade, picnic areas with BBQs, and a paved path, check out Robb Field, across from Dog Beach. **Amenities:** lifeguards, parking (no fee), showers, toilets. **Best for:** surfing, swimming, walking. ⊠ *Newport Ave. at Abbott St., 7 miles from downtown San Diego, Ocean Beach* ⊕ *www. sandiego.gov/lifeguards/beaches/ob.shtml.*

MISSION BAY

FAMILY **Mission Beach.** With a roller coaster, artificial wave park, and hotdog stands, this 2-mile long beach has a carnival vibe and is the closest thing you'll find to Coney Island on the West Coast. It's lively year-round but draws a huge crowd on hot summer days. A wide boardwalk paralleling the beach is popular with walkers, joggers, roller skaters, rollerbladers, and bicyclists. To escape the crowds a bit, head to South Mission Beach. It attracts surfers, swimmers, and scantily-clad volleyball players, who often play competitive pick-up games on the courts near the N. Jetty. The water near the Belmont Park roller coaster can be a bit rough but makes for good boogie boarding and body surfing. For parking, you can try for a spot on the street, but your best bets are the two big lots at Belmont Park. **Amenities:** lifeguards, parking (no fee), showers, toilets. **Best for:** swimming, surfing, walking. ⊠ *3000 Mission Blvd., parking near roller coaster at West Mission Bay Dr., Mission Bay* ⊕ *www. sandiego.gov/lifeguards/beaches/mb.shtml.*

Pacific Beach/North Pacific Beach. This beach, known for attracting a young college-age crowd, runs from the northern end of Mission Beach to Crystal Pier. The scene here is lively on weekends, with nearby restaurants, beach bars, and nightclubs providing a party atmosphere. In P.B. (as the local call it) Sundays are known as "Sunday Funday,"

and pub crawls can last all day. So although drinking is no longer allowed on the beach, it's likely you'll see people who have had one too many. The mood changes just north of the pier at North Pacific Beach, which attracts families and surfers. Although not quite pillowy, the sand at both beaches is nice and soft, which makes for great sunbathing and sand-castle building. ■TIP→ **Kelp and flies can be problem on this stretch, so choose your spot wisely.** Parking at Pacific Beach can also be a challenge. A few coveted free angle parking spaces are available along the boardwalk, but you'll most likely have to look for spots in the surrounding neighborhood. **Amenities:** food and drink, lifeguards, parking (no fee), showers, toilets. **Best for:** partiers, swimming, surfing. ✉ *4500 Ocean Blvd., Pacific Beach* ⊕ *www.sandiego. gov/lifeguards/beaches/pb.shtml.*

SNACK TIP

Trader Joe's. On your way to Pacific Beach? Head to Trader Joe's for sandwiches, sandwich fixings, chips, dried fruits, nuts, beverages, and tasty cheeses. ✉ *1211 Garnet Ave., Pacific Beach* ☎ *858/272-7235* ⊕ *www. traderjoes.com.*

Tourmaline Surfing Park. Offering slow waves and frequent winds, this is one of the most popular beaches for beginning surfers, longboarders, windsurfers, and kiteboarders. The 175-space parking lot at the foot of Tourmaline Street normally fills to capacity by midday. Just like Pacific Beach, Tourmaline has soft, tawny colored sand, but when the tide is in the beach becomes narrow, making finding a good sunbathing spot a bit of a challenge. **Amenities:** seasonal lifeguards, parking (no fee), showers, toilets. **Best for:** windsurfing, surfing. ✉ *600 Tourmaline St., Pacific Beach.*

LA JOLLA

FAMILY **Children's Pool.** Due to the groups of harbor seals that have claimed it as their own, this shallow cove, protected by a seawall, is closed to the public for the winter pupping season, December 15 through May 15. People may access its calm, protected waters the other seven months of the year, however, and the beach's small waves make it an ideal place for children to splash and play. Adults will appreciate the view. Because of its location at the tip of La Jolla peninsula, you can actually look east to get unmatched panoramic views of the coastline and ocean. The area just outside the pool is popular with scuba divers, who explore the offshore reef when the surf is calm. Although you may not be able

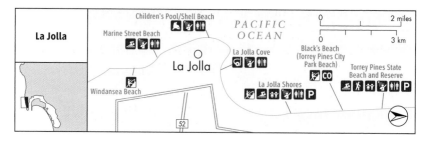

to go on the beach during the winter months, it's still worth a peak to see the seals and their pups from above. **Amenities:** lifeguards, showers, toilets. **Best for:** walking. ⊠ *850 Coast Blvd., La Jolla* ⊕ *www.sandiego. gov/lifeguards/beaches/pool.shtml.*

FAMILY

Fodor'sChoice

★

La Jolla Cove. This shimmering blue-green inlet surrounded by cliffs is what first attracted everyone to La Jolla, from Native Americans to the glitterati. "The Cove," as locals refer to it, beyond where Girard Avenue dead-ends into Coast Boulevard, is marked by towering palms that line a promenade where people strolling in designer clothes are as common as Frisbee throwers. Ellen Browning Scripps Park sits atop cliffs formed by the pounding of the waves and offers a great spot for picnics with a view. The Cove has beautiful white sand that is coarse near the water's edge, but the beach is still a great place for lounging. At low tide, the pools and cliff caves are a destination for explorers. This is also the best place in San Diego for snorkeling, and snorkelers can spot bright-orange Garibaldi fish and other marine life in the waters of the **San Diego–La Jolla Underwater Park Ecological Reserve.** The cove is also a favorite of rough-water swimmers. **Amenities:** lifeguards, showers, toilets. **Best for:** snorkeling, swimming, walking. ⊠ *1100 Coast Blvd., east of Ellen Browning Scripps Park, La Jolla* ⊕ *www.sandiego. gov/lifeguards/beaches/cove.shtml.*

FAMILY

La Jolla Shores. This is one of San Diego's most popular beaches due to its wide sandy shore, gentle waves, and incredible views of La Jolla peninsula. There's also a largy grassy park, and adjacent to La Jolla Shores lies the **San Diego La Jolla Underwater Park Ecological Reserve,** 6,000 acres of protected ocean bottom and tide lands. The white powdery sand at La Jolla Sands is some of San Diego's best, and several surf and scuba schools teach here. Kayaks can also be rented nearby. A concrete boardwalk parallels the beach, and a boat launch for small vessels lies 300 yards south of the lifeguard station at Avenida de Playa. Arrive early to get a parking spot in the lot at the foot of Calle Frescota. **Amenities:** lifeguards, parking (no fee), showers, toilets. **Best for:** surfing, swimming, walking. ⊠ *8200 Camino del Oro, 2 miles north of downtown La Jolla, La Jolla* ⊕ *www.sandiego.gov/lifeguards/beaches/ shores.shtml.*

Marine Street Beach. This wide expanse of white sand is famous for bodysurfing due to its powerful shorebreak, but it also teems with sunbathers, swimmers, walkers, joggers, and folks just out for the incredible views. The sand is soft and fluffy and feels wonderful as it squishes through your toes. Swimmers need to beware; waves break in extremely shallow water and you need to watch out for riptides. There are no amenities at the beach, but picnic tables, showers, and toilets are available at the nearby cove. **Amenities:** lifeguards. **Best for:** solitude, swimming, walking. ⊠ *Marine St. at Vista Del Mar Ave., 3 blocks west of La Jolla Blvd., La Jolla.*

12

Shell Beach. The small cove north of the Children's Pool remains remarkably under the radar and is typically less crowded than nearby beaches like La Jolla Cove and La Jolla Shores. The secluded beach is accessible by stairs and has clear water and tidepools. The reef comes all the way up to the shore, making it a less-than-ideal spot for swimming, but children love to wade in the shallow water. As the name would imply, tiny shells make up the sand near the water's edge. It's beautiful but coarse and can be hard on people's feet. Your visit is better spent exploring than sunning. The exposed rocks off the coast have been designated a protected habitat for sea lions; you can watch them frolic in the water. Picnic tables, showers, and toilets are available near the cove. **Amenities:** none. **Best for:** solitude. ⊠ *Coast Blvd, north of Children's Pool and south of Ellen Browning Scripps Park, La Jolla.*

Fodor'sChoice
★

Torrey Pines State Beach and Reserve. With sandstone cliffs and hiking trails adjacent to the beach rather than urban development, Torrey Pines State Beach feels far away from the SoCal sprawl. The beach and reserve encompasses 1,600 acres of sandstone cliffs and deep ravines, and a network of meandering trails lead to the wide, pristine beach below. Along the way enjoy the rare Torrey pine trees, found only here and on Santa Rosa Island, offshore. Guides conduct tours of the nature preserve on weekends. Torrey Pines gets crowded in summer, but you'll find more isolated spots heading south under the cliffs leading to Black's Beach. Smooth rocks often wash up on stretches of the beach making it a challenge, at times, to go barefoot. If you can find a patch that is clear of debris, you'll encounter the soft, golden sand San Diego is known for. There is a paid parking lot at the entrance to the park but also look for free angle parking along N. Torrey Pines Rd. **Amenities:** lifeguards, parking (fee), showers, toilets. **Best for:** swimming, surfing, walking. ⊠ *12600 N. Torrey Pines Rd.* ☎ *858/755-2063* ⊕ *www.torreypine.org* 🅿 *Parking $12–$15 per vehicle depending on day and season.*

Fodor'sChoice
★

Windansea Beach. With its rocky shoreline and strong shore break, Windansea stands out among San Diego beaches for its dramatic natural beauty. It's one of the best surf spots in San Diego County. Professional surfers love the unusual A-frame waves the reef break here creates. Although the large sandstone rocks that dot the beach might sound like a hinderance, they actually serve as protective barriers from the wind, making this one of the best beaches in San Diego for sunbathing. The beach's palm-covered surf shack is a protected historical landmark, and a seat here at sunset may just be one of the most romantic spots on the West Coast. The name Windansea comes from a hotel that burned down in the late 1940s. You can usually find nearby street parking. **Amenities:** seasonal lifeguards, toilet. **Best for:** sunset, surfing, solitude. ⊠ *Neptune Pl. at Nautilus St., La Jolla* ⊕ *www.sandiego.gov/lifeguards/beaches/windan.shtml.*

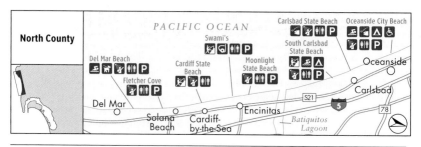

NORTH COUNTY BEACHES

DEL MAR

FAMILY **Del Mar Beach.** This famously clean 2-mile-long beach is the perfect place for long barefoot walks and sunbathing due to its fine, soft sand and lack of seaweed. Del Mar Beach is also a great place for families. It has year-round lifeguards and areas clearly marked for swimming and surfing. Depending on the swell, you may see surfers at the 15th Street surf break; volleyball players love the courts at the beach's far North end. The section of beach south of 15th is lined with cliffs and tends to be less crowded than Main Beach, which extends from 15th north to 29th. Leashed dogs are permitted on most sections of the beach, except Main Beach, where they are prohibited from June 15 through the Tuesday after Labor Day. For the rest of the year, dogs may run under voice control at North Beach, just north of the River Mouth, also known locally as Dog Beach. Food, hotels, and shopping are all within an easy walk of Del Mar beach. Parking costs from $1.50 to $3 per hour at meters and pay lots on Coast Boulevard and along Camino Del Mar. **Amenities:** food and drink, lifeguards, parking (fee), showers, toilets. **Best for:** swimming, walking. ⊠ *Main Beach, 1700 Coast Blvd., North Beach 3200–3300 Camino Del Mar, Del Mar* ☎ *858/755–1556* ⊕ *www.delmar.ca.us/203/Beaches-Parks.*

SOLANA BEACH

Fletcher Cove. Most of the beaches in the little city of Solana Beach are nestled under cliffs, and access is limited to private stairways. However, at the west end of Lomas Santa Fe Drive, where it turns into Plaza Street, there's an entrance to this small beach, along with parking lot, picnic area, playground, and restrooms. The softest sand can be found by the cliffs and it gets a bit coarser as you near the water's edge. During low tide it's an easy walk under the cliffs to nearby beaches, but high tide can make some of the beach impassable. At the northern end of town there are also restrooms, a pay lot, and easy beach access. The City of Solana Beach and the Belly Up Tavern host free summer concerts at Fletcher Cove (⊕ *www.cityofsolanabeach.org*) and there are plenty of great restaurants nearby on Highway 101 and on Cedros Avenue. Tides and surf conditions are posted at a kiosk by this parking lot. **Amenities:** lifeguards, parking (no fee), showers, toilets. **Best for:** surfing, solitude, swimming, walking. ⊠ *Plaza St. at S. Sierra Ave., Solana Beach.*

Check out the scene along Carlsbad State Beach's pedestrian walkway.

CARDIFF-BY-THE-SEA

Cardiff State Beach. A reef break draws surfers to this beach, popularly known as George's, and there are great cafés and restaurants nearby, such as Las Olas and Ki's. Stones run along the highway but then give way to a nice swath of sand. A walk south provides access to some of Solana Beach's secluded coves. ■TIP→ Pay attention to the incoming tide, or you may have to wade or swim back to the parking lot. The beach begins at the parking lot immediately north of the cliffs at Solana Beach. **Amenities:** lifeguards, parking (fee), showers, toilets. **Best for:** surfing, swimming. ⊠ *Hwy. 101 (Rte. S21), 1 mile south of Cardiff, Cardiff-by-the-Sea* ☎ *760/753–5091* ⊕ *www.parks.ca.gov* ⊠ *$10 per vehicle; $15 peak weekends/holidays.*

ENCINITAS

Moonlight State Beach. Its large parking areas, many facilities, and proximity to the quaint coastal town of Encinitas make this beach tucked into a break in the cliffs a great getaway. The volleyball courts on the northern end attract many competent players, and professionals can be spotted surfing the break known locally as "D Street." Moonlight is easily accessible from the Encinitas Coaster train station and S. Coast Highway 101, which runs right through town, is lined with great shops, restaurants and bars. There's a large free parking lot near the corner of 3rd and B Street. **Amenities:** food and drink, lifeguards, parking (no fee), showers, toilets. **Best for:** sunset, surfing, swimming. ⊠ *399 C St., Encinitas* ✛ *To get to beach from I–5, take Encinitas Blvd. west until it ends* ⊕ *www.parks.ca.gov.*

Swami's. The palms and the golden lotus-flower domes of the nearby Self-Realization Center temple and ashram earned this picturesque beach, also a top surfing spot, its name. Extreme low tides expose tide pools that harbor anemones, starfish, and other sea life. The only access is by a long stairway leading down from the cliff-top Seaside Roadside Park, where there's free parking. On big winter swells, the bluffs are lined with gawkers watching the area's best surfers take on—and be taken down by—some of the county's best big waves. The beach has flat, packed sand and can accumulate seaweed and some flies, so if laying out is your main objective you might want to head north to Moonlight Beach. Offshore, divers do their thing at North County's underwater park, Encinitas Marine Life Refuge. Sea Cliff, the small park next to the Swami's parking lot, offers shade trees, picnic tables, barbecues, and bathrooms. **Amenities:** lifeguards, parking (no fee), showers, toilets. **Best for:** snorkeling, surfing, swimming. ⊠ *1298 S. Coast Hwy. 101 (Rte. S21), 1 mile north of Cardiff, Encinitas.*

CARLSBAD

South Carlsbad State Beach/Carlsbad State Beach. There are fine street- and beach-level promenades at South Carlsbad State Beach, and although it may be rockier than most beaches in Southern California, it's still a good swimming spot. There's overnight camping for self-contained RVs (☎ *800/444–7275*). Farther north at the foot of Tamarack Avenue is Carlsbad State Beach. You can't camp here, but there's fishing and jogging trails and the beach has separate swimming and surfing sections. In summer, the south swell creates good surf when other San Diego beaches are bereft. The cement walkway that borders the beach continues into downtown Carlsbad, which has plenty of restaurants. Carlsbad State Beach has a paid parking lot on Tamarack Ave. **Amenities:** lifeguards, parking (fee), showers, toilets. **Best for:** walking, swimming, surfing. ⊠ *South Carlsbad Beach, 7201 Carlsbad Blvd., Carlsbad Beach; Tamarack Ave. at Carlsbad Blvd., Carlsbad* ☎ *760/438–3143* ⊕ *www.parks.ca.gov* ⊠ *$10–$15 per vehicle.*

OCEANSIDE

Oceanside City Beach. This long, straight beach is popular with swimmers, surfers, and U.S. Marines from nearby Camp Pendleton. The impressive wooden Oceanside Pier extends a quarter of a mile into the ocean, and there's a '50s-style diner called Ruby's at the end. The sand here is a bit course, and smaller rocks can be found in some sections, but due to its width (a quarter mile from street to surf near 1200 N. Pacific Street) nice patches can almost always be found. There is surfing around the pier, but the waves are bigger and better just north at Oceanside Harbor, which gets a south swell in the summer. Self-serve RV camping is permitted in the parking lot at the northernmost end of Harbor Beach, but there's no tent camping. Pay lots and meters are located around the pier and also in the Oceanside Harbor area. A free two-hour lot can be found east of the pay lots on Harbor Drive South. Wyndham Oceanside Pier Resort is steps away. **Amenities:** seasonal lifeguards, food and drink, parking (fee), toilets, showers. **Best for:** surfing, swimming, walking. ⊠ *200 N. the Strand, Oceanside* ⊠ *$8 parking.*

SPORTS AND
THE OUTDOORS

SURFING SAN DIEGO

Head to a San Diego beach on any given day and chances are you'll see a group of surfers in the water, patiently waiting to ride a memorable break. Spectators as well as enthusiasts agree that catching a perfect wave is an unforgettable experience.

(above) La Jolla Shores is a good beach for beginner surfers. *(lower right)* Surfer at the end of a good ride. *(upper right)* Instructors at Surf Diva Surf School cater to women.

Surfing may have originated in Hawaii, but modern surfing culture is inextricably linked to the Southern California lifestyle. From the Malibu setting of *Gidget* to the surf-city sounds of Jan and Dean and the Beach Boys, and TV's *Laguna Beach* and *The OC*, the entertainment industry brought a California version of surfing to the landlocked, and in the process created an enduring mystique.

San Diego surfing in particular is unique. Underwater kelp beds help keep waves intact, preventing the choppiness that surfers bemoan. Santa Ana winds that begin to arrive in fall and throughout early winter bring coveted offshore winds that contribute to morning and evening "glass" (the stillness of the water that encourages smooth waves).

BEST TIME TO GO

In San Diego the biggest swells usually occur in winter, although good-size waves can form year-round. Generally, swells come from a northerly direction in winter and from the south in summer. Certain surf spots are better on different swells. In winter, try beaches like Swami's or Black's Beach. Summer spots are La Jolla's Windansea and nearby Tourmaline Surfing Park.

TYPES OF BREAKS

Beach break: Waves that break over sandbars and the seafloor and are usually tamer and consistently long, thus typically the best type for beginners, with the exception of Black's Beach, which is legendary for its uniquely large beach breaks. **La Jolla Shores, Mission Beach,** and **Pacific Beach** are destinations for gentler, more forgiving waves.

Point break: Created as waves that hit a point jutting into the ocean. Surfers then peel down the swell it creates. With the right conditions, this can create very consistent waves. **Swami's** has an excellent point break.

Reef break: Waves break as they hit reef. It can create great (but dangerous) surf. There's a good chance of getting smashed and scraped over extremely sharp coral or rocks. Many of San Diego's best breaks occur thanks to underwater reefs, as at **San Elijo, La Jolla Cove,** and **Windansea**.

SAN DIEGO SURF FINDER

Get a closer view of surfers doing their thing from any municipal pier, such as at **Oceanside, Pacific,** and **Mission beaches.** The high bluffs of **Black's Beach** are also excellent points to watch surfers.

Swami's: Famous for its point break and beautiful waters.

Black's Beach: This is where to go for beach breaks. Serious surfers carry their boards and take a hike to reach the beach.

Windansea Beach: A dual beach for surf and romance. Known for its reef breaks.

Tourmaline Surfing Park: Windsurfers and surfers share Tourmaline's smooth waves.

La Jolla Shores: First-timers head here for more modest waves.

SURF SLANG

Barrel: The area created when a wave breaks onto itself in a curl.

Close out: When a wave breaks all at once, rather than breaking steadily in one direction.

Cutback: The most basic turn in surfing; executed to maintain position close to the barrel.

Dropping in: A severe breach of etiquette wherein a second surfer joins the wave later and cuts off the original rider.

Goofy foot: Having a right-foot-forward stance on the surfboard. The opposite is known as natural.

Grom: An affectionate term for those sun-bleached kids with tiny surfboards.

Hollow: Not all barrels create hollows, which are barrels big enough to create a tube that a surfer can ride within—also called the green room.

Lineup: A group of surfers waiting beyond the breakers for waves to come in.

Turtle roll: A maneuver in which the surfer rolls over on the surfboard, going underwater and holding the board upside down.

13

Updated
by Casey
Hatfield-Chiotti

With average daily temperatures of 70.5 degrees Fahrenheit, San Diego is built for outdoor activities year-round. As you'd expect, the ocean is one of San Diego's most popular natural attractions. Surfers, swimmers, kayakers, divers, snorkelers, and paddleboarders have 70 miles of shorefront to explore. What might surprise you is there is also great hiking, horseback riding, rock-climbing, biking, and more. The possibilities for outdoor activity really are endless and evidence of San Diego's outdoorsy spirit is apparent everywhere; you'll likely see runners swarming the waterfront and Balboa Park, groups of surfers bobbing in the water at dawn, hang gliders swooping off sandstone cliffs, and white sails gliding gracefully along the shore. Outdoor enthusiasts are as much a part of San Diego's landscape as the sea, sand, and hills, and if you want to get in on the action, it's easy. Companies offering kayak and snorkeling tours and rentals are prevalent, especially in the beach communities of La Jolla, Mission Beach, and on Coronado. If you want to learn to surf, sign up for a lesson at one of the many surf schools in La Jolla or rent a board in Mission Beach and go out on your own. If sightseeing is more your style you can head out on a fishing or whale-watching excursion aboard a charter boat or take a sunset stroll on a wide, sandy beach. At the end of the day at any beach in the county, you'll surely see a local ritual: everyone stops what they're doing to watch the sun's orange orb slip silently into the blue-gray Pacific.

SPORTS AND THE OUTDOORS PLANNER

SAN DIEGO BY THE SEASONS

San Diego has miles of beaches and bays, numerous lakes, mountains, and deserts to explore. With balmy average temperatures and less than a foot of rain per year, the lure to go play outside is hard to resist. That said, Southern California isn't as seasonless as some claim. Although the weather is generally mild and sunny year-round, the seasons do bring different outdoor activities.

Summer is the best time to plan your trip from an outdoor activities point of view (this is peak tourist season for a reason). San Diego's proximity to the ocean offers an almost endless selection of water activities. Rent kayaks at La Jolla Cove, take a charter boat off Point Loma for deep-sea tuna fishing, or simply hit the beach and go for a swim. The Bahia Resort at Mission Bay offers Jet Ski and sailboat rentals to help

TOP OUTDOOR EXPERIENCES

Kayak La Jolla's caves: Join a tour to explore the seven caves off La Jolla Cove; you can see lots of wildlife, including seals, sea lions, and maybe leopard sharks and dolphins.

Bike the boardwalk: Rent a beach cruiser and pedal along the Mission Bay boardwalk. You'll be in good company among the scene-making muscle men and babes in bikinis.

Catch a wave: Surf La Jolla Cove's famous reef breaks or watch the surfers at Swami's beach from the Self-Realization Foundation's meditation gardens on the cliffs above.

Horseback ride in the surf: San Diego Beach Rides offers sunset horseback rides in Border Field State Park.

Hit the links: With so many courses in San Diego, there's sure to be something for every golfer. Add to that the perfect weather and sweeping views of the ocean and it's tee time.

you enjoy the shimmering bay. Visitors planning a trip in early summer should be aware of the phenomenon known as "May Gray and June Gloom," when fog often blankets the coast in the morning. Things usually clear up by the afternoon, but occasionally the fog lasts all day, making a trip to the beach a damp and chilly affair.

The temperature begins to cool down for winter, but before it does, Santa Ana winds usher a warm dry spell throughout Southern California through the **fall**. It's the perfect time to shoot 18 holes at the Park Hyatt Aviara in Carlsbad, or take a hike at the Bayside Trail at Cabrillo National Monument—fall's cloudless skies allow for a crisp, clear vision of the Pacific. And although the foliage in San Diego doesn't turn into burnished reds and golds, you can appreciate the rare species of evergreen at Torrey Pines State Reserve.

Winter in California is hardly bitter or harsh, but the weather certainly gets too cold for water sports. Serious surfers love the breaks best in winter, when the swells are high. Black's Beach continues to be one of the most challenging surfing beaches in San Diego. Winter is also when gray whales migrate to warmer waters. Charter boats offer whale-watching trips between December and March. View the whales with San Diego Harbor Excursion or with one of the more intimate sailboat charters offered around town. Sunsets can be particularly spectacular during the winter months.

In **spring**, wildflowers begin to appear at Anza-Borrego Desert Park. At peak months, the desert terrain blooms with vibrant colors.

If you're interested in something sportier, Escondido's lakes are filled with bass, bluegill, and catfish waiting to be hooked.

PARTICIPATION SPORTS

BALLOONING

Enjoy views of the Pacific Ocean, the mountains, and the coastline south to Mexico and north to San Clemente from a hot-air balloon at sunrise or sunset; most excursions include beverages and snacks, too. The conditions are perfect: wide-open spaces and just enough wind to breeze you through them.

California Dreamin'. Head here for hot-air balloon rides, specializing in Temecula wine country flights and Del Mar sunset coastal excursions. ✉ *33133 Vista del Monte Rd., Temecula* ☎ *800/373–3359* ⊕ *www.californiadreamin.com.*

Skysurfer Balloon Company. Lift off for a one-hour champagne and sunset flight in Del Mar ($210 per person).■ TIP➔ Ask if they're running any special rates for couples. ✉ *3755 Townsgate Dr., Del Mar* ☎ *858/481–6800* ⊕ *www.sandiegohotairballoons.com.*

WORD OF MOUTH

"If you are adventuresome, my two favorite recommendations are [first,] kayaking in La Jolla Cove. You are likely to see and maybe even be surrounded by leopard sharks, which are completely harmless. It is a stunning experience. [Second,] hiking at the Torrey Pines State Park. My favorite is the beach hike." —ncounty

BICYCLING

San Diego offers bountiful opportunities for bikers, from casual boardwalk cruises to strenuous rides into the hills. The mild climate makes biking in San Diego a year-round delight. Bike culture is respected here, and visitors are often impressed with the miles of designated bike lanes running alongside city streets and coastal roads throughout the county.

BIKE PATHS

Lomas Santa Fe Drive. Experienced cyclists follow this route in Solana Beach east into Rancho Santa Fe, perhaps even continuing east on Del Dios Highway, past Lake Hodges, to Escondido. These roads can be narrow and winding in spots.

Mission Beach Boardwalk. A ride here is a great way to take in a classic California scene. Keep in mind this route is more for cruising than hardcore cycling, as the gawkers and crowds often slow foot- and bike traffic to a crawl. ✉ *Mission Beach.*

Route S21. On many summer days, Route S21, aka Old Highway 101, from La Jolla to Oceanside looks like a freeway for cyclists. About 24 miles long, it's easily the most popular and scenic bike route around, never straying far from the beach. Although the terrain is fairly easy, the long, steep Torrey Pines grade is famous for weeding out the weak. Another Darwinian challenge is dodging slow-moving pedestrians and cars pulling over to park in towns like Encinitas and Del Mar. ✉ *La Jolla.*

Coast Highway 101 is a haven for bicyclists from Oceanside down to La Jolla.

BIKE TOURS AND RENTALS

Bike & Kayak Tours. This bike and kayak outfitter, with locations in La Jolla and on Coronado, is your one-stop shop for biking fun. It offers bike rentals and tours like La Jolla Freefall tour that starts at Mt. Soledad, La Jolla's highest point, and continues down the mountain, past mansions and along the coastline. Bike & Kayak Tours also offers a hotel delivery service, via which they drop off Gary Fisher mountain bikes or Scott Racing road bikes right at your doorstep. ⊠ *2158 Ave. De La Playa, La Jolla* ☎ *858/454–1010* ⊕ *bikeandkayaktours.com.*

The Bike Revolution. Choose from a wide array of rentals, from road bikes to cruisers, and embark on a ride along the downtown waterfront, up the hill to Balboa Park, or hop on the ferry to Coronado Island for a leisurely ride around the idyllic island. ⊠ *522 6th Ave., Downtown* ☎ *619/238–2444* ⊕ *www.thebikerevolution.com.*

Cheap Rentals Mission Beach. A little over a block off the boardwalk, this place has good daily and weekly prices for surfboards, stand-up paddleboards, kayaks, skateboards, ice chests, umbrellas, chairs, and bike rentals, including beach cruisers, tandems, hybrids, and two-wheeled baby carriers. Demand is high during the busy season (May through September), so call to reserve equipment ahead of time. ⊠ *3689*

Mission Blvd., Mission Beach ☎ *858/488–9070, 800/941–7761* ⊕ *www.cheap-rentals.com.*

Hike Bike Kayak San Diego. This outfitter offers a wide range of guided bike tours, from easy excursions around Mission Bay and Coronado Island to slightly more rigorous trips through coastal La Jolla. Tours last up to two and a half hours, and cost $30–40 per person. The company also rents bikes and can even deliver them to your hotel. ✉ *2222 Ave. de la Playa, La Jolla* ☎ *858/551–9510* ⊕ *www.hikebikekayak.com.*

Holland's Bicycles. This is a great bike rental source on Coronado Island. It also has another store (**Bikes and Beyond** ☎ 619/435–7180) located at the ferry landing, so you can jump on your bike as soon as you cross the harbor from downtown San Diego. ✉ *977 Orange Ave., Coronado* ☎ *619/435–3153* ⊕ *www.hollandsbicycles.com.*

Wheel Fun Rentals. Surreys, cruisers, mountain bikes, tandems, and electric bicycles, among other two-, three-, and four-wheeled contraptions, are available at the downtown Holiday Inn and a number of other locations around San Diego; call or visit the website for details. ✉ *1355 N. Harbor Dr., Downtown* ☎ *619/342–7244* ⊕ *www.wheelfunrentals.com.*

DIVING AND SNORKELING

The kelp forests and protected marine areas off the San Diego coast are easily accessible and offer divers ample opportunities to explore. Classes are available for beginners, while experienced divers will appreciate the challenges of local wreck and canyon dives. Water temperatures can be chilly, so check with a local outfitter for the appropriate gear before setting out.

San Diego City Lifeguard Service. Call this hotline for pre-recorded, up-to-date diving information and conditions. ☎ *619/221–8824* ⊕ *www.sandiego.gov/lifeguards.*

DIVE SITES

Mission Beach. The HMCS *Yukon*, a decommissioned Canadian warship, was intentionally sunk off Mission Beach to create the main diving destination in San Diego. A mishap caused the ship to settle on its side, creating a surreal, M.C. Escher–esque diving environment. This is a technical dive and should be attempted only by experienced divers; even diving instructors have become disoriented inside the wreck, and a few have even died trying to explore it. ✉ *Mission Beach.*

San Diego–La Jolla Underwater Park Ecological Preserve. Diving enthusiasts the world over come to San Diego to snorkel and scuba dive off La

Jolla at the underwater preserve. Because all sea life is protected here, this 533-acre preserve (all of La Jolla Cove to La Jolla Shores) is the best place to see large lobster, sea bass, and sculpin (scorpion fish), as well as numerous golden garibaldi damselfish, the state marine fish. It's common to see hundreds of beautiful (and harmless) leopard sharks schooling at the north end of the cove, near La Jolla Shores, especially in summer. ⊠ *La Jolla Shores and Ellen Browning Scripps Park, La Jolla.*

Scripps Canyon. Off the south end of Black's Beach, the rim of Scripps Canyon lies in about 60 feet of water and comprises the Marine Life Refuge. The canyon plummets more than 900 feet in some sections.

13

DIVE TOURS AND OUTFITTERS

Ocean Enterprises Scuba Diving. Stop in for everything you need to plan a diving adventure, including equipment, advice, and instruction. ⊠ *7710 Balboa Ave., Suite 101, Clairemont Mesa* ☎ *858/565–6054* ⊕ *www. oceanenterprises.com.*

Scuba San Diego. This center is well regarded for its top-notch instruction and certification programs, as well as for guided dive tours. Trips include dives to kelp reefs in La Jolla Cove, and night diving at La Jolla Canyon. ⊠ *San Diego Hilton Hotel, 1775 E. Mission Bay Dr., Mission Bay* ☎ *619/260–1880* ⊕ *www.scubasandiego.com.*

FISHING

San Diego's waters are home to many game species; you never know what you'll hook. Depending on the season, a half- or full-day ocean charter trip could bring in a yellowfin, dorado, sea bass, or halibut. Longer trips to Mexican waters can net you bigger game like a marlin or a bigeye tuna. Pier fishing doesn't offer as much excitement, but it's the cheapest ocean fishing option available. No license is required to fish from a public pier, which includes those at Ocean Beach, Imperial Beach, and Oceanside.

Public lakes are frequently stocked with a variety of trout and large-mouth bass, but also have resident populations of bluegill and catfish.

California Department of Fish and Game. A fishing license, available at most bait-and-tackle and sporting-goods stores, is required for fishing from the shoreline. Nonresidents can purchase an annual license or a 10-day, 2-day, or 1-day short-term license. Licenses can also be purchased online through the department's website or at the San Diego headquarters. Children younger than 16 do not need a license. Note that some city reservoirs no longer sell snacks, drinks, bait, or fishing licenses, nor do they rent pedal boats or electric motors. They also accept cash only for day-use fees. Make sure to check updated concession availability for your specific destination, or obtain a fishing license in advance. ■ TIP➜ You do not need a license to fish from public piers. ⊠ *3883 Ruffin Rd.* ☎ *858/467–4201* ⊕ *www.wildlife.ca.gov.*

FRESHWATER FISHING

Dixon, Hodges, and Wohlford. These three freshwater lakes surround the North County city of Escondido.

Lake Jennings. County-operated Lake Jennings is stocked with trout in winter and catfish during the summer; it's a popular fly-fishing spot and also offers camping and great picnicking. ✉ *9535 Harritt Rd., Lakeside* ☎ *619/443–2510* ⊕ *www.lakejennings.org.*

Lake Morena. This spot is popular for fishing, camping, and hiking. ✉ *2550 Lake Morena Dr., Campo* ☎ *619/579–4101, 619/478–5473 recorded information* ⊕ *www.sdcounty.ca.gov/parks/Camping/lake_ morena.html.*

Sutherland. This city-operated reservoir, open March through September on weekends, is a good spot for catching largemouth bluegill and bass. There's also turkey hunting during the spring and fall. ✉ *22850 Sutherland Dam Rd., Ramona* ☎ *619/668–2050.*

SALTWATER FISHING

Fisherman's Landing. You can book space on a fleet of luxury vessels from 57 feet to 124 feet long and embark on multiday trips in search of yellowfin tuna, yellowtail, and other deep-water fish. Half-day fishing and whale-watching trips are also available. ✉ *2838 Garrison St., Point Loma* ☎ *619/221–8500* ⊕ *www.fishermanslanding.com.*

H&M Landing. Join one of the West's oldest sportfishing companies for year-round fishing trips plus whale-watching excursions from December through March. ✉ *2803 Emerson St., Point Loma* ☎ *619/222–1144* ⊕ *www.hmlanding.com.*

Helgren's Sportfishing. Your best bet in North County, Helgren's offers trips from Oceanside Harbor. ✉ *315 Harbor Way South, Oceanside* ☎ *760/722–2133* ⊕ *www.helgrensportfishing.com.*

FRISBEE GOLF

Morley Field Disc Golf Course. Disc golf is a popular local sport that's like golf, except it's played with Frisbees. The Morley Field course, in Balboa Park, is open daily from dawn to dusk. Frisbees are available to rent for a small fee, and there's also a small fee for using the course (it's first come, first serve). Rules are posted for those new to the sport. ✉ *3090 Pershing Dr., Balboa Park* ☎ *619/692–3607* ⊕ *www.morleyfield.com.*

GOLF

San Diego's climate—generally sunny, without a lot of wind—is perfect for golf, and there are some 90 courses in the area, appealing to every level of expertise. Experienced golfers can play the same greens as PGA-tournament participants, and beginners or rusty players can book a week at a golf resort and benefit from expert instruction. You'd also be hard-pressed to find a locale that has more scenic courses—everything from sweeping views of the ocean to verdant hills inland.

During busy vacation seasons it can be difficult to get a good tee time. Call in advance to see if it's possible to make a reservation. You don't necessarily have to stay at a resort to play its course; check if the one you're interested in is open to nonguests. Most public courses in the area provide a list of fees for all San Diego courses.

COURSES

Below are some of the best courses in the area. The adult public's greens fees for an 18-hole game are included for each course, as well as the courses' championship (blue) yardage; carts (in some cases mandatory), instruction, and other costs are additional. Rates go down during twilight hours, and San Diego residents may be able to get a better deal. Prices change regularly, so check with courses for up-to-date greens fees and deals.

Arrowood Golf Course. This Ted Robinson Jr.–designed course in Oceanside remains under the radar, but many San Diegans cite it as their favorite due to its challenging holes and tournament-style feel with year-round contests and prizes. The course, which opened in 2005, is quite scenic thanks to its location next to protected habitat and the signature 16th hole requires a challenging shot into an island green. ⊠ *5201 A Village Dr., Oceanside* ☎ *760/967–8400* ⊕ *www.arrowoodgolf.com* 🗩 *$87 Mon.–Thurs., $92 Fri., $110 weekends* ⚑ *18 holes, 6721 yards, par 71.*

Balboa Park Municipal Golf Course. San Diego's oldest public course is five minutes from downtown in the heart of Balboa Park and offers impressive views of the city and the bay. The course includes a 9-hole executive course and a challenging 18-hole course that weaves among the park's canyons with some tricky drop-offs. Finish off your round with biscuits and gravy and a mimosa at Tobey's 19th Hole Cafe, a greasy spoon that's also Balboa Park's best-kept secret. ⊠ *2600 Golf Course Dr., Balboa Park* ☎ *619/235–1184* ⊕ *www.balboagc.com* 🗩 *9 holes: $18 weekdays, $23 weekends. 18 holes: $40 weekdays, $50 weekends* ⚑ *27 holes, 6281 yards, par 72.*

Fodor's Choice ★ **Coronado Municipal Golf Course.** Spectacular views of downtown San Diego and the Coronado Bridge as well as affordable prices make this public course one of the busiest in the world. Bordered by the bay, the trick is to keep your ball out of the water. Wind can add some difficulty, but otherwise this is a leisurely course and a good one to walk. It's difficult to get on unless you reserve a tee time 3 to 14 days in advance. The course's Bayside Grill restaurant is well-known for its Thursday and Sunday night prime rib dinner. Reservations are recommended. ⊠ *2000 Visalia Row, Coronado* ☎ *619/435–3121* ⊕ *www.golfcoronado.com* 🗩 *$18 for 9 holes, $35 for 18 holes weekdays, $40 weekends* ⚑ *18 holes, 6590 yards, par 72.*

Cottonwood at Rancho San Diego Golf Club. This peaceful public golf club 20 minutes from downtown San Diego is set among rolling hills and offers two 18-hole courses—the Lakes, aptly name for the eight lakes that dot the course, and the not-too-challenging Ivanhoe course. Both are good walking courses with nice practice putting greens. On weekend mornings tee times include mandatory cart rental. If it's your birthday, you can play for free. ⊠ *3121 Willow Glen Rd., El Cajon* ☎ *619/442–9891, 800/455–1902* ⊕ *www.cottonwoodgolf.com* 🗩 *Ivanhoe: $16–$24 weekdays, $38–$42 weekends. Lakes: $18 weekdays, $16–$24 weekends. Cart is extra.* ⚑ *Ivanhoe: 18 holes, 6831 yards, par 72. Lakes: 18 holes, 6610 yards, par 71.*

Torrey Pines Golf Course has fantastic views to go along with its challenging holes.

Eastlake Country Club. Ted Robinson designed this fun public course a few miles from the Olympic Training Center in Chula Vista. Eastlake offers great views of Mount Miguel, and despite the water hazards and sandtraps, it's good for players of all skill levels. It's also a pretty course with waterfalls, six lakes, and hundreds of trees. Reservations can be made up to seven days in advance and you can save quite a bit by taking advange of the club's Twilight rates. ⊠ *2375 Clubhouse Dr., Chula Vista* ☎ *619/482–5757* ⊕ *www.eastlakecountryclub.com* ⊠ *$69 Mon.–Thurs., $79 Fri., $89 weekends* ⅃ *18 holes, 6606 yards, par 72.*

Encinitas Ranch. See the Pacific Ocean from virtually every vantage point at this course on bluffs in North County. Local golfers love it because low scores aren't that hard to come by. It's a forgiving course with wide-open fairways. Encinitas Ranch also has a 6,000-square-foot clubhouse with a bar and café. The adjoining patio has a stone fireplace and great ocean views. ⊠ *1275 Quail Gardens Dr., Encinitas* ☎ *760/944–1936* ⊕ *www.jcgolf.com* ⊠ *$81 Mon.–Thurs., $87 Fri., $103 weekends (cart included)* ⅃ *18 holes, 6587 yards, par 72* ☞ *Facilities: Driving range, putting green, golf carts, pull carts, rental clubs, pro shop, golf academy/ lessons, restaurant, bar.*

Mission Bay Golf Course and Practice Center. Making sure people have fun is the number-one goal at this city-run golf course. San Diego's only nightlighted course, the final tee time is at 7:45 pm for 9 holes, and the executive course with par 3 and 4 holes isn't too challenging. The golf course's scenic and breezy location next to Mission Bay helps keep it comfortably cool. ⊠ *2702 N. Mission Bay Dr., Mission Bay* ☎ *858/581–7880* ⊕ *www.sandiego.gov/park-and-recreation/golf/*

mbgolf.shtml 🔲 *$17 for 9 holes weekdays, $22 weekends; $29 for 18 holes weekdays, $36 weekends* 🏌 *18 holes, 2715 yards, par 58.*

Mount Woodson Golf Club. This beautiful, heavily wooded club in a hilly area off Highway 67 is set amid a grove of ancient oak trees and granite boulder-strewn hillsides with spectacular views of the historic Woodson Castle, a private residence built in 1921 that is now one of San Diego's most popular wedding venues. The course features some challenging holes like the par 5 Windinface, a deep, three-tiered green, where accuracy is a must. The course also features wooden bridges and good views, particularly from Hole 17. There is a pro shop and a small café. This is a popular local tournament site. ⊠ *16422 N. Woodson Dr., Ramona* ☎ *760/788–3555* ⊕ *mtwoodsoncastle.com* 🔲 *Members: $42 weekdays, $52 weekends. Nonmembers: $55 weekdays, $65 weekends* 🏌 *18 holes, 6004 yards, par 70.*

Riverwalk Golf Clubs. With three different 9-hole layouts that can be combined in a variety of ways, this course near the Fashion Valley shopping center is sort of a "choose your own adventure" one. The layouts, designed by Ted Robinson Sr. and Jr., feature natural terrain and oak and eucalyptus trees throughout. There are also a variety of water features including four lakes and the San Dieguito river. This course is challenging but suitable for players of all skill levels with multiple tees on each hole. ⊠ *1150 Fashion Valley Rd., Fashion Valley* ☎ *619/296–4653* ⊕ *www.riverwalkgc.com* 🔲 *9 holes: $27–$30 Mon.–Thurs., $35 Fri.–Sun. 18 holes: $89 Mon.–Thurs., $99 Fri.–Sun.* 🏌 *Presidio: 9 holes, 3397 yards, par 72. Mission: 9 holes, 3153 yards, par 72. Friars: 9 holes, 3230 yards, par 72.*

Fodor's Choice ★ **Torrey Pines Golf Course.** Due to its clifftop location overlooking the Pacific and its classic championship holes, Torrey Pines is one of the best public golf courses in the United States. The course was the site of the 2008 U.S. Open and has been the home of the Farmers Insurance Open since 1968. The par-72 South Course, redesigned by Rees Jones in 2001, receives rave reviews from touring pros; it is longer, more challenging, and more expensive than the North Course. Tee times may be booked from 8 to 90 days in advance (☎ *877/581–7171*) and are subject to an advance booking fee ($43). ⊠ *11480 N. Torrey Pines Rd., La Jolla* ☎ *858/452–3226, 800/985–4653* ⊕ *www.torreypinesgolfcourse.com* 🔲 *South: $183 weekdays, $229 weekends. North: $100 weekdays, $125 weekends; $40 for golf cart* 🏌 *South: 18 holes, 7227 yards, par 72. North: 18 holes, 6874 yards, par 72.*

RESORTS

Fodor's Choice ★ **Barona Creek Golf Course.** Rated among the top five courses nationwide, this 7,392-yard course won accolades from day one for its challenging slopes, strategically placed boulders, and native grass landscaping. Barona Creek golf course offers four tees to accommodate golfers of all skills and abilities. For those looking to be challenged at the expert level, the course provides a championship layout with four T configurations. ⊠ *1932 Wildcat Canyon Rd., Lakeside, Ramona* ☎ *888/722–7662* ⊕ *www.barona.com* 🔲 *$80 to $160, depending on time of day, midweek or weekend* 🏌 *Black: 18 holes, 7092 yards, par 72. Gold:*

13

18 holes, 6632 yards, par 72. Silver: 18 holes, 6231 yards, par 72. Burgundy: 18 holes, 5296 yards, par 70 ☞ Facilities: Driving range, putting green, pitching area, golf carts, rental clubs, pro shop, lessons, restaurant, bar.

Carlton Oaks Lodge and Country Club. Many prestigious qualifying events—including the U.S. Open and U.S. Amateur qualifiers—have been held at this difficult course that was built in 1958 and designed by Pete Dye. The historic course is considered a local landmark and has a picturesque setting, with sycamore and eucalyptus trees, several lakes, and a creek. The newly renovated Oaks Bar and Grill serves sandwiches and wraps and offers good Happy Hour specials between 4 and 7. ⊠ *9200 Inwood Dr., Santee* ☎ *619/448–4242* ⊕ *www.carltonoaksgolf. com* ✉ *For members: $35 Mon.–Thurs., $45 Fri., $60 Sat., $50 Sun. For nonmembers: $55 Mon.–Thurs., $65 Fri., $85 weekends* ⚐ *18 holes, 6700 yards, par 72.*

Omni La Costa Resort and Spa. One of the premier golf resorts in Southern California, La Costa over the years has hosted many of the best professional golfers in the world as well as prominent politicians and Hollywood celebrities. The resort recently remodeled both its courses. The Dick Wilson–designed Champions course has new bent grass greens, Bermuda fairways, and bunkers. The more spacious Legends Course received a complete makeover including a redesign of all 18 greens, as well as new bunkers and turfgrass plantings. After a day on the links you can wind down with a massage, steam bath, and dinner at the resort. ⊠ *2100 Costa del Mar Rd., Carlsbad* ☎ *800/854–5000* ⊕ *www. lacosta.com* ✉ *$210 Mon.–Thurs., $230 Fri.–Sun.* ⚐ *Champions: 18 holes, 6608 yards, par 72. Legends: 18 holes, 6524 yards, par 72.*

Fodor'sChoice
★

Park Hyatt Aviara Golf Club. This golf course consistently ranks as one of the best in California and is the only course in San Diego designed by Arnold Palmer. The course features gently rolling hills dotted with native wildflowers and views of the protected adjacent Batiquitos Lagoon and the Pacific Ocean. There are plenty of bunkers and water features for those looking for a challenge, and the golf carts, included in the cost, come fitted with GPS systems that tell you the distance to the pin. The two-story Spanish colonial clubhouse has full-size lockers, lounge areas, a bar, and a steak house. ⊠ *7447 Batiquitos Dr., Carlsbad* ☎ *760/603–6900* ⊕ *www.golfaviara.com* ✉ *Members: $130 Mon.–Thurs., $150 Fri.–Sun. Nonmembers: $225 Mon.–Thurs., $245 Fri.–Sun.* ⚐ *18 holes, 7007 yards, par 72.*

Rancho Bernardo Inn and Country Club. Designed by William Francis Bell in 1962, this 18-hole course has a traditional layout, but renovations in 2009 and 2010 have kept it feeling fresh and new. New bunkers were even added in 2013. The course has hosted both PGA and LPGA events and offers an oasis in Rancho Bernardo, with its tree-lined fairways and various water features. A challenging 18th hole requires an approach shot over a creek. Located at the esteemed Rancho Bernardo Inn, the property offers great amenities like a spa and several restaurants, including AVANT, where gourmet mustards are served on tap. ⊠ *17550 Bernardo Oaks Dr., Rancho Bernardo* ☎ *858/675–8470*

⊕ *www.ranchobernardoinn.com/golf* ✉ *Members: $55 Mon.–Thurs., $59 Fri., $85 weekends. Nonmembers: $100 Mon.–Thurs., $115 Fri., $135 weekends* ⚡ *18 holes, 6631 yards, par 72* ☞ *Facilities: Driving range, putting green, golf carts, rental clubs, pro shop, golf academy/ lessons, restaurant, bar.*

Sycuan Resort & Casino. With its three courses orginally designed by Cecil Holingsworth, this resort offers something for every golfer. Due to flooding in the late 1970s, the courses had to be redesigned by golf course architect Ted Robinson Sr., who added elevation changes and lakes to increase the difficulty. Hackers will love the executive par-3 course, while seasoned golfers can play the championship courses. Sycuan Golf Resort hosts a variety of tournaments, including the Junior World Golf Championships, U.S. Public Links Qualifying site, and the San Diego Junior Amateur. ✉ *3007 Dehesa Rd., El Cajon* ☎ *619/219– 6028, 800/457–5568* ⊕ *www.sycuanresort.com* ✉ *Willow Glen and Oak Glen: $55 for members Mon.–Thurs., $56 Fri., $66 weekends; $91 for nonmembers Mon.–Thurs., $96 Fri., $111 weekends. Pine Glen: $25 for members and nonmembers* ⚡ *Willow Glen: 18 holes, 6687 yards, par 72. Oak Glen: 18 holes, 6682 yards, par 72. Pine Glen: 18 holes, 2508 yards, par 54* ☞ *Facilities: Driving range, putting green, pitching area, golf carts, pull carts, rental clubs, pro shop, golf academy/ lessons, restaurant, bar.*

HANG GLIDING AND PARAGLIDING

Torrey Pines Gliderport. Perched on the cliffs overlooking the ocean north of La Jolla, this is one of the most spectacular spots to hang glide in the world. It's for experienced pilots only, but hang gliding and paragliding lessons and tandem rides for inexperienced gliders are available. Those who'd rather just watch can grab a bite at the Cliffhanger Cafe, which offers incredible views of the Pacific and of the paragliders taking off. There's live music on Saturday. ✉ *2800 Torrey Pines Scenic Dr., La Jolla* ☎ *858/452–9858* ⊕ *www.flytorrey.com.*

HIKING AND NATURE TRAILS

From beachside bluffs and waterfront estuaries to the foothills and trails of the nearby Laguna Mountains and the desert beyond, San Diego County has several vegetation and climate zones—and plenty of open space for hiking. Even if you lack the time to explore the outskirts, a day hike through the canyons and gardens of Balboa Park or the canyons and hills of Mission Trails Park is a great way to escape to nature without leaving the city.

Guided hikes are conducted regularly through Los Peñasquitos Canyon Preserve and the Torrey Pines State Beach and Reserve.

HIKING

Fodor'sChoice **Bayside Trail at Cabrillo National Monument.** Driving here is a treat in itself,
★ as a vast view of the Pacific unfolds before you. The view is equally enjoyable on Bayside Trail (2 miles round-trip), which is home to the same coastal sagebrush that Juan Rodriguez Cabrillo saw when he

first discovered the California coast in the 16th century. After the hike, you can explore nearby tide pools, the monument statue, and the Old Point Loma Lighthouse. Don't worry if you don't see everything on your first visit; your entrance receipt ($5 per car) is good for 7 days. ⊠ *1800 Cabrillo Memorial Dr., Point Loma* ⊹ *From I–5, take the Rosecrans exit and turn right on Canon St. then left on Catalina Blvd. (also known as Cabrillo Memorial Dr.); follow until the end.* ☎ *619/557–5450* ⊕ *www.nps.gov/cabr.*

Hike Bike Kayak San Diego. Join guided treks through Torrey Pines State Beach and Reserve, and Mission Trails Regional Park, which includes Cowles Mountain and Fortuna Mountain. ⊠ *Office, 2222 Ave. de la Playa, La Jolla* ☎ *858/551–9510* ⊕ *www.hikebikekayak.com.*

Los Peñasquitos Canyon Preserve. Trails at this inland park north of Mira Mesa accommodate equestrians, runners, walkers, and cyclists as well as leashed dogs. Look at maps for trails specific to bikes and horses. A small waterfall among large volcanic rock boulders is one of the park's most popular sites—it's an unexpected oasis amid the arid valley landscape. ⊠ *12020 Black Mountain Rd., Rancho Peñasquitos* ⊹ *From I–15, exit Mercy Rd,. and head west to Black Mountain Rd.; turn right then left at first light; follow road to Ranch House parking lot* ☎ *858/484–7504* ⊕ *www.sandiego.gov.*

Mission Trails Regional Park. This park 8 miles northeast of downtown encompasses nearly 5,800 acres of wooded hillsides, grasslands, chaparral, and streams. Trails range from easy to difficult; they include one with an impressive view of the city from Cowles Mountain and another along a historic missionary path. The park is also a popular place for rock climbing and camping (the Kumeyaay Lake Campground is open on weekends). Lake Murray is at the southern edge of the park, off Highway 8. ⊠ *1 Father Junípero Serra Trail, Mission Valley* ☎ *619/668–3281* ⊕ *www.mtrp.org.*

Torrey Pines State Reserve. Hikers and runners will appreciate this park's many winning features: switch-back trails that descend to the sea, an unparalleled view of the Pacific, and a chance to see the Torrey pine tree, one of the rarest pine breeds in the United States. The reserve hosts guided nature walks as well. All food is prohibited at the reserve, so save the picnic until you reach the beach below. Parking is $12–$15, depending on day and season. ⊠ *12600 N. Torrey Pines Rd., La Jolla* ⊹ *Exit I–5 at Carmel Valley Rd. and head west toward Coast Hwy. 101 until you reach N. Torrey Pines Rd.; turn left.* ☎ *858/755–2063* ⊕ *www.parks.ca.gov.*

NATURE TRAILS

Anza-Borrego Desert State Park. With more than 600,000 acres, this is the largest state park in California. There are 500 miles of dirt roads and countless trails for hiking. Visits here are especially popular during the two-week desert wildflower bloom, which happens between early February and late April. The exact timing depends on winter rains, so it's best to call the park ahead for advice. The park is about a two-hour drive east of downtown San Diego, at the far eastern end of San Diego

County. ✉ *200 Palm Canyon Dr., Borrego Springs* ☎ *760/767–4205* ⊕ *www.parks.ca.gov.*

San Dieguito River Park. This 55-mile corridor begins at the mouth of the San Dieguito River in Del Mar and heads from the riparian lagoon area through coastal sage scrub and mountain terrain to end in the desert, which is east of Volcan Mountain near Julian. It's open to hikers, bikers, and horses. The expansive park is also home to the Sikes Adobe Farmhouse, an 1880s farmstead that was almost completely destroyed by wildfire in 2007. After painstaking restoration it reopened in 2010 and is now home to a museum. The restored adobe creamery reopened in 2014. ✉ *18372 Sycamore Creek Rd., Escondido* ☎ *858/674–2270* ⊕ *www.sdrp.org.*

Tijuana Estuary. Mostly contained within Border Field State Park, this estuary is one of the last riparian environments in Southern California. The freshwater and saltwater marshes shelter migrant and resident waterfowl. Horse-riding trails fringe the south end of the Tijuana Estuary in Border Field State Park. The visitor center is open Wednesday through Sunday, but the trails are open daily. ✉ *301 Caspian Way, Imperial Beach* ⊹ *Exit I–5 at Coronado Ave., head west to 3rd St., turn left onto Caspian, which leads into estuary parking lot.* ☎ *619/575–3613* ⊕ *www.tijuanaestuary.com.*

HORSEBACK RIDING

Bright Valley Farms. Take riding lessons or join a trail ride on the winding paths of the Sweetwater River valley. ✉ *12310 Campo Rd., Spring Valley* ☎ *619/670–1861* ⊕ *www.brightvalleyfarms.com.*

The Ranch at Bandy Canyon. At this historic ranch in Escondido, you can ride horseback by taking group or private lessons. Trail rides go past old dairy farms and orange groves. ✉ *16251 Bandy Canyon Rd., Escondido* ☎ *760/871–6494* ⊕ *bandycanyon.com.*

Fodor'sChoice ★ **San Diego Beach Rides.** This family-owned business south of Imperial Beach has been operating for 30 years and offers mostly private rides by appointment. The quarter and painted horses are carefully matched to each person for rides that can include a jaunt through the Tijuana River Valley Preserve, a sunset ride along the beach, or a swimming adventure, where your horse actually goes with you into the water. The monthly moonlight ride starts with a campfire cookout, complete with barbecued tri-tip and baked beans, followed by a 1½-hour ride to the top of the Grand Mesa. ✉ *2180 Monument Rd.* ☎ *619/947–3152*

OVER-THE-LINE

A giant beach party as much as a sport, Over-the-Line is a form of beach softball played with two teams of just three people each. Every July, over two weekends that include wild beer drinking and partying, the world championships are held on Fiesta Island. Admission is free, but parking is impossible (shuttle buses are available). Check the Old Mission Beach Athletic Club's website (⊕ *www.ombac.org*) for more information.

13

A kayak trip is the best way to experience the sea caves off La Jolla Cove.

⊕ *www.happytrailssandiego.com* ✉ *$50 per person for Riverbed Rides, $100 for Sunset Rides, and $150 for Swim Adventure Rides.*

Sweetwater Farms. Join the farm's guides for horse rides through the stunning nature trails of inland San Diego County's Bonita area. Sweetwater Farms also offers lessons and training. ✉ *3051 Equitation La., Bonita* ☎ *619/475–3134* ⊕ *www.sweetwaterhorses.com.*

Vineyard Trail Rides. Forty-five minutes northeast of San Diego, this company offers 90-minute horseback rides through Milagro Farm Vineyards and Winery, a 110-acre private estate with 100-year-old oak trees and wide valley views. The ride includes a wine tasting paired with a selection of chocolates. ✉ *18750 Littlepage Rd., Ramona* ☎ *951/595–3503* ⊕ *vineyardtrailrides.com* ✉ *$100 per person, $160 per couple.*

JET SKIING

Jet Skis can be launched from most ocean beaches, although you must ride beyond surf lines, and some beaches have special regulations governing their use.

California Watersports. Waveless Mission Bay and the smaller Carlsbad Lagoon, east of the intersection of Tamarack Avenue and I–5, are easy to reach from this water recreation center, which has a private beach and landing ramp. You can rent ski boats, jet skis, canoes, and stand-up paddle boards. ✉ *4215 Harrison St., Carlsbad* ☎ *760/434–3089* ⊕ *www.carlsbadlagoon.com.*

El Capitan Reservoir. The only freshwater lake that allows Jet Skis is 30 miles northeast of the city near Lake Jennings. ✉ *El Monte Rd.*

✛ *Take I–8 north to Lake Jennings Park Road, head east on El Monte Road, and follow signs.* ☎ 619/465–3474 ⊕ *www.sandiego.gov/water/ recreation/reservoirs/elcapitan.shtml* 🖛 *$10 day-use fee, per person.*

San Diego Jet Ski Rentals. The shop is open daily in spring, summer, and fall; in winter, call ahead for a reservation. In addition to Jet Skis the outfitter rents jet boats, kayaks, and paddleboards. ✉ *4275 Mission Bay Dr., Pacific Beach* ☎ *858/272–6161* ⊕ *www.sdjetski.com.*

Seaforth Boat Rentals. You can rent Yamaha WaveRunners and explore San Diego Bay or Mission Bay from Seaforth Boat Rentals' five different San Diego locations. On most Fridays, Saturdays, and Sundays you can join a two-hour waverunner tour of La Jolla's coast, departing from the Mission Bay location. ✉ *1715 Strand Way, Coronado* ☎ *888/834–2628* ⊕ *www.seaforthboatrental.com.*

13

JOGGING

Running is a very popular San Diego pastime and organized races like the Rock'n'Roll Marathon (⊕ *runrocknroll.competitor.com*) and La Jolla Half (⊕ *www.lajollahalfmarathon.com*) bring thousands of visitors to San Diego each year. You don't have to sign up for one of these races, though, to get in on the action. Just get out and pound the pavement by going for an easy jog along the San Diego Waterfront (do as the locals do and add in a stair workout at the Convention Center), or hit the trails in Balboa Park.

Balboa Park. Balboa Park offers 65 miles of hiking, biking, and running trails of various difficulty. Joggers can start out from any parking lot, but it's probably easiest to start anywhere along the 6th Avenue side. Entry to the numerous lots is best where Laurel Street connects with 6th Avenue. Trails are clearly marked and color coded and if you really want to follow a designated "route" that informs you of the distance you've gone start from one of five gateways in the park: Golden Hill, Marston Point, Morley Field, Park Boulevard, and Sixth and Upas. ✉ *1549 El Prado* ⊕ *www.balboapark.org.*

Del Mar. Park your car near 15th Street and run south along the cliffs for a gorgeous view of the ocean. ✉ *15th Street, Del Mar.*

Embarcadero. The most popular run downtown is along the Embarcadero, which stretches for 2 miles along the bay. ✉ *N. Harbor Dr., Downtown.*

Mission Bay. This area is popular with joggers for its wide sidewalks and basically flat landscape. Trails head west around Fiesta Island, providing distance as well as a scenic route. ✉ *1590 E. Mission Bay Dr.*

Mission Beach boardwalk. This is a great place to run while soaking up the scenery and beach culture. ✉ *Ocean Front Walk.*

Roadrunner Sports. Stop in at Roadrunner for all the supplies and information you'll need for running in San Diego. ✉ *5553 Copley Dr.* ☎ *858/974–4475* ⊕ *www.roadrunnersports.com.*

KAYAKING

There are several places to kayak throughout San Diego. You can spend an especially memorable afternoon exploring the Seven Caves off La Jolla Cove, where you can often see seals, sea lions, and even dolphin.

Bike & Kayak Tours. La Jolla's location of Bike & Kayak Tours offers a Leopard Shark Encounter snorkeling tour ($39 a person), where adventuresome travelers can see the shy spotted creatures up close. The Coronado location has you embarking on a kayak tour ($32 per person) underneath the Coronado Bridge at dusk to enjoy incredible views of Downtown San Diego. The Coronado location also offers stand-up paddleboards for as little as $14 a person. ⊠ *1201 1st St., #215, Coronado* ☎ *858/454–1010* ⊕ *bikeandkayaktours.com.*

Everyday California. This action-on-the-water sports company also has its own clothing line offering beach casual styles inspired by La Jolla. Tours with expert guides, many of whom are former college-level athletes, include a sunset kayak tour, where wildlife to see includes sea lions, seals, pelicans, and dolphin; the tour combines kayaking and snorkeling. If you'd rather go out on your own, Everyday California rents kayaks, stand-up paddleboards, surfboards, snorkel equipment, and bodyboards. ⊠ *2243 Ave. De La Playa, La Jolla* ☎ *858/545–6195* ⊕ *www.everydaycalifornia.com* ⊡ *Sunset Kayak Tour from $80 for a single and $150 for a double, prices can change depending on season.*

Hike Bike Kayak San Diego. This shop offers several kayak tours, from easy excursions in Mission Bay that are well suited to families and beginners to more advanced jaunts. Tours include kayaking the caves off La Jolla coast, whale-watching (from a safe distance) December through March, moonlight and sunset trips, and a cruise into the bay to see SeaWorld's impressive fireworks shows over the water in the summer. Tours last two to three hours and require a minimum of four people. ⊠ *2222 Ave. de la Playa, La Jolla* ☎ *858/551–9510* ⊕ *www.hikebikekayak.com.*

La Jolla Kayak. This family-owned company offers kayak tours of the Seven Caves of La Jolla as well as snorkel and biking adventures. Several guides have extensive backgrounds in marine biology and ecology. ⊠ *2199 Ave. De La Playa, La Jolla* ☎ *858/459–1114* ⊕ *www.lajollakayak.com* ⊡ *From $39 for singles, $69 for doubles.*

ROCK CLIMBING

Solid Rock Gym. With plenty of belay stations and holds that are regularly changed, the three locations of Solid Rock Gym appeal to all skill levels. There are indoor top-roping, bouldering, and lead climbing areas. ⊠ *2074 Hancock St., Old Town* ☎ *619/299–1124* ⊕ *www.solidrockgym.com.*

SAILING AND BOATING

The city's history is full of seafarers, from the ships of the 1542 Cabrillo expedition to the America's Cup that once had a home here. Winds in San Diego are fairly consistent, especially in winter. You can rent a slip at one of several marinas if you're bringing your own boat. If not, you can rent vessels of various sizes and shapes—from small paddleboats and kayaks to Hobie Cats—from various vendors. In addition, most bayside resorts rent equipment for on-the-water adventures. Kayaks are one of the most popular boat rentals, especially in La Jolla, where people kayak around the Underwater Park and Ecological Reserve at the cove. Most of what's available from these outlets is not intended for the open ocean—a dangerous place for the inexperienced.

For information, including tips on overnight anchoring, contact the **Port of San Diego Mooring Office** (☎ *619/686–6227* ⊕ *www.portofsan diego.org*).

For additional information contact the **San Diego Harbor Police** (☎ *619/686–6272*).

BOAT RENTALS

Bahia Resort Hotel. This facility and its sister location, the **Catamaran Resort Hotel** (E*3999 Mission Blvd., Mission Beach* ☎ *858/488–2582*), rent paddleboats, kayaks, powerboats, and sailboats from 14 to 22 feet. Thanks to their location on the calm waters of Mission Bay, both are great places for beginners to try paddleboarding. ⊠ *998 W. Mission Bay Dr., Mission Bay* ☎ *858/488–2582* ⊕ *www.bahiahotel.com*.

Seaforth Boat Rentals. You can book charter tours and rent kayaks, Jet Skis, fishing skiffs, powerboats and sailboats at Seaforth's five locations around town. The outfitter also can hook you up with a skipper for a deep-sea fishing trip. Seaforth also rents paddleboards at their Mission Bay and Coronado locations. ⊠ *1715 Strand Way, Coronado* ☎ *888/834–2628* ⊕ *www.seaforthboatrentals.com*.

BOAT CHARTERS

California Cruisin'. Contact California Cruisin' for sail boat or power boat charter excursions and dinner cruises. ⊠ *1450 Harbor Island Dr., Downtown* ☎ *619/296–8000* ⊕ *www.californiacruisin.com*.

Flagship Cruises & Events. Get on board here for harbor tours, two-hour dinner and brunch cruises, and a ferry to Coronado. ⊠ *1050 N. Harbor Dr., Embarcadero* ☎ *619/234–4111, 800/442–7847 reservations* ⊕ *www.flagshipsd.com*.

The Gondola Company. You don't have to travel to Venice to be serenaded by a gondolier. This company in the picturesque Coronado Cays features authentic Venetian gondola rides that depart daily from the Loews Coronado Bay Resort marina. ⊠ *503 Grand Caribe Causeway, Suite C, Coronado* ☎ *619/429–6317* ⊕ *www.gondolacompany.com* ⊠ *From $95 for 2 people.*

Harbor Sailboats. You can rent sailboats from 22 to 45 feet long here for open-ocean adventures. The company also offers skippered charter boats for whale-watching, sunset sails, and bay tours. ⊠ *2040 Harbor*

Island Dr., Harbor Island ☎ *619/291–9568, 800/854–6625* ⊕ *www.harborsailboats.com.*

Hornblower Cruises and Events. This outfit operates harbor cruises, sunset cocktail and dining cruises, whale-watching excursions, and yacht charters. ⊠ *1066 N. Harbor Dr., Embarcadero* ☎ *619/686–8700, 619/686–8715 ticket booth* ⊕ *www.hornblower.com.*

SURFING

If you're a beginner, consider paddling in the waves off Mission Beach, Pacific Beach, Tourmaline Surfing Park, La Jolla Shores, Del Mar, or Oceanside. More experienced surfers usually head for Sunset Cliffs, La Jolla reef breaks, Black's Beach, or Swami's in Encinitas. All necessary equipment is included in the cost of all surfing schools. Beach-area Ys offer surf lessons and surf camp in the summer months and during spring break.

Hike Bike Kayak San Diego. Sign up for group and private lessons in La Jolla year-round. If you know what you're doing but didn't bring your stick, this outfitter rents boards, too. ⊠ *2222 Ave. de la Playa, La Jolla* ☎ *858/551–9510* ⊕ *www.hikebikekayak.com.*

Kahuna Bob's Surf School. "Kahuna Bob" himself, one of San Diego's veteran surf instructors, conducts two-hour lessons at Beacon's Beach in Encinitas seven days a week; in summer there's a surf camp for kids. ⊠ *Beacon's Beach, 948 Neptune Ave., Encinitas* ☎ *760/721–7700, 800/524–8627* ⊕ *www.kahunabob.com.*

Menehune Surf School. This surf school, founded by local schoolteachers, provides surf lessons as well as paddleboard and surfboard rentals. Private or family lessons can be aranged (from $70 per person for one hour). Menehune Surf also offers popular surf camps for kids every summer from June through August at three locations: La Jolla Shores, Del Mar, and Mission Beach. ⊠ *2222 Ave. De La Playa, La Jolla* ☎ *866/425–2925* ⊕ *www.menehunesurf.com.*

San Diego Surfing Academy. Choose from private and group lessons and customizable surf camps for teens, kids, and adults. Instructional videos are also available online. The academy, which has been running since 1995, is based near South Carlsbad State Beach and meets for lessons at Seapointe Resort in Carlsbad. ⊠ *Near South Carlsbad State Beach, Carlsbad* ☎ *760/230–1474, 800/447–7873* ⊕ *www.surfing academy.com.*

Surf Diva Surf School. Check out clinics, surf camps, and private lessons especially formulated for girls and women. Most clinics and trips are for women only, but there are some co-ed options. Guys can also book private lessons from the nationally recognized staff. Surf Diva is also home to a boutique that sells surf and standup paddle board equipment, as well as sundresses and clothing for men and and children. ⊠ *2160 Ave. de la Playa, La Jolla* ☎ *858/454–8273* ⊕ *www.surfdiva.com.*

CLOSE UP

Longboarding vs. Shortboarding

Longboarders tend to ride boards more than 8 feet long with rounded noses. Shortboarders ride lightweight, high-performance boards from 5 to 7 feet long with pointed noses. (Funboards are a little longer than shortboards, with broad, round noses and tails that make them good for beginners who want something more maneuverable than a longboard.) A great longboarder will have a smooth, fluid style and will shuffle up and down the board, maybe even riding on the nose with the toes of both feet on the very edge ("hanging 10"). Shortboarders tend to surf faster and more aggressively. The best short-boarders surf perpendicular to the wave face and may even break free of the wave—known as "aerials" or "catching air." Nonsurfers are often most impressed and amused by the mistakes. "Wipeouts," the sometimes spectacular falls, inevitably happen to all surfers.

13

SURF SHOPS

Cheap Rentals Mission Beach. Many local surf shops rent both surf and bodyboards. Cheap Rentals Mission Beach is right off the boardwalk, just steps from the waves. It rents wet suits, bodyboards, and skimboards in addition to soft surfboards and long and short fiberglass rides. It also has good hourly to weekly pricing on paddleboards and accessories. ✉ *3689 Mission Blvd., Mission Beach* ☎ *858/488–9070, 800/941–7761* ⊕ *www.cheap-rentals.com.*

Hansen's. A short walk from Swami's beach, Hansen's is one of San Diego's oldest and most popular surf shops. It has an extensive selection of boards, wet suits, and clothing for sale, and a rental department as well. ✉ *1105 S. Coast Hwy. 101, Encinitas* ☎ *760/753–6595* ⊕ *www.hansensurf.com.*

TENNIS

Most of the more than 1,300 courts around the county are in private clubs, but a few are public.

Balboa Tennis Club at Morley Field. Practice your backhand at this historic tennis club with 25 hard courts, which are available on a first-come, first-served basis for a daily $6-per-person fee. Heaviest use is 9 am and 11 am and after 5 pm; at other times you can usually arrive and begin playing. Pros offer clinics and classes. ✉ *2221 Morley Field Dr., Balboa Park* ☎ *619/295–9278* ⊕ *www.balboatennis.com.*

La Jolla Tennis Club. This historic club has 9 public courts near downtown; 5 are lighted; the daily fee is $10. The club is first-come first-serve for non-members. Members are able to call one to three days ahead to reserve a court. ✉ *7632 Draper Ave., La Jolla* ☎ *858/454–4434* ⊕ *www.ljtc.org.*

Omni La Costa Resort and Spa. This tennis complex has 17 hard and clay courts, 7 of them lighted, plus professional instruction, clinics, and workouts. ✉ *2100 Costa Del Mar Rd., Carlsbad* ☎ *760/931–7501* ⊕ *www.lacosta.com.*

Several San Diego resorts have top-notch tennis programs staffed by big-name professional instructors.

Rancho Valencia Resort. One of the top resorts in the country has unveiled brand-new tennis facilities, which feature 18 revamped hard-court tennis courts backed by bouganvillia and citrus groves, a new pro shop, and spacious restrooms and lockers with added showers for guests and members. Rancho Valencia's tennis director is two-time U.S. Open Doubles Champion Robin White, and many of the other instructors have played at the professional level. Sign up for private lessons or tennis clinics, or try cardio tennis, where drills are set to music. Tennis shoes and tennis attire (no T-shirts) are required. ✉ *5921 Valencia Circle, Rancho Santa Fe* ☎ *858/756–1123* ⊕ *www.ranchovalencia.com.*

VOLLEYBALL

Ocean Beach, South Mission Beach, Del Mar Beach, Moonlight Beach, and the western edge of Balboa Park are major congregating points for volleyball enthusiasts. These are also the best places to find a pickup game.

WATERSKIING

Mission Bay is popular for waterskiing, although the bay is often polluted, especially after a heavy rain. As a general rule, it's best to get out early, when the water is smooth and the crowds are thin.

Seaforth Boat Rentals. Boats and equipment can be rented at the Mission Bay or Coronado locations. ✉ *1715 Strand Way, Coronado* ☎ *888/834–2628* ⊕ *www.seaforthboatrental.com.*

WHALE-WATCHING CRUISES

Whale-watching season peaks in January and February, when thousands of gray whales migrate south to the warm weather, where they give birth to their calves. Head to Cabrillo National Monument's Whale Overlook to see the whales pass through Point Loma. If you want a closer look, charter boats and cruises host whale-watching excursions.

Flagship Cruises & Events. Join one of the twice-daily whale-watching trips during the season from December through April. Rates start at $37 for adults on weekdays and $42 on weekends. ✉ *1050 N. Harbor Dr., Embarcadero* ☎ *619/234–4111, 800/442–7847 reservations* ⊕ *www. flagshipsd.com.*

Hornblower Cruises and Events. Yachts take passengers to catch a glimpse of gray whales and perhaps an occasional school of dolphins on weekends. Live narraton is provided by experts from the San Diego Natural History Museum. Rates start at $75 for adults and $40 for children. ✉ *1066 N. Harbor Dr., Embarcadero* ☎ *619/686–8700, 619/686–8715 ticket booth* ⊕ *www.hornblower.com.*

A kiteboarder joins the surfers waiting for a wave at Pacific Beach.

WINDSURFING

Also known as sailboarding, windsurfing is a sport best practiced on smooth waters, such as Mission Bay. More experienced windsurfers will enjoy taking a board out on the ocean. Wave jumping is especially popular at the Tourmaline Surfing Park in La Jolla and in the Del Mar area, where you can also occasionally see kiteboarders practice their variation on the theme.

Mission Bay Aquatic Center. The world's largest instructional waterfront facility offers lessons in wakeboarding, sailing, surfing, waterskiing, rowing, kayaking, and windsurfing. Equipment rental is also available, but the emphasis is on instruction, and most rentals require a minimum 2-hour orientation lesson before you can set out on your own. Reservations are recommended, particularly during the summer. Skippered keelboats and boats for waterskiing or wakeboarding can be hired with reservations. Free parking is available. ⊠ *1001 Santa Clara Pl., Mission Beach* ☎ *858/488–1000* ⊕ *www.mbaquaticcenter.com* ☉ *Sept.–May, Tues.–Sun. 8–5; June–Aug., daily 8–7.*

SPECTATOR SPORTS

BASEBALL

Fodor's Choice
★

Long a favorite spectator sport in San Diego, where games are rarely rained out, baseball gained even more popularity in 2004 with the opening of PETCO Park, a stunning 42,000-seat facility in the heart of downtown. The ballpark underwent a huge effort recently to improve dining in the park, and local food vendors and craft breweries now dominate the dining options. Although the Padres have not had the winning record many fans had hoped for in recent years, PETCO is a great place to spend an afternoon win or lose.

San Diego Padres. From April into October, the Padres slug it out for bragging rights in the National League West. Home games are played at PETCO Park. Tickets are usually available on game day, but rival matchups against the Los Angeles Dodgers and the San Francisco Giants often sell out quickly. For an inexpensive day at the ballpark, go for "The Park at the Park" tickets ($10 and up, depending on demand; available for purchase at the park only) and have a picnic on the grass while watching the game on one of several giant-screen TVs. You also get access to the full concourse. Head to the fifth floor to find a Stone Brewing outdoor beer garden with sweeping views of downtown and the San Diego Bay. ⊠ *100 Park Blvd., East Village* ☎ *619/795–5000, 877/374–2784* ⊕ *sandiego.padres.mlb.com.*

FOOTBALL

Holiday Bowl. One of college football's most-watched playoff games takes place in Qualcomm Stadium around the end of December. ⊠ *9449 Friars Rd.* ☎ *619/283–5808* ⊕ *www.holidaybowl.com.*

San Diego Chargers. Part of the NFL's West division, the offensive-minded San Diego–based Chargers play their home games at Qualcomm Stadium. Particularly intense are the Chargers' games with AFC West rivals the Oakland Raiders. The team began in 1960, with its first season in L.A. but then in San Diego since 1961. Its iconic lightning bolt has stayed with the team and uniforms through the decades. ⊠ *9449 Friars Rd., Mission Valley* ☎ *858/874–4500 Charger Park, 877/242–7437 season tickets* ⊕ *www.chargers.com.*

GOLF

Farmers Insurance Open. This tournament brings the pros to the Torrey Pines Golf Course in late January or early February. ⊠ *11480 North Torrey Pines. Rd., La Jolla* ☎ *858/886–4653 Year-round, 858/452–0362 During tournament* ⊕ *www.farmersinsuranceopen.com.*

HORSE RACING

Del Mar Thoroughbred Club. The racetrack attracts the best horses and jockeys in the country—Seabiscuit even won a much-talked-about race here in 1938. And, thanks to a newly added fall season, spectators can enjoy 11 weeks of racing annually at the historic Del Mar Racetrack. The summer season starts in mid-July and runs through early September and includes a summer concert series and opening and closing day celebrations. The fall season lasts for a month starting in November. The track, which opened in 1937, was founded in part by singer and actor Bing Crosby. ⊠ *2260 Jimmy Durante Blvd., Del Mar* ✛ *Take I–5 north to Via de la Valle exit* ☎ *858/755–1141* ⊕ *www.dmtc.com.*

SHOPPING

Updated
by Casey
Hatfield-Chiotti

San Diego's retail landscape has changed radically in recent years with the opening of several new shopping centers—some in historic buildings—that are focused more on locally owned boutiques than national retailers. Where once the Gaslamp was the place to go for urban apparel and unique home decor, many independently owned boutiques have decided to set up shop in the charming neighborhoods east of Balboa Park known as North Park and South Park. Although downtown is still thriving, any shopping trip to San Diego should include venturing out to the city's diverse and vibrant neighborhoods. Not far from downtown, Little Italy is the place to find contemporary art, modern furniture, and home accessories.

Old Town is a must for pottery, ceramics, jewelry, and handcrafted baskets. Uptown is known for its mélange of funky bookstores, off-beat gift shops, and nostalgic collectibles, and the beach towns have the best swimwear and sandals. La Jolla's chic boutiques offer a more intimate shopping experience along with some of the classiest clothes, jewelry, and shoes in the county. Point Loma's Liberty Station shopping area in the former Naval Training Center has art galleries, restaurants, and home stores. Trendsetters will have no trouble finding must-have handbags and designer apparel at the world-class Fashion Valley mall in Mission Valley, a haven for luxury brands such as Hermès, Jimmy Choo, and M Missoni.

Enjoy near-perfect weather year-round as you explore shops along the scenic waterfront. The Headquarters at Seaport District is a new open-air shopping and dining center in the city's former Police Headquarters building. Here there are some big names but mostly locally owned boutiques selling everything from gourmet cheese to coastal-inspired home accessories. Just next door, Seaport Village is still the place to go for trinkets and souvenirs. If you don't discover what you're looking for in the boutiques, head for Westfield Horton Plaza, the downtown mall with more than 100 stores. The sprawling mall has been going through a major restoration project that included demolishing an unused section and putting in a public plaza.

Most malls have free parking in a lot or garage, and parking is not usually a problem. Westfield Horton Plaza and some of the shops in the Gaslamp Quarter offer validated parking or valet parking.

SHOPPING PLANNER

OPENING HOURS

Shops near tourist attractions and the major shopping malls tend to open early and close late. Standard hours are typically 10 to 9 on weekdays and 10 to 10 on weekends. Smaller shops may close as early as 5 on weekdays and Sunday. It's best to call ahead to confirm hours if you have your heart set on visiting a particular shop.

FINDING UNIQUE GIFTS

The city's major attractions have gift shops with more than just stuffed animals and T-shirts. The museum shops at Balboa Park (☎ 619/239–0512) brim with affordable treasures. The ZooStore and Ituri Forest Outpost (☎ 619/231–1515) at the San Diego Zoo carry international crafts, world music, and hats, while the San Diego Safari Park's Bazaar (☎ 760/738–5055) sells authentic African artifacts, books, home-decor items, and apparel. The Big Shop (☎ 760/918–5346) at LEGOLAND is great for collectors and collectors-in-training, with the largest selection of LEGO sets in the nation.

14

SNAG A BARGAIN AT OUTLET MALLS

Some hotels offer free shuttles to shopping centers, outlet malls, and nearby casinos. Check with the concierge for schedules.

Carlsbad Premium Outlets. A 40-minute drive north of downtown San Diego, this complex contains 90 outlet stores, including Le Creuset, Banana Republic, DKNY, Kate Spade New York, Michael Kors, and a new Nike Factory Store. ■ TIP→ On Tuesdays, many stores offer shoppers a 10 percent discount. ⊠ *5620 Paseo del Norte, Ste. 100, Carlsbad* ☎ *760/804–9000* ⊕ *www.premiumoutlets.com.*

Las Americas Premium Outlets. Near the international border in San Ysidro, this outlet mall has about 120 shops, including two duty-free outlets and a clutch of fast-food and sit-down restaurants. The usual brand names are here, including Adidas, Hurley J. Crew, Polo/Ralph Lauren, and a new North Face for high-quality outerwear. ■ TIP→ Shuttle service to Las Americas is available from many San Diego area hotels, and the San Diego Trolley's San Ysidro stop is a five-minute walk from the mall. ⊠ *4211 Camino de la Plaza, off I–5, San Ysidro* ☎ *619/934–8400* ⊕ *www.premiumoutlets.com.*

FAMILY **Viejas Outlet Center.** Head east 30 miles from Mission Valley to reach this mall across the street from Viejas Casino. Major brands represented here include Coach, Chico's, Levi's, Osh Kosh, and Eddie Bauer. ■ TIP→ Free entertainment is offered year-round at the ShowCourt. Kids enjoy the FunZone arcade, bowling, and mini-golf. ⊠ *5000 Willow Rd., off I–8, Exit 33, Alpine* ☎ *619/659–2070* ⊕ *www.viejasoutletcenter.com.*

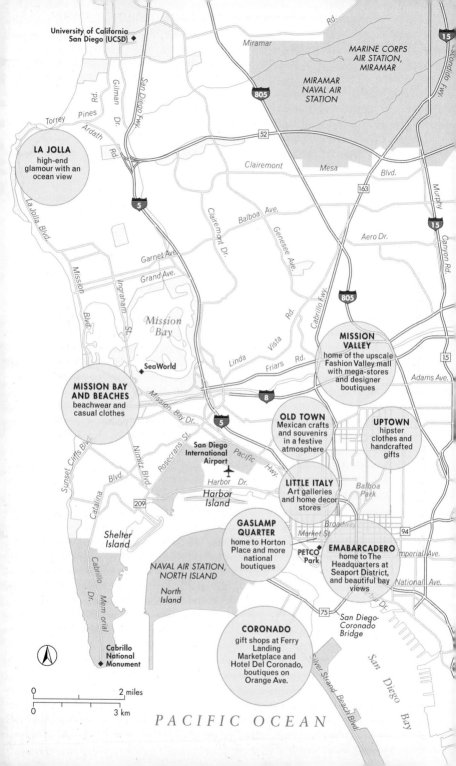

University of California
San Diego (UCSD) ◆

Miramar

**MARINE CORPS
AIR STATION,
MIRAMAR**

**MIRAMAR
NAVAL AIR
STATION**

🛣 **805**
🛣 **15**

Torrey   Pines
Ardath   Rd.
Gilman   Dr.
San Diego Fwy.
Escondido Fwy.

52

Clairemont   *Mesa*   *Blvd.*

163

LA JOLLA
high-end
glamour with an
ocean view

La Jolla Blvd.

🛣 **5**

Balboa   Ave.
Clairemont Dr.
Genesee Ave.
Aero Dr.

805

🛣 **15**

Murphy
Canyon Rd.

Adams Ave.

Garnet Ave.
Grand Ave.
Mission   St.
Ingraham   St.

*Mission
Bay*

Vista   Rd.
Cabrillo Fwy.

**MISSION
VALLEY**
home of the upscale
Fashion Valley mall
with mega-stores
and designer
boutiques

Linda   *Friars   Rd.*

8

◆ **SeaWorld**

**MISSION BAY
AND BEACHES**
beachwear and
casual clothes

Mission   Bay Dr.

🛣 **5**

OLD TOWN
Mexican crafts
and souvenirs
in a festive
atmosphere

UPTOWN
hipster
clothes and
handcrafted
gifts

Sunset Cliffs Blvd.
Catalina   Blvd.
Nimitz Blvd.
Rosecrans St.

**San Diego
International
Airport**
✈

Pacific   Hwy.
Harbor   Dr.

LITTLE ITALY
Art galleries
and home decor
stores

*Balboa
Park*

*Harbor
Island*

209

*Shelter
Island*

**GASLAMP
QUARTER**
home to Horton
Place and more
national
boutiques

Broadway
Market St

94

**NAVAL AIR STATION,
NORTH ISLAND**

*North
Island*

Cabrillo   Mem orial   Dr.

**PETCO
Park**

EMBARCADERO
home to The
Headquarters at
Seaport District,
and beautiful bay
views

Imperial Ave.
National Ave.

75

*San Diego-
Coronado
Bridge*

▲
**Cabrillo
National
◆ Monument**

CORONADO
gift shops at Ferry
Landing
Marketplace and
Hotel Del Coronado,
boutiques on
Orange Ave.

*San
Diego
Bay*

Silver Strand Beach Blvd.

◈

0		2 miles
0		3 km

PACIFIC   OCEAN

TOP SHOPPING EXPERIENCES

Fashion Valley: Bloomingdale's, Nordstrom, Neiman Marcus, and haute boutiques are all under one roof.

Gaslamp Quarter: Gaslamp's trendy shops carry everything from vintage clothing to antiques and art.

La Jolla: At the ocean-side enclave of the rich and famous, prices might leave your credit card reeling—but browsing is free.

North Park: Transform yourself from tourist into hipster in no time with finds from this neighborhood's edgy boutiques.

Old Town: No need for a passport. Mexico's finest crafts, artwork, and jewelry are all in this neighborhood north of the border.

The Headquarters: Locally owned boutiques rule at this new shopping center in a former jail.

14

SHOPPING BY NEIGHBORHOOD

DOWNTOWN

The city's ever-changing downtown offers a variety of shopping venues including the open-air Westfield Horton Plaza, a traditional mall; the eclectic-to-mainstream shops of the Gaslamp Quarter; and the upscale shopping at the Headquarters at Seaport District. Within easy walking distance of the Convention Center and downtown hotels, the area is a shopper's delight.

GASLAMP QUARTER

The mix of retailers in the historic heart of San Diego changes frequently but there are always boutiques in the Victorian buildings and renovated warehouses along 4th and 5th avenues. Also in the quarter are the usual mall stores and gift shops. Some stores close early, starting as early as 5 pm, and many are closed Sunday or Monday.

CLOTHING AND ACCESSORIES

Blends. Minimalist decor provides a perfect backdrop for the wild colors and patterns featured on limited-edition sneakers from Nike, Reebok, Vans, and other in-demand brands. Prices are steep, but many of the styles are unique. ⌧ *719 8th Ave., Gaslamp Quarter* ☎ *619/233–6126* ⊕ *blendsus.com.*

Dolcetti Boutique. With everything from flirty dresses to casual daytime outfits and a full-service salon on-site, this Gaslamp Quarter boutique is a one-stop shop for getting ready for a night on the town. Owned by style-savvy sisters, the lofty space has redbrick walls and also carries menswear, including jeans, collared shirts, and graphic tees. ⌧ *635 5th Ave., Gaslamp Quarter* ☎ *619/501–1559* ⊕ *www.dolcettiboutique. com* ☾ *Closed Mon.*

Goorin Bros. Hats. This company, first established in Pennsylvannia in 1895, has helped make hats hip again with its stylish takes on fedoras, bowlers, and Panama hats. The San Diego location occupies the first floor of the historic Yuma building, a former brothel. ⊠ *631 5th Ave., Gaslamp Quarter* 🕾 *619/450–6303* ⊕ *www.goorin.com.*

Ron Stuart. Sharp-dressed men flock to this men's shop for slim-fitting suits and shirts from brands like Privé and Stone Rose. It also offers Tommy Bahama shirts, custom Jack Victor suits, and expert on-site tailoring. ⊠ *225 A St., Gaslamp Quarter* 🕾 *619/232–8850* ⊕ *www. ronstuartmensclothing.com* ⊙ *Closed Sun.*

HOME ACCESSORIES AND GIFTS

Bubbles Boutique. Budget-conscious fashionistas will love this Gaslamp Quarter spot, where many items, including floral dresses, straw hats, and harem pants, are priced under $100. The boutique also stocks leather belts, strappy purses, and jewelry designed by local designers, such as turquoise pieces from Solana Beach–based Cat Max Jewels. ⊠ *226 5th Ave., Gaslamp Quarter* 🕾 *619/236–9003* ⊕ *www. bubblesboutique.com.*

Cuban Cigar Factory. San Diego Padres fans and other aficionados flock to this store and lounge that provides a comfy spot to savor a fine cigar—crafted from tobacco grown from Cuban seed—with a beer or a glass of wine. ⊠ *551 5th Ave., Gaslamp Quarter* 🕾 *619/238–2496* ⊕ *www.cubancigarfactory.net.*

Gaslamp Garage. Crammed floor to ceiling with merchandise and decorated to look like a 1950s auto repair shop, the city's largest gift shop is the place to head for Padres gear and quirky knickknacks like a San Diego refrigerator magnet decorated with pink flamingos. The store also stocks a wide variety of surf apparel from brands like Quiksilver and Roxy, and the Kidz Garage has toys, electronics, and apparel from infant to size 12. ⊠ *301 5th Ave., Gaslamp Quarter* 🕾 *619/241–4240.*

SHOPPING CENTERS

Westfield Horton Plaza. Macy's, Nordstrom, and a new natural foods grocer called Jimbo's anchor this multilevel complex that has 100 smaller stores, plus fast-food and upscale dining, cinemas, and a game arcade. The plaza garage is a maze so make sure to note where you parked. ▮**TIP→** Horton Plaza offers three hours of free parking between 9:30 am and 9 pm. Just validate your ticket at one of the machines in the mall. ⊠ *324 Horton Plaza, Gaslamp Quarter* 🕾 *619/239–8180* ⊕ *www. westfield.com/hortonplaza.*

EAST VILLAGE

Just a hop, skip, and a jump from the Gaslamp Quarter, the 130-block East Village neighborhood contains shops catering to local hipsters and visitors looking for edgy street wear, novelty T-shirts, and offbeat accessories. Some of the best shopping can be found from 8th to 10th avenues between Broadway and J Street. During the convivial "Evenings in the East Village" events (⊕ *www.sdeastvillage.com*), residents, and visitors stroll the area and enjoy art, music, and food.

CLOTHING AND ACCESSORIES

5&A Dime. This popular men's and women's clothing shop owned by a brother and sister features labels like Rich & Rude, Brixton, Dekline, Motor Union, and Herschel. Choose from a fun selection of hats, shoes, sweaters, and tees for guys and gals, and don't miss the sunglasses and jewelry. ⊠ *701 8th Ave., East Village* ☎ *619/236–0364* ⊕ *www.5andadime.com.*

GIFT AND SOUVENIRS

Central Library Library Shop. One of the highlights of San Diego's new eight-story central library in the East Village neighborhood is the well-curated gift shop, which carries gourmet cookbooks, jewelry, home accessories, and children's items. Mementos like shirts, totes, magnets, and notecards make great souvenirs. The shop, which is open daily, supports San Diego- or California-based vendors whenever possible. ⊠ *330 Park Blvd., East Village* ⊕ *libraryshopsd.org.*

LITTLE ITALY

14

With more than 33,500 square feet of retail, Little Italy is an especially fun place to visit during holiday celebrations and special events like ArtWalk in April and Taste of Little Italy in June. The weekly Saturday farmers market is one of the city's best and brings people from all over the county to the neighborhood (⊕ *www.sdweeklymarkets.com*). Many shops have a strong European ambience, and shoppers will find enticing wares that include colorful ceramics, hand-blown glassware, modern home accents, and designer shoes. Kettner Boulevard and India Street north of Grape Street are considered the North Little Italy Art and Design District. The website Little Italy San Diego (⊕ *www.littleitalysd.com*) has detailed info about neighborhood shops and events.

CLOTHING AND ACCESSORIES

Azzurra Capri. Walking into this white shop with blue trim will transport you instantly to Italy's stylish and sophisticated Amalfi Coast. Inspired by the island of Capri, this upscale boutique stocks resort wear, silk scarves, and handmade Italian leather sandals adorned with things like Swarovski crystals and turquoise. ⊠ *1840 Colombia St., Little Italy* ☎ *619/230–5116* ⊕ *azzurracapri.com.*

Kapreeza. Owner Renata Carlseen stocks her elegant boutique with upscale lingerie and sexy swimwear from European designers. ⊠ *1772 Kettner Blvd., Little Italy* ☎ *619/702–6355* ⊕ *www.kapreeza.com.*

Rosamariposa. This charming jewelry shop specializes in necklaces, earrings, and bracelets crafted by Indonesian artists using natural fibers, wood, seeds, and recycled glass. ⊠ *611 W. Fir St., Little Italy* ☎ *619/237–8064* ⊕ *www.rosamariposasd.com.*

Vocabulary Boutique. A local favorite for its friendly vibe and stylish inventory, this cozy boutique often stars in regional fashion shoots. It's known for unique, affordable outfits for women, men, and kids. ⊠ *414 W. Cedar St., Little Italy* ☎ *619/544–1100* ⊕ *www.vocabulary boutique.com.*

FOOD AND WINE

Bottlecraft Beer Shop. This boutique beer shop stocks the best craft beer from around the world as well as San Diego, from Belgian Sour Cherry Ale to local brewery Alesmith's award-winning Speedway Stout. Owner Brian Jensen offers a wealth of knowledge on the local craft beer scene. Bottlecraft now has a second location in North Park. ⊠ *2161 India St.* ☎ *619/487–9493* ⊕ *store.bottlecraftbeer.com.*

HOME ACCESSORIES AND GIFTS

Architectural Salvage of San Diego. If you have any interest in home design and renovation, this shop that specializes in reusing old materials should be a stop on your shopping tour. The warehouse space is filled with unusual home building and decorating materials, as well as items that come from various time periods throughout the 1900s. Products range from stained-glass windows to vintage water canisters to doors in styles ranging from Victorian to Craftsman. ⊠ *2401 Kettner Blvd., Little Italy* ☏ *619/696–1313* ⊕ *www.architecturalsalvagesd.com.*

Boomerang for Modern. This well-curated furniture store in the North Little Italy Design District is a shrine to mid-century modern design. Discover now-classic furniture and accessories like George Nelson star clocks, womb chairs and sofas, and stools by legendary designers Charles and Ray Eames. ⊠ *2475 Kettner Blvd., Little Italy* ☏ *619/239–2040* ⊕ *www.boomerangformodern.com* ◷ *Closed Sun.*

Casa Artelexia. This colorful shop specializing in Mexican gifts and art started as a booth at a farmers' market but has since evolved into a large retail space with its own art gallery and event space. Products— hand picked and imported from different parts of Mexico—include sacred heart wall hangings, artworks depicting Frida Kahlo, and Dia de Los Muertos screen-printed tanks. Casa Artelexia also offers weekly art classes. ⊠ *2400 Kettner Blvd., #102, Little Italy* ☏ *619/544–1011* ⊕ *www.artelexia.com* ◷ *Closed Mon.*

French Garden Shoppe. Specializing in European home and garden furnishings, this inviting store also offers great gift items like pottery, cookware, candles, and imported gourmet foods. ⊠ *2307 India St., Little Italy* ☏ *619/238–4700.*

Masquerade Art of Living. Masquerade's collections include fine art and wearable art, as well as gifts and mirrors, lamps, and other home accessories. ⊠ *1608 India St., Little Italy* ☏ *619/235–6564* ◷ *Closed Mon.*

Vitreum. The Japanese artist Takao owns this gallery-like shop that sells beautifully handcrafted home-decor items—tableware, vases, and decorative gifts. The shop has irregular hours on Sunday. ⊠ *619 W. Fir St., Little Italy* ⊕ *www.vitreum-us.com.*

EMBARCADERO

The new Headquarters at Seaport District shopping district is breathing new life into the somewhat touristy San Diego Waterfront. Spanning 14 acres and offering more than 50 shops and 18 restaurants, Seaport Village remains popular for souvenirs and entertainment.

SHOPPING CENTERS

Fodor'sChoice ★   **The Headquarters at Seaport District.** This new upscale shopping and dining center is in the city's former Police Headquarters, a beautiful and historic Mission-style building featuring a large open courtyard and water fountains. Restaurants and shops, many locally owned, occupy former jail cells and offices. Pop into the San Diego outpost of the trendy L.A.-based boutique **Kitson** for art and fashion books and clothing items that epitomize West Coast style like designer denim and soft button-down blouses. The **Aaron Chang Ocean Art Gallery** showcases the Encinitas-based photographer's heirloom quality photography and photo-wrapped surfboards. **Dallman Fine Chocolates** sells truffles in flavors like bacon with applewood smoked salt. **Vennissimo Cheese** sells the best cheese from around the world, from double cream herbed d'affinois from France to tangy ricotta from Pomona, California. There's also a second location of Coronado favorite **Seaside Paper Home.** Every Sunday the shopping center courtyard is home to a farmers' market. ⊠ *789 W. Harbor Dr., Downtown* ☏ *619/235–4014* ⊕ *the-headquarters.com.*

Seaport Village. This complex of shops and restaurants is a bit kitschy, but upping the hip factor here are some new boutiques—like wine bar, bamboo clothing–maker **Cariloha** and **FROST ME Gourmet Cupcakes,** a bakery from the champions of Cupcake Wars Season 9. Still if you're looking for trinkets and souvenirs, this is the place. In the East Plaza, keep an eye out for **Silver Crossing,** for rings, charms, chains, and jewelry, and **Seaport Village Shell Company,** for shells, coral, jewelry, and craft items. In addition to shopping, the village has views of the bay, fresh breezes, and great strolling paths. A hand-carved 1895 Looff carousel and frequent public entertainment are among the attractions. Restaurants are mediocre but redevelopment plans are in the works. ■TIP➔ **Get two hours of parking for $3 with a $10 purchase at any Seaport Village establishment.** ⊠ *849 W. Harbor Dr., at Pacific Hwy., Downtown* ☏ *619/235–4014* ⊕ *www.seaportvillage.com/shopping.*

BALBOA PARK

HOME ACCESSORIES AND GIFTS

Mingei International Museum Store. The shop at the Mingei showcases an international collection of textiles, jewelry, apparel, and home decor items. Artworks are displayed on a rotating basis in the store's gallery, and there's a nice selection of books on craft and folk art. If you're in San Diego during the first part of the year, watch out for the store's annual Treasure Sale, when some items that have been donated to the museum are put on sale, from baskets made in Africa to handmade jewelry. ⊠ *1439 El Prado, Balboa Park* ☏ *619/239–0003* ⊕ *www.mingei. org/store* ⊘ *Closed Mon.*

OLD TOWN AND UPTOWN

OLD TOWN

Tourist-focused Old Town, north of downtown off I–5, has festival-like ambience that also makes it a popular destination for locals. At Old Town Historic Park, you may feel like a time traveler as you visit shops housed in restored adobe buildings. Farther down the street are stores selling Mexican blankets, piñatas, and glassware. Old Town Market offers live entertainment, local artists selling their wares from carts, and a market crammed with unique apparel, home-decor items, toys, jewelry, and food. Dozens of stores sell San Diego logo merchandise and T-shirts at discounted prices; there are great deals on handcrafted jewelry, art, and leather accessories. When you've tired of shopping, there are plenty of Mexican restaurants where you can dine, down a margarita, or both.

14

SHOPPING CENTERS

Fodor's Choice ★ **Bazaar del Mundo Shops.** An arcade with a Mexican villa theme, the Bazaar hosts riotously colorful gift shops such as **Ariana,** for ethnic and artsy women's fashions; **Artes de Mexico,** which sells handmade Latin American crafts and Guatemalan weavings; and **The Gallery,** which carries handmade jewelry, Native American crafts, collectible glass, and original serigraphs by John August Swanson. The **Laurel Burch Gallerita** carries the complete collection of the northern California artist's signature jewelry, accessories, and totes. ⊠ *4133 Taylor St., at Juan St., Old Town* ☎ *619/296–3161* ⊕ *www.bazaardelmundo.com.*

Fiesta de Reyes. Within the Old Town San Diego State Historic Park, Fiesta de Reyes exudes the easy feel of Old California. Friendly shopkeepers dressed in period attire host a collection of boutiques and eateries around a flower-filled square whose design reflects Old Town circa the 1850s. Many of the shops stock items reminiscent of that era. Visit **Silver Lily** for one-of-a-kind silver pieces with semi-precious stones, **Fiesta Cocina** for festive kitchenware, **Temecula Olive Oil** for local olive oils and artisan foods, and **Hot Licks** for gourmet hot sauces. The **Tile Shop** carries hand-painted Mexican tiles, **Geppetto's** specializes in classic wooden toys, and **La Panaderia** sells baked goods made using early Mexican cooking methods. Two restaurants, **Casa de Reyes** and the **Barra Barra Saloon,** serve Mexican food. ⊠ *2754 Calhoun St., Old Town* ☎ *619/297–3100* ⊕ *www.fiestadereyes.com.*

Old Town Market. The atmosphere is colorful, upbeat, and Latin-centric at this eclectic market. Local artisans create some of the wares for sale, everything from dolls and silver jewelry to gourmet foods, home-decor items, and apparel. ⊠ *4010 Twiggs St., Old Town* ☎ *619/278–0955* ⊕ *www.oldtownmarketsandiego.com.*

Old Town Saturday Market. San Diego's largest artisan market presents live music and local artists selling jewelry, paintings, photography, handblown glass, apparel, pottery, and decorative items. The San Diego Trolley's Old Town stop is two blocks north of the market. ⊠ *Harney St. and San Diego Ave., Old Town* ☎ *858/272–7054* ⊕ *www.oldtownsaturdaymarket.com* ⊡ *Free* ☉ *Sat. 9–4:30.*

OFF THE BEATEN PATH   **Kobey's Swap Meet.** Not far from Old Town, San Diego's premier flea market seems to expand every week. Sellers display everything from African arts and gifts to fresh flowers at the open-air event. The back section, with secondhand goods, is great for bargain hunters. ⊠ *Valley View Casino Center parking lot, 3500 Sports Arena Blvd., Sports Arena* ☎ *619/226–0650* ⊕ *www.kobeyswap.com* ⊡ *$2 weekends, $1 Fri.* ☉ *Fri.–Sun. 7–3.*

HOME ACCESSORIES AND GIFTS

Four Winds Art. The excellent arts and crafts sold here include paintings, pottery, dolls, jewelry, and rugs created by Native Americans. ⊠ *2448 San Diego Ave., Old Town* ☎ *619/692–0466.*

Tafoya & Son Pottery. This shop in an historic adobe building specializes in Talavera pottery and Mexican folk art. Look for sterling silver jewelry designed by owner Chris Tafoya. ⊠ *2769 San Diego Ave., Old Town* ☎ *619/574–0989* ⊕ *www.tafoyaandson.com.*

Tienda de Reyes. This festive "store of the kings" stocks Old Town's largest selection of Day of the Dead art and carries sculpture, handbags, and barware from Mexico and Peru. ✉ *2754 Calhoun St., Old Town* ☎ *619/491–0611* ⊕ *www.tiendadereyes.com.*

Ye Olde Soap Shoppe. The mere scent of Ye Olde's hand-fashioned soaps conjures up a relaxing bath. If you want to craft your own soaps, you'll find a full line of supplies as well as soaps and lotions from around the world and wax sachets to put in your top drawer. ✉ *2497 San Diego Ave., Old Town* ☎ *800/390–9969* ⊕ *www.soapmaking.com.*

JEWELRY

The Diamond Source. Specializing in fashionable diamond and precious gemstone jewelry, this shop showcases the creations of master jeweler Marco Levy. There's a second location in La Jolla. ✉ *2474 San Diego Ave., Old Town* ☎ *619/299–6900* ⊕ *www.thediamondsource. com* ⊘ *Closed Mon.*

HILLCREST

The Uptown neighborhood of Hillcrest has many avant-garde apparel shops alongside gift, book, and music stores.

BOOKS

Adams Avenue Bookstore. Literature, history, philosophy, and theology are the specialties of this popular bookstore that carries used, rare, and out-of-print titles. ✉ *3502 Adams Ave., Hillcrest* ☎ *619/281–3330* ⊕ *www.adamsavebooks.com.*

CLOTHING AND ACCESSORIES

Mint. Affordably priced ballet flats and wild stilettos share space here with urban sneakers, retro boots, and colorful espadrilles. ✉ *525 University Ave., Hillcrest* ☎ *619/291–6468* ⊕ *www.mintshoes.com.*

HOME ACCESSORIES AND GIFTS

Babette Schwartz. This zany pop-culture store sells toys, books, T-shirts, and magnets. ✉ *421 University Ave., Hillcrest* ☎ *619/220–7048* ⊕ *www.babette.com.*

MISSION HILLS

The shops and art galleries in Mission Hills, west of Hillcrest, have a modern and sophisticated ambience that suits the well-heeled residents.

CLOTHING AND ACCESSORIES

Le Bel Age Boutique. A neighborhood staple for more than 28 years, this charming boutique carries maxi dresses, Capri pants, and handbags, as well as jewelry designed by the owner, Valeri. Just down the street sister boutique, **Chateau Bel Age,** features hard-to-find French designers and exotic-looking caftans. ✉ *1607 W. Lewis St., Mission Hills* ☎ *619/297–7080* ⊘ *Closed Sun. and Mon.*

HOME ACCESSORIES AND GIFTS

Maison en Provence. This adorable little shop located in a Mission Hills bungalow is the place for Francophiles to get their French fix in San Diego. The French proprietors Pascal and Marielle Giai stock linen tablecloths and dishes from Provence. There are also fine soaps, antique postcards, and Laguiole cutlery, the most elegant of pocket knives. ■ TIP ➜ For French inspiration and information about French events

14

Old Town is the place to go for colorful Mexican wares.

in San Diego, check the store's great blog. ⊠ *820 Ft. Stockton Dr., Mission Hills* ☎ *619/298–5318* ⊕ *maisonenprovence.skynetblogs.be* ⏱ *Closed Mon.*

M-Theory Music. This locally owned record store in Mission Hills carries new and often rarely used vinyl. It regularly hosts in-store performances. ⊠ *915 Washington St., Mission Hills* ☎ *619/220–0485* ⊕ *www.mtheorymusic.com.*

Taboo Studio. This upscale gallery displays and sells the handcrafted jewelry of an international group of artists. The stars here are the limited-edition pieces that incorporate precious metals and gemstones. The shop will also repurpose your old jewelry into something new. ⊠ *1615½ W. Lewis St., Mission Hills* ☎ *619/692–0099* ⊕ *www.taboostudio.com* ⏱ *Closed Sun.–Mon.*

MISSION VALLEY

Northeast of downtown near I–8 and Route 163, Mission Valley holds two major shopping centers and a few smaller strip malls. Fashion Valley hosts an impressive roster of high-end department stores—among them Neiman Marcus, Nordstrom, and Bloomingdale's—and a passel of luxury boutiques. Westfield Mission Valley is home to mainstays like Macy's and Old Navy, plus bargain-hunter favorites like Marshall's and Nordstrom Rack. The San Diego Trolley and city buses stop at both centers.

SHOPPING CENTERS

Fodor's Choice

★

Fashion Valley. More than 18 million shoppers visit Fashion Valley each year. That's more than the combined attendance of SeaWorld, LEGO-LAND, the San Diego Padres, the San Diego Chargers, and the San

Diego Zoo. San Diego's best and most upscale mall has a contemporary Mission theme, lush landscaping, and more than 200 shops and restaurants. Acclaimed retailers like Nordstrom, Neiman Marcus, and Tiffany are here, along with boutiques from fashion darlings like Michael Kors, Jimmy Choo, Tory Burch, and James Perse. H&M is a favorite of fashionistas in search of edgy and affordable styles. Free wireless Internet service is available throughout the mall. Select "Simon WiFi" from any Wi-Fi–enabled device to log onto the network. ■ **TIP→ If you show this Fodor's book at Simon Guest Services (lower level, along the walkway between Prada and Banana Republic), you will get a complimentary Style Pass, which can get you savings at more than 70 of Fashion Valley's stores, boutiques, and restaurants.** ⊠ *7007 Friars Rd., Mission Valley* ☎ *619/688–9113* ⊕ *www.simon.com/mall/fashion-valley.*

Off 5th. Across from Westfield Mission Valley, Off 5th sells bargain-price fashions by Ralph Lauren, Armani, and Burberry seen at Saks the previous season. ⊠ *1750 Camino de la Reina, Mission Valley* ☎ *619/296–4896* ⊕ *www.saksoff5th.com.*

FAMILY **Westfield Mission Valley.** The discount stores at San Diego's largest outdoor mall sometimes reward shoppers with the same merchandise as that sold in Fashion Valley, the mall up the road, but at lower prices. Shops include Macy's, American Eagle Outfitters, DSW Shoe Warehouse, and Victoria's Secret. ⊠ *1640 Camino del Rio, Mission Valley* ☎ *619/296–6375* ⊕ *www.westfield.com/missionvalley.*

UNIVERSITY HEIGHTS
University Avenue is good for furniture, gift, and specialty stores appealing to college students, singles, and young families.

NORTH PARK
North Park, east of Hillcrest, is a retro buff's paradise, with resale shops, trendy boutiques, and stores that sell mostly handcrafted items.

CLOTHING AND ACCESSORIES
Fodor's Choice **Aloha Sunday Supply Co.** This clean, white boutique with high ceilings
★ and blond-wood accents carries no Billabong or Quicksilver, but make no mistake, this is a surf shop. The store sells only hand-crafted pieces like Matuse wetsuits, American-made Thorogood leather boots and the store's own brand of tailored men's clothing designed by co-owner and former professional surfer Kahana Kalama. ⊠ *3039 University Ave.* ☎ *619/269–9838* ⊕ *alohasunday.com.*

Gym Standard. This footwear and design goods shop carries street-savvy brands like Converse, PF Flyers, Clae, and Vans, as well as design magazines, ceramics, and succulents. ⊠ *2903 El Cajon, Unit #2, North Park* ☎ *619/501–4996* ⊕ *www.gymstandard.com.*

Mimi & Red Boutique. Laid-back ambience, friendly service, and racks full of moderate to high-end women's fashions have made this shop a favorite with cool San Diegans. Nixon and Everly are here along with RVCA, BB Dakota, and affordably priced bath and body products. ⊠ *3032 University Ave., North Park* ☎ *619/298–7933* ⊕ *www.mimiandred.com.*

14

FOOD

Original Paw Pleasers. At this bakery for dogs and cats there are oatmeal "dogolate" chip cookies, peanut butter dog treats, and "itty bitty kitty treats." Paw Pleasers will also custom make a birthday cake for your four-legged friend. ⊠ *2818 University Ave., North Park* ☎ *619/293–7297* ⊕ *www.pawpleasers.com.*

HOME ACCESSORIES AND GIFTS

Fodor's Choice
★

Pigment. This light-filled shop carries a wide variety of design-conscious goods for the home, including geometric print pillows, outdoor bistro chairs, and home bar accessories. Pigment's "build your own" terrariums, where you select a glass vessel and fill it with succulents and colorful sand to make a great souvenir. ⊠ *3801 30th St., North Park* ☎ *619/501–6318* ⊕ *www.shoppigment.com.*

SOUTH PARK

South Park's 30th, Juniper, and Fern streets have everything from eco-friendly fashions to gourmet chocolate to craft supplies.

CLOTHING AND ACCESSORIES

Graffiti Beach. This indie boutique in South Park's historic 30th and Fern building is filled with quirky art, jewelry, and clothing from emerging designers and artists with a conscience as well as earth-friendly companies like Mukee, a Denver-based company that makes jewelry and accessories from reclaimed skateboards, and WeWood Watches, a company that plants a tree for every watch purchased. This is a great place to pick up souvenirs if you're into supporting local: 75% of the designers are from California. ⊠ *2220 Fern St., South Park* ☎ *858/433–0950* ⊕ *shopgraffitibeach.com* ☉ *Closed Mon.*

HOME ACCESSORIES AND GIFTS

The Grove. Crafters stock up on fabric trims, pattern books, and knitting and crochet supplies at this popular shop, which also offers instruction classes. Also here are organic clothing, children's apparel, fiber arts, kitchen and homeware items, and travel supplies like luggage and passport carriers. ⊠ *3010 Juniper St., South Park* ☎ *619/284–7684* ⊕ *www.thegrovesandiego.com* ☞ *Call ahead on Mon.*

Progress. This home store has its own line of modern furniture as well as hanging planters, wine decanters, and wall art. ⊠ *2225 30th St., South Park* ☎ *619/280–5501* ⊕ *www.progresssouthpark.com.*

Stone Brewing Co. This beer-tasting room and company store from the local brewery that put San Diego craft beer on the map also sells T-shirts and growlers—great souvenirs to have from this beer-loving city. ⊠ *2215 30th St., South Park* ☎ *619/501–3342* ⊕ *www.stonebrew.com.*

MISSION BAY AND THE BEACHES

Mission, Grand, and Garnet are the big shopping avenues in the beach towns. Souvenir shops are scattered up and down the boardwalk, and along Mission Boulevard there are surf, skate, and bike shops, bikini boutiques, and stores selling hip T-shirts, jeans, sandals, and casual apparel. Garnet Avenue is the hot spot for resale boutiques, thrift stores, and pawn shops. The Ocean Beach Antique District in the 4800 block of

Newport Avenue invites browsing with several buildings housing multiple dealers under one roof. Independent stores showcase everything from vintage watches and pottery to linens and retro posters.

MISSION BAY

HOME ACCESSORIES AND GIFTS

Ocean Gifts & Shells. This huge beach-theme store is filled with seashells of every size and shape, nautical-decor items, wind chimes, swimwear, toys, and souvenirs. ⊠ *4934 Newport Ave., Mission Bay* ☎ *619/224–6702* ⊕ *www.oceangiftsandshells.com.*

MISSION BEACH

CLOTHING AND ACCESSORIES

Gone Bananas Beachwear. When you first walk into this swimwear store it's a bit overwhelming. There are more than 15,000 pieces and swimsuits lining the walls from floor to ceiling. To make shopping a bit easier, swimsuits have been arranged by color. Browse through mix-and-match pieces from the most fashion-forward swimwear designers like Mikoh, Tori Praver, and Vitamin A. It's worth taking the time to peruse what is simply San Diego's best selection of swimwear. ⊠ *3785 Mission Blvd., Mission Beach* ☎ *858/488–4900* ⊕ *https://gonebananasbeachwear.com.*

PACIFIC BEACH

HOME ACCESSORIES AND GIFTS

Great News! Cookware and Cooking School. Cooks drool over the bakeware, cutlery, tools, cookbooks, and gadgets sold here. There's an on-site cooking school, and the shop's customer service is excellent. ⊠ *1788 Garnet Ave., Pacific Beach* ☎ *858/270–1582* ⊕ *www.great-news.com.*

CARLSBAD

Fodor's Choice
★ **Omni La Costa Resort Spa.** Bring your swimsuit to one of the top wellness spas in the country and join friends in the picture-perfect Mediterranean garden, where you can swim, sun, and shower. Recently remodeled, this spa is the core of the resort wellness program that offers weight loss and fitness programs, plus yoga, pilates, and meditation at the Chopra Center. Price: body treatments $160–$295. ⊠ *2100 Costa Del Mar Rd., Carlsbad* ☎ *760/931–7570* ⊕ *www.lacosta.com.*

LA JOLLA AND DEL MAR

San Diego's answer to Rodeo Drive in Beverly Hills, La Jolla has chic boutiques, art galleries, and gift shops lining narrow, twisty streets that attract well-heeled shoppers and celebrities and their gawkers Farther north in Del Mar it's equally upscale, but a little less pretentious. Stroll the cute boutiques in Del Mar Village or head to Flower Hill Promenade, an outdoor shopping center that has become one of San Diego's most thriving retail destinations, with an eclectic mix of locally owned retailers. In La Jolla, Prospect Street and Girard Avenue are the primary shopping stretches, and North Prospect is packed with art galleries (*see* Chapter 11: The Arts, for information on art galleries). The Upper Girard Design District stocks home decor accessories and luxury furnishings. Store hours vary widely, so it's wise to call in advance. Most

Stores on Prospect Street in La Jolla buzz with activity until late in the evening.

shops on Prospect Street stay open until 10 pm on weeknights to accommodate evening strollers.

There's free angled parking downtown, but if you're having trouble, head to one of the Prospect Street garages, between Wall and Silverado, or along Herschel, Girard, and Fay. Rates range from $1.50 for 20 minutes to a maximum of $15 per day. After 4 pm, there's a flat rate of $10.

SHOPPING CENTERS

Westfield UTC. This popular outdoor mall on the east side of I–5 has more than 150 shops and 28 eateries, plus an ArcLight Cinemas and a kids play area. **Nordstrom, Macy's,** and **Sears** anchor the center, and specialty stores of note include **Madewell** (☏ 858/458–0012), for high-quality basics; **Pottery Barn Kids** (☏ 858/453–1249), for children's bedding and accessories; **Crate & Barrel** (☏ 858/558–4545) for kitchenware, china, and furniture; and an **Apple Store** (☏ 858/795–6870). One of the country's greenest shopping centers, UTC has lush gardens, open-air plazas, and pedestrian-friendly walkways. Additional eco-friendly cred: Tesla, maker of electric automobiles, shows off its models here. ✉ 4545 La Jolla Village Dr., between I–5 and I–805, La Jolla ☏ 858/546–8858 ⊕ www.westfield.com/utc.

Flower Hill Promenade. At first glance, this open-air shopping center anchored by a **Whole Foods** might look like your typical upscale SoCal mall, but take a closer look, because there's way more to it than meets the eye. There's not only some great shopping, much of it locally owned and eco-minded, but also some of San Diego's best restaurateurs like Tracy Borkum and Matt Gordon have opened restaurants here (CUCINA enoteca and Sea & Smoke, respectively). **Sweet Pea** stocks children's clothing from brands like Burberry, Petit Bateau, and Mimi & Maggie. **Studio Penny Lane** makes keepsake pieces out of pennies. **Pink Soul Boutique** sells "vegan" leather jewelry and hand-painted yoga pants and shirts. The second outpost of San Diego's beloved record store **M-Theory Music** just opened in the Row Collective, a section of Flower Hill that caters to a younger demographic. ✉ *2720 Via De La Valle, Del Mar* ☎ *858/481–2904* ⊕ *www.flowerhill.com.*

SPECIALTY STORES

BOOKS

Warwick's. This independently owned bookstore has been a La Jolla fixture since 1896 and often hosts big-name author signings. ✉ *7812 Girard Ave., La Jolla* ☎ *858/454–0347* ⊕ *www.warwicks.com.*

14

CLOTHING AND ACCESSORIES

Ascot Shop. The classic Ivy League look is king in this traditional haberdashery that sells menswear by Hugo Boss, Robert Talbott, and Robert Graham. In-house same-day tailoring is available. ✉ *7750 Girard Ave., La Jolla* ☎ *858/454–4222* ⊕ *www.ascotshop.com* ☽ *Closed Sun.*

Blended Industries. Both a posh boutique and wine bar, this trendy shop is owned by Summer Albertsen and *Bachelorette* star Jesse Kovacs. Browse through brands like Black Halo, J Brand, Parker, BCBG Maxazria, and Clover Canyon, then take a seat at the elegant wine bar and try winemaker Kovacs' Sauvignan Blanc or Meritage Rhone Blend. ✉ *1025 Prospect St., Suite 220, La Jolla* ☎ *858/255–8205* ⊕ *blendedindustries.com.*

Cinderella Shoe Clinic. Whether they're repairing pricey Louboutins or mending the straps on well-worn Louis Vuitton handbags, the staffers at this trusted shoe-repair shop work miracles. ✉ *929 Silverado St., La Jolla* ☎ *858/454–0806* ☽ *Closed Sun.*

Fresh Produce. Sunny and spirited Fresh Produce sells beach-inspired clothing made from comfy fabrics. The boutique's easy-to-wear pieces are perfect for vacations and weekends away. ✉ *1147 Prospect St., La Jolla* ☎ *858/456–8134* ⊕ *freshproduceclothes.com.*

KERUT. This fashion-forward boutique, featured in magazines such as *Elle* and *Condé Nast Traveller*, makes it easy to get the coveted Bohemian look thanks to its mix of edgy yet beach-appropriate designs, from brands like Rag & Bone, A.L.C, Mother, and Alexander Wang. ✉ *7944 Girard Ave., La Jolla* ☎ *858/456–0800* ⊕ *www.kerut.com.*

La Jolla Surf Systems. One block from La Jolla Shores Beach, this local institution stocks hip beach and resort wear plus top-brand surfboards, boogie boards, and wetsuits. The shop also rents surf and stand-up paddle boards, beach chairs, kayaks, and snorkel gear. ✉ *2132 Ave. de la Playa, La Jolla* ☎ *858/456–2777* ⊕ *www.lajollasurfsystems.com.*

Poppy Boutique. This boutique in upscale Rancho Santa Fe just east of Del Mar is worth seeking out for its great selection of wearable pieces like brightly colored silk tops and tailored demin that epitomize easygoing West Coast Style. Designers include Diane von Furstenberg, Rebecca Taylor, Milly, Haute Hippie, and Paige Denim. The bright-white boutique with orange dressing room curtains and round pink chairs feels like a modern boudoir. The boutique also carries gift items like books, dog leashes, coasters, lotions, and perfumes. ⊠ *16087 San Dieguito Rd., Suite D2, Rancho Santa Fe* ☎ *858/756–5528* ⊕ *www.poppyrsf.com.*

Rangoni of Florence. The boutique carries its own house brand as well as other, mostly Italian men's and women's footwear labels, including Icon, and Pele Moda. ⊠ *7870 Girard Ave., La Jolla* ☎ *858/459–4469* ⊕ *www.rangonistore.com.*

Sauvage. This luxurious boutique sells sexy and sophisticated swimsuits, beachwear, jewelry, and accessories for women; and swim trunks, surf shorts, and workout wear for men. ⊠ *1025 Prospect St., Ste. 140, La Jolla* ☎ *858/729–0015* ⊕ *www.sauvageswimwear.com.*

Sigi's Boutique. Women seeking high-end European designer fashions and accessories love this shop's fine cashmere from Scotland, stylish classics from Italy and France, and sportswear from Max Mara. ⊠ *7888 Girard Ave., La Jolla* ☎ *858/454–7244* ⊕ *www.sigislajolla.com* ☉ *Closed Sun.*

HOME ACCESSORIES AND GIFTS

Africa and Beyond. This La Jolla art gallery carries tradtional and contemporary African art including Shona stone sculptures and ceremonial masks as well as ceramics, fair trade gifts, and furniture like a bed from the Ivory Coast carved out of a single piece of wood. Not everything at the shop comes from Africa. Look for oceanic art from Papua New Guinea and sterling and gold-plated jewelry from across the world. ⊠ *1250 Prospect St., La Jolla* ☎ *858/454–9983* ⊕ *www. africaandbeyond.com.*

Fair Trade Decor. This home store with a conscience in Del Mar Village stocks only fair trade items from 37 countries, including goat wool rugs from Mexico, colorful telephone wire baskets from South Africa, and throws made from recycled saris. ⊠ *1412 Camino Del Mar, Del Mar* ☎ *858/461–1263* ⊕ *www.fairtradedecor.com.*

Everett Stunz. Add a little luxury to your life with the lotions, linens, robes, and sleepwear in cashmere, silk, and Swiss cotton sold here. ⊠ *7616 Girard Ave., La Jolla* ☎ *800/883–3305* ⊕ *www.everettstunz. com.*

La Jolla Cove Gifts. At the ocean end of Girard and one block from La Jolla Cove, this gift shop sells T-shirts, souvenirs, seashells, jewelry, and nautical items. ⊠ *8008 Girard Ave., #120, La Jolla* ☎ *858/454–2297* ⊕ *www.lajollacovegifts.com.*

Muttropolis. Dogs (and their owners) love the chic chew toys sold here. They also love the accessories, such as high-fashion coats and hoodies for strutting La Jolla's sun-splashed streets. There's haute cat-ture for felines here as well, and lots of catnip toys. ⊠ *7755 Girard Ave., La Jolla* ☎ *858/459–9663* ⊕ *www.muttropolis.com.*

Seaside Home. This luxury home furnishings shop went through a rebranding recently and is now focusing more on interior design services and bespoke furnishings than retail. However, in the elegant showroom, which nows feels more like a salon in a beach bungalow than a store, there's plenty to shop for: furniture, bedding, crystal, and Ralph Lauren accessories, as well as hostess gifts, candles, and scents. ⊠ *1055*

Wall St., La Jolla ☎ 858/454–0866 ⊕ *www.seaside-home.com* ⊙ *Closed weekends.*

JEWELRY

CJ Charles. An exquisitely appointed shop selling designer and estate jewelry, CJ Charles specializes in Cartier, and Bulgari watches, along with stunning fine jewelry, Baccarat crystal, and gift items. ⊠ *1135 Prospect St., La Jolla* ☎ 858/454–5390 ⊕ *www.cjcharles.com.*

Pomegranate. Since 1983 Pomegranate has paired contemporary and antique jewelry with fashions by American, European, and Asian designers. ⊠ *1152 Prospect St., La Jolla* ☎ 858/459–0629 ⊕ *www.pomegranatelajolla.com.*

Swiss Watch Gallery. One of the largest watch dealers on the West Coast, this family-owned shop carries all the top brands, including Omega, Charriol, Cartier, and Tag Heuer. ⊠ *8867 Villa La Jolla Dr., #600B, La Jolla* ☎ 858/622–9000.

14

POINT LOMA AND CORONADO

POINT LOMA

The laid-back Point Loma peninsula offers incredible views of downtown San Diego and some great shopping away from the large crowds you often find downtown and at Fashion Valley.

CLOTHING AND ACCESSORIES

Men's Fashion Depot. San Diego insiders head to this warehouse-style men's store for discounted suits and affordable tuxedos. Speedy alterations are available. ⊠ *3730 Sports Arena Blvd., Point Loma* ☎ 619/222–9570 ⊕ *www.mensfashiondepot.net.*

HOME ACCESSORIES AND GIFTS

Fodor'sChoice ★ **SCOUT at Quarters D.** Located in the old Naval Commander's quarters at Liberty Station, Scout at Quarters D feels more like a private home than a retail space. The home-furnishing and design store specializes in "artifact"-style items, including vintage maps, bungalow-modern furniture, and rich-hued Farrow and Ball paint. A local icon, the historic Hotel San Diego sign is a permanent fixture in the garden. ⊠ *2675 Rosecrans St., Point Loma* ☎ 619/518–8374 ⊕ *www.scout-home.com.*

SHOPPING CENTERS

Liberty Station. San Diego's former Naval Training Center is now a mixed-use facility with shops, restaurants, and art galleries. With its large grassy areas and Spanish colonial revival–style architecture, it's a great place to take a stroll. The section on Truxton Road between Womble and Roosevelt includes a **Trader Joe's**, a **Vons**, and restaurants like **Tender Greens** and **Panera**. To the north are more locally owned businesses lining the arcades in the area known as the NTC Promenade Arts and Culture District. **Casa Valencia Galeria Baja** is the only gallery in San Diego featuring art exclusively from Baja, **Chi Chocolat** sells handmade chocolates and truffles, and the **Yellow Book Road** is San Diego County's largest children's bookstore. ■ TIP➜ If you're in town on the first Friday of the month, check out Friday Night Liberty (5 to 8 pm), a free art walk featuring refreshments and entertainment.

✉ *2640 Historic Decatur Rd., Point Loma* ☎ *619/573–9300* ⊕ *libertystation.com.*

CORONADO

Coronado's resort hotels attract tourists in droves, but somehow the town has managed to avoid being overtaken by chain stores. Instead, shoppers can browse through family-owned shops, dine at sidewalk cafés along Orange Avenue, stroll through the arcade at the historic Hotel Del Coronado, and take in the specialty shops at Coronado Ferry Landing. Friendly shopkeepers make the boutiques lining Orange Avenue, Coronado's main drag, a good place to browse for clothes, home-decor and gift items, and gourmet foods.

SHOPPING CENTERS

Coronado Ferry Landing. A stunning view of San Diego's downtown skyline across the bay and a dozen boutiques make this a delightful place to shop while waiting for a ferry. **La Camisa** (☎ *619/435–8009*) is a fun place to pick up kitschy souvenirs, T-shirts, fleece jackets, and postcards. **The French Room** (☎ *619/889–9004*) specializes in comfy women's shoes and affordable casual wear. **Men's Island Sportswear** (☎ *619/437–4696*) sells hats, tropical sportswear, and accessories to complete your seaside getaway outfit. ✉ *1201 1st St., Coronado* ☎ *619/435–8895* ⊕ *www.coronadoferrylandingshops.com* ⌖ *Farmers' market Tues. 2:30–6; some restaurants daily late-afternoon happy hour.*

Celtic Corner Scottish Treasures. Get in touch with your Celtic roots with imported apparel, gifts, tableware, and jewelry from Ireland, Scotland, England, and Wales. You can even order a custom-made kilt. ✉ *916 Orange Ave., Coronado* ☎ *619/435–1880* ⊕ *www.scottishtreasures.net*

Fodor's Choice
★

Hotel Del Coronado. At the dozen gift shops within the peninsula's main historic attraction, you can purchase sportswear, designer handbags, jewelry, and antiques. **Babcock & Story Emporium** carries an amazing selection of home decor items, garden accessories, and classy gifts. **Blue Octopus** is a children's store featuring creative toys, gifts, and apparel. **Spreckels Sweets & Treats** offers old-time candies, freshly made fudge, and decadent truffles. **Kate's** has stylish fashions and accessories, while **Brady's for Men,** with its shirts and jackets, caters to well-dressed men. **Crown Jewels Coronado** features fine jewelry, some inspired by the sea. ✉ *1500 Orange Ave., Coronado* ☎ *619/435–6611 plus extension* ⊕ *hoteldel.com/activities/coronado-shopping.*

BOOKS

FAMILY **Bay Books.** This old-fashioned bookstore is the spot to sit, read, and sip coffee on an overcast day by the sea. Great for international travelers, there's a large selection of foreign-language magazines and newspapers, and for youngsters, there's a section in the back devoted to children's books and games. Bay Books also has regular book-signing events; it has hosted a wide array of authors, from Newt Gingrich to Captain Chesley "Sully" Sullenberger. ✉ *1029 Orange Ave., Coronado* ☎ *619/435–0070* ⊕ *www.baybookscoronado.com.*

You can rent bikes at Coronado Ferry Landing to tour around Coronado.

CLOTHING AND ACCESSORIES

Dale's Swim Shop. All things beachy catch your eye in this shop crammed with swimsuits, hats, sunglasses, and sunscreen. ✉ *1150 Orange Ave., Coronado* ☎ *619/435–1757.*

Island Birkenstock. Do your feet a favor and check out the comfy sandals and walking shoes sold here. All the latest Birkenstock styles are available in sizes to fit men, women, and children. ✉ *1350 Orange Ave., Coronado* ☎ *619/435–1071* ⊕ *www.birkenstocksd.com.*

Kippys. If you've ever envied the studded and bejeweled belts worn by celebs like Beyoncé and Steven Tyler, Kippys will help you custom-design your very own. Choose from a rainbow of Swarovski crystals to adorn your choice of belt styles and patterns. Prices range from $200 to $800 (or more), and belts are ready in two to three weeks. ✉ *1114 Orange Ave., Coronado* ☎ *619/435–6218* ⊕ *www.kippys.com.*

Noon Design Shop. Affordable handmade jewelry and American-made home accessories like tea towels and glassware fill the shelves at this whimsical boutique and design studio in Ocean Beach. Noon also stocks fresh-smelling soaps and perfumes, and letterpress. ✉ *4993 Niagara Ave., #105, Ocean Beach* ☎ *619/523–1744* ⊕ *www.noondesignshop.com.*

HOME ACCESSORIES AND GIFTS

The Attic. Modern and vintage home-decor items and accessories are The Attic's specialties; the shop also sells stylish Will Leather Goods bags as well as jewelry and affordable gifts. ✉ *1011 Orange Ave., Coronado* ☎ *619/435–5432* ⊕ *theatticgirls.blogspot.com.*

Seaside Papery. This sister store of Seaside Paper Home at The Headquarters carries high-end wedding invitations, greeting cards, wrapping papers, and luxury personal stationery. ⊠ *1162 Orange Ave., Coronado* ☎ *619/435–5565* ⊕ *www.seasidepapery.com.*

Shorelines Gallery. A few blocks from the Hotel Del Coronado, this gallery sells reasonably priced wall art, jewelry, and mixed-media pieces created by dozens of American artists. It's also the only San Diego retailer that carries item by Sticks, an Iowa company that makes furniture and art out of driftwood. ⊠ *918 Orange Ave., Coronado* ☎ *619/727–4080* ⊕ *www.slsdgallery.com.*

Wine A Bit. Part store and part wine bar, the popular Wine A Bit carries hundreds of boutique wines, along with craft beers and decadent desserts. Cigars, gifts, and wine-related accessories are for sale as well. ⊠ *928 Orange Ave., Coronado* ☎ *619/365–4953* ⊕ *www.wineabit coronado.com.*

JEWELRY

D Forsythe Jewelry. Stepping into D Forsythe is like taking a quick spin around the world. The one-of-a-kind pieces sold here feature sapphires, emeralds, moonstones and Baroque pearls from such faraway places as Denmark, Cambodia, Turkey, Bali, India, England, and Thailand. ⊠ *1136 Loma Ave., Coronado* ☎ *619/435–9211* ⊕ *www.dforsythe.com* ☽ *Closed Sun.*

SAN MARCOS

Golden Door. Considered by many to be the world's best destination spa, the venerable Golden Door occupies a serene canyon. The serenity here will awaken your soul. Explore it from your zen-like, Honjin inn–inspired room, where you have a traditional private shrine, secluded garden, and deck. Set on 377 wooded acres, the spa offers massages, beauty treatments, fitness work with a personal trainer, and healthy cuisine. Signature experience: your surroundings. Price: $8,250 per week. Check the website for specialty weeks. ⊠ *777 Deer Springs Rd., San Marcos, California, United States* ☎ *760/744–5777, 866/420–6414* ⊕ *www.goldendoor.com.*

VISTA

Cal-a-Vie Health Spa. Celebrities like Julia Roberts and Oprah Winfrey have stayed at Cal-a-Vie, and so can you. Services are wide-ranging: fitness, beauty treatments, health and wellness guidance, and nutrition counseling, plus golf and tennis. Signature experience: the yin/yang of romping through the hillsides and then cooling off in your antiques-filled villa, and being rubbed and wrapped. Price: all-inclusive is $8,595 to $8,795 per week, $5,795 for four days, and $3,995 for three days. Suites cost extra. ⊠ *29402 Spa Havens Way, Vista, California, United States* ☎ *760/945–2055, 866/772–4283* ⊕ *www.cal-a-vie.com.*

NORTH COUNTY AND AROUND

WELCOME TO NORTH COUNTY

TOP REASONS TO GO

★ **Talk to the animals:** Get almost nose to nose with giraffes, lions, tigers, and rhinos at the San Diego Zoo Safari Park in Escondido.

★ **Build a dream at LEGOLAND California Resort:** Explore model cities built with LEGO bricks, including New Orleans, Washington, D.C., and New York City.

★ **Be a beach bum:** Surf Swami's for towering blue-water breaks, tiptoe through the sand at Moonlight Beach, cruise the coast in a sailboat, or spot a whale spouting.

★ **Tour SoCal-style wineries:** Savor the red and white wines while touring in Temecula, home to more than 35 wineries as well as boutique lodging and classy restaurants.

★ **Discover the desert wilderness:** Anza-Borrego Desert State Park encompasses more than 600,000 acres, most of it wilderness. Springtime, when the wildflowers are in full bloom, is glorious.

1 North Coast. From Del Mar to Oceanside the quintessential beach towns march north along I-5. These coastal cities have grown up recently and offer sophisticated shopping, art galleries, dining, and accommodations, but there are also great beaches where you can watch surfers testing the breaks in winter. LEGOLAND California Resort and other attractions are just east of I-5.

2 Inland North County and Temecula. Historically this is the citrus- and avocado-growing belt of San Diego County. Since the opening of the San Diego Zoo Safari Park in Escondido and expansion of the wine-making industry in Temecula Valley more than 20 years ago, visitors have added inland North County to their must-see lists.

3 The Backcountry and Julian. The backcountry consists of the mountain ranges that separate metropolitan San Diego and the North Coast from the desert. It's where San Diegans go to hike, commune with nature, share a picnic, and study the night sky. Julian, the only real community within these mountains, is famous for its apple pies and July 4 parade.

4 The Desert. The Anza-Borrego Desert is desert at its best: vast, mostly untracked wilderness where you can wander and camp where you wish; a huge repository of prehistoric beasts, illustrated by a large collection of life-size sculptures along desert roadsides; and the best wildflower display in Southern California in the springtime.

Oceanside

Carlsbad

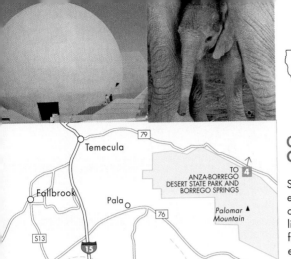

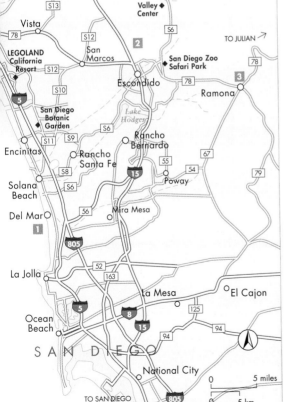

Temecula

79

TO
ANZA-BORREGO
DESERT STATE PARK AND
BORREGO SPRINGS

4

Fallbrook

Pala

76

Palomar ▲
Mountain

S13

15

Bonsall

76

S13

Valley ◆
Center

S6

Vista

78

S12

TO JULIAN ↗

San
Marcos

2

San Diego Zoo
◆ Safari Park

78

LEGOLAND
California
Resort   S12

Escondido

78

3

S10

Ramona

5

San Diego
Botanic
Garden   S6

*Lake
Hodges*

Encinitas

S11 S9

Rancho
Bernardo

67

S8

Rancho
Santa Fe

15

55

54

79

Solana
Beach   S6

Poway

Del Mar

56

Mira Mesa

1

805

52

La Jolla

163

La Mesa

El Cajon

5

8

125

Ocean
Beach

15

94

94

S A N   D I E G O

National City

0   5 miles

805

0   5 km

TO SAN DIEGO

GETTING
ORIENTED

San Diego's North County, encompassing the portion of San Diego County that lies north of the metro area from the ocean to the desert, has some of the same attractions of the city to the south: perpetual sunshine, great beaches, and entertainment, including the ever-growing LEGOLAND Resort complex and the San Diego Zoo's Safari Park. A visit to North County offers a chance to escape the metro area and find a little quiet in the backcountry, serious wine tasting and good eating in Temecula, several luxury resorts and golf courses, some world-class destination spas, art and historic centers, a bit of Gold Rush–era history, and a more laid-back lifestyle.

15

Updated by
Bobbi Zane

A whole world of scenic grandeur, fascinating history, and scientific wonder lies just beyond San Diego's city limits. If you travel north along the coast, you'll encounter the great beaches for which the region is famous, along with some sophisticated towns holding fine restaurants, great galleries, and museums.

Learn about sea creatures and the history of music in Carlsbad, home of LEGOLAND, LEGOLAND Water Park, and Sea Life Aquarium. If you travel east, you'll find fresh art hubs in Escondido, home of the San Diego Zoo Safari Park, a pair of world-class destination spas, a selection of challenging golf courses, and nightlife in bucolic settings. Inspiring mountain scenery plus beautiful places to picnic and hike can be found in the Cuyamaca Mountains, the historic gold-rush-era town of Julian (now known far and wide for its apple pies), and Palomar Mountain, home of the world-famous telescope. The vast wilderness of the Anza-Borrego Desert holds a repository of ancient fossils like no other, and is also home to one of the most colorful displays of native spring flowers. Just beyond the county limits in Temecula you can savor Southern California's only developed wine country, where more than three dozen wineries offer tastings and tours.

PLANNER

GETTING HERE AND AROUND
BUS AND TRAIN TRAVEL
The Metropolitan Transit System covers the city of San Diego up to Del Mar.

Buses and trains operated by North County Transit District (NCTD) serve all coastal communities in San Diego County, going as far east as Escondido; the NCTD Sprinter runs a commuter service between Oceanside and Escondido. Routes are coordinated with other transit agencies serving San Diego County. Amtrak stops in Solana Beach and Oceanside.

Coaster operates commuter rail service between San Diego and Oceanside, stopping en route in Old Town, Sorrento Valley, Solana Beach, Encinitas, and Carlsbad. The last Coaster train leaves San Diego at about 7 each night.

Bus and Train Contacts Metropolitan Transit System ☎ *619/233–3004* ⊕ *www.sdmts.com.* **North County Transit District** ☎ *760/966–6500* ⊕ *www. gonctd.com.* **Amtrak** ✉ *235 S. Tremont St., Oceanside* ☎ *760/722–4622 in Oceanside, 800/872–7245* ⊕ *www.amtrakcalifornia.com.* **Coaster** ☎ *760/996–6500* ⊕ *Transit.511sd.com.*

CAR TRAVEL

Interstate 5 is the main freeway artery connecting San Diego to Los Angeles, passing just east of the beach cities from Oceanside south to Del Mar. Running parallel west of I–5 is Route S21, also known and sometimes indicated as historic Highway 101, Old Highway 101, or Coast Highway 101, which never strays too far from the ocean. An alternate, especially from Orange and Riverside counties, is I–15, the inland route through Temecula, Escondido, and eastern San Diego County.

A loop drive beginning and ending in San Diego is a good way to explore the backcountry and Julian area. You can take the S1, the Sunrise National Scenic Byway (sometimes icy in winter) from I–8 to Route 79 and return through Cuyamaca Rancho State Park (also sometimes icy in winter). If you're only going to Julian (a 75-minute trip from San Diego in light traffic), take either the Sunrise Byway or Route 79, and return to San Diego via Route 78 past Santa Ysabel to Ramona and Route 67; from here I–8 heads west to downtown.

Escondido sits at the intersection of Route 78, which heads east from Oceanside, and I–15, the inland freeway connecting San Diego to Riverside, which is 30 minutes north of Escondido. Route 76, which connects with I–15 north of Escondido, veers east to Palomar Mountain. Interstate 15 continues north to Fallbrook and Temecula.

To reach the desert from downtown San Diego, take I–8 east to Highway 79 north, to Highway 78 east, to routes S2 and S22 east.

RESTAURANTS

Dining in the North County tends to reflect the land where the restaurant is located. Along the coast, for example, there is one luxury fine-dining spot after another. Most have dramatic water views and offer platters of exquisite fare created by graduates of the best culinary schools. Right next door you can wander into a typical beach shack or diner for the juiciest hamburger you've ever tasted. Locally sourced food can be found at restaurants throughout the area, although a few chefs have adopted molecular gastronomic techniques. Backcountry cuisine is generally served in huge portions and tends toward home-style cooking, steak and potatoes, burgers, and anything fried.

HOTELS

Like the restaurants, hotels in the North County reflect the geography and attractions where they are set. There are a number of luxury resorts that offer golf, tennis, entertainment, and classy service. For those who

15

want the ultimate pampered vacation, the North County holds two world-class spas: Cal-a-Vie and the Golden Door. Along the beach, there are quite a few stand-alone lodgings that attract the beach crowd; while some lack in appeal and service, they still charge a big price in summer. Lodgings in the Carlsbad area are family-friendly, some with their own water parks. In Temecula, some of the best and most delightful lodgings are tied to wineries; they offer a whole experience: accommodations, spa, dining, and wine. One-of-a-kind bed-and-breakfasts are the rule in the Julian area.

For expanded hotel reviews, facilities, and current deals, visit Fodors. com.

WHAT IT COSTS				
	$	$$	$$$	$$$$
Restaurants	under $18	$18–$27	$28–$35	over $35
Hotels	under $161	$161–$230	$231–$300	over $300

Restaurant prices are for a main course at dinner, excluding 8% tax. Hotel prices are for a standard double room in high (summer) season, excluding 9% to 10.5% tax.

VISITOR INFORMATION
San Diego Tourism Authoritiy ☎ 619/232–3101 ⊕ www.sandiego.org.

NORTH COAST: DEL MAR TO OCEANSIDE

Once upon a time, to say that the North Coast of San Diego County was different from the city of San Diego would have been an understatement. From the northern tip of La Jolla up to Oceanside, a half dozen small communities developed separately from urban San Diego—and from one another. Del Mar, because of its 2 miles of wide beaches, splendid views, and Thoroughbred horse-racing complex, was the playground of the rich and famous. Up the road, agriculture played a major role in the development of Solana Beach and Encinitas.

Carlsbad, too, rooted in the old Mexican rancheros, has agriculture in its past, as well as the entrepreneurial instinct of a late-19th-century resident, John Frazier, who promoted the area's water as a cure for common ailments and constructed a replica of a European mineral-springs resort. Oceanside was a beachside getaway for inland families in the 19th century; its economic fortunes changed considerably with the construction of Camp Pendleton as a Marine Corps training base during World War II. Marines still train at the huge base today.

What these towns shared was at least a half-century's worth of Southern California beach culture—think Woodies (wood-bodied cars), surfing, the Beach Boys, alternate lifestyles—and the road that connected them. That was U.S. Highway 101, which nearly passed into oblivion when I–5 was extended from Los Angeles to the Mexican border.

Then began an explosion of development in the 1980s, and the coast north of San Diego has come to resemble a suburban extension of the

city itself. Once-lovely hillsides and canyons have been bulldozed and leveled to make room for bedroom communities in Oceanside, Carlsbad, and even such high-price areas as Rancho Santa Fe and La Jolla.

If you venture off the freeway and head for the ocean, you can discover remnants of the old beach culture surviving in the sophisticated towns of Del Mar, Solana Beach, Cardiff-by-the-Sea, Encinitas, Leucadia, Carlsbad, and Oceanside, where the arts, fine dining, and elegant lodgings also now rule. As suburbanization continues, the towns are reinventing themselves—Carlsbad, for instance, is morphing from a farming community into a tourist destination with such attractions as LEGOLAND California, several museums, and an upscale outlet shopping complex. Oceanside, home of one of the longest wooden piers on the West Coast (its first pier was built in the 1880s), promotes its beach culture with a yacht harbor and beachside resort hotels.

DEL MAR

23 miles north of downtown San Diego on I–5, 9 miles north of La Jolla on Rte. S21.

Del Mar comprises two sections: the small historic village adjacent to the beach west of I–5 and a growing business center surrounded by multimillion-dollar tract housing east of the freeway. Tiny Del Mar village, the smallest incorporated city in San Diego County, holds a population of 4,500 tucked into a 2.1-square-mile beachfront. It's known for its quaint half-timbered Tudor-style architecture, 2 miles of accessible beaches, and the Del Mar

> **DID YOU KNOW?**
>
> San Diego County consists of 18 incorporated cities and several unincorporated communities, and is about the same size as the state of Connecticut.

racetrack and San Diego County Fairgrounds complex. The village attracted rich and famous visitors from the beginning; they still come for seclusion and to watch the horses run. Its new face is the Del Mar Gateway business complex with high-rise hotels and fast-food outlets east of the interstate at the entrance to Carmel Valley. Both Del Mars, old and new, hold expensive homes belonging to staff and scientists who work in the biotech industry and at UC San Diego in adjacent La Jolla. Access to Del Mar's beaches is from the streets that run east–west off Coast Boulevard; access to the business complex is via Highway 56.

TOUR OPTIONS

Barnstorming Adventures conducts excursions aboard restored 1920s-vintage open-cockpit biplanes and military-style *Top Dog* air combat flights on prop-driven Varga VG-21s. Flights are from Montgomery Field and start at $219 per couple for 20 minutes. Civic Helicopters gives whirlybird tours of the area along the beaches. The cost varies according to the model of helicopter and the number of passengers, so call for pricing.

Tour Contacts Barnstorming Adventures ✉ *3750 John J. Montgomery Dr., Ste. D, San Diego* ☎ *760/930–0903, 800/759–5667* ⊕ *www.barnstorming.com.* **Civic Helicopters** ✉ *2206 Palomar Airport Rd., Ste. H, Carlsbad* ☎ *760/438–8424* ⊕ *www.civichelicopters.com/flight-service.html.*

EXPLORING

FAMILY **Del Mar Fairgrounds.** The Spanish Mission–style fairground is the home of the **Del Mar Thoroughbred Club** (☎☎ *858/755–1141* ⊕ *www.dmtc. com*). Crooner Bing Crosby and his Hollywood buddies—Pat O'Brien, Gary Cooper, and Oliver Hardy, among others—organized the club in the 1930s, and the racing here (usually July through September, Wednesday through Monday, post time 2 pm) remains a fashionable affair. Del Mar Fairgrounds hosts more than 100 different events each year, including the San Diego County Fair, the Del Mar National Horse Show in April and May, and the fall Scream Zone that's popular with local familes. ✉ *2260 Jimmy Durante Blvd.* ☎ *858/755–1161* ⊕ *www. delmarfairgrounds.com.*

Del Mar Plaza. Along with its collection of shops, the plaza contains outstanding restaurants and landscaped plazas and gardens with Pacific views. The shops and restaurants are pricey, but the view—best enjoyed from the upper-level benches and chairs—is free. ✉ *1555 Camino del Mar* ⊕ *www.delmarplaza.com.*

FAMILY **Freeflight.** This small exotic-bird training aviary adjacent to the Del Mar Fairgrounds houses a collection of parrots and other exotic birds—a

The San Diego County Fair comes to Del Mar Fairgrounds every June to July.

guaranteed child pleaser. ⊠ *2132 Jimmy Durante Blvd.* ☎ *858/481–3148* ✉ *$5* ⏱ *Thurs.–Tues. 10–4, Wed. 10–2.*

Seagrove Park. Free summer evening concerts take place monthly at the west end of this small stretch of grass overlooking the ocean. ⊠ *15th St.* ☎ *858/755–1524.*

WHERE TO EAT

$$$$
FRENCH
Fodor'sChoice
★

✕ **Addison.** The sophisticated and stylish dining room and adjacent bar feel Italian and clubby, with intricately carved dark-wood motifs, and the tables, by contrast, are pure white, adorned with a single flower. Acclaimed chef William Bradley serves up explosive flavors in his 4-, 7-, and 10-course prix-fixe dinners, such as Prince Edward Island mussels with chickpeas, garlic confit, and saffron. Entrées might include red pepper Tart Tatan or salmon with sauce beets, apples, and fennel. Addison delights wine lovers with 160 pages of choices from around the world. ⓢ *Average main: $98* ⊠ *5200 Grand Del Mar Way* ☎ *858/314–1900* ⊕ *www.addisondelmar.com* ⌖ *Reservations essential* ⏱ *Closed Sun. and Mon. No lunch.*

$$
VIETNAMESE

✕ **Le Bambou.** Small, carefully decorated, and more elegant than any Vietnamese restaurant in San Diego proper, Le Bambou snuggles into the corner of a neighborhood shopping center and is easy to overlook. Those in the know, however, seek it out for authoritative versions of such classics as ground shrimp grilled on sugarcane; Imperial rolls generously stuffed with shrimp and noodles; and make-your-own meat wraps at the table. The menu also lists many vegetarian items. ⓢ *Average main: $19* ⊠ *2634 Del Mar Heights Rd.* ☎ *858/259–8138* ⊕ *www.lebamboudelmar.com* ⏱ *Closed Mon. No lunch Sat.–Sun.*

> **WORD OF MOUTH**
>
> "We took our son to San Diego when he was 12 years old. We visited the Zoo and the Wild Animal Park, and he loved them both. We also went to LEGOLAND because our son was always a huge LEGO fan. While he might have been a little old for LEGOLAND, we still had a fun day. The LEGO structures were impressive." —mikesmom

$$$ AMERICAN Fodor's Choice ★ 🍴 **Market Restaurant + Bar.** Carl Schroeder, one of California's hottest young chefs, draws well-heeled foodies to sample his creative and fun California fare, much of it with an Asian flare. The menu changes regularly depending upon what's fresh. Schroeder's seasonally inspired dishes have a playful spirit, whether it's a blue cheese soufflé with seasonal fruit, a Maine lobster salad with mango, or coriander-spiced red snapper with prawn dumplings. A well-edited wine list offers food-friendly wines by the best and brightest young winemakers around the world. Desserts are exquisite, such as the salty-sweet "S'Mores Bar" or the chocolate butterscotch trio. [$] *Average main: $30* ✉ *3702 Via de la Valle* ☎ *858/523–0007* 🌐 *www.marketdelmar.com* ✍ *Reservations essential* 🕒 *No lunch.*

$$ AMERICAN **Nickel Beer Co.** Some of the best brew in San Diego is served at this little beer bar that occupies an old jail in Julian. Owner Tom Nickel is considered one of the most creative brewers in the region and is always cooking up new recipes that win accolades from judges and fans. There are 12 taps and contents change regularly. On the weekends there's entertainment, and the patio is dog-friendly. ✉ *1458 Hollow Glen Rd., Julian* ☎ *760/765–2337* 🌐 *www.nickelbeerco.com* 🕒 *Thurs. 2–6, Fri.–Sun. 11:30–6.*

$$$ SEAFOOD 🍴 **Pacifica Del Mar.** The view of the shimmering Pacific from this lovely restaurant perched atop Del Mar Plaza is one of the best along the coast, and complements the simply prepared, beautifully presented seafood. The highly innovative menu is frequently rewritten to show off such creations as barbecue sugar-spice salmon with mustard sauce and mustard catfish with Yukon Gold potato–corn succotash. The crowd ranges from young hipsters at the bar to well-dressed businesspeople on the outdoor terrace overlooking the surf, where glass screens block any hint of a chilly breeze. [$] *Average main: $30* ✉ *Del Mar Plaza, 1555 Camino del Mar* ☎ *858/792–0476* 🌐 *www.pacificadelmar.com* ✍ *Reservations essential.*

WHERE TO STAY

$$$$ RESORT FAMILY Fodor's Choice ★ 🏨 **The Grand Del Mar.** Mind-blowing indulgence in serene surroundings, from drop-dead gorgeous guest accommodations to myriad outdoor adventures, sets the opulent Mediterranean-style Grand Del Mar apart from any other luxury hotel in San Diego. **Pros:** ultimate luxury; secluded, on-site golf course. **Cons:** service can be slow; hotel is not on the beach. [$] *Rooms from: $595* ✉ *5200 Grand Del Mar Ct., San Diego* ☎ *858/314–2000, 866/305–1528* 🌐 *www.thegranddelmar.com* 🛏 *218 rooms, 31 suites* 🍽 *No meals.*

$$$$ HOTEL 🏨 **L'Auberge Del Mar Resort and Spa.** This sophisticated beach estate is bright and airy with an outdoor feel, even when you're indoors, and most guest rooms, accented by sea grass–color walls and carpeting, have

balconies or patios. **Pros:** sunset views from the Waterfall Terrace; excellent service; walk to the beach. **Cons:** even with good soundproofing the Amtrak train can be heard as it roars through town; adult atmosphere; ground-level rooms surrounding the terrace are very public. $ *Rooms from: $375* ✉ *1540 Camino del Mar* ☎ *858/259–1515, 800/245–9757* ⊕ *www.laubergedelmar.com* ⤳ *112 rooms, 8 suites* ⦿ *No meals.*

$$ ⚏ **San Diego Marriott Del Mar.** Convenient for business travelers, this
HOTEL Marriott has guest rooms that are quiet and warmly decorated, and public areas that are homey, with comfortable sofas and fireplaces. **Pros:** friendly ambience in public areas; lots of wonderful art; within walking distance of companies in the Carmel Valley Corporate Center. **Cons:** freeway noise in outside public areas; rooms are on the small side. $ *Rooms from: $209* ✉ *11966 El Camino Real* ☎ *858/523–1700* ⊕ *www.marriott.com* ⤳ *281 rooms, 3 suites* ⦿ *No meals.*

SOLANA BEACH   15

1 mile north of Del Mar on Rte. S21, 25 miles north of downtown San Diego on I–5 to Lomas Santa Fe Dr. west.

Once-quiet Solana Beach is *the* place to look for antiques, collectibles, and contemporary fashions and artwork. The Cedros Design District, occupying four blocks south of the Amtrak station, contains shops, galleries, designers' studios, restaurants, and a popular jazz and contemporary music venue, the Belly Up Tavern. The town is known for its excellent restaurants, but most area lodging is in adjacent Del Mar and Encinitas. Solana Beach was the first city in California to ban smoking on its beaches. Now most cities in San Diego have followed suit.

WHERE TO EAT

$ ✕ **Don Chuy.** Family-run and utterly charming, Don Chuy serves authen-
MEXICAN tic Mexican cuisine to patrons who, before dining here, may have tasted only a pale version of the real thing. The flavors are savory and convincing, and the portions sufficient to banish hunger until the following day. For something straight from the soul of Mexican home cooking, try the *nopales con chorizo y huevos*, a scramble of tender cactus leaves, crumbled spicy sausage, and eggs; this is served with piles of rice and beans as well as a warm tortilla and the palate-warming house salsa. $ *Average main: $12* ✉ *650 Valley Ave.* ☎ *858/794–0535* ⊕ *www. donchuymexicanrestaurant.com* ⊗ *No lunch Mon.–Thurs., breakfast on Sun. only.*

$$$ ✕ **The Fish Market.** There's no ocean view at the North County branch of
SEAFOOD downtown's waterfront restaurant, but this eatery remains popular with
FAMILY residents and tourists for its simple preparations of very fresh fish, shellfish, and sushi from a menu that changes daily. The oyster bar here is popular. The scene is lively, crowded, and noisy—a great place to bring the kids. $ *Average main: $31* ✉ *640 Via de la Valle* ☎ *858/755–2277* ⊕ *www.thefishmarket.com.*

$$$$ ✕ **Pacific Coast Grill.** This casual beachy-style eatery offers a sweeping
SEAFOOD ocean view and seasonal Pacific Coast fare that reflects California's Mexican and Asian influences. Lunch in the spacious dining room or on the dog-friendly sunny patio brings sashimi ahi salad with greens,

seaweed and mango, plum-ginger–braised short ribs, or perfect fried-fish tacos washed down with a margarita that sings with fresh lime and lemon juice. Evenings are a scene, as attractive beachy types sip microbrews and well-priced wines along with enjoying morsels from the sushi bar. $ *Average main: $37* ⊠ *2526 S. Hwy. 1010, Cardiff-by-the-Sea* ☎ *760/479–0721* ⊕ *www.pacificcoastgrill.com.*

$$$$
FRENCH
Fodor'sChoice
★

X **Pamplemousse Grille.** One of North County's best restaurants, across the street from the Del Mar Fairgrounds and racetrack, offers casual French-country dining California style. Chef-proprietor Jeffrey Strauss brings a caterer's sensibilities to the details, like a mix-or-match selection of sauces—such as wild mushroom, grain mustard, or peppercorn—to complement the simple but absolutely top-quality grilled meats and seafood. Appetizers can be very clever, like the Kim Chee seafood martini. Whatever you do, save room for dessert; you can watch the pastry chef build it for you at the demonstration area in the dining room. Popular sweet endings include pear tarte tatin and chocolate peanut-butter bombe. The comfortable rooms are painted with murals of bucolic country scenes, and the service is quiet and professional. $ *Average main: $36* ⊠ *514 Via de la Valle* ☎ *858/792–9090* ⊕ *www.pgrille.com* ⌃ *Reservations essential* ⊗ *No lunch Sat.–Thurs.*

$
PIZZA
FAMILY

X **Pizza Port.** Local families flock here for great pizza and handcrafted brews. Pick a spot at one of the long picnic-type tables, choose traditional or whole-grain beer crust for your pie and any original topping—such as the Monterey, with pepperoni, onions, mushrooms, and artichoke hearts—and tip back a brew from one of the longest boutique lists in San Diego. $ *Average main: $15* ⊠ *135 N. Hwy. 101* ☎ *858/481–7332* ⊕ *www.pizzaport.com* ⌃ *Reservations not accepted.*

$$$
STEAKHOUSE

X **Red Tracton's.** Across the street from the Del Mar racetrack, this deluxe old-fashioned steak and seafood house is a high-roller's heaven. Everyone from the bar pianist to the exceptional waitresses is well aware that smiles and prompt service can result in tips as generously sized as the gigantic Australian lobster tails that the menu demurely lists at "market price." The food is simple but good, and the menu highlights roasted prime rib in addition to prime New York ribeye, panfried scallops, and such starters as lobster bisque and "jumbo" shrimp on ice. $ *Average main: $31* ⊠ *550 Via de la Valle* ☎ *858/755–6600* ⊕ *www. redtractonssteakhouse.com* ⌃ *Reservations essential* ⊗ *Sun. lunch late summer only.*

NIGHTLIFE

Belly Up Tavern. A fixture on local papers' "best of" lists, Belly Up has been drawing crowds since it opened in the mid-'70s. Its longevity attests to the quality of the eclectic entertainment on its stage. Within converted Quonset huts, critically acclaimed artists play everything from reggae and folk to—well, you name it. ⊠ *143 S. Cedros Ave., Solana Beach* ☎ *858/481–8140* ⊕ *www.bellyup.com.*

SHOPPING

Amba Gallery. Handwoven scarves, shawls, clothing, and textiles are on offer at this gallery that reinvests profits to develop the skills of its India-based artisans so they'll become self-sustaining. ⊠ *143 S. Cedros,*

Solana Beach, San Diego ☎ *858/259–2622* 🌐 *www.ambagallery.com* 🕑 *Tues.–Sat. 11–6, Sun. 11–5.*

Antique Warehouse. More than 100 booths here carry American and European and Asian furniture, mid-century items, and folk and country art. ✉ *212 S. Cedros Ave.* ☎ *858/755–5156* 🕑 *Closed Tues.*

Cedros Design District. A collection of more than 85 shops, along a two-block stretch of S. Cedros Avenue, this district specializes in interior design, apparel, jewelry, and gifts. Local chefs shop the Sunday Farmers' Market from 1 to 5 pm. ✉ *District office, 444 S. Cedros Ave.* 🌐 *www.cedrosavenue.com.*

Curve Couture. "Runway styles for real sizes" describes the mission of this upscale boutique that stocks designer fashions size 12 and above, including casual, office, and evening wear. ✉ *415 S. Cedros Ave., Ste. 160* ☎ *858/847–9100* 🌐 *www.curve-couture.com.*

Muttropolis. This shop stocks cool accessories, such as designer beds, toys, hats and coats, as well as totes for haute dogs and grain-free food. ✉ *227 S. Cedros Ave.* ☎ *858/755–3647* 🌐 *www.muttropolis.com* 🕑 *Weekdays 10–7, Sat. 10–6, Sun. 10–5:30.*

15

RANCHO SANTA FE

4 miles east of Solana Beach on Rte. S8, Lomas Santa Fe Dr., 29 miles north of downtown San Diego on I–5 to Rte. S8 east.

Groves of huge, drooping eucalyptus trees cover the hills and valleys of this affluent and exclusive town east of I–5. Rancho Santa Fe and the areas surrounding it are primarily residential, where there are mansions at every turn in the road. It's also common to see entire families riding horses on the many trails that crisscross the hillsides.

Modeled after a Spanish village, the town was designed by Lilian Rice, one of the first women to graduate with a degree in architecture from the University of California. Her first structure, a 12-room house built in 1922, evolved into the Inn at Rancho Santa Fe, which became a gathering spot for celebrities such as Bette Davis, Errol Flynn, and Bing Crosby in the 1930s and 1940s. The challenging Rancho Santa Fe Golf Course, the original site of the Bing Crosby Pro-Am, is considered one of the best courses in Southern California.

WHERE TO EAT AND STAY

$$$ FRENCH 🍴 **Mille Fleurs.** From its location in the heart of wealthy, horsey Rancho Santa Fe to the warm Gallic welcome extended by proprietor Bertrand Hug and the talents of chef Martin Woesle, Mille Fleurs is a winner. The quiet dining rooms are decorated like a French villa. Menus are written daily to reflect the market and Woesle's mood, which means you may find some interesting seasonal choices, such as Maine lobster salad with avocado, mango, and lemon dressing; green herb crusted lamb chops; or Wiener Schnitzel with quail egg and arugula salad. Save room for desserts, which might include chocolate-caramel delice or peach melba. [$] *Average main: $35* ✉ *Country Squire Courtyard, 6009 Paseo Delicias* ☎ *858/756–3085* 🌐 *www.millefleurs.com* ✍ *Reservations essential* 🕑 *No lunch Sat.–Mon.*

$$$$
MEDITERRANEAN
Fodor's Choice
★

🍴 **Restaurant at Rancho Valencia.** It always feels like spring when dining in the garden room at Veladora, the main restaurant at Rancho Valencia. Bouquets of fresh flowers are everywhere, potted plants fill nooks and crannies, and furnishings complete the mood. This is a serious restaurant, however, where you're likely to dine on Brandt farm filet mignon with grilled asparagus or seared George's bank scallops with shishito and parsley crust. And that's just dinner. The restaurant serves a selection of entrée salads and sandwiches at lunch and a full breakfast. The restaurant is refined without being stuffy; service is beyond attentive. [$] *Average main: $42* ✉ *5921 Valencia Circle* ☎ *858/756–1123* 🌐 *www.ranchovalencia.com* ✍ *Reservations essential* ⏲ *Closed Mon.*

$$$$
RESORT
FAMILY
Fodor's Choice
★

🏨 **Rancho Valencia Resort and Spa.** Elegant, two-level, Spanish-style casitas, appointed with corner fireplaces, luxurious carpeting, and shuttered French doors leading to private patios, are tucked into 40 acres in one of Southern California's most affluent neighborhoods. **Pros:** splendid surroundings; impeccable service; large rooms. **Cons:** secluded; expensive. [$] *Rooms from: $483* ✉ *5921 Valencia Circle* ☎ *858/756–1123, 866/233–6708* 🌐 *www.ranchovalencia.com* 🛏 *49 suites* 🍽 *No meals.*

SHOPPING

The Country Friends. Operated by a nonprofit foundation, The Country Friends is a great place for unusual gifts and carries collectibles, silver, and antiques donated or consigned by community residents. ✉ *6030 El Tordo* ☎ *858/756–1192* 🌐 *www.thecountryfriends.org* ⏲ *Tues.–Sat. 10–4.*

Vegetable Shop. This is the place to buy the same premium (and very expensive) fruits and rare baby vegetables that the Chino Family Farm grows for many of San Diego's upscale restaurants, and for such famed California eateries as Chez Panisse in Berkeley and Spago in Los Angeles. ✉ *6123 Calzada del Bosque* ☎ *858/756–3184* ⏲ *Closed Mon.*

ENCINITAS

6 miles north of Solana Beach on Rte. S21, 7 miles west of Rancho Santa Fe on Rte. S9, 28 miles north of downtown San Diego on I–5.

Flower breeding and growing has been the major industry in Encinitas since the early part of the 20th century; the town now calls itself the Flower Capital of the World, thanks to the large number of nurseries operating here. The city, which encompasses the coastal towns of Cardiff-by-the-Sea and Leucadia as well as inland Olivenhain, is home to Paul Ecke Poinsettias (open only to the trade), which tamed the wild poinsettia in the 1920s and today is the largest producer and breeder of the Christmas blossom in the world. During the spring blooming season some commercial nurseries east of I–5 are open to the public. The palms and the golden domes of the Self-Realization Fellowship Retreat mark the southern entrance to downtown Encinitas.

U.S. 101—now Route S21—was the main route connecting all the beach towns between southern Orange County and San Diego before the I–5 freeway was constructed to the east of Encinitas. Local civic efforts are bringing back the historic California–U.S. 101 signs and restoring the boulevard's historic character.

GETTING HERE AND AROUND

From San Diego, head north on I–5. If you're already on the coast, drive along Route S21. Lodgings, restaurants, and the beach pop up along Route S21 (Old Highway 101) west of the freeway. The San Diego Botanic Gardens and commercial plant nurseries lie to the east of the freeway.

EXPLORING

FAMILY **San Diego Botanic Gardens.** More than 4,000 rare, exotic, and endangered plants are on display on 35 landscaped acres. Displays include plants from Central America, Africa, Australia, the Middle East, the Mediterranean, the Himalayas, Madagascar, and more; the most diverse collection of bamboo in North America; California native plants; and subtropical fruits. The park contains the largest interactive children's garden on the West Coast, where kids can roll around in the Seeds of Wonder garden, explore a baby dinosaur forest, discover a secret garden, or play in a playhouse. An Under the Sea Garden displays rocks and succulents that uncannily mimic an underwater environment. ⊠ *230 Quail Gardens Dr.* ☎ *760/436–3036* ⊕ *www.sdbgarden. org* ☞ *$14* ☉ *Daily 9–5.*

San Elijo Lagoon Conservancy. Between Solana Beach and Encinitas, this is the most complex of the estuary systems in San Diego North County. A 7-mile network of trails surrounds the 979 reserve, where more than 700 species of plants, fish, and birds (many of them migratory) live. Be sure to stop by the LEED-certified gold New San Elijo Lagoon Nature Centre. The center, open 9 to 5 daily, offers museum-quality exhibits about the region and a viewing deck overlooking the estuary. Docents offer free public walks every Saturday at 10 a.m. ⊠ *2710 Manchester Ave., Cardiff-by-the-Sea* ☎ *760/436–3944* ⊕ *www.sanelijo.org* ☞ *Free* ☉ *Daily dawn–dusk.*

WHERE TO EAT

$ ✕ **Bubby's Gelato.** A hardworking French couple makes the region's best
CAFÉ gelato and sorbets in this unassuming little shop tucked away in the Lumberyard Shopping Center. The flavors are different every day, and each is clear and intense, with a dense creaminess. Sit on the sunny patio whiling away the afternoon while enjoying a flavor like honey-lavender, cookies and cream, chocolate-hazelnut, or vanilla tinged with rose. On the lighter side, try the sunset-color apricot sorbet or the deep-red raspberry. Bubby's also serves an assortment of tasty sandwiches. $ *Average main: $5* ⊠ *937 S. Coast Hwy. 101* ☎ *760/436–3563* ▭ *No credit cards.*

$$ ✕ **Ki's Restaurant.** Veggies with a view could be the subtitle for this vener-
VEGETARIAN able Cardiff-by-the-Sea restaurant that grew from a simple juice shack. Ki's is well known for heart-healthy, gluten-free, vegan, locally sourced, ovo-lacto, vegetarian-friendly dishes like huevos rancheros, filling tofu scrambles, taco plates, chopped salads with feta and nuts, watermelon juice, and carrot ice-ream smoothies. The menu also includes turkey wraps piled on wheat bread and dinner entrées such as Thai seafood curry, roasted Jidori chicken, or Asian salmon salad on a bed of organic

greens, all prepared with minimal fat. Get a table up top for incomparable ocean views, but be prepared for a wait, as service is rather slow. $ *Average main: $20* ⊠ *2591 S. Coast Hwy. 101, Cardiff-by-the-Sea* ☎ *760/436–5236* ⊕ *www.kisrestaurant.com.*

$ ✕ **La Especial Norte.** Casual to the point of funkiness, this Mexican café MEXICAN is a great hit with locals who flock here to slurp up large bowls of delicious homemade soups. Try the chicken, beans, and rice, or the Seven Seas fish soup accompanied by tortillas and a dish of cabbage salad. You can also order renditions of the standard burrito, fajitas, seafood, and tacos, washed down with premium margaritas. $ *Average main: $15* ⊠ *644 N. Coast Hwy. 101* ☎ *760/942–1040.*

WHERE TO STAY

$ 🏨 **Moonlight Beach Motel.** This folksy, laid-back motel looks better on the HOTEL outside than inside, but it's just steps from the surf and rooms are spacious FAMILY cious and clean, and most have balconies and ocean views. **Pros:** within walking distance of the beach; kitchenettes in rooms; public barbecues. **Cons:** plain motel with limited service; reserve ahead in summer; two- or three-night minimum in season. $ *Rooms from: $140* ⊠ *233 2nd St.* ☎ *760/753–0623, 800/323–1259* ⊕ *www.moonlightbeachmotel.com* ⇱ *24 rooms* ❢◯❢ *No meals.*

$ 🏨 **Rodeway Inn North Encinitas.** Across from the train tracks on the main HOTEL drag through the north end of Leucadia, this basic motel is apt to be somewhat noisy. **Pros:** basic motel; close to beach. **Cons:** on busy highway, perfunctory service. $ *Rooms from: $69* ⊠ *1444 N. Coast Hwy. 101* ☎ *760/436–1988* ⊕ *www.rodewayinn.com* ⇱ *50 rooms* ❢◯❢ *Breakfast.*

SHOPPING

Souvenir items are sold at shops along U.S. 101 and in the Lumberyard Shopping Center. Encinitas also abounds in commercial plant nurseries, where you can pick up a bit of San Diego to take home.

Anderson's La Costa Nursery. Come here for rare and hard-to-find orchids, bromeliads, cactus, and succulents. ⊠ *400 La Costa Ave.* ☎ *760/753–3153* ⊕ *www.andersonslacostanursery.com.*

Hansen's. One of San Diego's oldest surfboard manufacturers is owned by Don Hansen, surfboard shaper extraordinaire, who came here from Hawaii in 1962. The store also stocks a full line of surf apparel, wet suits, surf cams, and casual wear. ⊠ *1105 S. Coast Hwy. 101* ☎ *800/480–4754, 760/753–6596* ⊕ *www.hansensurf.com* ⏱ *Mon., Tues., Sat. 9–6, Wed.–Fri. 9–9, Sun. 10–5.*

Weideners' Gardens. Begonias, fuchsias, and other flowers are for sale here. ⊠ *695 Normandy Rd.* ☎ *760/436–2194* ⊕ *www.weidners.com.*

CARLSBAD

6 miles from Encinitas on Rte. S21, 36 miles north of downtown San Diego on I–5.

Once-sleepy Carlsbad, lying astride I–5 at the north end of a string of beach towns extending from San Diego to Oceanside, has long been popular with beachgoers and sun-seekers. On a clear day in this village you can take in sweeping ocean views that stretch from La Jolla to Oceanside by walking the 2-mile-long sea walk running between the Encina power plant and Pine Street. En route, you can get closer to the water via several stairways leading to the beach; quite a few benches are here as well.

More recently, however, much of the attention of visitors to the area has shifted inland, east of I–5, to LEGOLAND California and other attractions in its vicinity—two of the San Diego area's most luxurious resort hotels, one of the last remaining wetlands along the Southern California coast, a discount shopping mall, golf courses, the cattle ranch built by movie star

> **DID YOU KNOW?**
>
> Carlsbad village owes its name to John Frazier, who dug a well for his farm here in the 1880s. The water bubbling from it was soon found to have the same properties as water from the mineral wells of Karlsbad, Bohemia (now Karlovy Vary, Czech Republic, but then under the sway of the Austro-Hungarian Empire). When Frazier and others went into the business of luring people to the area with talk of the healing powers of the local mineral water, they changed the name of the town from Frazier's Station to Carlsbad, to emphasize the similarity to the famous Bohemian spa.

Leo Carrillo, and colorful spring-blooming Flower Fields at Carlsbad Ranch. Until the mid-20th century, when suburban development began to sprout on the hillsides, farming was the main industry in Carlsbad, with truckloads of vegetables shipped out year-round. Some agriculture remains. Area farmers develop and grow new varieties of flowers, including the ranunculus that transform a hillside into a rainbow each spring, and Carlsbad strawberries are among the sweetest in Southern California; in spring you can pick them yourself in fields on both sides of I–5.

GETTING HERE AND AROUND

LEGOLAND California Resort, off Cannon Road east of I–5, is surrounded by the Flower Fields, hotels, and the Museum of Making Music. On the west side of the freeway is beach access at several points and quaint Carlsbad village shops.

ESSENTIALS

Visitor Information Carlsbad Convention and Visitors Bureau ⊠ *400 Carlsbad Village Dr.* ☎ *760/434–6093, 800/227–5722* ⊕ *visitcarlsbad.com.*

EXPLORING

Batiquitos Lagoon. Development has destroyed many of the lagoons and saltwater marsh wildlife habitats that used to punctuate the North County coastline, but this 610-acre lagoon has been restored to support fish and bird populations. A stroll along the 2-mile trail from the Batiquitos Lagoon Foundation Nature Center along the north shore of the lagoon reveals nesting sites of the red-winged blackbird, lagoon birds such as the great blue heron, the great egret, and the snowy egret; and life in the mud flats. This is a quiet spot for contemplation or a picnic. ⊠ *7380 Gabbiano La.* ✦ *Take the Poinsettia Lane exit off I–5,* *go east, and turn right onto Batiquitos Drive, then right again onto Gabbiano Lane.* ☎ *760/931–0800* ⊕ *www.batiquitosfoundation.org* ⊙ *Mon.–Fri. 9–noon, Sat.–Sun. 9–3.*

Carlsbad Mineral Water Spa. Remnants from late 1800s, including the original well dug by John Frazier and a monument to him, are found here. The elaborately decorated stone building houses a small day spa and the Carlsbad Water Company, a 21st-century version of Frazier's waterworks, where the Carlsbad water is still sold. Spa treatment packages range from one hour to three hours; treatments include combinations of wraps, alkaline mineral baths, mud facials, and full-body massages at prices from $99 to $249. ⊠ *2802 Carlsbad Blvd.* ☎ *760/434–1887* ⊕ *www.carlsbadmineralspa.com.*

FAMILY
Fodor's Choice
★

Flower Fields at Carlsbad Ranch. The largest bulb production farm in Southern California has hillsides abloom here each spring, when thousands of Giant Tecolote ranunculus produce a stunning 50-acre display of color against the backdrop of the blue Pacific Ocean. Other knockouts include the rose gardens—with examples of every All-American Rose Selection award-winner since 1940—and a historical display of Paul Ecke poinsettias. Open to the public during this time, the farm offers family activities that include a LEGO Flower Garden and a kids' playground. ⊠ *5704 Paseo del Norte, east of I-5* ☎ *760/431–0352* ⊕ *www.theflowerfields.com* 🎟 *$12* ⊙ *Mar.–May, daily 9–6.*

FAMILY
Fodor's Choice
★

LEGOLAND California Resort. The centerpiece of a development that includes resort hotels, a designer discount shopping mall, an aquarium, and a waterpark, LEGOLAND has rides and diversions geared to kids ages 2 to 12. Bring bathing suits; there are lockers at the entrance and at Pirate Shores. The main events are as follows:

Movie Experience: Take a behind-the-scenes view of movie making LEGOLAND style.

Lost Kingdom Adventure: Armed with a laser blaster, you'll journey through ancient Egyptian ruins in a desert roadster, scoring points as you hit targets.

Star Wars **Miniland:** Follow the exploits of Yoda, Princess Leia, Obi-Wan, Anakin, R2, Luke, and the denizens of the six *Star Wars* films. Some kids loop back several times to take it all in.

Miniland U.S.A.: This miniature, animated, interactive collection of U.S. icons was constructed out of 24 million LEGO bricks!

Soak-N-Sail: Hundreds of gallons of water course through 60 interactive features, including a pirate shipwreck–theme area. You'll need your swimsuit for this one.

Dragon Coaster: Little kids love this popular indoor/outdoor steel roller coaster that goes through a castle. Don't let the name frighten you—the motif is more humorous than scary.

Driving School: Kids ages 6 to 13 can drive speed-controlled cars (not on rails) on a miniature road; driver's licenses are awarded after the course. Volvo Junior is the pint-size version for kids 3 to 5.

▓ TIP→ **The best value is one of the Hopper Tickets that give you one admission to LEGOLAND plus Sea Life Aquarium and/or the LEGOLAND**

The spring blooms at the Flower Fields at Carlsbad Ranch are not to be missed.

Water Park. These can be used on the same day or on different days. Purchase tickets online for discounted pricing. Go midweek to avoid the crowds.

LEGOLAND Hotel: Opened in 2013, this is the place for the family that eats, sleeps, and lives LEGO. Family rooms are themed Pirate, Adventure, and Kingdom, with corresponding LEGO-style decor. Each room has sleeping quarters for up to three kids. The hotel has interactive play areas, a restaurant, bar, and swimming pool, but best of all, guests get early admission to the park.

Be sure to try Granny's Apple Fries, Castle Burgers, and Pizza Mania for pizzas and salads. The Market near the entrance has excellent coffee, fresh fruit, and yogurt. ⊠ *1 Legoland Dr.* ✛ *Exit I–5 at Cannon Rd. and follow signs east ¼ mile* ☎ *760/918–5346* ⊕ *california.legoland. com* 🖥 *LEGOLAND $83 adults, $73 children; parking $15* ⏲ *Park: late May–early Sept., daily (hrs vary), early Sept.–late May, Thurs.–Sun. Water Park: May–Aug. Aquarium: Daily. Check website or call for specifics* ⏲ *Closed Tues. and Wed. except holiday weeks.*

Leo Carrillo Ranch Historic Park. This was a real working ranch with 600 head of cattle owned by actor Leo Carrillo, who played Pancho in the *Cisco Kid* television series in the 1950s. Before Carrillo bought the spread, known as Rancho de Los Kiotes, in 1937, the rancho was the home of a band of Luiseno Indians. Carrillo's hacienda and other buildings have been restored to reflect the life of the star when he hosted his Hollywood friends for long weekends in the country. Four miles of trails take visitors through colorful native gardens to the cantina, washhouse, pool and cabana, barn, and stable that Carrillo used. You can see the insides of these buildings on weekends when guided tours are offered. After Carrillo's death in 1961, the ranch remained in the family until 1979, when part of the acreage was acquired by the city for a park. ✉ *6200 Flying Leo Carrillo La.* ☎ *760/476–1042* 🌐 *www.leocarrilloranch.org* 🎟 *Free* 🕒 *Tues.–Sat. 9–5, Sun. 11–5.*

FAMILY **Museum of Making Music.** Take an interactive journey through 100 years of popular music with displays of more than 500 vintage instruments and samples of memorable tunes from the past century. Hands-on activities include playing a digital piano, drums, guitar, and electric violin. ✉ *5790 Armada Dr., east of I–5* ☎ *760/438—5996* 🌐 *www.museumofmakingmusic.org* 🎟 *$8* 🕒 *Tues.–Sun. 10–5.*

FAMILY **Sea Life Aquarium.** Offering an educational and interactive underwater experience, the walk-through exhibits focus on creatures found in local waters including California lakes and streams and the cold water marine animals that live along the California coast. Other exhibits include an underwater acrylic tunnel that affords a deep sea (but dry) look at sharks, fish, and invertebrates. There's a seahorse kingdom, interactive tide pools, jelly fish discovery (opened in 2014) and a chance for kids to build a LEGO coral reef. This park has a separate admission from LEGOLAND, although one- and two-day tickets including both venues are available. ✉ *1 LEGOLAND Dr.* ☎ *760/918–5346* 🌐 *www.visitsealife.com/california* 🎟 *$20* 🕒 *Daily, call for hrs.*

WHERE TO EAT

$$$$ AMERICAN 🍴 **Argyle Steakhouse.** Even if you don't play golf, the Argyle, occupying the Aviara Golf clubhouse, is a good choice for dining on a sunny day. The 18th green, Batiquitos Lagoon, and the Pacific Ocean create beautiful vistas from nearly every table, whether you are inside at the clubby bar or outside on the deck. The breakfast menu lists classics like smoked salmon, omelettes, and breakfast burritos, while soups, salads, a renowned hamburger, and "lite" entrées fill the bill at lunch. By dinnertime the Argyle becomes a steak house purveying dry-aged locally-sourced prime beef. [$] *Average main: $46* ✉ *7447 Batiquitos Dr.* ☎ *760/603–9608* 🌐 *www.parkhyattaviara.com* ✍ *Reservations essential* 🕒 *Closed Mon.*

$$ AMERICAN 🍴 **Bistro West.** This busy spot, part of the West Inn complex, might be called the boisterous bistro, especially if you get there during happy hour, when it appears that all of Carlsbad is tipping back a few. The bistro specializes in comfort food; a huge chicken pot pie tops the list that also includes meat loaf, several burger variations, pastas, and pizza. Many of the ingredients come from a nearby farm tended by Bistro chefs. You can select from a long wine list of mostly California products at fair prices; many are available by the glass. [$] *Average main: $27* ✉ *4960 Ave. Encinas* ☎ *760/930–8008* 🌐 *www.bistrowest.com* ✍ *Reservations essential* 👔 *Jacket required.*

$$$ MEDITERRANEAN 🍴 **BlueFire Grill.** Fire and water drama defines this signature restaurant that's part of La Costa resort complex. The centerpiece of the resort's entrance plaza, the grill has an outdoor patio with fire pits, fountains, and a year-round floral display. Inside is a contemporary Mission-style room surrounding a green bottle glass fountain that extends the length of the main dining room. The menu features local

seafood and vegetables combined in exciting ways. As a starter, try the Baja ceviche, followed by shortrib bourguignon. $ *Average main: $34* ⊠ *2100 Costa Del Mar Rd.* ☎ *760/929–6306* ⊕ *www.dine bluefire.com* ⌖ *Reservations essential* ⊙ *Closed Sun.–Tues. No lunch.*

15

WHERE TO STAY

$$
HOTEL
FAMILY
Carlsbad Inn Beach Resort. On the main drag and with direct access to the beach, this sprawling inn and time-share condominium complex is popular with families and has a variety of rooms, ranging from cramped to large, including many with ocean views, balconies, and kitchenettes, and some with fireplaces and hot tubs. **Pros:** easy walk to the beach; casual service; warm ambience. **Cons:** lots of kids; can be noisy; near crowds. $ *Rooms from: $189* ⊠ *3075 Carlsbad Blvd.* ☎ *760/434–7020, 800/235–3939* ⊕ *www.carlsbadinn.com* ⇆ *54 rooms, 7 suites* ⦿ *No meals.*

$$
HOTEL
FAMILY
Grand Pacific Palisades Resort & Hotel. With direct access to LEGO-LAND, the Grand Pacific has a LEGO-decorated lobby and caters to families, offering one-, two-, and three-bedroom villas that surround a swimming pool. **Pros:** close walk to LEGOLAND; two pools—one for kids, one for adults; nice views of the Flower Fields at Carlsbad Ranch. **Cons:** some rooms are small; a lot of kids and tour groups. $ *Rooms from: $179* ⊠ *5805 Armada Dr.* ☎ *800/725–4723* ⊕ *www.grandpacificpalisades.com* ⇆ *90 rooms, 162 time-share villas* ⦿ *No meals.*

$$
HOTEL
FAMILY
Hilton Carlsbad Oceanfront Resort & Spa. Sea and sand loom large here, where the fitness center has an ocean view and guest rooms have sitting areas so you can easily enjoy the sea views and breezes when you're not exploring South Carlsbad State Park nearby. **Pros:** afternoon coastal breezes; state park across the highway. **Cons:** on main highway. $ *Rooms from: $229* ⊠ *1 Ponto Dr.* ☎ *760/602–0800* ⊕ *www.hiltoncarlsbadoceanfront.com* ⇆ *215 rooms* ⦿ *No meals.*

$$
HOTEL
FAMILY
Fodor's Choice
★
Legoland Hotel. Created for the entertainment and pleasure of small children, Legoland Hotel hits the mark everywhere. **Pros:** ocean views from some rooms; dive-in movies at the pool; tempting hands-on activities throughout the hotel. **Cons:** frequently sells out; no romance here. $ *Rooms from: $170* ⊠ *5885 The Crossings Dr.* ☎ *887/534-6526* ⊕ *www.legoland.com* ⇆ *250.*

$$$$
RESORT
FAMILY
Fodor's Choice
★
Omni La Costa Resort and Spa. This chic Spanish colonial oasis on 400 tree-shaded acres has ample guest rooms, two golf courses, and is known for being family-friendly, with plenty of kids' activities (including a kids' club, teen lounge, seven swimming pools, three waterslides, and a water play zone). **Pros:** adult-only pool; excellent kids' facilities; spa under the stars. **Cons:** very spread out, making long walks necessary; lots of kids; parking spread all over the property. $ *Rooms from:*

$349 ✉ 2100 Costa del Mar Rd. ☎ 760/438–9111, 800/854–5000 🌐 www.lacosta.com 🛏 607 rooms, 137 villas 🍴 No meals.

$$$ RESORT FAMILY Fodor's Choice ★ 🏨 **Park Hyatt Aviara Resort.** The quietly elegant hilltop retreat with a golf course is one of the most luxurious hotels in the San Diego area, where oversized rooms have every possible amenity (including private terraces and deep soaking tubs) and one of the most sublime views in Southern California, overlooking Batiquitos Lagoon and the Pacific. **Pros:** unbeatable location; tram rides; many nature trails. **Cons:** $25 resort fee; $35 parking. [$] *Rooms from: $279 ✉ 7100 Aviara Resort Dr. ☎ 800/233–1234, 760/448–1234 🌐 www.parkhyattaviara.com 🛏 329 rooms, 44 suites 🍴 No meals.*

$$$ HOTEL 🏨 **Sheraton Carlsbad Resort & Spa.** If location is everything, you have it two ways here: you can walk right into LEGOLAND's Castle Hill through a private back entrance directly from the hotel, or you can walk to the Crossings at Carlsbad golf course. **Pros:** lovely views from many rooms; expansive bathrooms with soaking tubs; happy hour. **Cons:** high noise level in public areas; many conventions. [$] *Rooms from: $259 ✉ 5480 Grand Pacific Dr. ☎ 760/827–2400, 800/444–3515 🌐 www.sheratoncarlsbadresort.com 🛏 250 rooms 🍴 No meals.*

$$ B&B/INN FAMILY 🏨 **West Inn and Suites.** Everything in this family- and pet-friendly inn near beaches exudes a warm and friendly atmosphere, right down to the milk and cookies served in the lobby each night. **Pros:** full buffet breakfast; organized activities; guest shuttle service for Carlsbad area; near beaches. **Cons:** adjacent to railroad tracks and freeway. [$] *Rooms from: $189 ✉ 4970 Av. Encinas ☎ 760/448–4500, 866/431–9378 🌐 www.westinnandsuites.com 🛏 86 rooms, 36 suites 🍴 Breakfast.*

SHOPPING

Carlsbad Premium Outlets. Part of the growing LEGOLAND complex, this outlet center is one of two designer factory outlets in the San Diego area. Within this attractively landscaped complex you can find Brooks Brothers, Tahari, Le Creuset, and Polo Ralph Lauren plus a food court. Some nearby hotels offer Shop and Stay packages. *✉ 5620 Paseo Del Norte ☎ 760/804–9000, 888/790–7467 🌐 www.premiumoutlets.com/carlsbad ⏲ Mon.–Sat. 10–9, Sun. 10–7.*

Saratoga Saddlery. Sidle on up to the Saddlery for a peek at the store's handsome lines of riding and hiking boots, belts, accessories, and clothing from Emu Australia, Lucchese, Joules, and DuBarry. You could drop a bundle here, but the quality is impeccable. *✉ 1555 Camino Del Mar, Ste. 117, Del Mar ☎ 858/755–7752 🌐 www.saratogasaddlery.com.*

OCEANSIDE

8 miles north of Carlsbad on Rte. S21, 37 miles north of downtown San Diego on I–5.

The beach culture is alive and well in Oceanside, despite redevelopment activities that are changing the face of the waterfront. Mixed-use hotels and residences are under construction to enhance the beach culture and make it more accessible. Visitors to this part of downtown Oceanside can stay within walking distance of the city's best swimming and surfing beaches: Harbor Beach, brimming with beach activities and fun, and Buccaneer Beach, home to some of the best surfing in North County. Many who have been in the military link Oceanside with Camp Pendleton, the sprawling U.S. Marine base that lies at the north end of the city. Until recently the military was Oceanside's main industry, but now that's being eclipsed by tourism. Proximity to the base still has its benefits, as most businesspeople offer discounts to active military personnel and their families. Also home to the largest and one of the best-preserved California missions, Mission San Luis Rey, Oceanside's history extends back to the 1700s, when the Spanish friars walked along the California coast founding missions as they went. Today Oceanside celebrates its historic culture with the regionally exciting Oceanside Museum of Art, displaying the works of San Diego area artists. Residents and visitors gather weekly at the farmers' market and Sunset Market, where shopping for fresh-picked produce is a pleasant pastime.

GETTING HERE AND AROUND

The northernmost of the beach towns, Oceanside, lies 8 miles north of Carlsbad via I–5; exit the freeway on Mission Avenue. If you go west, you'll come to the redeveloped downtown and harbor where you'll find most of the restaurants, lodgings, and attractions. Downtown Oceanside is quite walkable from the Transportation Center, where Amtrak, the Coaster, and Sprinter stop. Buses and taxis are also available at the Transportation Center.

ESSENTIALS

Visitor Information **Oceanside Welcome Center** ✉ *928 N. Coast Hwy., Ste. A* ☎ *760/721–1101, 800/350–7873* ⊕ *www.californiawelcomecenter.org* ☽ *Daily 9–5.*

EXPLORING

TOP ATTRACTIONS

California Surf Museum. A large collection of surfing memorabilia, going back to the earliest days of the sport, is on display here, along with old black and white photos, vintage boards, apparel, and accessories. ✉ *312 Pier View Way* ☎ *760/721–6876* ⊕ *www.surfmuseum.org* ☐ *$5; free on Tues.* ☽ *Daily 8– 4.*

Camp Pendleton. The nation's largest amphibious military training complex encompasses 17 miles of Pacific shoreline. It's not unusual to see herds of tanks and flocks of helicopters maneuvering through the dunes and brush alongside I–5. You may also see herds of sheep keeping the bushland down and fertile fields growing next to the Pacific coastline. You can make advance arrangements to tour historic sites on the base by contacting the community relations office. ☎ *760/725–5799* ⊕ *www. mccscamppendleton.com.*

FAMILY

Fodor's Choice

★

Old Mission San Luis Rey. Known as the King of the Missions, the 18th, the largest, and the most prosperous of California's missions was built in 1798 by Franciscan friars under the direction of Father Fermin Lasuen to help educate and convert local Native Americans. The *sala* (parlor), the kitchen, a friar's bedroom, a weaving room, and a collection of religious art and old Spanish vestments convey much about early mission life. A location for filming Disney's 1950's *Zorro* TV series, the well-preserved mission is still owned by the Franciscans. ✉ *4050*

15

Mission Ave. ☎ *760/757–3651* 🌐 *www.sanluisrey.org* 🎟 *$5* 🕓 *Mon.–Fri. 9:30–5, Sat.–Sun. 10–5.*

Oceanside Pier. At 1,600 feet, this is one of the longest piers on the West Coast. The water surrounding it is known for its surf breaks and good fishing. A restaurant, Ruby's Diner, stands at the end of the wooden pier's long promenade. ✉ *Pier View Way.*

WORTH NOTING

Oceanside Harbor. With 1,000 slips, this is North County's fishing, sailing, and water-sports center. There's a small dining and retail area at the north end of the harbor where you can linger and watch the boats coming and going. ✉ *1540 Harbor Dr. N* ☎ *760/435–4000* 🌐 *www.ci.oceanside.ca.us.*

Oceanside Museum of Art. Housed in side-by-side buildings designed by two Southern California modernist architects—the old City Hall designed by Irving Gill and the Central Pavilion designed by Frederick Fisher—the museum showcases works by San Diego area artists, including paintings and photography. ✉ *704 Pier View Way* ☎ *760/435–3720* 🌐 *www.oma-online.org* 🎟 *$8* 🕓 *Tues.–Sat. 10–4, Sun. 1–4.*

Wave Waterpark. A 3-acre water park run by the city of Vista is one of the few places in the country with a flow-rider, a type of standing wave that allows riders on bodyboards to turn, carve, and slash almost as though they were surfing on a real wave. If you haven't learned how to do that, you can tube down the park's own river or slip down the 35-foot waterslide. There's even a lap pool for serious swimmers. ✉ *101 Wave Dr., Vista* ☎ *760/760/940–9283* 🌐 *www.thewavewaterpark.com* 🎟 *$17* 🕓 *Memorial Day–Labor Day, Mon.–Fri. 10–4, Sat.–Sun. noon–5:30; Labor Day–Sept., Sat.–Sun. noon–5.*

WHERE TO EAT

$ AMERICAN FAMILY

🍴 **101 Cafe.** A diner dating back to 1928 is both a local hangout and the headquarters of the historic Highway 101 movement. Find all kinds of Highway 101 memorabilia here along with breakfast and lunch. The bountiful breakfast menu lists omelets, eggs any way you want, pancakes, and French toast. On offer at lunchtime are burgers, sandwiches, and salads. Families like the the ambience, food, and prices. [$] *Average main: $8* ✉ *631 S. Coast Hwy.* ☎ *760/722–5220* 🌐 *www.101cafe.net* ✍ *Reservations not accepted* 💳 *No credit cards* 🕓 *Closed for dinner.*

$ SEAFOOD

🍴 **Harbor Fish & Chips.** Pick up a basket of fresh-cooked fish-and-chips at this dive and you're in for a treat. The shop has been serving the combo—and clam chowder, shrimp cocktail, and fish sandwiches—to boaters and visitors for more than 40 years. It looks like it, too, with fish trophies hung on walls and from the ceiling. Outdoor tables offer terrific views of the Oceanside Marina. [$] *Average main: $12* ✉ *276 S. Harbor Dr.* ☎ *760/722–4977* 🌐 *www.harborfishandchips.net.*

WHERE TO STAY

$ HOTEL

🏨 **Oceanside Marina Suites.** Come for the proximity to water: these unusually large rooms and one- and two-bedroom suites, with fireplaces and expansive balconies in many, are on a spit of land, surrounded by water and cool ocean breezes on all sides. **Pros:** best sunsets; spacious rooms; free parking. **Cons:** marina location apt to be busy on weekends. $ *Rooms from: $109* ✉ *2008 Harbor Dr. N* ☎ *760/722–1561, 800/252–2033* ⊕ *www.omihotel.com* ⤴ *6 rooms, 51 suites* ◎| *Breakfast.*

$ ⛱ **Wyndham Oceanside Pier Resort.** Just steps from the beach and
HOTEL Oceanside Pier, these spacious two-bedroom suites with views are
FAMILY ideal for families. **Pros:** beachfront location; family-friendly. **Cons:** no spa; limited hotel rooms; two-night minimum stay. $ *Rooms from: $129* ✉ *333 N. Myers* ☎ *760/901–1200, 800/210–0948* ⊕ *www. wyndhamoceansidepier.com* ⤴ *24 rooms, 132 suites* ◎| *No meals.*

SHOPPING
Oceanside Photo & Telescope. This is the place to pick up a telescope or binoculars for viewing San Diego County's dazzling night sky. Call for information about stargazing parties the store holds regularly in the San Diego area. ✉ *918 Mission Ave.* ☎ *800/483–6287* ⊕ *www.optcorp.com.*

15

INLAND NORTH COUNTY AND TEMECULA

Long regarded as San Diego's beautiful backyard, replete with green hills, quiet lakes, and citrus and avocado groves, inland San Diego County and the Temecula wine country are among the fastest-growing areas in Southern California. Subdivisions, many containing palatial homes, now fill the hills and canyons around Escondido and Rancho Bernardo. At the northern edge of this region, Fallbrook (longtime self-proclaimed Avocado Capital of the World) has morphed into an emerging arts community. Beyond Fallbrook is Temecula, the premium winemaking area of southern Riverside County. Growth notwithstanding, inland San Diego County still has such natural settings as the San Diego Zoo Safari Park, Rancho Bernardo, and the Welk Resort. The region is also home to a number of San Diego County's Indian casino resorts, among them Pala, Harrah's Rincon, Valley View, and Pauma. Pachanga lies just over the county line near Temecula.

RANCHO BERNARDO

23 miles northeast of downtown San Diego on I–15.

Rancho Bernardo straddles a stretch of I–15 between San Diego and Escondido and is technically a neighborhood of San Diego. Originally sheep- and cattle-grazing land, it was transformed in the early 1960s into a planned suburban community, one of the first, and a place where many wealthy retirees settled down. It's now home to a number of high-tech companies, the most notable of which is Sony. If you want to spend some time at the nearby San Diego Zoo Safari Park, this community, home of the Rancho Bernardo resort, makes a convenient and comfortable headquarters for a multiday visit.

WHERE TO EAT
$$$ ✕ **Bernard'O.** Intimate despite its shopping-center location, Bernard'O is
FRENCH the choice for a romantic dinner. Sit fireside in the small dining room, dine by candlelight, and savor contemporary versions of California

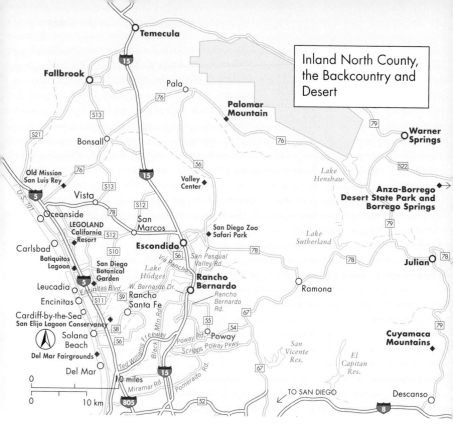

Inland North County,
the Backcountry and
Desert

bouillabaisse or grilled Scottish salmon with asparagus. Many items also appear on the reduced price Happy Hour menu, served from 4:30 to 7. $ *Average main: $33* ✉ *12457 Rancho Bernardo Rd.* ☎ *858/487–7171* ⌚ *Reservations essential* ☉ *Closed Sun. No lunch Sat.–Mon.*

$ ✕ **Chin's Szechwan Cuisine.** Locals pick Chin's for special occasions. It
SICHUAN feels rich, with dark-red walls, blooming orchids everywhere, and heavy
FAMILY wooden furnishings. The extensive menu lists popular items such as Kung Pao chicken, sizzling beef and scallops, and tangerine crispy beef. $ *Average main: $17* ✉ *15721 Bernardo Heights Pkwy.* ☎ *858/676–0166* ⊕ *www.govisitchins.com.*

$$ ✕ **French Market Grille.** The flower-decked dark-wood dining room and
FRENCH patio with twinkling lights will help you forget that you're eating in a shopping center. The French fare changes with the seasons; typical entrées include rack of lamb, oven-roasted swordfish and lobster with vermouth, or Pacific Coast bouillabaisse. If you love desserts, save room for one of the French classics offered here, apple tarte tatin, crêpes suzette, and crème brûlée. $ *Average main: $25* ✉ *15717 Bernardo Heights Pkwy.* ☎ *858/485–8055* ⊕ *www.frenchmarketgrille.com* ⌚ *Reservations essential.*

WHERE TO STAY

$$ RESORT FAMILY **Rancho Bernardo Inn Resort and Spa.** The gorgeous, flower-decked 265-acre grounds draw a sophisticated clientele looking for a golf getaway. **Pros:** excellent service; popular golf course; good value in off-season. **Cons:** walking required in spacious grounds; distance from most visitor attractions. [$] *Rooms from: $189* ✉ *17550 Bernardo Oaks Dr.* ☎ *858/675–8500, 888/476-4417* 🌐 *www.ranchobernardoinn.com* 🛏 *287 rooms, 15 suites* 🍴 *No meals.*

SHOPPING

Bernardo Winery. A trip to the oldest operating winery in Southern California, founded in 1889 and run by the Rizzo family since 1928, feels like traveling back to early California days; some of the vines on the former Spanish land-grant property have been producing grapes for more than a hundred years. Most of the grapes now come from other wine-growing regions. A collection of quaint shops surrounds the winery. Cafe Merlot serves lunch daily except Monday, and shops sell cold-pressed olive oil and other gourmet goodies, as well as apparel, home-decor items, and arts and crafts. A glassblowing artist is often working at the outdoor furnace. ✉ *13330 Paseo Del Verano Norte* ☎ *858/487–1866* 🌐 *www.bernardowinery.com* 🎫 *Winery free, tastings $10* ⏲ *Mon.–Fri. 9–5, Sat.–Sun. 9–6, shop hrs vary.*

ESCONDIDO

8 miles north of Rancho Bernardo on I–15, 31 miles northeast of downtown San Diego on I–15.

Escondido and the lovely rolling hills around it were originally a land grant bestowed by the governor of Mexico on Juan Bautista Alvarado in 1843. The Battle of San Pasqual, a bloody milestone in California's march to statehood, took place just east of the city. For a century and a half, these hills supported citrus and avocado trees, plus large vineyards. The rural character of the area began to change when the San Diego Zoo established its Safari Park in the San Pasqual Valley east of town in the 1970s. By the late 1990s suburban development had begun to transform the hills into housing tracts. The California Center for the Arts, opened in 1993, now stands as the downtown centerpiece of a burgeoning arts community that includes a collection of art galleries along Grand Avenue. Despite its urbanization, Escondido still supports several pristine open-space preserves that attract nature lovers, hikers, and mountain bikers.

ESSENTIALS

Visitor Information Visit Esconidido ✉ *235 E. Grand Ave.* ☎ *760/839–4777* 🌐 *www.VisitEscondido.com* ⏲ *Tues.–Fri. 10–4.*

EXPLORING

TOP ATTRACTIONS

FAMILY **California Center for the Arts.** An entertainment complex with two theaters, an art museum, and a conference center, the center presents operas, musicals, plays, dance performances, and symphony and chamber music concerts. Performers conduct free workshops for children; check the

15

website for dates. The museum, which focuses on 20th-century art, occasionally presents blockbuster exhibits such as the glass art of Dale Chihuly or photos by Ansel Adams, making a side trip here worthwhile. ✉ *340 N. Escondido Blvd.* ☎ *800/988–4253 box office, 760/839–4138 museum* ⊕ *artcenter.org* ☉ *Hrs vary, call ahead.*

FAMILY **Daley Ranch.** A 3,058-acre conservation area and historic ranch site is laced with more than 20 miles of multipurpose trails for hikers, mountain bikers, and equestrians. The 2.4-mile Boulder Loop affords sweeping views of Escondido, and the 2.5-mile Ranch House Loop passes two small ponds, the 1928 Daley family ranch house, and the site of the original log cabin. Private cars are prohibited on the ranch, but a Sunday shuttle service is provided from the parking area to the entrance. Free naturalist-guided hikes are offered on a regular basis; call for schedule. Leashed dogs permitted. ✉ *3024 La Honda Dr.* ☎ *760/839–4680* ⊕ *www.ci.escondido.ca.us* ✉ *Free* ☉ *Daily dawn–dusk.*

FAMILY
Fodor's Choice
★
San Diego Zoo Safari Park. A branch of the San Diego Zoo, 35 miles to the south, the 1,800-acre preserve in the San Pasqual Valley is designed to protect endangered species from around the world. Exhibit areas have been carved out of the dry, dusty canyons and mesas to represent the animals' natural habitats in various parts of Africa and Asia.

The best way to see these preserves is to take the 25-minute, 2½-mile Africa tram safari, included with admission. As you pass in front of the large, naturally landscaped enclosures, you can see animals bounding across prairies and mesas as they would in the wild. More than 3,500 animals of more than 400 species roam or fly above the expansive grounds. Predators are separated from prey by deep moats, but only the elephants, tigers, lions, and cheetahs are kept in enclosures. Good viewpoints are at the Elephant Viewing Patio, African Plains Outlook, Kilmia Point. ■TIP➔ Prepare for summer heat. Wear a hat, cool clothing, and drink plenty of water; water refills are free. Also walk in the shade whenever possible. In summer, when the park stays open late, the trip is especially enjoyable in the early evening, when the heat has subsided and the animals are active and feeding. When the tram travels through the park after dark, sodium-vapor lamps illuminate the active animals. Photographers with zoom lenses can get spectacular shots of zebras, gazelles, and rhinos.

For a more focused view of the park, you can take one of several other safaris that are well worth the additional charge. You can choose from several behind-the-scenes safaris, fly above it all via the Zip-line safari, or get up close to giraffes and rhinos on a Caravan safari.

The park is as much a botanical garden as a zoo, serving as a "rescue center" for rare and endangered plants. Unique gardens include cacti and succulents from Baja California, a bonsai collection, a fuchsia display, native plants, and protea.

The Lion Camp gives you a close-up view of the king of beasts in a slice of African wilderness complete with sweeping plains and rolling hills. As you walk through this exhibit, you can watch the giant cats lounging around through a 40-foot-long window. The last stop is a research station, where you can see them all around you through glass panels.

The ticket booths at Nairobi Village, the park's center, are designed to resemble the tomb of an ancient king of Uganda. Animals in the Petting Kraal here affectionately tolerate tugs and pats and are quite adept at posing for pictures with toddlers. At the Congo River Village 10,000 gallons of water pour each minute over a huge waterfall into a large lagoon. Hidden Jungle, an 8,800-square-foot greenhouse, is a habitat for creatures that creep, flutter, or just hang out in the tropics. Gigantic cockroaches and bird-eating spiders share the turf with colorful butterflies and hummingbirds and oh-so-slow-moving two-toed sloths. Lorikeet Landing holds 75 of the loud and colorful small parrots—you can buy a cup of nectar at the aviary entrance to induce them to land on your hand. The park's newest project is the Tull Family Tiger Trail, a Sumatran tiger habitat opened in 2014, where you can get face-to-face (with a glass between) with the gorgeous cats. The 5-acre exhibit features a waterfall and swimming hole, and addresses poaching and other environmental threats to the species.

All the park's walk-to exhibits and animal shows (included in admission) are entertainingly educational. The gift shops are well worth a visit for their limited-edition items. There are lots of restaurants, snack bars, and some picnic areas. Rental lockers, strollers, and wheelchairs are available. You can also arrange to stay overnight in the park in summer on a Roar and Snore Sleepover ($140 and up, plus admission). ⊠ *15500 San Pasqual Valley Rd.* ⊹ *Take I–15 north to Via Rancho Pkwy. and follow signs, 6 miles* ☎ *760/747–8702* ⊕ *www.sdzsafaripark.org* ☑ *$46 one-day pass including Africa tram ride; multipark and multiday passes are available; special safaris are extra starting at $50 per person; parking $12* ☉ *Daily 9–dusk.*

WORTH NOTING

Escondido Arts Partnership Municipal Gallery. This gallery showcases works by local artists, with regular exhibitions and year-round special events. ⊠ *262 E. Grand Ave.* ☎ *760/480–4101* ⊕ *www.escondidoarts.org* ☉ *Tues.–Sat. 11–4.*

Escondido History Center. This outdoor museum adjacent to the California Center for the Arts in Grape Day Park consists of several historic buildings moved here to illustrate local development from the late 1800s, when grape growing and gold mining supported the economy. Exhibits include the 1888 Santa Fe Depot, Escondido's first library, the Bandy Blacksmith shop, a furnished 1890 Victorian house, and other 19th-century buildings. ⊠ *321 N. Broadway* ☎ *760/743–8207* ⊕ *www.escondidohistory.org* ☑ *$3 suggested donation* ☉ *Tues.– Thurs., Sat. 1–4.*

Orfila Vineyards. Visitors here can taste award-winning Syrah, Sangiovese, and Viognier produced from grapes harvested from the 10,000-acre vineyard. The Rose Arbor has a picnic area, and there's a gift shop with wine-related merchandise. ⊠ *13455 San Pasqual Rd.* ☎ *760/738– 6500* ⊕ *www.orfila.com* ☑ *Tastings $10* ☉ *Daily 10–6, free guided tours at noon.*

FAMILY **Queen Califia's Magical Circle.** The last work by sculptor Niki de Saint Phalle (1930–2002), this sculpture garden designed for entertaining

Enjoying the wine at Orfila Vineyards in Escondido

children consists of nine totemic figures up to 21 feet tall. Adorned with stylized monsters, animals, protective deities, geometric symbols, and crests, the pieces evoke ancient tales and legends. Youngsters can climb on the giant fanciful figures. ✉ *Kit Carson Park, Bear Valley Pkwy. and Mary La.* ☎ *760/839–4691* ⊕ *www.queencalifia.org* ✉ *Free* ☉ *Tues.– Sun., 8–dusk except when raining.*

FAMILY   **San Dieguito River Park.** The park maintains several hiking and walking trails in the Escondido area. These are part of an intended 70-mile-long Coast to Crest Trail that will eventually link the San Dieguito Lagoon near Del Mar with the river's source on Volcan Mountain, north of Julian. Among the existing trails are three that circle Lake Hodges: the **North Shore Lake Hodges Trail;** the **Piedras Pintadas Trail,** which informs about native American Kumeyaay lifestyles and uses for native plants; and the **Highland Valley Trail,** the first mile of which is the Ruth Merrill Children's Walk. Three trails in **Clevenger Canyon** lead to sweeping views of the San Pasqual Valley. Visit the website for a list of upcoming guided hikes. ✉ *18372 Sycamore Creek Rd.* ☎ *858/674–2275* ⊕ *www.sdrp.org* ✉ *Free* ☉ *Daily dawn–dusk.*

FAMILY   **Stone Brewing Co.** One of the fastest-growing companies in the United States, Stone staked out a hilltop overlooking Escondido to create, brew, and sell its beloved craft beer. It's a huge, gorgeous facility, filled with massive stainless steel tanks used in beer-making. You can take a tour to see how the beer is made and get a taste, dine on farm-to-table fare at the on-site bistro, and purchase signature items in the company store. Thirty-six craft and specialty beers are always on tap in the tasting bar and the bistro, which has indoor and garden seating for lunch and dinner. ✉ *1999 Citracado Pkwy.* ☎ *760/294–7866* 🌐 *www.stoneworldbistro.com* 🕒 *Daily 11–11.*

OFF THE BEATEN PATH

Keys Creek Lavender Farm. In spring a visit to this organic lavender farm is worth a detour. A self-guided walk takes you through 6 acres planted with 28 varieties of lavender and to an area where plants are distilled into essential oils. A gift shop sells lavender products and plants. The farm serves a three-course English High Tea at 2 on Sunday. ✉ *12460 Keys Creek Rd., Valley Center* ☎ *760/742–3844* 🌐 *www.keyscreeklavenderfarm.com* 🎟 *$5* 🕒 *Wed.–Sun. 10–3, open May–June only.*

WHERE TO EAT AND STAY

With the exception of the Welk Resort, which is now primarily a time-share property, Escondido has little to offer in the way of accommodations.

$$$ FRENCH

🍴 **Vincent's.** This French restaurant is an excellent choice for lunch or dinner before an event at the nearby California Center for the Arts. Original paintings decorate the walls and crisp white tablecloths cover the tables, adorned with fresh flowers. The menu changes frequently; offerings might include tournedos Merlot, sweet potato ravioli, beef Wellington, or duck à l'orange. The wine list is serious, as are the desserts. The service is friendly and attentive. [$] *Average main: $28* ✉ *113 W. Grand Ave.* ☎ *760/745–3835* 🌐 *www.vincentsongrand.com* ✍ *Reservations essential* 🕒 *Closed Sun.–Mon. No lunch Sat.–Sun.*

$ ITALIAN

🍴 **Vinz Wine Bar.** A bit pizza joint, a bit deli, and a lot wine bar, Vinz is the place to go for beautiful salads, pizzas that range from margherita to barnyard rustica, sandwiches to panini. Occupying a two-storefront corner, it has a cozy, friendly ambiance, attentive service, and delicious food. The two venues inside are the dining room and the wine lounge, a small room where you're surrounded by bottles. During happy hours, the chef makes puppy pizza and terrier tapas for visiting dogs. There's live music and entertainment on weekends. [$] *Average main: $16* ✉ *201 E. Grand Ave.* ☎ *760/743–8466* 🌐 *www.vinzwinebar.com.*

$$ RESORT FAMILY

🏨 **Welk Resort.** Built by bandleader Lawrence Welk in the 1960s, the property sprawls over 600 acres of rugged, oak-studded hillside and is family-friendly, with abundant children's activities. **Pros:** excellent theater; popular golf course; near the Safari Park. **Cons:** located outside the city; very spread-out; rooms may not always be available due to time-sharing. [$] *Rooms from: $198* ✉ *8860 Lawrence Welk Dr.* ☎ *760/749–3000, 800/932–9355* 🌐 *www.welkresorts.com* 🛏 *574 suites* 🍽 *No meals.*

SHOPPING

Although farmland began to give way to suburbs in the 1990s, and the area's fruit, nut, and vegetable bounty has diminished, you can still find overflowing farm stands in the San Pasqual Valley and in Valley Center, just east of the city.

FAMILY

Bates Nut Farm. Home of San Diego's largest pumpkin patch each fall, this family farm is where you might find 200-pound squash. It also sells locally grown pecans, macadamia nuts, and almonds. On the 100 acres, there's a farm zoo, a picnic area, and a gift shop. ✉ *15954 Woods*

Valley Rd., Valley Center ☎ *800/642–0348* ⊕ *www.batesnutfarm.biz* ⊙ *Daily 9–5.*

Canterbury Gardens. Occupying an old winery, this shop specializes in giftware and seasonal decorative accessories for the home, plus it has a year-round selection of Christmas ornaments and collectibles by Christopher Radko, Mark Robert's Fairies, and Department 56. ⊠ *2402 S. Escondido Blvd.* ☎ *760/746–1400* ⊕ *www.canterburygardens.com.*

FALLBROOK

19 miles northwest of Escondido on I–15 to Mission Rd., Rte. S13, to Mission Dr.

A quick 5-mile detour off I–15 between Temecula and San Diego, Fallbrook bills itself as the Avocado Capital of the World. Avocado orchards fill the surrounding hillsides, and guacamole is served in just about every eatery. You can even pig out on avocado ice cream at the annual Avocado Festival in April. But this small agricultural town is also morphing into an interesting arts center. The art and cultural center showcases the work of local and regional painters, sculptors, and fiber artists. The National Gourd and Fiber Show in June draws lovers of this art from all over Southern California. You'll find several intriguing galleries displaying antiques, jewelry, watercolors, and photography on Main Avenue. Innovative restaurants now supplement the staple fast-food joints, and the Fallbrook Winery is making a name for itself in the South Coast wine region.

ESSENTIALS

Visitor Information Fallbrook Chamber of Commerce ⊠ *111 S. Main St.* ☎ *760/728–5845* ⊕ *www.fallbrookchamberofcommerce.org.*

EXPLORING

Brandon Gallery. This Fallbrook art institution that has been showing works of regional emerging and professional artists for more than 30 years is the place to find excellent quality watercolors, ceramics, jewelry, and baskets. It's a cooperative in which all work shown is judged and artists showing are members. ⊠ *105 N. Main St.* ☎ *760/723–1330* ⊕ *www.fallbrookbrandongallery.org.*

Fallbrook Art Center. Housed in a typical mid-century modern building that served as the Rexall Pharmacy for 30 years, the spacious center mounts 10 to 12 local and regional art shows yearly, including the annual Galaxy of Glass, World of Watercolor, and Reflections of Nature. The center also hosts a number of national touring art shows, among them the National Watercolor Society Show. The Café des Artistes, tucked into a back corner of the center, serves salads and sandwiches, and occasional dinners. ⊠ *103 S. Main St.* ☎ *760/728–1414* ⊕ *www.fallbrookartcenter.org* 🏷 *$6* ⊙ *Mon.–Sat. 10–4, Sun. noon–3; occasionally closed between shows. Café: Closed Sun.*

Fallbrook Winery. It's worth visiting this winery, perched on a lovely hillside outside Fallbrook, where winemaker Vernon Kindred and owners Ira Gourvitz and Rebecca Wood produce bottles that bring back medals from state and national competitions. They make wine from grapes grown on 36 hilly acres surrounding the winery and from other areas in California. Try the estate-bottled fruity 33°N Sauvignon Blanc, Bordeaux style 33°N BDX Red Blend, or the unusual North Rosato-Rosé of Sangiovese. ✉ *2554 Via Rancheros* ☎ *760/728–0156* ⊕ *www.fallbrookwinery.com* 🎫 *$20 midweek tours, $30 Sat.–Sun.* ☉ *By appointment only.*

WHERE TO EAT AND STAY

$$$
SEAFOOD

✗ **AquaTerra.** This pleasant room in the Pala Mesa Golf Resort is popular with locals. Most come for the seafood selections on the wide-ranging menu that lists Angus Certified Beef, house-made gnocchi, and Tuscan rosemary chicken. Tables here offer good golf-course views, and in warm weather you can dine outside on the patio. $ *Average main: $30* ✉ *2001 Old Hwy. 395* ☎ *760/728–5881* ⊕ *www.palamesa.com.*

$$
MEDITERRANEAN

✗ **Brothers Bistro.** Everything from sauces to breads is made in-house at this cozy bistro that's tucked into a back corner of the Major Market Shopping Center. Owner/chef Ron Nusser has a New York touch with Italian specialties such as Alla Diana Pasta, an antipasto-like Monterey seafood salad, and roasted halibut. But the most popular item on the menu is homemade lasagna, nearly a pound per serving with house-made marinara and three cheeses. Eat in the small dining room, where huge paintings adorn every wall, or on the tree-shaded patio outdoors. $ *Average main: $24* ✉ *835 S. Main St., Suite A* ☎ *760/731–9761* ⊕ *www.brothersbistro.net* ☜ *Reservations essential* ☉ *No lunch Sat.–Sun.*

$
MEXICAN

✗ **La Caseta.** The "little cottage" serves up small surprises. Chef Delos Eyer brings traditional Mexican fare up to date with options including grilled chicken wrap with achiote sauce and savory black beans, San Filipe fish tacos, charbroiled shrimp diablo, and meatless black bean quesadillas. The casual cottage with wraparound windows and colorful murals is bright and cheerful, and in good weather you can dine outside on the patio. $ *Average main: $13* ✉ *111 N. Vine St.* ☎ *760/728–9737* ⊕ *www.lacasetafinemexicanfood.com* ☉ *Closed Sun.*

$
RESORT

🏨 **Pala Casino Resort Spa.** Lovely spacious rooms and suites, a big selection of dining options, a tranquil spa, and an enticing entertainment schedule are all designed to pamper guests drawn to the casino. **Pros:** classy ambience; cabanas at pool; casual service; all rooms with mountain or pool views. **Cons:** remote location; challenging drive from I–15. $ *Rooms from: $139* ✉ *11154 Hwy. 76* ☎ *877/946-7275* ⊕ *www.palacasino.com* ⚲ *425 rooms, 82 suites* 🍽 *No meals.*

$
HOTEL

🏨 **Pala Mesa Golf Resort.** A vague Hawaiian feel prevails at this friendly and popular two-story resort, where large, simply furnished rooms have floor-to-ceiling windows and most have balconies, some with great fairway, garden, or mountain views. **Pros:** attractive grounds; spacious rooms; dog-friendly. **Cons:** adjacent to freeway; many convention-goers; resort's age is showing. $ *Rooms from: $119* ✉ *2001 Old Hwy. 395* ☎ *760/728–5881, 800/722–4700* ⊕ *www.palamesa.com* ⚲ *133 rooms* 🍽 *Some meals.*

15

TEMECULA

29 miles from Escondido, 60 miles from San Diego on I–15 north to Rancho California Rd. east.

Once an important stop on the Butterfield Overland Stagecoach route and a market town for the huge cattle ranches surrounding it, Temecula (pronounced teh-*mec*-yoo-la) is now a developed wine region, designated the South Coast region, which also includes some wineries in San Diego County. Known for its gently rolling hills, the region is studded with ancient oak trees and vernal pools. Until recently the offering at many of the wineries were just okay, but things have changed in the last decade as winemakers discovered that French and Italian grapes thrive in the valley's hot climate. Vines were replanted with the European varieties, and now winemakers are creating luscious blended reds and whites that resemble rich Rhones and Tuscan vintages. Because most of the wineries sell their bottles only at the wineries, it pays to stock up if you find something you especially enjoy. Most of the wineries that line both sides of Rancho California Road as it snakes east from downtown offer tours and tastings (for a fee) daily and have creatively stocked boutiques, picnic facilities, and restaurants on the premises. Lately, visitors will also find that some wineries have opened luxury boutique lodgings and fine dining restaurants. Several with sprawling elegant facilities host weekend weddings. Meanwhile, local developers have created an Old Town along historic Front Street on the west side of I–15. This section is home to boutique shops, good restaurants, a children's museum, and a theater. In addition to its visitor appeal, Temecula is also a suburban bedroom community for many who work in San Diego North County.

TOUR OPTIONS

Several companies offer individual and group tours of the Temecula wine country with departures from San Diego and Temecula. Some include lunch or refreshments as part of the package.

Limousine Tours Destination Temecula. Let someone else do the driving and enjoy this tour service that takes groups of 1 to 15 in luxury vans for tasting and touring Temecula wineries. ✉ *28475 Old Town Front St.* ☎ *951/695–1232, 800/584–8162* ⊕ *www.destem.com.* **Grapeline Wine Country Shuttle.** Daily Vineyard Picnic Tours offer tasting, picnic lunches, and behind-the-scenes vintner tours. Shuttles depart from Temecula hotels, wineries, and other locations. ✉ *Office, 43500 Ridge Park Dr., Suite 204* ☎ *951/693–5755* ⊕ *www.gogrape. com* 🎟 *Tours, $88–$118.* **Temecula Carriage Company.** Horse-drawn shuttles run between Ponte, Wiens, Lorimar, and South Coast wineries. Shuttle trips, drawn by handsome Percheron horses, are $99 per person including a picnic, or $30 per person for transportation only. Couples/special occasion winery tours, by reservation, include a two-hour ride, wine, and a picnic lunch ($250 per couple). ✉ *40001 Berenda Rd.* ☎ *858/205–9161* ⊕ *www.temeculacarriageco. com* ⊙ *Fri.–Sun. 10–2.*

ESSENTIALS

Visitor Information Visit Temecula Valley ✉ *28690 Mercedes St., Suite A* ☎ *951/491–6085* ⊕ *www.visittemecula.org.*

Temecula Valley Winegrowers Association. A good resource for information on Temecula's 35-some wineries, this group distributes brochures and sells tickets to special wine events. ✉ *29377 Rancho California Rd., Suite 203* ☎ *951/699–6586, 800/801–9463* ⊕ *www.temeculawines.org* ⊙ *Weekdays 9–5.*

EXPLORING

Old Town Temecula. Once a hangout for cowboys, Old Town has been updated and expanded while retaining its Old West appearance. A walking tour put together by the **Temecula Valley Historical Society**, starting at the Temecula Valley Museum, covers some of the old buildings; most are identified with bronze plaques. ⊕ *www.oldtowntemecula.com.*

FAMILY
Fodor's Choice
★
Pennypickle's Workshop: Temecula Children's Museum. This is the imaginary home of Professor Phineas Pennypickle, where kids accompanied by parents enter a time machine that carries them through six rooms of interactive exhibits demonstrating perception and illusion, music making, flight and aviation, chemistry and physics, plus power and electricity. The shop stocks an array of educational toys, games, and books. Reservations are not taken, so be sure to get there early, especially during school vacations. ✉ *42081 Main St.* ☎ *951/308–6376* ⊕ *www.pennypickles.org* ⊠ *$5* ⊙ *2-hr sessions Tues.–Sat. at 10, 12:30, and 3; Fri., also at 5:30; Sun. at 12:30 and 3.*

FAMILY
Santa Rosa Plateau Ecological Reserve. This 9,000-acre wooded preserve provides a glimpse of what this countryside was like before the developers took over. Trails wind through ancient oak forests and past vernal pools and rolling grassland. A visitor and operations center has interpretive displays and maps; some of the reserve's hiking trails begin here. There are designated trails for leashed dogs, horses, and mountain bikers. ✉ *39400 Clinton Keith Rd., Murrieta* ⊕ *Take I–15 south to Clinton Keith Road exit and head west 5 miles.* ☎ *951/677–6951* ⊕ *www.santarosaplateau.org* ⊠ *$3* ⊙ *Daily dawn–dusk; visitor center Tues.–Sun. 9–5.*

FAMILY
Temecula Valley Museum. Adjacent to Sam Hicks Monument Park, this museum focuses on Temecula Valley history, including early Native American life, Butterfield stage routes, and the ranchero period. A hands-on interactive area for children holds a general store, photographer's studio, and ride-a-pony station. Outside there's a playground and picnic area. ✉ *28314 Mercedes St.* ☎ *951/694–6450* ⊕ *www.temeculavalleymuseum.org* ⊠ *$2 suggested donation* ⊙ *Tues.–Sat. 10–4, Sun. 1–4.*

WINERIES

Europa Village. You'll find three tasting rooms here, reflecting three European-style wineries: French, cabernet sauvignon; Spanish, tamperanillo; and Italian, pinot grigio. You can walk through lush gardens and enjoy weekend entertainment. The Inn at Europa Village, perched on an adjacent hilltop, offers 10 guest rooms. ✉ *3347 La Serena Way* ☎ *951/216–3380* ⊕ *www.europavillage.com* ⊠ *Tastings $15* ⊙ *Daily 10–7.*

Fodor's Choice
★
Hart Family Winery. A perennial crowd-pleaser, this winery specializes in well-crafted red wines made by father-son winemakers Joe and Jim Hart. Joe, who started the winery in the 1970s with his wife, Nancy,

focuses on growing grapes suited to the Temecula region's singular climate and soils—Zinfandel, Cabernet Sauvignon, and Sangiovese as might be expected, but also little known varietals such as Aleatico, used in the winery's marvelous dessert wine. The reds are the stars, though, along with the amiable Hart family members themselves. ☒ *41300 Avenida Biona* ☎ *951/676–6300* ⊕ *www.hartfamilywinery.com* 🍷 *Tasting $10* ☾ *Daily 9–4:30.*

Leoness Cellars. Rhone- and Tuscan-style blends—along with killer views—are the specialties of this mountaintop facility. Winemaker Tim Kramer and his staff produce about a dozen and a half wines each year, of which you can select six. If you like reds, be sure to try the Syrahs, which are almost always winners. Winery tours take in the vineyards and the wine-making areas. The tours require a reservation, as do wine-and-food pairing sessions that might include fruits and cheeses or, in the case of dessert wines, some chocolates. ☒ *38311 DePortola Rd.* ☎ *951/302–7601* ⊕ *www.leonesscellars.com* 🍷 *Tasting $15–$18, tours with tasting $18–$85* ☾ *Daily 11–5.*

Miramonte Winery. At Temecula's hippest winery, perched on a hilltop, listen to Spanish-guitar recordings while sampling the slightly pricy Opulent Meritage, a supple Roussanne, or the sultry Syrah. Owner Cane Vanderhoof's wines have earned dozens of awards. While you're enjoying your wine on the deck, order an artisan cheese plate. On Friday and Saturday nights from 7 to 10, the winery turns into a local hot spot with tastings of signature wines ($17) and beer, live music, and dancing that spills out into the vineyards. ☒ *33410 Rancho California Rd.* ☎ *951/506–5500* ⊕ *www.miramontewinery.com* 🍷 *Tastings $15–17, tours $75 (reservations required Sat.–Sun.)* ☾ *Sun.–Thurs. 11–6, Fri.–Sat. 11–10 p.m.*

Mount Palomar Winery. One of the original Temecula Valley wineries, opened in 1969, Mount Palomar introduced Sangiovese grapes, a varietal that has proven perfectly suited to the region's soil and climate. New owners have transformed the homey winery into a grand Mediterranean villa with acres of gardens and trees. Some of the wines are made from grapes brought from Italy nearly 50 years ago. Try the dry Sangiovese or Bordeaux-style Meritage. Shorty's Bistro, open for lunch daily and for dinner Friday through Sunday, presents live entertainment on Friday nights. ☒ *33820 Rancho California Rd.* ☎ *951/676–5047* ⊕ *www.mountpalomar.com* 🍷 *Winery free, tasting $12 Mon.–Thurs., $16 Fri.– Sun.* ☾ *Daily 10:30–6.*

Fodor's Choice
★
Wiens Family Cellars. A visit to this serious winery can be an enlightenment; request information cards for a full description of each vintage you taste, combinations of cabernet sauvignon, cabernet franc, petite syrah, zinfandel, and pinot noir. The winery is known for its so-called Big Reds, which include Crowded, a four-grape blend; lighter Infinite Perspective, a three-grape blend; and a jammy Zinfandel. ☒ *35055 Via Del Ponte* ☎ *951/694–9892* ⊕ *www.wienscellars.com* 🍷 *Main Taisting Room Tastings, $15.*

Wilson Creek Winery & Vineyards. One of Temecula's busiest tasting rooms sits amid inviting, parklike grounds. Wilson is known for its

Almond Champagne, but the winery also produces appealing still wines. The Viognier, Reserve Syrah, Reserve Zinfandel, and late-harvest Zinfandel all merit a taste. The on-site Creekside Grill Restaurant serves sandwiches, salads, and entrées such as Mexican white sea bass and gluten-free vegetable potpie. Dine inside or select a picnic spot, and the servers will deliver your meal to you. ✉ *35960 Rancho California Rd.* ☎ *951/699–9463* 🌐 *www.wilsoncreekwinery.com* 🎟 *Tasting $15 Mon.–Fri., $20 Sat.–Sun. and holidays* 🕓 *Daily 10–5, restaurant Mon.–Fri. 11–4, Sat. 11–5, Sun. 10–3.*

WHERE TO EAT

$$ EUROPEAN 🍴 **Baily's.** A genteel clientele and attentive service mark this fine-dining restaurant on the second floor of Baily's Old Town Dining establishment (downstairs is the Front Street Bar & Grill). Tall windows draped in red frame a town-and-country view. Contemporary cuisine leans heavily on fresh interpretations of classics such as rack of lamb, ribeye, and salmon Wellington. The menu changes frequently to take advantage of locally grown produce. There's an impressive wine list. [$] *Average main: $26* ✉ *28699 Old Town Front St.* ☎ *951/676–9567* 🌐 *www.oldtowndining.com* ✍ *Reservations essential* 🕓 *No lunch.*

15

$$ AMERICAN FAMILY 🍴 **Baily's Front Street Bar & Grill.** The easy-on-the-budget menu lists eight gourmet burgers, chipotle-braised barbecued ribs, chili-stuffed chicken, and jambalaya. You can also nosh on Irish nachos and jalapeño-calamari tempura. On weekend evenings, the place turns into a locally popular nightclub. Breakfast is offered on weekends only. It's a good place for casual fare,;however, note that some diners have complained about service. [$] *Average main: $26* ✉ *28699 Old Town Front St.* ☎ *951/676–9567* 🌐 *www.oldtowndining.com* ✍ *Reservations essential.*

$$$ CONTEMPORARY 🍴 **Café Champagne.** The spacious patio, with its bubbling fountain, flowering trellises, and vineyard views, at this Thornton Winery cafe is the perfect place to lunch on a sunny day. Inside, the dining room is decked out in French country style, and the open kitchen turns out such dishes as braised beef short ribs and cioppino. The reasonably priced wines served here include the signature Thornton Winery sparklers. [$] *Average main: $34* ✉ *Thornton Winery, 32575 Rancho California Rd.* ☎ *951/699–0099* 🌐 *www.thorntonwine.com* ✍ *Reservations essential.*

$$$$ MODERN AMERICAN FAMILY 🍴 **Vineyard Rose.** Big and barnlike, the Vineyard Rose is a good choice for family dining, one that will give the kids a chance to sample some excellent cooking. Consider lamb duo with caulifulower, sea scallops with confetti quiona, or Shelton Farms chicken. The restaurant, part of the South Coast Winery complex, serves three meals daily. [$] *Average main: $47* ✉ *34843 Rancho California Rd.* ☎ *951/587–9463, 866/994–6379* 🌐 *www.wineresort.com* ✍ *Reservations essential.*

WHERE TO STAY

$$ B&B/INN 🏨 **Inn at Europa Village.** Offering a lovely hillside setting for an escape to the wine country, this 10-room bed-and-breakfast delights guests. **Pros:** privacy; delicious home-cooked breakfast; scenery. **Cons:** long walk to wineries. [$] *Rooms from: $180* ✉ *33350 La Serena Way* ☎ *877/676–7047* 🌐 *www.europavillage.com/inn* 🛏 *10 rooms* 🍽 *Breakfast.*

$$ HOTEL 🏨 **Ponte Vineyard Inn.** Comfortable and relaxed digs offer vineyard and garden views and have an Old California feel, with lots of dark wood,

leather furnishings, and open spaces. **Pros:** fire pits in garden; excellent service; live music on weekends. **Cons:** many weekend weddings. [$] *Rooms from: $200* ✉ *35001 Rancho California Rd.* ☎ *951/587–6688* 🌐 *www.pontevineyardinn.com* 🛏 *60 rooms* 🍴 *No meals.*

$$ HOTEL 🏨 **South Coast Winery Resort & Spa.** The Temecula wine country's resort offers richly appointed and highly private rooms surrounded by 38 acres of vineyards. **Pros:** elegantly appointed rooms; full-service resort; good value. **Cons:** spread out property requires lots of walking; poor service; $15 resort fee. [$] *Rooms from: $169* ✉ *34843 Rancho California Rd.* ☎ *951/587–9463, 866/994–6379* 🌐 *www.wineresort.com* 🛏 *76 rooms, 2 suites* 🍴 *Breakfast.*

$ RESORT 🏨 **Temecula Creek Inn.** Each room at this spacious inn has a private patio or balcony overlooking the championship golf course. **Pros:** beautiful grounds; top golf course; great views. **Cons:** simple furnishings; shows its age; location away from Old Town and wineries. [$] *Rooms from: $139* ✉ *44501 Rainbow Canyon Rd.* ☎ *951/694–1000, 888/976–3404* 🌐 *www.temeculacreekinn.com* 🛏 *130 rooms, 1 guesthouse* 🍴 *No meals.*

SPORTS AND THE OUTDOORS

A Grape Escape Balloon Adventure. Enjoy a morning hot-air balloon lift-off from Europa Village Winery. ✉ *33475 La Serena Way* ☎ *951/699–9987, 800/965–2122* 🌐 *www.hotairtours.com* 🎫 *$156.*

Balloon and Wine Festival. Temecula draws thousands of people to its Balloon and Wine Festival at Lake Skinner Recreation Area in late spring. Festivities include concerts with headliner entertainment and wine tasting and pairing. ✉ *37701 Warren Rd., Winchester* ☎ *951/676–6713* 🌐 *www.tvbwf.com.*

California Dreamin'. Leave on a hot-air balloon ride from a private Temecula vineyard. Rates range from $148 to $168. ✉ *33133 Vista Del Monte Rd.* ☎ *800/373–3359* 🌐 *www.californiadreamin.com.*

SHOPPING

Temecula Lavender Co. Owner Jan Schneider offers an inspiring collection of the herb that fosters peace, purification, sleep, and longevity. Bath salts, hand soaps, essential oil, even dryer bags to freshen up the laundry—she's got it all. ✉ *28561 Old Town Front St.* ☎ *951/676–1931* 🌐 *www.temeculalavenderco.com* 🕒 *Daily 10–6.*

Temecula Olive Oil Company. Tastings of locally pressed olive oil are offered at the Temecula Olive Oil Company, where you can find a selection of oils seasoned with garlic, herbs, and citrus. This Old Town shop has dipping and cooking oils, locally crafted oil-based soaps and bath products, and a selection of preserved and stuffed olives. ✉ *28653 Old Town Front St.* ☎ *951/693–0607* 🌐 *www.temeculaoliveoil.com.*

THE BACKCOUNTRY AND JULIAN

The Cuyamaca and Laguna mountains to the east of Escondido—sometimes referred to as the backcountry by county residents—are favorite weekend destinations for hikers, bikers, nature lovers, stargazers, and apple-pie fanatics. Most of the latter group head to Julian, a historic

Ready for lift-off at the Temecula Valley Balloon and Wine Festival

mining town now better known for apple pie than for the gold once extracted from its hills. Much of nearby Cuyamaca Rancho State Park, once a luscious ancient oak and pine forest, burned in a 2003 fire, but many of the park's ancient oak trees have come back to life.

CUYAMACA MOUNTAINS

The Cuyamaca and Laguna mountains separate coastal and inland San Diego from the desert. In most years abundant winter rainfall here produces thick oak and pine forests, year-round streams, and sparkling waterfalls. The mountains were also home to a small gold rush in the 1870s, remnants of which can be seen throughout the region. Wildlife, including deer, coyotes, and mountain lions, is abundant.

Cuyamaca Rancho State Park. Spread over more than 25,000 acres of open meadows, oak woodlands, pine forests, and mountains and rising to 6,512 feet at Cuyamaca Peak, much of the park burned during California's biggest wildfire in 2003. A study in reforestation, most of the park offers a beautiful outdoor experience. Camps, picnic areas, and trails are open daily. There are more than 100 miles of trails for hiking, mountain biking, and horse riding. For an inspirational desert view, stop at the lookout about 2 miles south of Julian on Route 79; on a clear day you can see several mountain ranges in hues ranging from pink to amber stepped back behind the Salton Sea. ⊠ *13652 Hwy. 79* ☎ *760/765–3020* ⊕ *www.parks.ca.gov.*

FAMILY **Lake Cuyamaca.** Behind a dam constructed in 1888 (the second oldest in California), this 110-acre lake offers fishing, boating, picnicking, nature

CLOSE UP

Casino Country

San Diego County, along with Temecula, is the Indian gaming capital of California, with more than 13 tribes operating casinos in the region. The casinos range from resorts with headliner entertainment and golf courses, to rooms tucked away on a crossroads with slot machines. Although the gaming options resemble what you find in Las Vegas, the action is different. The casinos stand alone on back roads, so it's not practical to travel from one to another. The big casinos—Viejas, Barona, Sycuan, Rincon, Pala, and Pachanga—are popular with local seniors and visitors. Many casinos offer bus transport; gambling age is 18 years, 21 in some casinos.

Barona Valley Ranch Resort and Casino. This is an all-in-one Western-style destination, with gaming, hotel, restaurants, and golf course. In the casino are 2,000 slots and more than 80 gaming tables, including blackjack. You can also play roulette, craps, and baccarat. The 400-room Barona Valley Ranch hotel has a fitness center, day spa, and pool. ⊠ *1932 Wildcat Canyon Rd., Lakeside* ☎ *619/443–2300, 888/722–7662* ⊕ *www.barona.com.*

Harrah's Rincon Casino & Resort. In the shadow of Palomar Mountain, this resort has 662 rooms and five entertainment venues with almost nightly entertainment, seven restaurants, a spa, a pool, and a casino with 2,000 slot machines and 60 table games. ⊠ *777 Harrah's Rincon Way, Valley Center* ☎ *760/751–3100* ⊕ *www. harrahs.com.*

Pechanga Resort & Casino. This resort hotel, with some of the vicinity's best accommodations, has 517 rooms, plus 45 sites in its RV park, as well as

seven restaurants and a food court, a gym, sauna, swimming pool, spa, and golf course. The casino has 3,800 slot machines, more than 132 table games, a high-limit gaming area with salon, and no-smoking poker room. Several night clubs offer live entertainment nightly. The casino presents championship boxing matches year-round. ⊠ *45000 Pechanga Pkwy., Temecula* ☎ *951/693–1819* ⊕ *www. pechanga.com.*

Sycuan Casino. More compact than other area casinos, Sycuan Casino has 2,000 slot machines; 40 table games such as blackjack, poker, and pai gow, and a bingo parlor. The smoke-free casino is the closest to downtown San Diego. The tribe also owns the nearby Sycuan Resort. ⊠ *5469 Casino Way, El Cajon* ☎ *619/320–6078, 800/279–2826* ⊕ *www.sycuan.com.*

Viejas Casino. A Native American–theme entertainment and shopping complex, Viejas Casino has more than 2,500 slot machines, plus blackjack, poker, bingo, pai gow, and off-track wagering. There are six restaurants and a cocktail lounge, plus a high-end bar and VIP lounge. The Viejas Outlet Center across from the casino has more than 50 shops, restaurants, an amphitheater, and the California Welcome Center. ⊠ *5000 Willows Rd., Alpine* ☎ *619/445–5400, 800/847–6537* ⊕ *www.viejas.com* ☉ *Casino, daily; Outlet, Mon.–Sat. 10–9, Sun. 11–8.*

—Bobbi Zane

hikes, and wildlife-watching. Anglers regularly catch trout, smallmouth bass, and sturgeon. A shaded picnic area occupies the lakeshore. Families can rent small motorboats, rowboats, and paddleboats by the hour. Free fishing classes for adults and kids are held Saturday at 10 am. Fishing licenses and advice are available at the tackle shop. Chambers Park on the east side of the lake holds two rental condominiums, three sleeping cabins, 20 RV campsites with hookups, and 21 tent sites are available with reservations (call Monday through Thursday). ✉ *15027 Hwy. 79* ☎ *760/765–0515, 877/581–9904* 🌐 *www.lakecuyamaca.org* 🎟 *$6 per vehicle for picnic area* 🕒 *Daily dawn–dusk.*

Sunrise National Scenic Byway. In the Cleveland National Forest, this route is the most dramatic approach to Julian—its turns and curves reveal amazing mountain views of the desert from the Salton Sea all the way to Mexico. You can spend an entire day roaming these mountains; an early-morning hike to the top of Garnet Peak (mile marker 27.8) is the best way to catch the view. Springtime wildflower displays are spectacular, particularly along Big Laguna Trail from Laguna Campground. There are picnic areas along the highway at Desert View and Pioneer Mail. The National Forest Visitor Center, open weekends, has maps and hiking guides. The Blue Jay Lodge, open weekends, has a rustic restaurant straight out of a western movie. ✉ *Hwy. 79, Descanso* 🌐 *www.byways.org.*

15

WHERE TO EAT

$ AMERICAN

🍴 **Lake Cuyamaca Restaurant.** This tidy lakefront café specializes in hearty breakfasts, burgers, salads, and sandwiches. A new owner who took over in 2013 and is serving home-style American food, is getting good reviews from locals. The lakeside view from the deck can't be beat. [$] *Average main: $14* ✉ *15027 Hwy. 79* ☎ *760/765–0700.*

JULIAN

62 miles from San Diego to Julian, east on I–8 and north on Rte. 79.

Gold was discovered in the Julian area in 1869, and gold-bearing quartz a year later. More than $15 million worth of gold was taken from local mines in the 1870s. Many of the buildings along Julian's Main Street and the side streets today date back to the gold-rush period; others are reproductions.

When gold and quartz became scarce, the locals turned to growing apples and pears. During the fall harvest season you can buy fruit, sip apple cider (hard or soft), eat apple pie, and shop for local original art, antiques, and collectibles. But spring is equally enchanting (and less congested), as the hillsides explode with wildflowers—thousands of daffodils, lilacs, and peonies. More than 50 artists have studios tucked away in the hills surrounding Julian; they often show their work in local shops and galleries. The Julian area comprises three small crossroads communities: Santa Ysabel, Wynola, and historic Julian. You can find bits of history, shops, and dining options in each community. Most visitors come to spend a day in town, but the hillsides support small bed-and-breakfast establishments for those who want to linger longer.

ESSENTIALS

Visitor Information Julian Chamber of Commerce ✉ *Town Hall, 2129 Main St.* ☎ *760/765–1857* ⊕ *www.julianca.com* ⊙ *Daily 10–4.*

EXPLORING

TOP ATTRACTIONS

FAMILY
Fodor's Choice
★

California Wolf Center. This center, just outside Julian, is one of the few places in North America where you can get an up-close view of the gray wolves that once roamed much of the continent. The center participates in breeding programs and houses several captive packs, including some rare Mexican grays, a subspecies of the North American gray wolf that came within seven individuals of extinction in the 1970s. The animals are kept secluded from public view in 3-acre pens, but some may be seen by visitors during educational tours. Private tours are by appointment. ✉ *Hwy. 79 at KQ Ranch Rd.* ☎ *619/234–9653* ⊕ *www. californiawolfcenter.org* 🖅 *$20, reservations required* ⊙ *Tours: Mon. and Fri. 10 a.m., Sat. 2 and 4:30 pm, Sun. 10 am.*

The Feed Store–Antiques and Such at the Santa Ysabel Store. A local landmark, the Santa Ysabel General Store has been updated and backdated to 1884, when it was an important stop on the road between the mountains and San Diego. The store sells heirloom seeds and bulbs, do-it-yourself cheese or craft beer–making kits, and specialty honey, pickled vegetables, and preserves put up in micro batches by food artisans. It's also a resource for those looking for salvaged architectural elements and vintage home and garden furnishings. ✉ *30275 Hwy. 78, Santa Ysabel* ☎ *760/765–1270* ⊙ *Fri.–Sun. 11–5.*

FAMILY **Julian Pioneer Museum.** When the gold mines in Julian played out, the mobs of gold miners who had invaded it left, leaving behind discarded mining tools and empty houses. Today the Julian Pioneer Museum, a 19th-century brewery, displays remnants of that time, including pioneer clothing, a collection of old lace, mining tools, and original photographs of the town's historic buildings and mining structures. ✉ *2811 Washington St.* ☎ *760/765–0227* ⊕ *julianpioneermuseum.org* 🖅 *$3* ⊙ *Thurs.–Sun., 10–4.*

Observer's Inn. One of the best ways to see Julian's star-filled summer sky is by taking a sky-tour at Mike and Caroline Leigh's observatory, with research-grade telescopes. The hosts guide you through the star clusters and galaxies, pointing out planets and nebulae. The guides also offer solar tours at 11 a.m., when you can get a good look at the sun using a telescope designed for this purpose. It's also an inn, if you wish to stay the night. Reservations are necessary for tours and lodging. ✉ *3535 Hwy. 79* ☎ *760/765–0088* ⊕ *www.observersinn.com* 🖅 *$25* ⚠ *Reservations essential.*

Volcan Mountain Wilderness Preserve. The Volcan Mountain Foundation and San Diego Parks and Recreation manage this 3,000-acre preserve, where hikes challenge your stamina and views are stunning. A 1¼-mile trail through the preserve passes through Engelmann oak forest, native manzanita, and rolling mountain meadows to a viewpoint where the panorama extends north all the way to Palomar Mountain. On a clear day you can see Point Loma in San Diego. At the entrance you pass through gates designed by James Hubbell, a local artist known for his ironwork, wood carving, and stained glass. You can see splendid views from the 5-mile Volcan Summit Trail. Guided hikes on the Sky Island Trail and the Oak Walk Trail are offered regularly. ✉ *Foundation office, 2015 Main St.* ⚓ *From Julian take Farmer Rd. to Wynola Rd., go east a few yards, and then north on continuation of Farmer Rd.* ☎ *760/765–2300* ⊕ *www.volcanmt.org* 🎫 *Free* ☾ *Daily dawn–dusk.*

WORTH NOTING

Banner Queen Trading Post Gallery. A step inside what was the mine superintendent's home in the run-down-looking remnant of an old gold mine dug into a hillside on Banner Grade, 5 miles east of Julian, reveals a wealth of contemporary art. Five rooms are filled with paintings, photos, sculpture, ceramics, stained glass, and woven pieces by Julian artists. Prices range from $30 or less for photos and pottery to hundreds of dollars for paintings. Closed Monday through Thursday. ✉ *36766 Hwy. 78* ☎ *760/765–2168* ☾ *Fri.–Sun. 1–5.*

FAMILY

Fodor's Choice

★

Eagle Mining Company. Five blocks east of the center of Julian you can take an hour-long tour of an authentic family-owned gold mine. Displays along the route include authentic tools and machinery, gold extraction process, and gold quartz bearing veins. A small rock shop and gold-mining museum are also on the premises. ✉ *Box 624* ☎ *760/765–0036* 🎫 *$10* ☾ *Daily 10–3, weather permitting.*

Mission Santa Ysabel. West of Santa Ysabel, this tiny late-19th-century adobe mission continues to serve several local Native American communities. A small museum on the premises (*Daily 8–3*) houses memorabilia from local families, Native Americans, and the parish. ✉ *23013 Hwy. 79* ☎ *760/765–0810.*

Santa Ysabel Preserve. Three Native American tribes live in this valley, which looks pretty much the way the backcountry appeared a century ago, with sweeping meadows surrounded by oak-studded hillsides. The tribes operate small farms and run cattle here. The San Dieguito River (Santa Ysabel Creek) emerges from Volcan Mountain here and winds its way 55 miles to Dog Beach at Del Mar. A hiking, biking, and equestrian trail system follows the river from Farmer Road in Julian to the West Entrance just west of Santa Ysabel. Legacy oak tree shade the trail, waterfalls provide a background sound, there are spectacular views along the way, and picnic tables abound. ☎ *760/765–4089* ⊕ *www.sdparks.org.*

WHERE TO EAT

$$

MODERN

AMERICAN

FAMILY

Fodor's Choice

★

✕ **Jeremy's on the Hill.** For a quiet dinner, pleasant surroundings, and some of the best burgers around, Jeremy's is the place to go. Although the menu features grilled steak, rack of lamb, and locally grown pork and veggies, the stars are burgers, particularly the San Diego burger stuffed with blue cheese cream and Dijon cream sauce bacon-wrapped bison burger made with locally raised meat. Jeremy specializes in local produce, wine, and brews such as Julian Hard Cider, Stone Brewing Levitation Ale, and Shadow Mountain Viognier. There's entertainment weekend nights, although it's not a late-night place: Jeremy's closes by 8 pm Sunday through Thursday, and 9 pm Saturday. $ *Average main:*

15

$27 ✉ *4354 Hwy. 78* ☎ *760/765–1587* 🌐 *www.jeremysonthehill.com* ✍ *Reservations essential.*

$ CAFÉ 🍴 **Julian Pie Company.** The apple pies that made Julian famous come from the Smothers family bakery in a one-story house on Main Street. In pleasant weather you can sit on the front patio and watch the world go by while savoring a slice of hot pie—from Dutch apple to apple mountain berry crumb—topped with homemade cinnamon ice cream. The Smothers family has been making pies in Julian since 1986; by 1989 the family had bought its own orchard, and by 1992 it had built a larger bakery in Santa Ysabel that makes and serves only pies. Daily at lunchtime the Julian location also serves soups and sandwiches inside and in their tree-shaded backyard. [$] *Average main: $8* ✉ *2225 Main St.* ☎ *760/765–2449* 🌐 *www.julianpie.com.*

JULIAN'S BLACK HISTORY

According to local history and old photos, the Julian area had a large population of African Americans in the years following the Civil War. Indeed, it was a black man, Fred Coleman, who discovered gold in Julian, and the Julian Hotel was founded and operated by Albert and Margaret Robinson, also black. Headstones recognizing the contributions of Julian's black pioneers continue to be placed in the old section of the Pioneer Cemetery.

$ CAFÉ FAMILY 🍴 **Julian Tea & Cottage Arts.** Sample finger sandwiches, scones topped with whipped cream, and lavish sweets, which are served during afternoon tea inside the Clarence King House, built by Will Bosnell in 1898. Regular sandwiches, soups, salads, and a children's tea are also available. Victorian teas are presented during the holiday season. [$] *Average main: $15* ✉ *2124 3rd St.* ☎ *760/765–0832, 866/765–0832* 🌐 *www.juliantea.com* 🕒 *Closed Tues.–Wed. No dinner.*

$$ SICILIAN 🍴 **Romano's Dodge House.** You can gorge on huge portions of antipasto, pizza, pasta, sausage sandwiches, and seafood in a cozy old house. Start with the generous antipasto platter that's big enough for the whole table. Specialties include pork Juliana simmered in apple cider, pasta Pacifica, and brasciole. This is a casual, red-checked-tablecloth kind of place, where you can dine outside in good weather. There's a small bar that's popular with locals. [$] *Average main: $20* ✉ *2718 B St.* ☎ *760/765–1003* 🌐 *www.romanosrestaurantjulian.com.*

$ CAFÉ 🍴 **Soups 'n Such Cafe.** It's worth the wait for breakfast or lunch at this cozy café, where everything is fresh and made to order. The breakfast standout is eggs Benedict, both classic and vegetarian. For lunch you can chose among several classic salads and homemade soups. [$] *Average main: $15* ✉ *2000 Main St.* ☎ *760/765–4761* 🕒 *Closed Tues.–Wed. No dinner.*

$ PIZZA FAMILY 🍴 **Wynola Pizza & Bistro.** Locals and San Diegans come to this quaint and casual indoor-outdoor restaurant for delicious, single-portion pies, such as pesto pizza, Thai chicken pizza, vegan pizza, and tostada pizza. Other items include chili, lasagna, seared Cajun salmon, and a killer fire-roasted artichoke dip served with homemade buffalo crackers. Entertainers usually perform on weekends in the adjacent Red Barn or, in good weather, outdoors. $ *Average main: $15* ✉ *4355 Hwy. 78, Santa Ysabel* ☎ *760/765–1004* ⊕ *www.wynolapizzaexpress.com.*

WHERE TO STAY

$ 🏨 **Butterfield Bed and Breakfast.** This beautifully landscaped inn on a
B&B/INN 3-acre hilltop is cordial and romantic, with knotty-pine ceilings, Laura Ashley accents, and rooms with nice touches, such as fireplaces or woodstoves and private entrances. **Pros:** great food; interesting and helpful hosts; secluded. **Cons:** very quiet; no room phones. $ *Rooms from: $135* ✉ *2284 Sunset Dr.* ☎ *760/765–2179, 800/379–4262* ⊕ *www.butterfieldbandb.com* ⌁ *5 rooms* ⦿| *Breakfast.*

$ 🏨 **Julian Gold Rush Hotel.** Built in 1897 by freed slave Albert Robinson
B&B/INN and his wife, Margaret, this old hotel is Julian's only designated national landmark and offers antiques-filled rooms and cottage accommodations with private entrances and fireplaces. **Pros:** genuine historic hotel; convivial atmosphere. **Cons:** small rooms; no TV. $ *Rooms from: $155* ✉ *2032 Main St.* ☎ *760/765–0201, 800/734–5854* ⊕ *www.julianhotel. com* ⌁ *14 rooms, 2 suites* ⦿| *Breakfast.*

$ 🏨 **Julian Lodge.** Near shops, this bed and breakfast is a replica of a
B&B/INN late-19th-century inn and has rooms and public spaces furnished with antiques. **Pros:** in-town location; free parking. **Cons:** simple appointments; reserve well in advance for fall; busy surroundings. $ *Rooms from: $120* ✉ *2720 C St.* ☎ *760/765–1420, 800/542–1420* ⊕ *www. julianlodge.com* ⌁ *23 rooms* ⦿| *Breakfast.*

$$ 🏨 **Orchard Hill Country Inn.** On a hill above town, this inn with a lodge
B&B/INN and five Craftsman-style cottages offers luxurious accommodations decorated with antiques, original art, and handcrafted quilts, complemented by sweeping views of the countryside. **Pros:** most luxurious digs in Julian; good food. **Cons:** limited amenities; not good for children. $ *Rooms from: $195* ✉ *2502 Washington St., PO Box 2410* ☎ *760/765–1700, 800/716–7242* ⊕ *www.orchardhill.com* ⌁ *10 rooms, 12 suites* ⦿| *Breakfast.*

$ 🏨 **Viejas Casino & Resort Hotel.** The last thing you expect to find at a
HOTEL hotel in the back country (albeit one steps from the casino and its res-
Fodor's Choice taurants) is sophisticated art and furnishings created by local artists
★ and valet parking. **Pros:** free internet; business center; attentive service. **Cons:** close to freeway; far from metro San Diego. $ *Rooms from: $129* ✉ *5000 Willows Rd.* ☎ *619/445-5400, 800/938-2532* ⊕ *www.viejas. com* ⌁ *99, 29 suites* ⦿| *No meals.*

$$ 🏨 **Wikiup Bed and Breakfast.** Best known for its herd of llamas, this
B&B/INN contemporary cedar-and-brick inn is decorated with romantic furnishings and offers guest rooms with fireplaces and outdoor hot tubs for stargazing. **Pros:** private entrances; pleasant surroundings. **Cons:** limited facilities; decor may be a bit much for some; two-night minimum. $ *Rooms from: $185* ✉ *1645 Whispering Pines Dr.* ☎ *760/765–1512, 800/694–5487* ⊕ *www.wikiupbnb.com* ⌁ *5 rooms* ⦿| *Breakfast.*

SHOPPING

The Julian area has a number of unique shops that are open weekends, but midweek hours vary considerably. In autumn locally grown apples, pears, nuts, and cider are available in town and at a few roadside stands.

15

The best apple variety produced here is a Jonagold, a hybrid of Jonathan and Golden Delicious.

Birdwatcher. Wild-bird lovers can shop for birdhouses, birdseed, hummingbird feeders, guidebooks for serious birding, and bird-theme accessories, such as jewelry, apparel, and novelties. ⊠ *2775 B St.* ☎ *760/765–1817* ⊕ *www.thebirdwatcher.net.*

E. Barrett General Store. Scores of earth-friendly items fill the inside of this old-fashioned shop. It's stocked with delightful fragrances, from French milled soaps, scented candles, bath ice, lotions, and lip balm to books, outdoor clothing, vintage kitchen items, and more. The shop is dog-friendly; ask about treats. ⊠ *2111 Main St.* ☎ *760/765–0123* ⊕ *www. ebarrettco.com* ⊙ *Daily 10–5.*

Falcon Gallery. A replica of one of Julian's original hotels, this gallery has works by local artists, books about area history including Native American history, and limited edition print books. ⊠ *2015A Main St.* ☎ *760/765–1509.*

Mountain Gypsy. This shop is popular area-wide for its extensive collection of jewelry, trendy apparel, and shoes in petite and plus sizes. ⊠ *2007 Main St.* ☎ *760/765–0643.*

Santa Ysabel Art Gallery. On display here are works fine art, including watercolors, stained glass, sculptures, fiber, and other creations by local artists. ⊠ *30352 Hwy. 78, Santa Ysabel* ☎ *760/765–1676* ⊕ *www. santaysabelartgallery.com.*

PALOMAR MOUNTAIN

35 miles northeast of Escondido on I–15 to Rte. 76 to Rte. S6, 66 miles northeast of downtown San Diego on Rte. 163 to I–15 to Rte. 76 to Rte. S6.

Palomar Mountain, at an altitude of 6,140 feet and with an average of 300 clear nights per year, has the distinction of being the home of one of the world's most significant astronomical observation sites, the Hale 200-inch telescope installed at the Palomar Observatory in 1947. Before that, the mountain played a role in San Diego County's rich African American history and culture. One of many who migrated to the area in the mid-19th century was Nathan Harrison, a former slave who owned a large swath of property on the mountain where he farmed and raised cattle, the importance of which is just being revealed through archaeological excavations conducted by local university students. According to local historians, Harrison and other former slaves made up a major segment of the backcountry population until about 1900.

EXPLORING

FAMILY **Mission San Antonio de Pala.** A living remnant of the mission era, built in 1816, this mission still ministers to the Native American community, making it the only original Spanish mission still serving its initial purpose. The old jail and cemetery are part of the original mission. The school, long operated by Sisters of the Blessed Sacrament and the Sisters of Precious Blood, is now a charter school operated by the Bonsall USD. You can take a self-guided tour of the mission and grounds.

✉ *Pala Mission Rd. off Rte. 76, 6 miles east of I–15, 3015 Pala Mission Rd., Pala* ☎ *760/742–3317* ⊕ *www.missionsanantonio.org* 🖃 *$2* ⊘ *Wed.–Sat. 9–4.*

FAMILY **Palomar Mountain State Park.** One of the few areas in Southern California with a Sierra-like atmosphere, the park is carpeted with a forest of pines, cedars, western dogwood, native azalea, and other plants. Wildflower viewing is good in spring. **Boucher Lookout,** on one of several nature/ hiking trails, affords a sweeping view to the west. There's trout fishing in Doane Pond. The Doane Valley campground offers 31 sites with tables, fire pits, and flush toilets. From May to October, reservations are strongly recommended and can be made seven months in advance. ✉ *Off Hwy. S6 at Hwy. S7, 19952 State Park Dr., Palomar Mountain* ☎ *760/742–3462 ranger station, 800/444–7275 campsite reservations* ⊕ *www.parks.ca.gov* 🖃 *Camping $30, $8 day use.*

Palomar Observatory. Atop 6,000-foot Palomar Mountain, the observatory is owned and operated by the California Institute of Technology, whose astronomy faculty conducts research here. The observatory houses the Hale Telescope, as well as 60-inch, 48-inch, 24-inch, 18-inch, and Snoop telescopes. Some of the most important astronomical discoveries of the 20th century were made here, and already in this century scientists using the observatory's 48-inch telescope have detected a 10th planet. ■TIP➡ The observatory closes without advance notice during inclement weather. Call in advance during winter. The small museum contains photos of some of these discoveries, as well as photos taken by NASA's Hubble Space Telescope and from recent NASA–European Space Agency missions to Mars and Saturn. A park with picnic areas surrounds the observatory. ✉ *Rte. S6 north of Rte. 76, east of I–15, 35899 Canfield Rd., Palomar Mountain* ☎ *760/742–2119* ⊕ *www. astro.caltech.edu/palomar* 🖃 *Free, $5 guided tours* ⊘ *Daily 9–4 during daylight savings time; 9–3 during standard time; guided tours Sat.–Sun. Apr.–Oct. at 11 and 1:30.*

15

WHERE TO EAT

$ ╳ **Mother's Kitchen.** This popular stop for motorcyclists (the road up to
VEGETARIAN the restaurant is the most popular biker route in Southern California)
FAMILY serves huge portions of vegetarian fare, including salads, mountain chili, Boca tacos, macaroni and cheese, and lasagna. Sides include steaming-hot soup, nachos, and quesadillas. The atmosphere is mountain casual, with open-beam ceilings, knotty-pine tables, and fresh flowers everywhere. Waitresses are friendly, and local musicians entertain on weekends. Ⓢ *Average main: $10* ✉ *Junction of Hwys. S6 and S7, Palomar Mountain* ☎ *760/742–4233* ⊕ *www.motherskitchenpalomar.com* ⊘ *Closed Tues.–Wed. Labor Day–Memorial Day. No dinner.*

THE DESERT

In most spring seasons the stark desert landscape east of the Cuyamaca Mountains explodes with colorful wildflowers. The beauty of this spectacle, as well as the natural quiet and blazing climate, lures many tourists and natives each year to Anza-Borrego Desert State Park, about a two-hour drive from central San Diego.

For hundreds of years the only humans to linger here were Native Americans of the Cahuilla and Kumeyaay tribes, who made their winter homes in the desert. It was not until 1774, when Mexican explorer Captain Juan Bautista de Anza first blazed a trail through the area seeking a shortcut from Sonora, Mexico, to San Francisco, that Europeans had their first glimpse of the oddly enchanting terrain.

The desert is best visited from October through May to avoid the extreme summer temperatures. Winter temperatures are comfortable, but nights (and sometimes days) are cold, so bring a warm jacket.

ANZA-BORREGO DESERT STATE PARK

88 miles from downtown San Diego (park border due west of Borrego Springs).

GETTING HERE AND AROUND

You'll need a car to visit the Anza-Borrego Desert and Borrego Springs, which is totally surrounded by wilderness. The trip from San Diego is about 88 scenic miles, and it takes about two hours. Once there be prepared to drive on dusty roads as there is no public transportation. The best route to Borrego Springs is via I–8 east out of San Diego; exit east on Highway 79 and take the scenic drive through the Cuyamaca Mountains to Julian, where Highway 79 intersects with Highway 78 going east. Follow Highway 78 into the desert to Yaqui Pass Road, turn left and follow the signs to Borrego Springs Christmas Circle. Take Borrego Palm Canyon west to reach the Anza-Borrego Desert State Park headquarters.

TOUR OPTIONS

California Overland Excursions offers day tours and overnight excursions into hard-to-reach scenic desert destinations using open-air, military-transport vehicles. Typical destinations include Font's Point, the Badlands, and 17-Palm Oasis.

Tour Information California Overland Excursions ⊠ *1233 Palm Canyon Dr., Borrego Springs* ☎ *760/767–1232, 866/639–7567* ⊕ *www.californiaoverland. com.*

ESSENTIALS

Visitor Information Anza-Borrego Desert State Park ⊠ *200 Palm Canyon Dr., Borrego Springs* ☎ *760/767–5311* ⊕ *www.parks.ca.gov.* **State Park Reservations** ☎ *800/444–7275* ⊕ *www.reserveamerica.com.* **Wildflower Hotline** ☎ *760/767–4684.*

CLOSE UP

Spring Wildflowers

Southern California's famous climate has blessed this corner of the continent with an ever-changing, year-round palette of natural color. It's hard to find a spot anywhere around the globe that produces as spectacular a scene as San Diego in spring—from native plant gardens found tucked away in mountain canyons and streambeds to carpets of wildflowers on the desert floor. You'll have to see it yourself to believe just how alive the deceptively barren desert really is.

WHEN TO GO
Spring debuts in late February or early March. Heavy winter rains always precede the best bloom seasons. And good blooms also bring even more beauty—a bounty of butterflies. A further boon: here in this generally temperate climate, the bloom season lasts nearly all year.

Some drought-tolerant plants rely on fire to germinate, and the years following wildfires generally produce a profusion of plant life not normally seen.

WHAT TO SEE
Look for rare western redbud trees erupting into a profusion of crimson flowers, sometimes starting as early as February. Native California lilacs (ceanothus) blanket the hillsides throughout the backcountry with fragrant blue-and-white blossoms starting in May and showing until August.

Native varieties of familiar names show up in the mountain canyons and streambeds. A beautiful white western azalea would be the star in anyone's garden. A pink California rose blooms along streambeds in spring and summer. Throughout the year three varieties of native dogwood show off white blooms and beautiful crimson fall foliage. The **Cuyamaca Mountains** usually put on a display of fall color as the native oaks turn gold and red. By winter the rare toyon, known as the California Christmas tree, lights up the roadside with its red berries.

Farther east in the **Anza-Borrego Desert State Park**, the spring wildflower display can be spectacular: carpets of pink, purple, white, and yellow verbena and desert primrose as far as the eye can see. Rocky slopes yield clumps of beavertail cactus topped with pink blossoms, clumps of yellow brittlebush tucked among the rocks, and crimson-tip ocotillo trees. For an introduction to desert vegetation, explore the visitor center demonstration garden, adjacent to the park's underground headquarters.

For a vivid view of both the mountain and desert spring flora, take I–8 east to Route 79, go north to Julian, and then east on Route 78 into Anza-Borrego park.

15

EXPLORING
Anza-Borrego State Park. Today more than 1,000 square miles of desert and mountain country are included in the Anza-Borrego Desert State Park, one of the few parks in the country where you can follow a trail and pitch a tent wherever you like. There are 110 miles of hiking and riding trails that allow you to explore canyons, capture scenic vistas, tiptoe through fields of wildflowers in spring, and see wildlife—the park is home to rare Peninsula bighorn sheep, mountain lions, coyotes,

black-tailed jackrabbit, and roadrunners. State Highway 78, which runs north and south through the park, has been designated the Juan Bautista de Anza National Historic Trail, marking portions of the route of the Anza Colonizing Expedition of 1775–76 that went from northern Mexico to the San Francisco Bay area. In addition, 28,000 acres have been set aside in the eastern part of the desert near Ocotillo Wells for off-road enthusiasts. General George S. Patton conducted field training in the Ocotillo area to prepare for the World War II invasion of North Africa.

Many of the park's sites can be seen from your vehicle, as 500 miles of paved and dirt roads traverse the park—note that you are required to stay on them so as not to disturb the park's ecological balance. On dirt roads it's easy to sink up to your wheel covers in dry sand, so rangers recommend using four-wheel-drive vehicles on the dirt roads. Also, carry the appropriate supplies: shovel and other tools, flares, blankets, and plenty of water. Canyons are susceptible to flash flooding; inquire about weather conditions before entering.

Wildflowers, which typically begin to bloom in January and are at their peak in mid-March, attract thousands of visitors each spring. A variety of factors, including rainfall and winds, determine how extensive the bloom will be in a particular year. However, good displays of low-growing sand verbena and white evening primrose can usually be found along Airport Road and DiGeorgio Road. Following wet winters, spectacular displays fill the dry washes in Coyote Canyon and along Henderson Canyon Road. ■TIP→ The best light for photography is in early morning or late afternoon.

Erosion Road is a self-guided, 18-mile auto tour along Route S22. The **Southern Emigrant Trail** follows the route of the Butterfield Stage Overland Mail, the route used by half of the argonauts heading for the gold fields in Northern California.

At **Borrego Palm Canyon,** a few minutes west of the visitor information center is a 1½-mile trail leads to a small oasis with a waterfall and palms. The Borrego Palm Canyon campground is the only developed campground with flush toilets and showers in the park. (Day use is $8 and camping is $25 in high season, $35 with hookup.)

International geology students visit the Fish Creek area of Anza-Borrego to explore a famous canyon known as **Split Mountain** (*Split Mountain Rd. south from Rte. 78 at Ocotillo Wells*), a narrow gorge with 600-foot perpendicular walls formed by an ancestral stream. Fossils in this area indicate that a sea covered the desert floor at one time. A 2-mile nature trail west of Split Mountain rewards hikers with a view of shallow caves created by erosion. ✉ *200 Palm Canyon Dr., Borrego Springs* ☎ *760/765–5311* ⊕ *www.parks.ca.gov*

Visitor Information Center. Rangers and displays at this excellent visitor's center can point you in the right direction. Most of the desert plants also can be seen in the demonstration desert garden here. ✉ *200 Palm Canyon Dr., Borrego Springs* ☎ *760/767–4205, 760/767–4684 wildflower hotline* ⊕ *www.parks.ca.gov* ☉ *Oct.–Apr. daily 9–5; May–Sept. Sat.–Sun. 9–5.*

BORREGO SPRINGS

31 miles from Julian, east on Rte. 78 and Yaqui Pass Rd., and north on Rte. S3.

A quiet town with a handful of year-round residents, Borrego Springs is set in the heart of the Anza-Borrego Desert State Park and is emerging as a destination for desert lovers. From September through June, temperatures hover in the 80s and 90s, and you can enjoy activities such as hiking, nature study, golf, tennis, horseback riding, and mountain-bike riding. Even during the busier winter season, Borrego Springs feels quiet. There are three golf resorts, two bed-and-breakfasts, and a community of winter residents, but the laid-back vibe prevails. If winter rains cooperate, Borrego Springs puts on the best wildflower displays in the low desert.

UNBURIED TREASURE

The Anza-Borrego Desert is one of the most geologically active spots in North America and a repository of paleontological treasure. Beneath the desert's surface are fossil-bearing sediments that provide clues to the geological activity that occurred in eras gone by, from climate change to tectonic activity and up-thrust. Reading the fossil record, scientists have learned that the badlands here were once a wonderland of green and home of saber-toothed tigers, flamingos, zebras, camels, the largest known mammoths, and a flying bird with a 16-foot wingspan.

15

ESSENTIALS

Visitor Information Borrego Springs Chamber of Commerce ✉ *786 Palm Canyon Dr.* ☎ *760/767–5555, 800/559–5524* 🌐 *www.borregospringschamber.com.*

EXPLORING

Galleta Meadows. Flowers aren't the only things popping up from the earth in Borrego Springs. At Galleta Meadows, camels, llamas, saber-toothed tigers, tortoises, and monumental gomphotherium (a sort of ancient elephant) appear to roam the earth again. These life-size bronze figures are of prehistoric animals whose fossils can be found in the Borrego Badlands. The collection of more than 130 sculptures created by Ricardo Breceda was commissioned by the late Dennis Avery, who installed the works of art on property he owned for the entertainment of locals. Maps are available from Borrego Springs Chamber of Commerce. ✉ *Borrego Springs Rd. from Christmas Circle to Henderson Canyon* ☎ *760/767–5555* 🌐 *www.galletameadows.com* 🎟 *Free.*

WHERE TO EAT

$ AMERICAN 🍴 **The Arches.** Set right on the edge of the Borrego Springs Golf Course, this is one of the most pleasant dining rooms in the area. Choose indoor or outdoor seating, and enjoy dishes that are mostly of the comfort food variety. They are surprisingly good—try the tortilla-crusted chicken for dinner. Service can be super casual. [$] *Average main: $17* ✉ *1112 Tilting T Dr.* ☎ *760/767–5700* 🌐 *www.borregospringsresort.com* 🕒 *Summer hrs vary; call ahead.*

$$ **✕ Carlee's Bar & Grill.** This local watering hole seems to collect characters
AMERICAN ranging from hippies to mountain men and is the place to go any night
of the week. A large, dimly lighted room houses the bar and dining
tables, and the menu lists pasta and pizza in addition to old-fashioned
entrées such as liver and onions, ribs and steaks, and a mixed grill.
$ *Average main: $21* ⊠ *660 Palm Canyon Dr.* ☎ *760/767–3262.*

$ **✕ Carmelita's Mexican Grill and Cantina.** A friendly family-run eatery
MEXICAN tucked into a back corner of what is called "The Mall," Carmelita's
draws locals and visitors all day whether it's for a hearty breakfast, a
cooked-to-order enchilada or burrito, or a brew at the bar. The menu
lists typical combination plates (enchiladas, burritos, tamales, and
tacos). Salsas have a bit of zing, and masas are tasty and tender. $ *Average main: $14* ⊠ *575 Palm Canyon Dr.* ☎ *760/767–5666.*

WHERE TO STAY

$$ **⊞ Borrego Springs Resort & Spa.** The large rooms at this quiet resort set
RESORT around a swimming pool and with golf, tennis, and golf options come
with either a shaded balcony or a patio with desert views. **Pros:** golf and
tennis; good desert views from most rooms. **Cons:** limited amenities;
average service. $ *Rooms from: $182* ⊠ *1112 Tilting T Dr.* ☎ *760/767–
5700, 888/826–7734* ⊕ *www.borregospringsresort.com* ⇨ *66 rooms,
34 suites* ⦿*No meals.*

$$$ **⊞ Borrego Valley Inn.** Those looking for desert landscapes may enjoy the
B&B/INN adobe Southwestern-style buildings here that house spacious rooms,
Fodor's Choice which boasts plenty of natural light, original art, pine beds, and double
★ futons facing corner fireplaces, plus have desert gardens of mesquite,
ocotillo, and creosote just outside. **Pros:** swimming under the stars in the
clothing-optional pool; exquisite desert gardens. **Cons:** potential street
noise in season; not a good choice for families with young children or
pets. $ *Rooms from: $235* ⊠ *405 Palm Canyon Dr.* ☎ *760/767–0311,
800/333–5810* ⊕ *www.borregovalleyinn.com* ⇨ *15 rooms, 1 suite*
⦿*Breakfast.*

$$ **⊞ Casa del Zorro.** With new owners, who have renovated and updated
RESORT the property, Casa del Zorro is once again a secret hideaway for those
FAMILY looking for spacious and comfortable accommodations—many with
Fodor's Choice private pools, surrounded by desert mountains—as well as beautifully
★ prepared meals. **Pros:** colorful gardens; summer stargazing; amenities
such as fitness center, spa, and two pools. **Cons:** summer heat; huge
campus; spotty service. $ *Rooms from: $200* ⊠ *3845 Yaqui Pass Rd.*
☎ *760/767–0100* ⊕ *www.lacasadelzorro.com* ⇨ *66 rooms* ⦿*All meals.*

$$ **⊞ The Palms at Indian Head.** Spectacular desert views can be had from
B&B/INN this small hotel that displays an authentic mid-century look, with hand-
crafted, Southwest lodgepole furniture and original art by local art-
ists. **Pros:** quiet, oasis-like atmosphere; star connection; great views.
Cons: somewhat remote location; simple decor; no room phones.
$ *Rooms from: $179* ⊠ *2220 Hoberg Rd.* ☎ *760/767–7788* ⊕ *www.
thepalmsatindianhead.com* ⇨ *12 rooms* ⦿*Breakfast.*

If you think the desert is just a sandy wasteland, the stark beauty of the Anza-Borrego Desert will shock you.

SPORTS AND THE OUTDOORS

Borrego Springs Resort and Country Club. Midwinter, when you can expect cool breezes, is the best time for a round of golf at the Borrego Springs Resort and Country Club. The public course here is fairly flat and dotted with palm trees. Rates vary from winter to summer. ✉ *1112 Tilting T Dr., Borreo Springs* ☎ *760/767–3330* 🌐 *www.borregospringsresort.com* *$55* *18 holes, 6760 yards, par 71* ⏲ *Closed Sept.–mid-Nov.* ☞ *Facilities: putting green, driving range, pitching area, golf carts; rental clubs, pro shop, lessons, restaurant, bar.*

OFF THE BEATEN PATH

Ocotillo Wells State Vehicular Recreation Area. The sand dunes and rock formations at this 70,000-plus acre haven for off-road enthusiasts are fun and challenging. Camping is permitted throughout the area, but water is not available. The only facilities are in the small town (really no more than a corner) of Ocotillo Wells. ✉ *Rte. 78, 18 miles east from Borrego Springs Rd., 5780 Hwy. 78* ☎ *760/767–5391* 🌐 *www.parks.ca.gov* *$5 day use.*

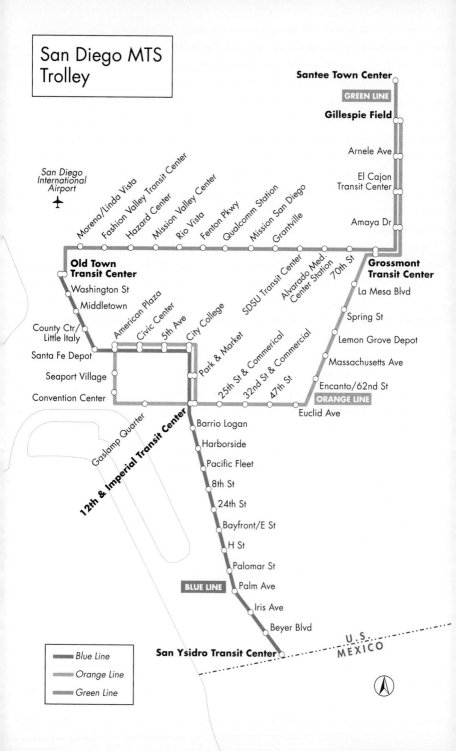

San Diego MTS Trolley

San Diego International Airport

GREEN LINE

ORANGE LINE

BLUE LINE

Santee Town Center

Gillespie Field

Arnele Ave

El Cajon Transit Center

Amaya Dr

Grossmont Transit Center

La Mesa Blvd

Spring St

Lemon Grove Depot

Massachusetts Ave

Encanto/62nd St

Euclid Ave

Morena/Linda Vista
Fashion Valley Transit Center
Hazard Center
Mission Valley Center
Rio Vista
Fenton Pkwy
Qualcomm Station
Mission San Diego
Grantville
SDSU Transit Center
Alvarado Med. Center Station
70th St

Old Town Transit Center
Washington St
Middletown
County Ctr/ Little Italy
Santa Fe Depot
Seaport Village
Convention Center

American Plaza
Civic Center
5th Ave
City College
Park & Market
25th St & Commercial
32nd St & Commercial
47th St

Gaslamp Quarter

12th & Imperial Transit Center

Barrio Logan
Harborside
Pacific Fleet
8th St
24th St
Bayfront/E St
H St
Palomar St
Palm Ave
Iris Ave
Beyer Blvd

San Ysidro Transit Center

U.S. MEXICO

Blue Line
Orange Line
Green Line

TRAVEL SMART
SAN DIEGO

GETTING HERE AND AROUND

When traveling in the San Diego area, consider the big picture to avoid getting lost. Water lies to the west of the city. To the east and north, mountains separate the urban areas from the desert. If you keep going south, you'll end up in Mexico.

Downtown San Diego is made up of several smaller communities, including the Gaslamp Quarter and Balboa Park that you can easily explore by walking, driving, riding the bus or trolley, or taking a taxi. In the heart of the city, numbered streets run west to east and lettered streets run north to south. The business district around the Civic Center, at 1st Avenue and C Street, is dedicated to local government and commerce.

▌ AIR TRAVEL

Flying time to San Diego is 5 hours from New York, 3½ hours from Chicago, 3½ hours from Dallas, and 45 minutes from Los Angeles.

Airline Security Issues Transportation Security Administration ⊕ www.tsa.gov.

AIRPORT

The major airport is San Diego International Airport (SAN), called Lindbergh Field locally. Major airlines depart and arrive at Terminal 1 and Terminal 2; commuter flights identified on your ticket with a 3000-sequence flight number depart from a third commuter terminal. A red shuttle bus provides free transportation between terminals. With only one runway serving two main terminals, San Diego's airport is too small to accommodate the heavy traffic of busy travel periods. Small problems including fog and rain can cause congested terminals and flight delays. Delays of 20–30 minutes in baggage claim aren't unusual.

Major construction, which took three years to complete in summer 2013, resulted in improved traffic flow, better parking, expanded waiting areas, 10 additional gates at Terminal 2, more shopping and dining options, and a public art collection that changes regularly. Shopping and dining options include these popular spots: Einstein Bros. Bagel, Best Buy Express, Brighton Collectibles, Be Relax Spa, Phil's Barbecue, and Stone Brewing. In addition, if you have a flight delay, consider catching a 10-minute cab ride downtown to go shopping or take one last stroll around the city.

If you need travel assistance at the airport, there are two Travelers Aid information booths, one in Terminal 1 and one in Terminal 2, open daily 6 am–11 pm.

Airlines and Airports Airline and Airport Links.com ⊕ www.airlineandairportlinks.com. **San Diego International Airport** ✉ 3225 N. Harbor Dr., off I-5 ☎ 619/400–2400 ⊕ www.san.org.

GROUND TRANSPORTATION

San Diego International Airport is 3 miles from downtown. Shuttle vans, buses, and taxis run from the Transportation Plaza, reached via the skybridges from Terminals 1 and 2. The cheapest and sometimes most convenient shuttle is the Metropolitan Transit System's Flyer Route 992, red-and-blue-stripe buses that serve the terminals at 10- to 15-minute intervals between 5 am and 11 pm. These buses have luggage racks and make a loop from the airport to downtown along Broadway to 9th Avenue and back, stopping frequently within walking distance of many hotels; they also connect with the San Diego Trolley and Amtrak. The $2.25 fare includes transfer to local transit buses and the trolley, and you should have exact fare (in coins or bills) handy. Information about the Metropolitan Transit System's shuttles and buses, the San Diego Trolley, and Coaster commuter train can all be found on the joint transit website www.transit.511sd.com.

If you're heading to North County, the Flyer can drop you off at the Santa Fe Depot, where you can take the Coaster commuter train as far north as Oceanside for $4–$5.50.

Of the various airport shuttles, only SuperShuttle has tie-downs for wheelchairs.

Ground shuttle service is available between LAX and San Diego, but can be prohibitively expensive, with rates for the two-hour trip starting at $275, so a car rental may be a more economical option. All of the shuttles listed at the end of this section offer the service.

Taxis departing from the airport are subject to regulated fares—($2.80 initial fee, $3 per mile). Taxi fare is about $16 plus tip to most downtown hotels. The fare to Coronado runs about $30 plus tip. Limousine rates vary and are charged per hour, per mile, or both, with some minimums established.

Contacts Cloud 9/SuperShuttle ✉ *123 Caminio de la Riena* ☎ *800/974-8885* ⊕ *www.cloud9shuttle.com.* **San Diego Transit** ☎ *619/233-3004* ⊕ *transit.511sd.com.*

■ BOAT TRAVEL

Many hotels, marinas, and yacht clubs rent slips short term. Call ahead, because available space is limited. The San Diego and Southwestern yacht clubs have reciprocal arrangements with other yacht clubs.

The San Diego Bay Ferry takes you between downtown and Coronado in a nostalgic, old-school ferry every hour from 9 am to 10 pm. The ride lasts about 15 minutes and costs $4.25 each way; bicycles and Segways are free. The Water Taxi is a great alternative for nighttime transit along San Diego Bay. It is on call daily from 3 to 10 and costs $8 each way.

SEAL Amphibious tours, operated by Old Town Trolley, combine the best of land and sea, departing from Seaport Village daily. After exploring picturesque

San Diego neighborhoods, the bus-boat hybrid rolls right into the water for a cruise around the bay. It's all narrated with fun facts, too.

Ferry Contacts San Diego Bay Ferry ✉ *1050 N. Harbor Dr.* ☎ *800/442-7847* ⊕ *www.sdhe.com.* **SEAL Amphibious tours** ⊕ *www.sealtours.com.* **Water Taxi** ✉ *1050 N. Harbor Dr.* ☎ *619/235-8294* ⊕ *www.sdhe.com.*

Marinas Best Western Island Palms Hotel & Marina ✉ *2051 Shelter Island Dr.* ☎ *619/222-0561.* **The Dana on Mission Bay** ✉ *1710 W. Mission Bay Dr.* ☎ *619/222-2141* ⊕ *www.thedana.com.* **Kona Kai Resort** ✉ *1551 Shelter Island Dr.* ☎ *619/224-7547* ⊕ *www.resortkonakai.com.* **San Diego Marriott Hotel and Marina** ✉ *3333 W. Harbor Dr.* ☎ *619/230-8955* ⊕ *www.marriott.com.* **San Diego Yacht Club** ✉ *1011 Anchorage La.* ☎ *619/221-6400* ⊕ *www.sdyc.org.* **Southwestern Yacht Club** ✉ *2702 Qualtrough St.* ☎ *619/222-0438.*

CRUISE TRAVEL

Cruise lines that make regular calls at San Diego include Holland American, Royal Caribbean, Princess, Disney, Regent 7 Seas, and Celebrity. Ships heading to and from Alaska, Mexico, and the Panama Canal arrive and depart from the Cruise Terminal, which is on the B Street Pier (1140 N. Harbor Drive). This is a busy spot, where you can get advice at the International Visitor Center and catch the Coronado Ferry or Water Taxi. San Diego Harbor Excursion bay cruises also dock here. The San Diego Maritime Museum and the Midway Museum are just steps away, and the terminal is a short taxi ride from Balboa Park, Little Italy, and the Gaslamp Quarter. Fares from the cruiseship terminal are $18 to Balboa Park, $15 to SeaWorld, and $14 to the Gaslamp Quarter.

Cruise Lines Celebrity ☎ *800/647-2251* ⊕ *www.celebrity.com.* **Holland America** ☎ *800/426-0327* ⊕ *www.hollandamerica.com.* **Princess Cruises** ☎ *800/774-6237* ⊕ *www.princess.com.* **Royal Caribbean International** ☎ *800/338-4962* ⊕ *www.royalcaribbean.com.*

▌ BUS AND TROLLEY TRAVEL

Under the umbrella of the Metropolitan Transit System, there are two major transit agencies in the area: San Diego Transit and North County Transit District (NCTD). You will need to buy a $2 compass card, available when you board for the first time, on which are loaded your destinations to use MTS. Day passes, available for 1 to 30 days and starting at $5, give unlimited rides on nonpremium regional buses and the San Diego Trolley. You can buy them from most trolley vending machines, at the downtown Transit Store, and at Albertsons markets. A $14 Regional Plus Day Pass adds Coaster service and premium bus routes.

The bright-red trolleys of the San Diego Trolley light-rail system operate on three lines that serve downtown San Diego, Mission Valley, Old Town, South Bay, the U.S. border, and East County. The trolleys operate seven days a week from about 5 am to midnight, depending on the station, at intervals of about 15 minutes. The trolley system connects with San Diego Transit bus routes—connections are posted at each trolley station. Bicycle lockers are available at most stations and bikes are allowed on buses and trolleys though space is limited. Trolleys can get crowded during morning and evening rush hours. Schedules are posted at each stop; on-time performance is excellent.

NCTD bus routes connect with Coaster commuter train routes between Oceanside and the Santa Fe Depot in San Diego. They serve points from Del Mar North to San Clemente, inland to Fallbrook, Pauma Valley, Valley Center, Ramona, and Escondido, with transfer points within the city of San Diego. NCTD also offers special express-bus service to Qualcomm Stadium for select major sporting events. The Sprinter light rail provides service between Oceanside and Escondido, with buses connecting to popular North County attractions.

San Diego Transit bus fares range from $2.25 to $5; North County Transit District bus fares are $4. You must have exact change in coins and/or bills. Pay upon boarding. Transfers are not included; the $5 day pass is the best option for most bus travel and can be purchased on board.

San Diego Trolley tickets cost $2.50 and are good for two hours, but for one-way travel only. Round-trip tickets are double the one-way fare.

Tickets are dispensed from self-service machines at each stop; exact fare in coins is recommended, although some machines accept bills in $1, $5, $10, and $20 denominations and credit cards. For trips on multiple buses and trolleys, buy a day pass good for unlimited use all day.

Bus and Trolley Information North County Transit District ☎ *760/966–6500* ⊕ *www. gonctd.com.* **San Diego Transit** ☎ *619/233– 3004* ⊕ *transit.511sd.com.* **Transit Store** ⊠ *102 Broadway* ☎ *619/234–1060* ⊕ *www. sdmts.com.*

▌ CAR TRAVEL

A car is necessary for getting around greater San Diego on the sprawling freeway system and for visiting the North County beaches, mountains, and Anza Borrego Desert. Driving around San Diego County is pretty simple: most major attractions are within a few miles of the Pacific Ocean. Interstate 5, which stretches from Canada to the Mexican border, bisects San Diego. Interstate 8 provides access from Yuma, Arizona, and points east. Drivers coming from the Los Angeles area, Nevada, and the mountain regions beyond can reach San Diego on I–15. During rush hours there are jams on I–5 and on I–15 between I–805 and Escondido.

There are border inspection stations along major highways in San Diego County. Travel with your driver's license, and passport if you're an international traveler, in case you're asked to pull into one.

Gas is widely available in San Diego County, except in rural areas. Outlets are generally open 24 hours and accept major credit cards that can be processed at the pump. Full service is not generally available, but you will usually find window-washing tools next to a pump; water and air are available somewhere on the property. All fuel in California is unleaded and sold at three price levels. Pricing is per gallon pumped and varies widely by season, location, and oil company provider. In San Diego gas tends to cost about 15% more than it does in many other California cities.

■TIP➔ Many Costco outlets sell gas to members at prices up to 20% less than the going rate.

PARKING

Meters downtown usually cost 50¢ to $1.25 an hour; enforcement is 8–6 every day but Sunday. ■TIP➔ If you are headed to Horton Plaza, the mall validates for three hours with no purchase required. Be extra careful around rush hour, when certain on-street parking areas become tow-away zones. Violations in congested areas can cost you $25 or more. In the evening and during events downtown, parking spaces are hard to find. Most downtown hotels offer valet parking service. The Convention Center has nearly 2,000 spaces that go for $15 to $25 for event parking. On game day at PETCO Park, expect to pay $17 or more for a parking space a short walk from the stadium, less for a space farther away. Other downtown lots cost $5–$35 per day.

Balboa Park and Mission Bay have huge free parking lots, and it's rare not to find a space, though it may seem as if you've parked miles from your destination. Old Town has large lots surrounding the transit center, but parking spaces are still hard to find. Parking is more of a problem in La Jolla and Coronado, where you generally need to rely on hard-to-find metered street spots or expensive by-the-hour parking lots.

ROAD CONDITIONS

Highways are generally in good condition in the San Diego area. From 6 to 8:30 am and 3:30 to 6 pm, traffic is particularly heavy on I–5, I–8, I–805, and I–15. Before venturing into the mountains, check on road conditions; mountain driving can be dangerous. Listen to radio traffic reports for information on the length of lines waiting to cross the border from Mexico. For roadside assistance, dial 511 from a mobile phone.

RENTAL CARS

In California you must be 21 to rent a car, and rates may be higher if you're under 25. Some agencies will not rent to those under 25; check when you book. Children up to age six or 60 pounds must be placed in safety or booster seats. For non–U.S. residents an international license is recommended but not required.

Rates fluctuate with seasons and demand, but generally begin at $39 a day and $250 a week for an economy car with air-conditioning, automatic transmission, and unlimited mileage. This doesn't include an 8.75% tax.

▮ TAXI TRAVEL

Fares vary among companies. If you are heading to the airport from a hotel, ask about the flat rate, which varies according to destination; otherwise you'll be charged by the mile (which works out to $15 or so from any downtown location). Taxi stands are at shopping centers and hotels; otherwise you must call and reserve a cab. The companies listed *below* don't serve all areas of San Diego County. If you're going somewhere other than downtown, ask if the company serves that area.

Taxi Companies Orange Cab ☎ *619/223-5555* ⊕ *www.orangecabsandiego.com.* **Silver Cabs** ☎ *619/280-5555* ⊕ *www.sandiegosilvercab.com.* **Yellow Cab** ☎ *619/444-4444* ⊕ *www.driveu.com.*

▌ TRAIN TRAVEL

Amtrak serves downtown San Diego's Santa Fe Depot with daily trains to and from Los Angeles, Santa Barbara, and San Luis Obispo. Connecting service to Oakland, Seattle, Chicago, Texas, Florida, and points beyond is available in Los Angeles. Amtrak trains stop in San Diego North County at Solana Beach and Oceanside. You can obtain Amtrak timetables at any Amtrak station, or by visiting the Amtrak website.

Coaster commuter trains, which run between Oceanside and San Diego Monday–Saturday, stop at the same stations as Amtrak as well as others. The frequency is about every half hour during the weekday rush hour, with four trains on Saturday (with additional Friday and Saturday night service in spring and summer). One-way fares are $4 to $5.50, depending on the distance traveled. The Oceanside, Carlsbad, and Solana Beach stations have beach access. The Sprinter runs between Oceanside and Escondido, with many stops along the way.

Metrolink operates high-speed rail service ($28) between the Oceanside Transit Center and Union Station in Los Angeles.

Amtrak and the Coaster vending machines accept all major credit cards. Metrolink requires cash. Many Amtrak trains require advance reservations, especially for long-distance routes. Reservations, which you can make online, are suggested for trains running on weekends between San Diego and Santa Barbara. For security reasons, Amtrak requires ticket holders to provide photo ID.

Information Amtrak ☎ *800/872–7245* ⊕ *www.amtrak.com.* **Coaster** ☎ *760/966–6500* ⊕ *www.gonctd.com/coaster.* **Metrolink** ☎ *800/371–5465* ⊕ *www.metrolinktrains.com.*

ESSENTIALS

▍ CUSTOMS AND DUTIES

Customs officers operate at the San Ysidro border crossing, at San Diego International Airport, and in the bay at Shelter Island.

You're always allowed to bring goods of a certain value back home without having to pay any duty or import tax. But there's a limit on the amount of tobacco and liquor you can bring back duty-free. If the total value of your goods is more than the duty-free limit, you'll have to pay a tax (most often a flat percentage) on the value of everything beyond that limit.

U.S. Information U.S. Customs and Border Protection ⊕ *www.cbp.gov.*

▍ MONEY

With the mild climate and proximity to the ocean and mountains, San Diego is popular with tourists and conventioneers and, accordingly, is a relatively expensive place to visit. Three-star rooms average between $200 and $280 per night in high season, but there is also a good variety of modest accommodations available. Meal prices compare to those in other large cities, and you can usually find excellent values by dining in smaller, family-run establishments. Admission to local attractions can cost anywhere from $10 to $70. Thankfully, relaxing on one of the public beaches or meandering through the parks and neighborhoods is free—and fun. ■TIP→ To save money on restaurants, spas, and boutiques, scour the coupon section at www.sdreader.com.

Prices here are given for adults. Substantially reduced fees are almost always available for children, students, and senior citizens. Many museums offer free admission one day of the month.

ITEM	AVERAGE COST
Cup of Coffee	$2
Glass of Wine	$11
Sandwich	$9
One-Mile Taxi Ride	$2.4
Museum Admission	$16

▍ PACKING

San Diego's casual lifestyle and year-round mild climate set the parameters for what to pack. You can leave formal clothes and cold-weather gear behind.

Plan on warm weather at any time of the year. Cottons, walking shorts, jeans, and T-shirts are the norm. Pack bathing suits and shorts regardless of the season. Few restaurants require a jacket and tie for men. Women may want to also bring something a little dressier than their sightseeing garb.

Evenings are cool, even in summer, so be sure to bring a sweater or a light jacket. Rainfall in San Diego isn't usually heavy; you won't need a raincoat except in winter, and even then, an umbrella may suffice.

Be sure you have comfortable walking shoes. Even if you don't walk much at home, you will probably find yourself covering miles while sightseeing on your vacation. Also bring a pair of sandals or water shoes for the beach.

Sunglasses and sunscreen are a must in San Diego. Binoculars can also come in handy, especially if you're in town during whale-watching season, from December through March, or planning to stargaze in the desert in the summer.

▪ RESTROOMS

Major attractions and parks have public restrooms. In the downtown San Diego area, you can usually use the restrooms at major hotels and fast-food restaurants. The Bathroom Diaries is a website that's flush with unsanitized information on restrooms the world over—each one located, reviewed, and rated.

Find a Loo The Bathroom Diaries ⊕ *www. thebathroomdiaries.com.*

TIPPING GUIDELINES FOR SAN DIEGO	
Bartender	$1 to $5 per round of drinks, depending on the number of drinks
Bellhop	$1 to $5 per bag, depending on the level of the hotel
Hotel Concierge	$5 or more, if he or she performs a service for you
Hotel Doorman	$1–$2 if he helps you get a cab
Hotel Maid	$1 to $3 a day (either daily or at the end of your stay, in cash)
Hotel Room-Service Waiter	$1–$2 per delivery, even if a service charge has been added
Porter at Airport or Train Station	$1 per bag
Skycap at Airport	$1 to $3 per bag checked
Taxi Driver	15%–20%, but round up the fare to the next dollar amount
Tour Guide	10% of the cost of the tour
Valet Parking Attendant	$1–$2, but only when you get your car
Waiter	15%–20%, with 20% being the norm at high-end restaurants; nothing additional if a service charge is added to the bill

▪ SAFETY

San Diego is generally a safe place for travelers who observe all normal precautions. Dress inconspicuously (this means removing badges when leaving convention areas) and know the routes to your destination before you set out. At the beach, check with lifeguards about any unsafe conditions such as dangerous riptides or water pollution. The San Diego Tourism Authority offers a print and web version of Visitor Safety Tips, providing sensible precautions for many situations, *see Visitor Information.*

▪ TOURS

BIKE TOURS

Biking is very popular in San Diego. You can find trails along the beach, in Mission Bay, and throughout the mountains. Pedal your way around San Diego with the Bike Revolution, which delivers bikes. Secret San Diego, by Where You Want To Be Tours, offers walking tours as well as tours on bike and Segway.

Contacts Secret San Diego. Taking in spectacular views of the beach, bay, and skyline, these bike rides, offered by Where You Want to Be Tours, cover everything from historic neighborhoods to historic Highway 101. The walking tours and Rent-a-Local custom tours are popular options as well. ⊠ *611 K St., #B224* ☎ *619/917–6037* ⊕ *www. wheretours.com* ⊠ *From $45.*

BOAT TOURS

Flagship Cruises and Events and Hornblower Cruises & Events both operate one- and two-hour harbor cruises departing from the Broadway Pier. No reservations are necessary for the tours, which cost $24–$31.04; both companies also do dinner cruises ($76.95) and brunch cruises. These companies also operate during whale-watching season, from December to March. Fishing boats that also do whale watches in season include H&M Landing and Seaforth Boat Rentals.

Contacts Flagship Cruises and Events. One- and two-hour tours of the San Diego harbor loop north or south from the Broadway Pier throughout the day. Other offerings include dinner and dance cruises, brunch cruises, and winter whale-watching tours. ✉ *990 N. Harbor Dr., Embarcadero* ☎ *619/234–4111* ⊕ *www. flagshipsd.com* 🚢 *From $23.* **H&M Landing.** From mid-December to March, this outfitter offers three-hour tours to spot migrating gray whales just off the San Diego coast. From June to October, six-hour cruises search for the gigantic blue whales that visit the California coast in summer. Winter gray whale cruises are offered daily; summer blue whale tours are available Thursday, Saturday, and Sunday. ✉ *2803 Emerson St.* ☎ *619/222–1144* ⊕ *www. hmlanding.com* 🚢 *From $45.* **Hornblower Cruises & Events.** One- and two-hour cruises around San Diego harbor depart from the Embarcadero several times a day and alternate between the northern and southern portion of the bay. If you're hoping to spot some sea lions, take the North Bay route. Dinner and brunch cruises are also offered, as well as whale-watching tours in winter. ✉ *970 N. Harbor Dr.* ☎ *619/234–8687, 800/668–4322* ⊕ *www.hornblower.com* 🚢 *From $23.* **San Diego Seal Tours.** This amphibious tour drives along the Embarcadero before splashing into the San Diego Harbor for a cruise. The 90-minute tours depart from Seaport Village year-round, and from outside the Maritime Museum seasonally. Call for daily departure times and locations. ✉ *500 Kettner Blvd., Embarcadero* ☎ *619/298–8687* ⊕ *www. sealtours.com* 🚢 *$39.* **Seaforth Boat Rentals.** For those seeking a private tour on the water, this company can provide a skipper along with your boat rental. Options include harbor cruises, whale-watching, and sunset sails. Seaforth has five locations and a diverse fleet of sail and motorboats to choose from. ✉ *1641 Quivira Rd., Mission Bay* ☎ *888/834–2628* ⊕ *www.seaforthboatrental.com* 🚢 *From $225.*

BUS AND TROLLEY TOURS

Old Town Trolley Tours takes you to 11 sites, including Old Town, Seaport Village, Horton Plaza and the Gaslamp Quarter, Coronado, Little Italy, and El Prado in Balboa Park. The tour is narrated, and for the price of the ticket ($35.10 for adults, $17.10 for children 4–12; under 4, free) you can get on and off as you please at any stop. The trolley leaves every 30 minutes, operates daily, and takes two hours to make a full loop.

DayTripper, San Diego Scenic Tours, and Five Star Tours do one-day or multiple-day bus tours of attractions in Southern California.

DayTripper. Single- and multiday trips throughout Southern California, the Southwest, and Baja depart from San Diego year-round. Popular day trips include the Getty Museum, and theater performances in Los Angeles. Call or check website for pickup locations. ☎ *619/299–5777, 800/679–8747* ⊕ *www. daytripper.com* 🚢 *From $75.*

Five Star Tours. Private and group sightseeing bus tour options around San Diego and beyond include everything from the San Diego Zoo to Brewery tours and trips to Baja, Mexico. ✉ *1050 Kettner Blvd.* ☎ *619/232–5040* ⊕ *www.fivestartours. com* 🚢 *From $48.*

Old Town Trolley Tours. Combining points of interest with local history, trivia, and fun anecdotes, this hop-on, hop-off trolley tour provides an entertaining overview of the city and offers easy access to all the highlights. The tour is narrated, and you can get on and off as you please. Stops include Old Town, Seaport Village, the Gaslamp Quarter, Coronado, Little Italy, and Balboa Park. The trolley leaves every 30 minutes, operates daily, and takes two hours to make a full loop. ☎ *619/298– 8687* ⊕ *www.trolleytours.com/san-diego* 🚢 *From $35.10.*

San Diego Scenic Tours. Half- and full-day bus tours of San Diego and Tijuana depart daily, and some include a harbor cruise. Tours depart from several hotels around town. ☎ *858/273–8687* ⊕ *www. sandiegoscenictours.com* 🚢 *From $38.*

GO CAR TOURS

These miniature talking cars offer the benefits of a guided tour, but taken at your own pace. Tour the city in a bright yellow three-seater, equipped with GPS navigation and accompanying narration. Go Cars Tours offers two routes: choose from Downtown, Balboa Park, Uptown, and Old Town or Point Loma, Cabrillo National Monument, and Ocean Beach. The tours can be driven straight through, or visitors can park and explore any of the sights en-route. Rentals are $54 for the first hour, $200 for five hours for two. There is a maximum daily charge of five hours if you want to keep the car for the entire day.

Contacts Go Car Tours ⊠ *2100 Kettner Blvd.* ☎ *800/914–6227* ⊕ *www.gocartours.com.*

WALKING TOURS

Several fine walking tours are available on weekdays or weekends; upcoming walks are usually listed in the *San Diego Reader.*

Coronado Walking Tours offers an easy 90-minute stroll ($12; Tuesday, Thursday, Saturday at 11 am) through Coronado's historic district, with departures from the Glorietta Bay Inn. Make reservations.

On Saturday at 10 am and 11:30 am, Offshoot Tours conducts free, hour-long walks starting at the Visitor Center through Balboa Park that focus on history, palm trees, and desert vegetation.

Urban Safaris, led by longtime San Diego resident Patty Fares, are two-hour-long Saturday walks ($10) through interesting neighborhoods such as Hillcrest, Ocean Beach, and Point Loma. The tours, which always depart from a neighborhood coffeehouse, focus on art, history, and ethnic eateries. Reservations are required.

The Gaslamp Quarter Historical Foundation leads two-hour historical walking tours of the downtown historic district from the William Heath Davis House on Saturday at 11 am ($15).

Balboa Park Offshoot Tours. On Saturday at 10 am, free, hour-long walks start from

the Balboa Park Visitor Center. The tour's focus rotates weekly, covering topics such as the park's history, palm trees, and desert vegetation. Reservations are not required, but no tours are scheduled between Thanksgiving and the New Year. ⊠ *1549 El Prado, Balboa Park* ☎ *619/239–0512* ⊕ *www.balboapark.org* ⊠ *Free.*

Coronado Walking Tours. Departing from the Glorietta Bay Inn at 11 am Tuesday, Thursday, and Saturday, this 90-minute stroll through Coronado's historic district takes in the island's mansions, old Tent City, the Hotel del Coronado, and the castles and cottages that line the beautiful beach. Reservations are recommended. ⊠ *1630 Glorietta Blvd.* ☎ *619/435–5993* ⊕ *coronadowalkingtour.com* ⊠ *$12.*

Gaslamp Quarter Historical Foundation. Two-hour walking tours of the downtown historic district depart from the William Heath Davis House at 11 am Tuesday, Thursday, and Saturday. ⊠ *410 Island Ave.* ☎ *619/233–4692* ⊕ *www. gaslampquarter.org* ⊠ *$15.*

Urban Safaris. Led by longtime San Diego resident Patty Fares, these two-hour Saturday walks through diverse neighborhoods like Hillcrest, Ocean Beach, and Point Loma are popular with tourists and locals alike. The tours, which always depart from a neighborhood coffeehouse, focus on art, history, and ethnic eateries, among other topics. Reservations are required, and private walks can be arranged during the week. ☎ *619/944–9255* ⊕ *www. walkingtoursofsandiego.com* ⊠ *$10.*

VISITOR INFORMATION

For general information and brochures before you go, contact the San Diego Tourism Authority, which publishes the helpful *San Diego Visitors Planning Guide.* When you arrive, stop by one of the local visitor centers for general information.

Citywide Contacts San Diego Tourism Authority ☎ 619/232-3101 ⊕ www.sandiego. org. San Diego Tourism Authority International Visitor Information Center ✉ 1140 N. Harbor Dr., Downtown ☎ 619/236-1212 ⊕ www.sandiego.org.

San Diego County Contacts Borrego Springs Chamber of Commerce and Visitor Center ☎ 760/767-5555 ⊕ www. borregospringschamber.org. The California Welcome Center Alpine ☎ 619/445-0180 ⊕ www.visitcwc.com. California Welcome Center Oceanside ✉ 928 N. Coast Hwy., Oceanside ☎ 760/721-1101, 800/350-7873 ⊕ www.visitcwc.com/oceanside. Carlsbad Convention & Visitors Bureau ✉ 400 Carlsbad Village Dr., Carlsbad ☎ 800/227-5722 ⊕ www.visitcarlsbad.com. Coronado Visitor Center ✉ 1100 Orange Ave., Coronado ☎ 619/435-7242 ⊕ www. coronadovisitorcenter.com. Encinitas Chamber of Commerce ✉ 527 Encinitas Blvd., Suite 116, Encinitas ☎ 760/753-6041 ⊕ www. encinitaschamber.com. Julian Chamber of Commerce ☎ 760/765-1857 ⊕ www.julianca. com.

Statewide Contacts California Travel and Tourism Commission ☎ 916/444-4429, 877/225-4367 ⊕ www.visitcalifornia.com.

INSPIRATION

Check out these books for further San Diego reading. The novel *Drift* by Jim Miller explores San Diego's boom time through the eyes of a college professor in the year 2000. *Leave Only Paw Prints: Dog Hikes in San Diego* offers myriad walking spots that are dog-friendly, along with smart travel tips for your furry friend. *San Diego Legends: Events, People and Places That Made History* goes beyond the typical history-book material to reveal little-known stories about San Diego.

San Diego has a rich film history, thanks to the city's unique geography and proximity to Los Angeles. Some of the better-known films made here include *Some Like it Hot, Top Gun, Traffic,* and *Almost Famous.* The bar scene in *Top Gun* was filmed at a local restaurant, Kansas City BBQ, on the corner of Kettner Boulevard and West Harbor Drive. And, of course, don't forget to take *Anchorman* Ron Burgundy's advice, and "Stay classy, San Diego."

ONLINE RESOURCES

For a dining and entertainment guide to San Diego's most popular nightlife district, check out Gaslamp.org. Visit the HillQuest.com guide to Hillcrest, a historic neighborhood with a large number of gay and lesbian households. For insider tips from a local perspective, try Local Wally's San Diego Tourist Guide. For information on the birthplace of California, search the Old Town San Diego organization's site. Browse the website of San Diego's premier upscale lifestyle magazine, *Ranch and Coast. San Diego magazine* also has a useful site. Search the site of Arts Tix for half-price show tickets. For a comprehensive listing of concerts, performances, and art exhibits, check out the local alternative paper *San Diego Reader.* For edgier arts and culture listings, pick up the *San Diego Citybeat* alt-weekly.

Websites Gaslamp Info ⊕ www.gaslamp. org. Hillcrest ⊕ www.hillquest.com. Local Wally ⊕ www.localwally.com. Old Town San Diego ⊕ www.oldtownsandiego.org. Ranch and Coast Magazine ⊕ www.ranchandcoast. com. San Diego Citybeat Newspaper ⊕ www. sdcitybeat.com. San Diego Magazine ⊕ www. sandiegomagazine.com. San Diego Reader Newspaper ⊕ www.sdreader.com. San Diego Union-Tribune ⊕ www.signonsandiego.com.

Half Price Tickets ⊕ sdartstix.com.

INDEX

A

A. R. Valentien ✕, *136*
Accommodations, *7, 162–178*
apartment rentals, 174
Balboa Park and Bankers Hill, 169
beaches, 163, 172, 217
bed and breakfasts, 174
best bets, 164
Borrego Springs, 328
Carlsbad, 297–298
children, 165, 167, 169, 170, 171, 172, 175, 176–177, 178
Del Mar, 287–287
Downtown San Diego, 163, 166–169
Encinitas, 292
Escondido, 307
Fallbrook, 309
Fodor's choice, 164
Julian, 321
La Jolla, 163, 172–173, 175
Mission Bay and Seaworld, 163, 171–173, 175
North Country and environs, 281–282, 286–287, 290, 292, 297–298, 300–301, 303, 307, 309, 313–314, 321, 328
Old Town, Mission Valley, and North Park, 163, 171–172
neighborhoods, 163
Oceanside, 300–301
parking, 165
Point Loma and Coronado with Harbor and Shelter Islands, 163, 175–178
price categories, 165, 282
Rancho Bernardo, 303
Rancho Santa Fe, 290
reservations, 165
services, 165
Temecula, 313–314
Uptown, 163
Achiote ✕, *126*
Adams Avenue Roots Unplugged (festival), *17*
Adams Avenue Street Fair, *17*
Addison ✕, *285*
Air travel, *332–333*
Airports, *332*
Alcazar Garden, *49, 50, 52*
Aloha Sunday Supply Co., *267*
AleSmith Brewing Co., *191*
Alpine Brewing Co., *191*
Amici Park, *28*

Amusement Parks
Belmont Park, 85, 86, 88
Legoland California Resort, 19, 294–295
SeaWorld San Diego, 19, 81, 82–83, 84, 85
Wave Waterpark, 300
Andaz San Diego 🏠, *166*
Anza-Borrego Desert State Park, *21, 244–245, 324–326*
Apartment rentals, *174*
Aquariums
Carlsbad, 296
La Jolla, 92–93
SeaWorld San Diego, 19, 81, 82–83, 84, 85
AquaTerra ✕, *309*
Arches, The ✕, *327*
Argyle Steakhouse ✕, *296*
Arrowood Golf Course, *237*
Arts, *200–208*
ArtWalk (festival), *17*
Azucar ✕, *147*

B

B Street Pier, *36*
Bahia Belle (stern-wheeler), *84–85, 195*
Baily's ✕, *313*
Baily's Front Street Bar & Grill ✕, *313*
Baja Betty's (gay club), *190, 192*
Balboa Park, *12, 18, 44–64*
accommodations, 169
children's activities, 50, 52, 54, 55–61, 62, 63, 64
nightlife, 189
restaurants, 45, 123
shopping, 51, 263
Balboa Park December Nights (festival), *17*
Balboa Park Inn 🏠, *171*
Balboa Theatre, *28, 35, 204*
Bali Hai ✕, *148*
Ballast Point Brewing Co., *191*
Ballet, *20, 202–203*
Ballooning, *20, 232, 314*
Bankers Hill
accommodations, 169
nightlife, 189
restaurants, 123–125
Bankers Hill ✕, *123*
Banner Queen Trading Post Gallery, *319*

Bar and Grill at the Wave House ✕, *81*
Barbarella ✕, *136–137*
Barona Creek Golf Course, *239–240*
Barona Valley Ranch Resort and Casino, *316*
Barrio Logan, *41*
Barrio Star ✕, *124*
Bars and pubs
Balboa Park and Bankers Hill, 189
Downtown, 183–185, 187, 188–189
La Jolla and Kearney Mesa, 196–197
Mission Bay and the beaches, 195, 196
Old Town and Uptown, 190, 192, 193, 194–195
Point Loma, Ocean Beach, and Coronado, 197, 198
Baseball, *40–41, 253–254*
Batiquitos Lagoon, *293–294*
Bay Books, *106*
Bayside Trail, *101, 241, 244*
Bazaar del Mundo Shops, *264*
Bea Evenson Fountain, *49, 52*
Beaches, *12, 18, 210–226*
accommodations, 163, 171, 172, 217
Black's Beach, 212
Cardiff-by-the-Sea, 225
Carlsbad, 226
Coronado, 99, 219
Del Mar, 224
Encinitas, 225–226
for children, 218–219, 220, 221–222, 224
La Jolla, 91, 93, 99, 221–223
Mission Bay, 81, 84–88, 220–221
nightlife, 195–196
North County and environs, 224–226
Oceanside, 226, 306–307
Point Loma, 102, 104, 219–220
restaurants, 211
shopping, 268–269
Ski Beach, 86
Solana Beach, 224, 287–289
South Bay, 218–219
Vacation Isle, 85–86
Bed and breakfasts, *174*
Belmont Park, *85, 86, 88*

Bencotto ✕, 118–119
Bernard'O ✕, 301–302
Bernini's Bistro ✕, 137
Bertrand at Mister A's ✕, 124
Best Western Plus Hacienda Hotel-Old Town 🏠, 170
Best Western Plus Island Palms Hotel & Marina 🏠, 176–177
BiCE Ristorante ✕, 111, 114
Bicycling, 105, 231, 232–234
tours, 233–234, 338
Birch Aquarium at Scripps, 92–93
Bistro Bijou ✕, 137
Bistro West ✕, 296
Black's Beach, 212
Blind Burro, The ✕, 117
Blind Lady Ale House, 193
Blue Water Seafood Market & Grill ✕, 125
BlueFire Grill ✕, 296–297
Boat and ferry travel, 106, 333
Boat tours, 338–339
night bay cruises, 188, 195
Boating, 249–250
BO-Beau kitchen + bar ✕, 143
BO-Beau kitchen + garden ✕, 144
Border Field State Park, 218
Borrego Springs, 327–329
Borrego Springs Resort and Country Club, 329
Borrego Springs Resort and Spa 🏠, 328
Borrego Valley Inn 🏠, 328
Botanical Building, 49, 50, 52
Brandon Gallery, 308
Bread & Cie Café ✕, 67, 127–128
Breweries and brewpubs, 191
Downtown, 188
Mission Bay and the beaches, 196
North County and environs, 307–308
Old Town and Uptown, 193, 194
Bristol, The 🏠, 166
Broadway Pier, 36
Brockton Villa ✕, 137
Brooklyn Girl ✕, 128
Brothers Bistro ✕, 309
Bubby's Gelato ✕, 291
Buon Appetito ✕, 119
Buona Forchetta ✕, 132
Burger Lounge ✕, 126

Bus travel, 334
North County and environs, 280–281
tours, 339
Butterfield Bed and Breakfast 🏠, 321

C

Cabarets, 185, 197
Cabrillo Bridge, 49, 50, 52
Cabrillo National Monument, 18, 100–101
Café Champagne ✕, 313
Café Chloe ✕, 117
Cafe 1134 ✕, 99
California Ballet Company, 202
California Center for the Arts, 303–304
California Department of Fish and Game, 234
California Surf Museum, 299
California Wolf Center, 318
Camp Pendleton, 299
Car rentals, 335
Car travel, 17, 334–335
Desert area, 324
North County and environs, 282
tours, 103
Cardiff-by-the-Sea, 225
Cardiff State Beach, 225
Carlee's Bar & Grill ✕, 328
Carlsbad, 226, 269, 292–298
Carlsbad Flower Fields, 18, 294
Carlsbad Inn Beach Resort 🏠, 297
Carlsbad Mineral Water Spa, 294
Carlsbad Premium Outlets, 298
Carlsbad State Beach, 226
Carlton Oaks Lodge and Country Club, 240
Carmelita's Mexican Grill and Cantina ✕, 328
Carnitas' Snack Shack ✕, 132
Carousels, 39, 49, 50, 52
Casa de Estudillo, 70
Casa del Zoro 🏠, 328
Casinos, 309, 316
Catamaran Resort Hotel 🏠, 172
Cedros Avenue Farmers' Market, 30
Chez Loma ✕, 149–150
Chicano Park, 41
Children's activities, 26
accommodations, 165, 167, 169, 170, 171, 172, 175, 176–177, 178

Balboa Park, 50, 52, 54, 55–61, 62, 63, 64
beaches, 218–219, 220, 221–222, 224
Carlsbad, 294–295, 296, 297–298
Coronado, 105
Cuyamaca Mountains, 315, 317
Del Mar, 284–285, 286
Downtown San Diego, 37, 39, 41, 42
Encinitas, 291, 292
Escondido, 303–305, 306–307, 308
Julian, 318, 319, 320–321
La Jolla, 92–93
Mission Bay, 85–86, 88
North Coast, 284–285, 286, 287, 288, 290, 291, 292, 294–295, 296, 297–298, 299–300, 301
North Country and environs, 284–285, 286, 287, 288, 290, 291, 292, 294–295, 296, 297–298, 299–300, 301, 302, 303–304, 305–307, 311, 313, 315, 317, 318, 319–320, 322–323, 328
Oceanside, 299–300, 301
Old Town, 69, 70, 73
Palomar Mountain, 322–323
Point Loma, 102, 105
restaurants, 110, 113, 117, 125, 128, 129–130, 131, 132, 133, 134–135, 139–140, 145–146, 147, 148
SeaWorld San Diego, 19, 81, 82–83, 84, 85
shopping, 257, 267, 274
Temecula, 311, 313
Children's Pool, 213, 221–222
China Max ✕, 142
Chin's Szechwan Cuisine ✕, 302
Clairemont, 96, 141
Climate, 16, 230–231
Coast Highway 101, 213
Cody's La Jolla ✕, 137
Coffeehouses
Downtown, 185, 189
La Jolla and Kearney Mesa, 197
Mission Bay and the beaches, 196
Old Town and Uptown, 190, 192, 194, 195
Point Loma, Ocean Beach, and Coronado, 198
Comedy and cabaret, 185, 197

Con Pane Rustic Breads & Cafe ✕, 144
Copley Symphony Hall, 204
Coronado, 14, 105–106
accommodations, 163, 177–178
beaches, 219
children's activities, 105, 219
restaurants, 99, 149–150
shopping, 274–276
Coronado Beach, 219
Coronado Farmers' Market, 30
Coronado Ferry Landing, 105, 106, 274
Coronado Island Marriott Resort ☂, 177
Coronado Municipal Golf Course, 237
Cosmopolitan Hotel, The ☂, 170
Cosmopolitan Hotel and Restaurant, 70
Costs, 7, 337
Courtyard by Marriott Mission Valley ☂, 170
Courtyard by Marriott San Diego Airport ☂, 176
Cowboy Star ✕, 117–118
Craft & Commerce ✕, 119
Credit cards, 7
Croce's Park West ✕, 124
Crown Barber Shop, 106
Crown City Inn & Bistro ☂, 177
Crowne Plaza San Diego ☂, 171
Cruise travel, 333
night bay cruises, 188, 195
whale-watching, 100, 252
Crystal Pier, 85, 88
Crystal Pier Hotel and Cottages ☂, 172
Cucina Urbana ✕, 124–125
Customs and duties, 337
Cuyamaca Mountains, 315, 317
Cuyamaca Rancho State Park, 315

D

Dae Jang Keum Korean BBQ ✕, 142
Daley Ranch, 304
Dana on Mission Bay, The ☂, 171
Dance, 20, 37, 202–203
Dance clubs, 186, 194
Davanti Enoteca Little Italy ✕, 119
Del Mar, 224, 269–273

Del Mar Beach, 224
Del Mar Fairgrounds, 17, 284
Del Mar Plaza, 284
Del Mar Thoroughbred Club, 254, 284
Desert, 278, 323–328
Desert Garden, 49, 51
Dining. ⇨ See Restaurants
Discounts and deals, 82
Diving and snorkeling, 213, 234–235
Don Chuy ✕, 287
Doubletree Hotel San Diego Mission Valley ☂, 170
Downtown San Diego, 12, 32–42
accommodations, 163, 166–169
children's activities, 37, 39, 41, 42
nightlife, 183–189
restaurants, 33, 111, 114, 116–122
shopping, 259–263
Dress code, 110, 182
Dumpling Inn ✕, 142
Duties, 337

E

Eagle Mining Company, 319
East Village, 40–41
accommodations, 168–169
restaurants, 117–118
Eddie V's Prime Seafood ✕, 121
El Campo Santo cemetery, 72
El Pescador Fish Market ✕, 138
El Zarape ✕, 131
Embarcadero, 17, 36–40
accommodations, 169
restaurants, 121–122
Embarcadero Marina Park North, 36
Embarcadero Marina Park South, 36
Embassy Suites-San Diego Bay ☂, 169
Empress Hotel ☂, 173
Encinitas, 225–226, 290–292
Escondido, 303–308
Escondido Arts Partnership Municipal Gallery, 305
Escondido History Center, 305
Estancia La Jolla Hotel & Spa ☂, 173
Europa Village, 311
Extraordinary Desserts (coffeehouse), 190

F

Fallbrook, 308–309
Fallbrook Art Center, 308
Fallbrook Winery, 308–309
Farmers Insurance Open, 17, 254
Farmer's Market, 30
Fashion Valley, 21, 266–267
Feed Store-Antiques and Such at the Santa Ysabel Store, The, 318
Festivals and seasonal events, 17, 20, 191, 254
North Country and environs, 20, 314
Old Town and Uptown, 67, 191
Field, The ✕, 114
Fiesta de Reyes, 21, 67, 69
Fiesta Island, 86
1500 Ocean ✕, 149
Film, 203
Firehouse Museum, 42
Fish Market, The ✕, 287
Fish tacos, 21
Fishing, 234, 235–236
500 West ☂, 166
Fletcher Cove, 224
Florida Canyon, 50
Flower Fields at Carlsbad Ranch, 18, 294
Flowers, 325, 326
Fodor's choice, 7
accommodations, 164
restaurants, 112
Fogo de Chao ✕, 114
Football, 254
Fort Rosecrans National Cemetery, 102–103
Fossils, 327
Free activities, 27, 48
Freeflight, 284–285
French Market Grille ✕, 302
Frisbee golf, 236

G

Galleries, 203–204, 305, 308, 319, 322
Gallery nights, 201–202
Galleta Meadows, 327
Gaslamp Museum at the William Heath Davis House, 35–36
Gaslamp Plaza Suites ☂, 166
Gaslamp Quarter, 34–36
accommodations, 166–168
restaurants, 111, 114, 116–117

Gay and lesbian nightlife, *190, 192, 194*
Geisel Library, *93, 96*
George's at the Cove ✕, *91, 138*
Glorietta Bay Inn ☑, *177–178*
Go car tours, *32, 340*
Goldfish Point Cafe ✕, *91*
Golf, *17, 20, 71, 231, 236–241, 254, 308*
Borrego Springs, 329
Old Town, 71
Grand Del Mar, The ☑, *286*
Grand Pacific Palisades Resort & Hotel ☑, *297*
Grande Colonial ☑, *173*
Grunion, *143*

H

Hamilton's Tavern, *193*
Hane Sushi ✕, *125*
Hang gliding, *241*
Harbor Fish & Chips ✕, *300*
Harbor Island, *14, 104–105*
accommodations, 163, 177
restaurants, 148–149
Hard Rock Cafe ✕, *34–35*
Hard Rock Hotel ☑, *166–167*
Harney Sushi ✕, *126, 127*
Harrah's Rincon Casino & Resort, *316*
Hart Family Winery, *311–312*
Hash House A Go Go ✕, *128*
Headquarters at Seaport District, *262–263*
Heritage Park, *69–70*
Hike Bike Kayak San Diego, *248*
Hiking and nature trails, *241, 244–245*
Hillcrest, *72, 75*
restaurants, 127–130
Hillcrest Farmers Market, *30, 73*
Hilton Carlsbad Oceanfront Resort & Spa ☑, *297*
Hilton La Jolla Torrey Pines ☑, *173*
Hilton San Diego Bayfront ☑, *167*
Hilton San Diego Gaslamp Quarter ☑, *167*
History, *28–29, 320*
Hodad's ✕, *126, 147*
Holiday Bowl, *254*
Holiday Inn Bayside ☑, *176*
Holiday Inn Express-Old Town ☑, *170*

Holiday Inn Express-SeaWorld Area ☑, *176*
Homewood Suites San Diego Airport ☑, *176*
Horse racing, *254, 284*
Horseback riding, *231, 245–246*
Hospitality Point, *85, 86*
Hotel Del Coronado ☑, *21, 105–106, 178, 274*
Hotel Indigo ☑, *168*
Hotel La Jolla ☑, *173*
Hotel Palomar San Diego ☑, *167*
Hotel Solamar ☑, *167*
Hotel Vyvant ☑, *169*
Hotels. ⇨ *See* Accommodations
House of Charm, *49*
House of Hospitality, *45, 49, 52*
House of Pacific Relations, *52, 63*
Humphrey's Half Moon Inn & Suites ☑, *177*
Humphreys Restaurant ✕, *148*
Hyatt Regency La Jolla ☑, *173*
Hyatt Regency Mission Bay Spa & Marina ☑, *171*

I

Imperial Beach, *178, 218–219*
Indigo Grill ✕, *119–120*
Inez Grant Parker Memorial Rose Garden, *49, 51, 52*
Inn at Europa Village ☑, *313*
Inn at Sunset Cliffs ☑, *176*
Inn at the Park ☑, *169*
International Cottages, *49*
International Visitor Information Center, *33, 91*
Ironside Fish & Oyster ✕, *120*
Isabel's Cantina ✕, *134*
Island Prime and C Level Lounge ✕, *105, 148–149*
Itineraries, *22–23*

J

Japanese Friendship Garden, *49, 51–52*
Jazz clubs, *188*
Jeremy's on the Hill ✕, *319–320*
Jet skiing, *246–247*
Jimmy's Famous American Tavern ✕, *144*
Jogging, *247*
JRDN ✕, *134*
Jsix ✕, *114*
Julian, *21, 317–322*
Julian Gold Rush Hotel ☑, *321*

Julian Lodge ☑, *321*
Julian Pie Company ✕, *320*
Julian Pioneer Museum, *318*
Julian Tea and Cottage Arts ✕, *320*
Juniper & Ivy ✕, *120*
Junípero Serra Museum, *72–73*

K

Karen Krasne's Extraordinary Desserts ✕, *120*
Kayaking, *213, 231, 233, 234, 248*
Kearny Mesa, *96*
nightlife, 197
restaurants, 142–143
Keating Building, *28*
Keating Hotel, The ☑, *34, 167*
Kebab Shop, The ✕, *118*
Keys Creek Lavender Farm, *307*
King's Fish House ✕, *130–131*
Ki's Restaurant ✕, *291–292*
Kona Kai Resort ☑, *177*
Kono's Surf Club Café ✕, *134–135*
Kous Kous Moroccan Bistro ✕, *128–129*

L

La Caseta ✕, *309*
La Costa Resort and Spa ☑, *21, 240, 297–298*
La Especial Norte ✕, *292*
La Jolla, *14, 18–19, 21, 90–96*
accommodations, 163, 172–173, 175
beaches, 91, 93, 221–223
children's activities, 92–93
nightlife, 196–197
restaurants, 91, 136–141
shopping, 269–273
La Jolla Caves, *93*
La Jolla Cove, *213, 222*
La Jolla Cove Suites ☑, *173, 175*
La Jolla Open Aire Market, *30*
La Jolla Playhouse, *20, 207–208*
La Jolla Shores, *222*
La Jolla Shores Hotel ☑, *175*
La Pizzeria Arrivederci ✕, *129*
La Valencia ☑, *175*
Lake Cuyamaca, *315, 317*
Lake Cuyamaca Restaurant ✕, *317*
Lanna ✕, *135*
L'Auberge Del Mar Resort and Spa ☑, *286–287*

Le Bambou ✕ , 285
Legoland California Resort, 19, 293, 294–295
Legoland Hotel 🏨 , 297
Leo Carrillo Ranch Historic Park, 295–296
Leoness Cellars, 312
LGBT Pride Festival, 17
Lighthouses, 101, 105
Little Italy, 21, 28, 41–42
accommodations, 169
restaurants, 118–121
Little Italy Mercato, 30, 41–42
Live music clubs
Downtown, 186, 188
Point Loma, Ocean Beach, and Coronado, 198
Lodge at Torrey Pines 🏨 , 175
Lodging. ⇨ See Accommodations
Loews Coronado Bay Resort 🏨 , 178
Lolita's Mexican Food ✕ , 126
Los Peñasquitos Lagoon, 93
Louis Bank of Commerce Building, 34
Lucha Libre Gourmet Taco Shop ✕ , 129
Lucky D's Hostel 🏨 , 168–169, 174
Lucky Liu's ✕ , 114, 116

M

Mama's Bakery & Lebanese Deli ✕ , 132–133
Manchester Grand Hyatt San Diego 🏨 , 169
Mardi Gras, 17
Marie Hitchcock Puppet Theater, 49, 52, 63
Marine Room ✕ , 138
Marine Street Beach, 222–223
Maritime Museum, 20, 36, 38
Market Restaurant + Bar ✕ , 286
Marketplace Deli ✕ , 125
Marriott Residence Inn Downtown 🏨 , 167
Marston Building, 28
Marston House Museum & Gardens, 63
McP's Irish Pub ✕ , 106
Michele Coulon Dessertier ✕ , 139
Mille Fleurs ✕ , 289
Mingei International Museum, 52, 52
Mingei International Museum Store, 263

Miniature Railroad, 49, 52, 63
Miramonte Winery, 312
Mission, The ✕ , 118, 126
Mission Basilica San Diego de Alcalá, 76–77
Mission Bay, 12, 80–88
accommodations, 163, 171–172
beaches, 81, 84–88, 220–221
children's activities, 85–86, 88
nightlife, 195
restaurants, 81, 134
shopping, 268–269
Mission Bay Park, 84, 85
Mission Beach, 86, 88, 134, 172, 220, 234
Mission Beach Boardwalk, 85, 88
Mission Hills, 76
Mission Hills Nursery, 76
Mission San Antonio de Pala, 322–323
Mission Santa Ysabel, 319
Mission Valley, 76–77
accommodations, 170–171
restaurants, 130–131
Money matters, 337
Moonlight Beach Motel 🏨 , 292
Moonlight State Beach, 225
Mootime Creamery ✕ , 99
Morton's, The Steakhouse ✕ , 116
Mother's Kitchen ✕ , 323
Mount Palomar Winery, 312
Mount Soledad, 96
Museum of Contemporary Art San Diego (MCASD), 20, 28, 37, 95
Museum of Making Music, 296
Museum of Photographic Arts, 52, 63–64
Museums, 20
Balboa Park, 52, 54, 63–64
Carlsbad, 296
Downtown San Diego, 35–36, 37, 38, 39–40, 42
Escondido 303–304, 305–306
Fallbrook, 308
Julian, 318, 319
La Jolla, 95
museum nights, 201–202
Oceanside, 299, 300
Old Town, 71, 72–73
Temecula, 311
Music, 20, 204, 206
Music clubs
Downtown, 186, 188
Point Loma, Ocean Beach, and Coronado, 198

N

Nature trails, 241, 244–245
Neighborhood ✕ , 118
Nesmith-Greeley Building, 34
New Children's Museum (NCM), 37, 39
Nickel Beer Co. (bar), 286
Night bay cruises, 188, 195
Nightlife, 180–198, 288
1906 Lodge at Coronado Beach 🏨 , 177
Nine-Ten ✕ , 139
Noble Experiment (piano bar), 188
Nobu ✕ , 116
North County and environs, 14, 278–329
accommodations, 281–282, 286–287, 290, 292, 297–298, 300–301, 303, 307, 309, 313–314, 321, 328
Backcountry and Julian, 278, 314–323
beaches, 224–225
children's activities, 284–285, 286, 287, 288, 290, 291, 292, 294–295, 296, 297–298, 299–300, 301, 302, 303–304, 305–307, 311, 313, 315, 317, 318, 319–320, 322–323, 328
Desert, 278, 323–329
Inland North County and Temecula, 278, 301–314
Legoland California Resort, 19, 293, 294–295
nightlife, 288
North Coast, 278, 282–301
price categories, 282
restaurants, 281, 285–286, 287–288, 289–290, 291–292, 296–297, 300, 301–302, 307, 309, 313, 317, 319–321, 323, 327–328
San Diego Zoo Safari Park, 304–305
shopping, 288–289, 290, 292, 298, 301, 303, 307–308, 314, 321–322
sports and the outdoors, 314, 328
tours, 284, 310, 314, 324
transportation, 280–281
visitor information, 282, 293, 299, 303, 308, 310, 318, 324, 326, 327
North Pacific Beach, 220–221

North Park, *21, 77–78*
accommodations, 171
restaurants, 132–133

O

Oakwood Apartments ☰, *174*
Observer's Inn, *318*
Ocean Beach, *102, 104, 219–220*
nightlife, 198
restaurants, 146–148
Ocean Beach Farmers' Market, *30*
Ocean Beach Pier, *104*
Oceanside, *226, 298–301*
Oceanside City Beach, *226*
Oceanside Harbor, *300*
Oceanside Marina Suites ☰, *300–301*
Oceanside Museum of Art, *300*
Oceanside Pier, *300*
Ocotillo Wells State Vehicular Recreation Area, *329*
Off-roading, *329*
Old Bridal Trail, *50*
Old City Hall, *28, 34*
Old Globe, The, *20, 208*
Old Mission San Luis Rey, *299–300*
Old Point Loma Lighthouse, *101*
Old Town, *12, 66–78*
accommodations, 170
children's activities, 69, 70, 73
nightlife, 190
restaurants, 67, 125, 127–133
shopping, 263–268
Old Town San Diego State Historic Park, *68, 70*
Old Town Temecula, *311*
Omni La Costa Resort Spa ☰, *21, 240, 269, 297–298*
Omni San Diego Hotel ☰, *167–168*
100 Wines ✕, *127*
101 Cafe ✕, *300*
Orange Avenue (Coronado), *106*
Orchard Hill Country Inn ☰, *321*
Orfila Vineyards, *305*
Ortega's Bistro ✕, *129*
Osteria Romantica ✕, *139*
Outlet malls, *257*
Over-the-Line, *245*

P

Pacific Beach, *88, 220–221*
accommodations, 172
restaurants, 134–136

Pacific Coast Grill ✕, *287–288*
Pacific Terrace Hotel ☰, *172*
Pacifica Del Mar ✕, *286*
Packing, *17, 337*
Pala Casino Resort Spa ☰, *309*
Pala Mesa Golf Resort ☰, *309*
Palm Canyon, *49, 50, 52*
Palms at Indian Head, The ☰, *328*
Palomar Mountain, *322–323*
Palomar Mountain State Park, *323*
Palomar Observatory, *323*
Pamplemousse Grille ✕, *288*
Pantai Inn ☰, *175*
Pappelucco ✕, *28, 33*
Paradise Point Resort & Spa ☰, *172*
Paragliding, *241*
Park Hyatt Aviara Golf Club, *240*
Park Hyatt Aviara Resort ☰, *20, 298*
Parks and gardens
Alcazar Garden, 49, 50
Amici Park, 28
Anza-Borrego Desert State Park, 21, 244–245, 324–326
Balboa Park, 12, 18, 45–64
Batiquitos Lagoon, 293–294
Belmont Park, 85, 86, 88
Border Field State Park, 218
Cabrillo National Monument, 18, 100–101
Chicano Park, 41
Cuyamaca Rancho State Park, 314
Desert Garden, 49
Embarcadero Marina Park North, 36
Embarcadero Marina Park South, 36
Flower Fields at Carlsbad Ranch, 18, 294
Heritage Park, 69–70
Inez Grant Parker Memorial Rose Garden, 49
Japanese Friendship Garden, 49
Keys Creek Lavender Farm, 307
Leo Carrillo Ranch Historic Park, 295–296
Mission Bay Park, 84, 85
Mission Hills Nursery, 76
Old Town, 68, 69–70, 71–72
Old Town San Diego State Historic Park, 68, 70

Palomar Mountain State Park, 323
Presidio Park, 71–72
San Diego Botanic Gardens, 291
San Diego-La Jolla Underwater Park Ecological Preserve, 222
San Dieguito River Park, 245, 307
San Elijo Lagoon Conservancy, 291
Santa Rosa Plateau Ecological Reserve, 311
Santa Ysabel Preserve, 319
Seagrove Park, 285
Torrey Pines State Natural Reserve, 19, 93, 213, 223, 244
Volcan Mountain Wilderness Preserve, 318–319
Zoro Garden, 54
Passport to Balboa discount passes, *24, 48*
Patio on Lamont, The ✕, *135*
Pearl Hotel, The ☰, *176*
Pechanga Resort & Casino, *316*
Pedicabs, *16, 32*
Pennypickle's Workshop: Temecula Children's Museum, *311*
Petco Park, *40–41*
Phil's BBQ ✕, *126, 144*
Phuong Trang ✕, *142–143*
Piano bars, *186, 188, 192–193*
Piatti Ristorante and Bar ✕, *139–140*
Pier South Resort ☰, *178*
Pigment (shop), *268*
Pizza Port ✕, *147, 288*
Pizzeria Mozza ✕, *122*
Plaza de Panama, *49*
Po Pazzo Bar and Grille ✕, *121*
Point Loma, *14, 98–99, 102–104*
accommodations, 163, 176
beaches, 102, 104, 219–220
children's activities, 102, 105
nightlife, 197–198
restaurants, 99, 143–146
shopping, 273–274
Point Loma Seafood's ✕, *145*
Ponte Vineyard Inn ☰, *313–314*
Porto Vista Hotel & Suites ☰, *169*
Prado, The ✕, *45, 123*
PrepKitchen La Jolla ✕, *140*

PrepKitchen Little Italy ✕, 120–121
Presidio Park, 71–72
Price categories, 7
accommodations, 165, 282
restaurants, 111, 282
Project Pie ✕, 129–130
Public transportation, 16, 24
Puerto La Boca ✕, 121
Puesto ✕, 122

Q

Queen Califia's Magical Circle, 305–306

R

Racine & Laramie, 70
Rancho Bernardo, 301–303
Rancho Bernardo Inn and Country Club, 241–242
Rancho Bernardo Inn Resort and Spa ☎, 303
Rancho Bernardo Resort & Spa, 20
Rancho Santa Fe, 289–290
Red Door, The ✕, 130
Red Tracton's ✕, 288
Reservations, 110, 165
Restaurant at Rancho Valencia ✕, 290
Restaurants, 7, 108–150
Balboa Park, 45, 123
Bankers Hill, 123–125
best bets, 112–113
Borrego Springs, 327–328
business hours, 110
Carlsbad, 296–297
children, 110, 113, 117, 125, 128, 129–130, 131, 132, 133, 134–135, 139–140, 145–146, 147, 148
Clairemont Mesa, 141
Coronado, 99, 149–150
Cuyamaca Mountains, 317
Del Mar, 285–286
Downtown San Diego, 33, 111, 114, 116–122
dress, 110
Encinitas, 291–292
Escondido, 307
Fallbrook, 309
Fodor's choice, 112
Harbor Island, 148–149
Hillcrest, 127–130
Julian, 320–321
Kearny Mesa, 142–143
Kensington, 131–132

La Jolla and Northern San Diego, 91, 136–141
mealtimes, 110
Mission Bay, 81, 134
Mission Beach, 134
Mission Valley, 130–131
Normal Heights, 131–132
North Park, 132–133
Ocean Beach, 146–148
Oceanside, 300
Old Town and Uptown, 67, 125, 127–133
Pacific Beach, 134–136
Palomar Mountain, 323
parking, 110
Point Loma, 99, 143–146
price categories, 111, 282
Rancho Bernardo, 301–302
Rancho Santa Fe, 289–290
reservations, 110
Shelter Island, 148
smoking, 111
Solana Beach, 287–288
South Bay, 150
South Park, 132–133
Temecula, 313
University Heights, 131–132
Restrooms, 338
Reuben H. Fleet Science Center, 52, 54
Robinson-Rose House, 71
Rock climbing, 248
Rodeway Inn North Encinitas ☎, 292
Romano's Dodge House ✕, 320
Romesco Mexiterranean Bistro ✕, 150
Rooftop bars, 185
Rooftop 600 @ Andaz (bar), 184
Roppongi Restaurant and Sushi Bar ✕, 140
Roy's Restaurant ✕, 122

S

Safety, 17, 223, 338
Saigon on Fifth ✕, 130
Sailing and boating, 249–250
Salk Institute, 96
Sammy's Woodfired Pizza ✕, 126
San Diego Air and Space Museum, 52, 54
San Diego Asian Film Festival, 203
San Diego Automotive Museum, 52, 64
San Diego Ballet, 20

San Diego Bay Parade of Lights, 17
San Diego Beach Rides, 245–246
San Diego Botanic Garden, 291
San Diego Chargers, 254
San Diego Convention Center, 36
San Diego County Fair, 17
San Diego History Center, 52, 64
San Diego-La Jolla Underwater Park Ecological Preserve, 222, 234–235
San Diego Maritime Museum, 20, 36, 38
San Diego Marriott Del Mar ☎, 287
San Diego Marriott Gaslamp Quarter ☎, 168
San Diego Model Railroad Museum, 52, 64
San Diego Mormon Battalion Historic Site, 73
San Diego Museum of Art, 52, 54
San Diego Museum of Man, 52, 54
San Diego Natural History Museum, 62
San Diego Opera, 20, 206
San Diego Padres, 40–41, 254
San Diego Surfing Academy, 21
San Diego Symphony Orchestra, 20
San Diego Zoo, 19, 55–61
San Diego Zoo Safari Park, 304–305
San Dieguito River Park, 245, 307
San Elijo Lagoon Conservancy, 291
Santa Fe Depot, 28
Santa Rosa Plateau Ecological Reserve, 311
Santa Ysabel Preserve, 319
Santa Ysabel Store, The, 318
Scott Street (Point Loma), 103–104
SCOUT at Quarters D. (shop), 273
Scripps Inn ☎, 175
Scuba diving, 213, 234–235
Sea Life Aquarium, 296
Sea 180 Coastal Tavern ✕, 145
Seagrove Park, 285

Seals, *213*
Seaport Village, *21, 36, 39*
shopping, 263
Seaport Village Carousel, *39*
Searsucker ✕, *116*
SeaWorld San Diego, *19, 81, 82–83, 84, 85*
accommodations, 171–172
Seeley Stable, *71*
Serra, Father Junípero, *75*
Sessions Public ✕, *145*
Seven Grand (bar), *194*
Shades ✕, *147–148*
Shell Beach, *223*
Shelter Island, *14, 104*
accommodations, 163, 176–177
restaurants, 148
Sheraton Carlsbad Resort & Spa ☞, *298*
Sheraton San Diego Hotel & Marina ☞, *177*
Shopping, *21, 256–276*
Balboa Park, 51, 263
beaches, 268–269
business hours, 257
Carlsbad, 269, 298
children, 257, 267, 274
Coronado, 274–276
Del Mar, 269–273
Downtown San Diego, 259–263
Encinitas, 292
Escondido, 307–308
Julian, 321–322
La Jolla, 91, 269–273
Mission Bay, 268–269
Oceanside, 301
Old Town, 263–269
outlet malls, 257
Point Loma, 273–274
Rancho Bernardo, 303
Rancho Santa Fe, 290
Seaport Village, 263
Solana Beach, 288–289
Temecula, 314
Uptown, 263–268
Shorehouse Kitchen ✕, *140*
Silver Strand State Beach, *219*
Slater's 50/50 ✕, *145*
Smoking, *182*
Snooze ✕, *130*
Snorkeling, *213*
Sofia Hotel, The ☞, *168*
Solana Beach, *224, 287–289*
Soups 'n Such Cafe ✕, *320*
South Bay, *150, 218–219*
South Carlsbad State Beach, *226*

South Coast Winery Resort & Spa ☞, *314*
South Park, *78*
restaurants, 132–133
Spanish Village Art Center, *49, 62*
Spas, *21, 276*
Spencer-Ogden Building, *28*
Sports and the outdoors, *228–254*
ballooning, 20, 232, 314
baseball, 253–254
beaches, 12, 18, 210–226
bicycling, 105, 231, 232–234
diving and snorkeling, 213, 234–235
fishing, 234, 235–236
football, 254
Frisbee golf, 236
Golf, 17, 20, 71, 231, 236–241, 254
hang gliding and paragliding, 241
hiking and nature trails, 241, 244–245
horse racing, 254, 284
horseback riding, 231, 245–246
jet skiing, 246–247
jogging, 247
kayaking, 213, 231, 233, 234, 248
off-roading, 329
over-the-line, 245
rock climbing, 248
sailing and boating, 249–250
surfing, 21, 229, 231, 250–251
tennis, 251–252
volleyball, 252
waterskiing, 252
whale-watching, 101, 252
windsurfing, 253
Sportsmen's Sea Foods ✕, *81*
Spreckels Organ Pavilion, *49, 52, 62–63*
Spruce Street Bridge, *73, 75*
Starlite (piano bar), *192–193*
Stone Brewing Co., *307–308*
Stone Brewing World Bistro and Gardens ✕, *145–146, 191*
Stuart Collection of Sculpture, *93*
Summer Shakespeare Festival, *17*
Sunrise National Scenic Byway, *317*
Sunset Cliffs, *102, 103*
Surf Diva Surf School, *21, 250*
Surfer Beach Hotel ☞, *172*

Surfing, *21, 229, 231, 250–251*
Sushi Diner ✕, *141*
Sushi Ota ✕, *136*
Swami's (beach), *226*
Sycuan Resort & Casino, *241, 316*
Symbols, *7*

T

Tacos, *21, 135*
Tacos El Gordo ✕, *150*
Taka ✕, *116*
Tapenade ✕, *140–141*
Taxis, *335*
Temecula, *278, 310–314*
Temecula Balloon & Wine Festival, *20, 314*
Temecula Creek Inn ☞, *314*
Temecula Valley Museum, *311*
Temecula Valley Winegrowers Association, *311*
Tender Greens ✕, *146*
Tennis, *251–252*
Theater, *20, 207–208*
3rd Corner Wine Shop and Bistro ✕, *146–147*
Thomas Whaley House Museum, *71, 72*
Tickets, *201*
Tide pools, *101*
Timing the visit, *16, 230–231*
Timken Museum of Art, *52, 64*
Tin Fish, The ✕, *116–117*
Tipping, *338*
Tom Ham's Lighthouse, *105, 149*
Top of the Market ✕, *122*
Torrey Pines Golf Course, *20, 239*
Torrey Pines State Natural Reserve, *19, 93, 213, 223, 244*
Tourmaline Surfing Park, *221*
Tours, *28–29, 49–50, 338–340*
Coronado, 106
Desert, 324
Inland North County and Temecula, 284, 310, 314, 324
North Coast, 284
Tower23 ☞, *172*
Train travel, *24, 336*
North County and environs, 280–281
Transportation, *16, 24, 332–336*
Desert, 324
North Coast, 291, 293, 299
North Country and environs, 280–281

Travel tips, 24, 49, 83
Trolley travel, 24, 32, 37, 334
tours, 339
Truluck's ✕ , 141
Tuna Harbor, 36

U

U. S. Grant ⌂ , 28, 168
University of California at San
  Diego, 93, 96
University Heights, 77
Upstart Crow & Co. (coffee-
  house), 33
Uptown, 12, 66–78
accommodations, 163
children's activities, 69, 70, 73
nightlife, 190, 192–195
restaurants, 67, 125, 127–133
shopping, 263–268
Urban Art Trail, 35
URBN Coal Fired Pizza ✕ , 133
USS Midway Museum, 36,
  39–40

V

Vacation Isle, 85–86
Venetian Point Loma, The ✕ ,
  146
Viejas Casino, 316
Viejas Casino & Resort Hotel
  ✕ , 321
Village Vino ✕ , 131–132
Vin de Syrah (wine bar), 187
Vincent's ✕ , 307
Vineyard Rose ✕ , 313

Vinz Wine Bar ✕ , 307
Visitor information, 341
Backcountry and Julian, 318
Desert, 324, 326
Inland North County and Tem-
  ecula, 303, 308, 310
North Country and environs,
  282, 293, 299, 303, 308,
  310, 318, 324, 326, 327
Viva el Café ✕ , 67
Viva Pops ✕ , 133
Volcan Mountain Wilderness
  Preserve, 318–319
Volleyball, 252

W

W Hotel ⌂ , 168
Wa Dining Okan ✕ , 143
Walking tours, 28–29, 340
Balboa Park, 49–50
Coronado, 106
Waterfront Bar & Grill, The,
  188
Waterskiing, 252
Wave Waterpark, 300
Waypoint Public ✕ , 133
Weather, 16, 230–231
Web sites, 17, 341
Welk Resort ⌂ , 307
West Inn and Suites ⌂ , 298
Western Metal Supply Co.
  Building, 41
Westfield Horton Plaza, 21,
  28, 33, 35
Westgate Hotel ⌂ , 168

Westgate Hotel Plaza Bar
  (piano bar), 186
Whale-watching, 101, 252
Whaley House, 71, 72
When to go, 16, 230–231
Whisknladle ✕ , 141
Wiens Family Cellars, 312
Wikiup Bed and Breakfast
  ⌂ , 321
William Heath Davis House, 28
Wilson Creek Winery & Vine-
  yards, 312–313
Windansea Beach, 223
Windsurfing, 253
Wine Bars, 187, 192, 307
Wine Cabana ✕ , 127
Wineries, 303, 308–309,
  311–313
Wyndham Oceanside Pier
  Resort ⌂ , 301
Wynola Pizza Express ✕ ,
  320–321

Y

Yuma Building, 34

Z

Zoos
California Wolf Center, 318
San Diego Zoo, 19, 45–61
San Diego Zoo Safari Park,
  304–305
Zoro Garden, 54

PHOTO CREDITS

ABOUT OUR WRITERS

Veteran traveler Claire Deeks van der Lee feels lucky to call San Diego home. An East Coast transplant, she never takes the near-perfect weather for granted. Claire loves playing tourist in her own city, exploring San Diego's cultural attractions as well as its myriad neighborhoods and Balboa Park—so it was a perfect fit for her to work on the Experience and Exploring chapters of this book. Claire has contributed to *Everywhere* magazine and several Fodor's guides.

When Maren Dougherty moved to Southern California in 2005, she thought she'd stay for one year—maybe two. To her East Coast family's dismay, she fell in love with the year-round beach scene, perfectly mixed margaritas, and a surfer who can't imagine life without the waves. Maren's freelance work has appeared in *San Diego Magazine* and *Alaska Airlines* magazine. She updated the Where to Stay chapter.

Longtime Southern Californian Bobbi Zane lives in the mountain hamlet of Julian, making her the perfect person to update our North County chapter. Bobbi's byline has appeared in the *Los Angeles Times*, the *Los Angeles Daily News*, *Westways* magazine, and the *Orange County Register*. She has written about the Palm Springs area for Fodor's for more than 20 years and is a contributor to the Fodor's *National Parks of the West* guidebook.

Jeff Terich is a culture-seeker and night owl who is most at home on a barstool, watching live music. He's the music editor at San Diego CityBeat and a freelance arts and music writer with 14 years of experience writing for publications like *American Songwriter, ALARM, Paste and Chord.* When he's not breaking in his earplugs at shows in San Diego, he's often traveling with his wife Candice or in search of a good bourbon cocktail. Jeff updated the Nightlife and Performing Arts chapters.

Casey Hatfield-Chiotti's passion for food and travel has taken her from Mount Kilimanjaro to Machu Picchu, but she also loves exploring her adopted home of Southern California. A multimedia journalist, Hatfield-Chiotti was a TV news reporter for five years before becoming a freelance food and travel writer. Hatfield-Chiotti's work has appeared in *Travel & Leisure, Sunset Magazine, Robb Report, Departures, Cooking Light* and on *BonAppetit.com.* She updated the Beaches, Shopping, and Sports and the Outdoors chapters.

Mary Hellman James is an award-winning journalist and editor who has lived in San Diego for 40 years. After a 29-year-career with the *San Diego Union-Tribune*, James currently is a contributor to *San Diego Home/Garden Lifestyles* magazine, executive editor of *California Garden*, and is co-publisher and editor of *Wine Dine & Travel Magazine*. With her husband, Ron, she updated the Where to Eat chapter.

Ron James is a veteran journalist and native San Diegan who has worked for Time Warner, *The San Diego Union-Tribune*, and *San Diego Magazine*. While leading the online editorial team at *The Union-Tribune*, Ron wrote a syndicated weekly column, "Perfect Pairings." For four years he published the award-winning online magazine *Wine & Dine San Diego*, which evolved to the current print and digital magazine *Wine Dine & Travel*. With his wife, Mary, he updated the Where to Eat chapter.